SMALL ENTERPRISES AND CHANGING POLICIES

SMALL ENTERPRISES AND CHANGING POLICIES

Structural adjustment, financial policy and assistance programmes in Africa

Edited by A.H.J. HELMSING and Th. KOLSTEE

IT PUBLICATIONS 1993

Intermediate Technology Publications
103–105 Southampton Row, London WC1B 4HH, UK

ISBN UK Hardback 1 85339 186 7
ISBN UK Paperback 1 85339 185 9

The research for this publication was financed by the Netherlands' Ministry for Development Cooperation.

Printed by SRP, Exeter, UK
Phototypeset by Tradespools Ltd., Frome, Somerset, UK

Contents

Preface

In 1990 the Directorate General for International Development Cooperation (DGIS) of the Netherlands' Ministry of Foreign Affairs was invited by the Committee of Donor Agencies for Small Enterprise Development to organize a conference on Small and Micro Enterprise Promotion in a Changing Policy Environment, with a special focus on Africa. Since the early 1980s DGIS has supported and sponsored a series of seminars, conferences and research in support of small enterprise development.

DGIS invited Dr A.H.J. Helmsing of the Institute of Social Studies to assist Drs Th. Kolstee and Bas van Noordenne (DGIS) in the organization of the conference. The conference was held in The Hague, at the Institute of Social Studies from 30 September — 2 October 1991 and was sponsored by DGIS as well as CIDA, SDC, ODA, NORAD, FINNIDA, KfW, IDB, UNIFEM and the World Bank. The Conference was attended by some one hundred participants which, in addition to the donor community and a few leading researchers from the donor countries, included a large number of African researchers and NGO practitioners.

In view of the success of the conference, it was decided that instead of simply publishing the proceedings, the best papers would be revised and made available for wider circulation in the form of this book.

The process of revision and editing has been somewhat longer than originally expected. Nevertheless, we would like to acknowledge the promptness with which most contributors have revised their papers and attended to further queries.

Last, but not least, we would like thank Gary Debus, ISS Publications Manager for his advice and Wang Yun for typing accurately all corrections. However, the editors remain responsible for any remaining errors and omissions.

The Hague, July 1992
Bert Helmsing
Theo Kolstee

Glossary

CIDA	Canadian International Development Agency
DANIDA	Danish International Development Agency
DFI	Development Finance Institution
DGIS	Directoraat Generaal voor Internationale Ontwikkelingssamenwerking (Directorate General for International Development Cooperation)
DRC	Domestic resource cost
EPR	Effective protection rate
FINNIDA	Finnish International Development Agency
GDP	Gross domestic product
IDB	Interamerican Development Bank
IMF	International Monetary Fund
ISI	Import-substituting industrialization
IVA	Industrial value added
KfW	Kreditanstalt für Wirtschaft
LA	Latin America
LME	Large and medium enterprises
LSE	Large-scale enterprises
MLE	Medium and large enterprises
NBFI	Near Bank Financial Institution
NGO	Non-government organization
NORAD	Norwegian Agency for Development
ODA	Overseas Development Administration
OGL	Open general licence
PVO	Private voluntary organization
ROSCA	Rotating Savings and Credit Association
SAL	Structural adjustment loan
SAP	Structural adjustment programme/policy
SE	Small enterprise
SIDA	Swedish International Development Authority
SME	Small and micro enterprises
SMIDA	Small and medium-size industrial development agency
SSA	Sub-Saharan Africa

SSE	Small-scale enterprise
SSME	Small-scale and micro enterprise
SSMI	Small-scale manufacturing industry
SDC	Swiss Development Corporation
UNIFEM	United Nations Development Fund For Women
USAID	United States Agency for International Development
VA	Value added
VSE	Very small enterprise

I

Introduction

Small enterprise promotion in a changing policy environment in Africa: raising issues and attempting answers

A.H.J. (BERT) HELMSING and THEO KOLSTEE

Introduction

From a number of directions donor agencies and development analysts are converging in small enterprise (SE) development as a (potential) priority area in development policy in general, and in Africa in particular. First of all, changing perceptions about state, market, and society are having substantial impact on the political economy of development. On the one hand the 'burden of proof' as regards public sector and parastatal solutions to development problems has shifted; on the other hand private sector, grassroots and NGO/PVO initiatives are receiving increased attention.

Second, experiences with structural adjustment have shown that macroeconomic adjustments do not always achieve the desired supply responses, especially as regards private investment.

Third, during the eighties there was a growing realization that non-agricultural activities in the rural areas and small towns play a much more substantial role than hitherto surmised. In view of the relatively restricted labour absorption in high input agriculture, these activities acquire more significance.

Fourth, the inability of the urban manufacturing, trade and services sector to provide a satisfactory rate of growth in employment, combined with informalization of large-scale production in some countries and with rapid growth of city populations, has put inordinate pressures on urban labour markets. The SE has as a result acquired new dimensions. Linkages with large-scale production and new forms of organization of industrial production are explored which may give SSE (small-scale enterprise) a new role in industrial development.

Finally, the appropriate technologies may give SE advantages in terms of greater efficiency in resource use and of environmental effects relative to imported technologies (e.g. high input agriculture, high energy manufacturing) (Romijn and de Wilde, 1991).

The key question is now not so much the advantages of SE *per se* but rather the extent to which the development of SE will assist in resolving major (economic and non-economic) development issues. The burden of proof is in this regard on SE analysts.

Over the past few years, SE promotion has come out of its confines and has begun to raise and answer some of the major development questions, in part aided by a cumulative wealth of experiences and evaluations of a great variety of promotional efforts and projects (Boomgard, 1989; UNIDO *et al.* 1988). Studies of past projects and programmes have shown that the effectiveness of micro-level efforts can be improved by addressing sectoral/regional and macro-economic factors. Thus, also from this angle there is a greater disposition to consider the wider policy framework for SE development (Stewart, Thomas, de Wilde, 1990).

The new Dutch policy for SE seeks to place SE in the context of a wider framework of development issues. It raises macro, meso and micro issues and seeks to differentiate objectives and policy instruments depending on the type of SE and situation (DGIS, 1992).

This volume seeks on the one hand to discuss main SE policy issues that African policymakers, donors, domestic and foreign NGOs and PVOs face. They may draw on such a discussion to guide their own respective SE policies and programmes. On the other hand, it is hoped that this volume will identify issues on which further research is most urgently needed in order to develop appropriate policies and strategies.

Small enterprise in Africa

It is increasingly realized that SE concerns in Africa do differ significantly from those in Latin America and Asia. Among the reasons cited are the differences in the level, pattern and rate of change in economic development. Other aspects refer to the nature of state and society (e.g. the level of institutional development and relative importance of and relation between public and private sectors) as well as cultural dimensions at macro- and micro-levels.

Although Africa has been the birthplace of important research on concepts of SE, for example the research on enterprise development and modernization in the sixties (Kilby, 1965 and Berry, 1977); the informal sector studies in the seventies (Hart, 1973; ILO, 1972; King, 1977); the non-agricultural enterprise research in the seventies and eighties (Anderson and Leiserson, 1980; Chuta and Liedholm, 1979; World Bank, 1978; Freeman and Norcliffe, 1985) and gender issues in relation to SE activities (Downing, 1990), SE has not been high on the development agenda of many African governments.

'Africanization' has always been associated with the promotion of small enterprise, but governments of a number of countries have chosen the state socialist road of nationalization and public enterprise expansion as the supposedly faster road to (another sort of) Africanization. The economic crisis of the eighties has questioned basic features of the prevailing economic structure and the structural adjustment reforms which are unfolding themselves, cause a gradual loss of legitimacy of this position. Are governments in Africa ready to embrace domestic SE development as an alternative? What margins are open? This would seem to vary considerably from country to country.

Heterogeneity of countries

Sub-Saharan Africa (SSA) consists of a rather heterogeneous group of countries in terms of population, level of economic development, per capita income and in sectoral composition of the economy. Some countries have a very small manufacturing sector (e.g. Malawi, Mozambique, Angola). In other countries it is more substantial (e.g Zimbabwe, Mauritius, Ivory Coast). Some are rather highly urbanized (Zambia) while others have a low degree and rate of urbanization, while again others are on the threshold of a process of rapid rural to urban shift (Zimbabwe). Some countries have a rather substantial parallel economy, are suffering from wars, serious civil strife and/or droughts (Sudan, Somalia, Ethiopia) and some are just beginning to recover from conflicts (Uganda, Mozambique). Some countries are already deeply engaged in a process of structural adjustment (Ghana) while others have barely started to implement it (Zimbabwe). This means that the importance, composition and role of SE is likely to vary considerably, and this will have to be taken into account when designing policies. Uniform policy prescriptions have to be treated with great caution.

Internal differentiation of SE

Increasingly, researchers and practitioners of SE promotion take into account the heterogeneity of SEs. The issue of definition of small enterprise has been dominated by the scale dimension to the detriment of other quantitative and qualitative aspects of a relatively small economic unit of operation including its relative place and function within the economy. The contributions to this volume do not attempt to resolve this issue. Most papers accept a basic distinction between: (a) microenterprise (household and survival sector; one-person operations), and (b) small to medium-sized as well as more formalized enterprises.

Across SSA there is considerable variation, although it is difficult to arrive at exact estimates. In addition there are considerable rural-urban differences. It seems that in countries like Kenya and Zimbabwe there is a much larger presence (in relative terms) of rural enterprises than in countries such as Ghana, Zambia or even Tanzania. Given the relatively low degree of urbanization and the current level of economic development in Tanzania one would expect a much larger role of rural SE than there is actually found. The importance of urban SE also fluctuates across SSA.

Research on SE in Africa needs to be more specific as regards the enterprise segment one is dealing with. By no means can one assume a priori similar impacts and reactions across all segments. Similarly, segment-specific comparisons may improve understanding more than aggregate comparisons.

To limit oneself to one single category, such as 'b' or excluding another, like 'a', would have considerable implications in terms of political priority as well as policy approach. The rural/urban dimension needs to be carefully taken into account when making choices in terms of policies.

Policy approach to SE

While many policy analysts and donor agencies may contend that there is an a priori case in favour of SE, it is not a panacea for African development. Nor can it a priori be assumed that SE has high priority on the African development agenda.

While SE (again depending on the subsectors covered) would have certain assumed economic advantages (relatively high labour intensity, low capital intensity, low import propensity, appropriate technology, etc.), it seems more appropriate to build up a case rather carefully. An approach that first seeks to examine what the impacts are of main policy reforms (e.g. international trade, debt, food security, social services) on SE subsectors and to determine if and to what extent SE development and SE policies are instrumental towards achieving (better) reforms would contribute considerably to bringing SE into the centre of current development debates — something that is crucial when seeking to establish a policy dialogue with African governments.

By concentrating on policies affecting SEs rather than only on specific programmes supporting SEs, one is not focusing on a miniscule number of beneficiary enterprises but rather on the position of SEs as a whole.

This approach is a relatively new one, and this volume will endeavour to apply it to a number of selected themes.

Greater African voice

Over the last decade it has become painfully clear that there can be no major progress in tackling Africa's development dilemmas without strong and clear participation by African policymakers, practitioners and researchers. This applies particularly to SE which in many countries has been relegated to the fringe of government policy, though in some countries donors and NGOs have made important initiatives. A careful look at SE publications in journals, newsletters etc. will show that the predominant share is published by researchers from the North.

There is a great need to build up and use research capacity in Africa capable of generating information regarding ongoing SE aggregate trends, of improving our knowledge about micro SE behaviour and of undertaking policy studies. This volume pursues the latter via the participation of a large number of African researchers.

Main issues

The general aim of this book is to discuss the state of our knowledge about the appropriate policy response for SE development in a changing environment in Africa.

The main themes selected for discussion are the following and are described below:

- impact of adjustment on SEs
- financial policy reforms and SE financial assistance
- policies for sustaining government and NGO assistance programmes (in particular in the field of technology and entrepreneurship programmes)

Chapters around each theme are organized in the three main parts of this book. These parts are preceded by an introductory section which contains, apart from the overall presentation of arguments in this chapter, two additional introductory chapters on policy perspectives. The first looks at small enterprise development in the context of historical patterns of African industrialization and the second aims to provide a framework for assessment of key policies and their effects on small enterpise development.

Policy perspectives

Bert Helmsing starts by noting that much of the current SE debate concentrates on immediate development problems and issues (unemployment, structural adjustment impacts) but pays insufficient attention to the role of SEs in the industrialization process in Africa. He examines three partly overlapping trends which have had a decisive influence on SE development, namely the effects of colonial policies on African craft and village industries, import-substituting industrialization and the effects of post-colonial industrialization policies, concentrating on Southern and Eastern Africa.

The pattern of industrialization in Southern and Eastern Africa has been distorted in several respects. The development of SEs, through the proliferation, expansion and transformation of indigenous artisan and village industries and by entry of new entrepreneurs has been severely weakened not only by the colonial urban and industrial policies but also by post-independence industrialization policies. There are significant differences however between countries, due to particular circumstances of the day as well as to ideologies.

By implanting factory-based mass production, import substituting industrialization was regarded as a faster road to progress without the apparent necessity of having to make large initial investments over an extended period of time in the techno-institutional support environment (human resources development, research and technology, economic and social infrastructure). The vertical integration of large firms with continued dependence on the import of inputs, together with the low level of labour division within the small firms, has created a fragmented industrial structure characterized by a low level of external division of labour as evidenced by limited linkages between firms, not only between large and small firms but also among large and among small firms.

In looking for a basis for SE in future industrialization, Helmsing discusses recent literature concerning flexible specialization particularly regarding the internal and external division of labour and the roles of central and local governments.

Can there be a SE-led industrialization process in Africa? This question begs for answers. The sheer growth in numbers of SEs is not a sufficient condition. One needs to differentiate further, examining the potential of different types of entrepreneurs and of enterprises. The very question however puts a different perspective on the rationales of current SE promotion practices.

William Steel presents a long standing practitioner's view on policy biases, market distortions and other factors which pre-empt or prevent the growth of SEs. The factors that affect the availability of opportunities and resources for SEs as well as of entrepreneurs' ability and willingness to respond are discussed under five headings, namely incentives, investors, environment, inputs and facilitating institutions.

With regard to incentives, Steel emphasizes policies which expand domestic demand in particular through agriculture. Many other measures designed to improve SE productive capabilities are likely to fail in the absence of growing demand. Trade policies are considered important in creating new opportunities for SEs. Further, by improving access to imported inputs SEs will be in a better position to adjust to new market conditions. With regard to investors, policies should redirect entrepreneurship away from rent-seeking and towards socially-relevant productive activities and give priority to training in entrepreneurial capabilities, especially technology and markets.

African policymakers should take into account the importance of the following as key issues which shape the SE environment: positive attitudes towards the private sector, stability of the economy and particularly economic policy and minimal regulations, as the latter can cause evasion and non-compliance.

SEs are small buyers of inputs. Efforts on the part of SEs to compensate for this disadvantage should not be thwarted by policies. Access to equipment should not be made more difficult by restrictive legislation (e.g. import licensing). Restrictive labour legislation may push SEs into non-compliance and prevent other SEs from growing.

With regard to facilitating institutions, Steel gives most attention to policies that can make the financial system more responsive to the needs of the SEs. Although the low propensity of banks to provide loans to SEs may be caused by preconceptions or sound business practices, measures can be adopted to improve the system for this market segment. For very small SEs informal schemes that provide credit and mobilize local savings are considered desirable. This theme will receive more attention in Part Three.

Fully in line with the overall tenet of this volume, Steel stresses the importance of the approach that looks at the policy regime affecting SE development and that seeks to effect policy changes to broader problems rather than a more micro-oriented approach that, after having identified specific problems, formulates specific interventions designed to remediate these but which by doing so creates new distortions.

Impact of adjustment on SEs

The short- and medium-term effects of structural adjustment on SE are by no means clear and there are many contrasting views (Stewart, Thomas and de Wilde, 1990). Some argue that trade liberalization may result in a flood of competing imports which would seriously reduce the market share of domestic SE production. Others maintain, however, that a strong reduction in the overvaluation of the exchange rate (through devaluation) would ensure that imported products would become sufficiently dear to prevent such an effect from occurring. Again others argue that much depends on the extent to which SE themselves are relying on imported inputs and/or producing either for the domestic market or for export. Some macroeconomists have predicted that these effects would be overshadowed by the demand contraction resulting from the implementation of adjustment reforms (lower real incomes due to adoption of higher (market) prices in agriculture (food), adoption of cost recovery measures for public services, reduction of public sector employment, etc.).

To what extent are adjustment processes and the greater reliance on market institutions effectively opening up new opportunities for SE? What are the dynamic effects: do new SEs enter, and above all, what kind of SE? Can SE as a result become the basis for a new industrialization strategy and, if so, what kind of SE? These issues are crucial in order to determine to what extent the established instruments for the promotion of SE, and the manner in which these are used, require reconsideration.

These are all questions in search of answers. Country case studies as well as reviews of major adjustment programme components would shed more light on the relative importance of the various factors and may assist in clarifying which and when policy measures should be taken.

Detailed evaluative studies are difficult to obtain for several reasons. First, there are methodological issues. Ideally, answers should be obtained by means of one of three methods: first, by comparing the situation 'before SAP' and 'after SAP'. This type of comparison is probably the most desirable but unfortunately also rarely feasible. Certainly in the case of SE development there are few base-line studies that could serve this purpose. The second method is counterfactual analysis of 'countries with SAP' and 'countries without SAP', which is becoming increasingly difficult as there are few countries that would fit a matching 'without SAP' control group in Africa. Not only is there considerable heterogeneity among SSA countries, as noted above, but also the majority of them (35) had started to undertake adjustment programmes in the eighties (Cornea, 1991). Third, large-scale versus small-scale enterprise impact comparison is a method which is frequently adopted in view of the (often implicit) assumption that pre-SAP distortions have been working to the benefit of LSE and to the disadvantage of SSEs. The elimination of these distortions would result in a better performance of SEs.

A second and partly overlapping reason as to why comparative studies are difficult to undertake is that there are problems of comparison of countries undergoing processes of structural adjustment due to differences in the timing, in contents (relative importance of stabilization versus reform, extent of reform) and the sequencing of stabilization measures and of institutional reforms.

The country case studies presented in this volume are to be considered as initial or preliminary assessments of structural adjustment impacts on small enterprises, their problems and potentials. Most authors use a combination of the first and the third mentioned methods. And in view of the limitations of single-visit surveys of SE entrepreneurs, qualitative assessments are the best that could be achieved.

In view of the above considerations, any generalization as to the impact of structural adjustment would be fraught with danger. At best one can signal similarities and dissimilarities in experiences so as to improve insight and understanding and raise issues which would require further investigation.

Of the four countries considered, Ghana has probably had the longest period of adjustment (as of the early eighties), while in Mali and Tanzania the adjustment processes really began in the second half of the eighties. Finally, in Zimbabwe implementation of adjustment measures only started in 1992. In 1987 the estimated per capita income of the four countries was as follows: Tanzania (US$180); Mali (US$210); Ghana (US$390) and Zimbabwe (US$580) (World Bank, 1989a). All except Mali were experiencing negative per capita growth rates in the 1980s. Table 1.1 gives additional general indicators demonstrating some similarities (low growth, importance of manufactured imports) and dissimilarities (importance of industry, structure of manufacturing and of exports).

For the purpose of the analysis of the impact of structural adjustment on small enterprises, the reforms may be summarized under the following main components: (a) external sector reforms including depreciation of the domestic currency, liberalization of foreign exchange control as well as allocation and trade liberalization; (b) fiscal reform and public sector restructuring including reduction of public sector expenditures, tax reforms and cost recovery, reduction of public sector employment, privatization of parastatals; (c) domestic de-regulation and liberalization of internal trade and finance including elimination of price controls, liberalization of banking regulation and interest rates, reduction of restrictive wage and labour regulations etc; and (d) demand management including demand control and reorientation from consumption to investment and from domestic demand to exports.

The external sector reform in Ghana, as reported by Osei *et al.* and by Dawson in this volume has been very substantial. The cedi depreciated some 8,000 per cent during the 1983–8 period. Foreign exchange controls and administrative allocation

Table 1 Selected economic indicators for Tanzania, Mali, Ghana and Zimbabwe (percentages)

	Tanzania	*Mali*	*Ghana*	*Zimbabwe*
GDP growth (1980–7)	1.7	3.4	1.4	2.4
GDP growth for industry (1980–7)	–2.4	9.8	0.1	1.4
Share of industry in GDP (1987)	5	6	10	20
Structure of the manufacturing sector (1986):				
– basic consumer(*)	54	69(**)	46(***)	44
– all other	46	31	54	56
Share of manufacturing in imports (1987)	75	71	73	79
Share of agriculture in exports (1987)	75	71	60	43
Share of manufacturing in exports (1987)	18	29	2	40

(*) food/agriculture processing plus textiles and clothing
(**) 1988 figures for Mali from Kessous and Lessard in this volume
(***) 1980 figures
Source: World Bank, 1989.

have been abolished and foreign exchange is auctioned to 'Foreign Exchange Bureaux'. In Tanzania, foreign exchange controls have been relaxed (e.g. own funds schemes) and the government intends to auction forex in a similar manner. According to Bagachwa, in this volume the Tanzanian shilling depreciated 1370 per cent in the period 1984–92 and is still considered to be 50 per cent overvalued. Since Mali is part of the CFA zone through which the Mali currency is convertible, Kessous and Lessard in this volume conclude that this country does not experience similar problems. Zimbabwe has depreciated its dollar continuously over the past few years but has only recently begun to relax its exchange control and allocation.

Countries with a relatively substantial manufacturing sector, such as Zimbabwe, are phasing their trade liberalization, concentrating initially on capital goods and intermediate inputs in order to give their consumer goods industries more time to adjust. The reduction of trade restrictions has improved the availability of inputs in all countries.

To what extent have these reforms impacted upon small enterprises? Bagachwa notes that most SEs do not apply themselves to foreign exchange and in as far as they have been relying on parallel foreign exchange and illegal imports, these reforms have had no direct impacts in terms of price. There is however greater availability of imports and their use has increased (e.g. in Mali). In so far as small enterprises relied on inputs imported by other firms, the improved availability came with considerable price hikes. As a result, the credit needs of small enterprises rise. The latter effect is also noted by Osei *et al.*

The availability of (better quality) inputs had a positive effect in the sense that it enabled small enterprises to improve, modify or diversify their product lines and in that way improve their ability to adjust to the changing market conditions. Kessous and Lessard found this to be a significant factor in Mali.

Has the reduction of trade restrictions led to a flood of competing imports which would have swept domestic producers from the market? Competing imports are on the whole harmful to small enterprises, but their impact tends to be restricted to particular sectors (e.g. garment and textiles, including second-hand clothing in Ghana, soap and tie-dye products in Tanzania). The Mali study clearly confirms that competing imports are a bigger threat to larger firms which originally were set up to substitute imports. On a more positive side, the rapidly-rising prices of imports also generate new opportunities for domestic producers (e.g. in metal products, food processing equipment, etc.), something which was particularly noted for Ghana.

With regard to fiscal reform and public sector restructuring, the studies presented in this volume concentrate on three issues. The first issue is demand contraction for SEs caused by diminishing purchasing power of their clients as a result of curbing of public sector expenditures (including the adoption of cost recovery measures). Several authors mention this but no direct evidence could be presented to determine its importance. The curtailment of public sector employment was singled out as a second issue. In Ghana some 100,000 public workers were fired in the 1983–9 period while Zimbabwe intends to eliminate 50,000 public sector jobs.

Apart from its associated demand effect, the reduction of public-sector employment has a supply side effect: redundant civil servants as well as aspiring young potential entrants exit the public sector labour market and establish their own small enterprise. Osei *et al.* found that 15 per cent of the small enterprises surveyed had been established by former civil servants.

The high influx of new enterprises has also had a harmful effect, causing intense competition among small enterprises. This has been observed for both Ghana (since the 1970s) and for Tanzania (since the mid-1980s), by Dawson and Bagachwa respectively. Although Kessous and Lessard do not specifically mention public sector retrenchment, they do find in their survey that 30 per cent of the enterprises covered in their sample were created because the entrepreneur was either dismissed from a previous (public or private) job (8 per cent) or could not find any employment (22 per cent). This still leaves, however, 70 per cent of the enterprises being established out of other motives.

The entry of (ex-)civil servants into small enterprise activity cannot be attributed solely to the adjustment measures. As Bagachwa pointed out, the decline of real public sector wages below 'living wage' level is of pre-SAP origin. There was already an outflow of skilled labour from the public sector and it induced many public employees to undertake all kinds of activities alongside (see also Maliyamkono and Bagachwa, 1990 and Tripp, 1989).

Lastly, the entry of former civil servants into businesses has positive connotations given their education and skill levels. To what extent ex-civil servants move into industry rather than trade and services could not be established; it provides the potential for a new type of small enterprise.

The restructuring of parastatals and the elimination of state monopolies has in several instances opened up new opportunities for small enterprises. Dawson emphasizes this for Ghana and Bagachwa also illustrates this via the case of the National Milling Corporation which created opportunities for small-scale processing of grains.

With regard to domestic de-regulation, the impacts expected or observed by the various authors differ considerably depending on the pre-SAP situation. Dawson argues that domestic deregulation in Tanzania would have a much stronger positive impact than in the case of Ghana, given the greater importance of state controls and parastatals and the much stronger repression of the private sector in the former as compared to the latter. In the case of Zimbabwe, where there is a strong private sector alongside a large parastatal sector, Mumbengegwi expresses the concern that private sector monopolies will be the chief beneficiary and will capture new opportunies, leaving little room for entry of new indigenous SEs.

The elimination of domestic price controls may result in considerable price hikes which may undo the intended effect of currency devaluation (i.e. namely raising prices of imports relative to domestic prices). The high levels of inflation have had the unintended effect of seriously eroding the capital base of many small enterprises which, in view of the difficulties of access to credit, diminishes their capacity to adjust to changing market conditions.

Most opportunities tend to be generated in trade, transport and services, while far fewer are taken up in manufacturing. On balance the result may be a net loss in industrial capacity or the 'informalization' of part of it.

With regard to demand, governments in the countries concerned introduced measures to reduce public spending, to stimulate agriculture through improving the terms of trade, especially for export crops, and to stimulate investment and manufacturing export (using tax incentives and forex retention schemes). The actual package and timing of these measures varied from country to country and the impacts on small enterprises are difficult to trace and no doubt vary by sector and type of enterprise. In the case of Ghana, Osei *et al.* found that only 2 per cent of the enterprises that were surveyed were engaged in exports. In the case of Mali 15 per cent of the enterprises were exporting (directly or indirectly) part of their output, notably textiles/clothing; particularly 'post-adjustment' small enterprises were actively seeking export outlets. For Tanzania there are no clear indications to this effect, although Bagachwa provides some examples.

Since small enterprises normally do not cater to (or have access to) public sector demand for goods and services, they are also not directly affected by cuts in public spending. Linkages with large firms and with other small enterprises are argued to be weaker in Tanzania than in Ghana. On this basis, Dawson concludes that the transmission of growth effects from growth sectors to small enterprises is a positive phenomenon in Ghana.

The studies could not ascertain to what extent demand switching away from larger enterprises and in favour of lower-priced (and lower quality) SE products has taken place as a result of declining purchasing power in the domestic market.

The number of small enterprises keeps growing but, in the absence of information on disappearance of enterprises, it is difficult to ascertain net growth attributable to pre- or post-SAP periods. Whatever governments and NGOs have done over the past years (as part of SAP or not) to assist SEs with credit barely constitutes a trickle, as the overwhelming majority of small enterprises (95 per cent in Ghana and 80 per cent in Mali) have been set up with own and family resources and are run with customer and/or supplier credit and working capital financed from profits. A similar conclusion may be drawn with regard to training, which is predominantly non-formal.

As to the overall effect, it appears that 53 per cent of the small enterprises surveyed in Ghana experienced increased output and sales, while in Mali 45 per cent experienced an increase since the reforms were adopted (particularly in textiles, soap and building materials). In Ghana, the experiences are more polarized than in Mali as there is also a greater proportion of enterprises with decreasing output (37 per cent versus 18 per cent). This may be explained by the fact that the adjustment process in Ghana has been under way longer while in Mali the reform process is not more than four years old.

Are smaller enterprises doing better than larger enterprises? This question is relevant in so far as this is sometimes taken to mean that small enterprises outperform large ones when distortions are removed. For Ghana findings are inconclusive.

Osei *et al.* report that increases in output and sales are more modest for smaller and microenterprises than for larger ones. Steel and Webster (1990) found the opposite to be true. In the case of Mali, smaller enterprises tend to do better in terms of output growth than larger firms. For Tanzania there are no figures to support either position, while in the case of Zimbabwe, it is too early to establish this yet.

As indicated earlier, competing imports are on the whole also harmful to small enterprises, but large enterprises tend to suffer more from this (in Ghana and Mali). On the other hand, the rapidly rising prices of imports also generate new opportunities for domestic producers (e.g. in metal products, food processing equipment etc.), particularly in the case of Ghana.

The surveys show that small enterprises do not experience serious competition from large enterprises except in some specific product sectors. The most important source of competition are other small enterprises. More than two-thirds of the surveyed enterprises report this. Typical sectors are food processing, leather/shoemaking, furniture/woodwork. This is not likely to apply to Zimbabwe which has the most extensive manufacturing base of all four countries and which produces a wide range of durable and non-durable consumer, intermediate and some capital goods. Competition between small and large firms is likely to be more important.

On the whole, since the introduction of the reforms, competition has increased in stagnating or marginally-growing domestic markets and the main contributing source is the large influx of small enterprises. Not surprisingly, the growth of domestic demand is singled out as a key priority in order to sustain development of small enterprises and to escape from meaningless cut-throat competition.

To what extent are results sustainable? Is the growth of the number of small enterprises temporary, as a means of survival, as Mumbengegwi suggests? Osei *et al.* are more optimistic. They purport that the enterprises are here to stay: three-quarters of the surveyed entrepreneurs would remain with his/her enterprise even if offered other employment. Liedholm in this volume comes to similar findings but adds that the vast majority of microenterprises will remain small and fail in the first three years and the majority will not 'graduate' to become a modern, highly-productive undertaking.

If these small enterprises are here to stay, then policymakers should take the growth in number of small enterpises as a given fact when formulating new industrialization strategies. At the same time, it should be recognized that one is not dealing with an undifferentiated mass of enterprises. They may all be – to varying degrees – small, but they vary in behaviour, in place in the economy (sector, rural/urban, domestic/export, linkages), in capacity to respond to changing circumstances and so on. Future attention should therefore focus on more specific types or groups of enterprises and their dynamics. Dawson makes some tentative suggestions in this direction.

The final chapter in this part, by Francisco Uribe, stands somewhat apart in dealing with SE policy regimes in the Andean countries of Latin America. It offers a comparative perspective as these countries in terms of their macroeconomic performance over the past decade or so come close to SSA countries. Uribe observes that in spite of considerable variety in the general economic environment in the 1970s, the three countries (Chile, Equador and Colombia) have had very similar specific SSE policy regimes both in terms of (multiple) objectives (employment, poverty alleviation and regional development) and instruments (subsidized credit, training and technical assistance programmes). They have also had very similar poor achievements which are attributed to, among others, limited impact of financial incentives, limited reach and poor quality of assistance programmes. The performance of small enterprises is not so much influenced by the specific SSE policy regime but rather by other factors such as structural, macroeconomic and sectoral issues which differed significantly between the three countries.

Economic liberalization has advanced most in the 1980s in Chile as compared to Colombia, while it is most recent in Equador. All three countries are revising their SE policy regimes, placing emphasis on the restructuring of the SE sector and focusing on internal firm efficiency and competitiveness. In Chile this takes place under a banner of modernization, with emphasis on access to technology and services (including for export). Governments do see a need for a specific SE policy regime in which there is room for subsidies, for example in support of certain services and as a reward incentive, but there is a greater awareness that support systems should not be supply-driven but primarily market-based.

Financial policies and financial assistance to SE

The availability of credit is a key constraint for small enterprises, as the studies in the previous part have reconfirmed. It is therefore justified to single it out as a specific policy area.

Over the past decades, a range of initiatives have been undertaken and a lot of experimentation has taken place to provide financial assistance to SE ranging from DFI (development finance institution) and bank-based special SE programmes, credit guarantee schemes to various kinds of mixed systems in which formal and informal financial institutions participate. In addition there are important NGO-based financial assistance schemes available.

Without wishing to underplay the significance of micro-level factors, it is important to look at the macro dimension, in particular the question as to which policy environment is more conducive to success, especially as regards which domestic finance policy. The latter has played an important role in the past. Reference is made here to issues of the financial regime such as interest rate policy, credit targeting, and relationships between central bank and financial institutions. How have the financial liberalization measures undertaken under structural adjustment affected this financial regime and have they resulted in an increased availability of credit to SEs?

If the answer to the latter question is affirmative, what is the future role, if any, for special credit institutions (like the DFIs) and programmes (like those undertaken by NGOs)?

The papers in this second part volunteer some clear answers. Ernest Aryeetey begins by examining Ghana's experience with the effectiveness of credit allocation policies in channelling resources towards small enterprises. He shows that the adoption of selective credit ceilings and controls was followed by a *decline* of credit allocated to priority sectors (including manufacturing). If credit to indigenous sole proprietorships is taken as representing the major portion of small enterprises in manufacturing, then it can be shown that its share in domestic credit has consistently declined between 1985 and 1990.

Research into a sample of 100 small enterprises which were all operating with a current and/or savings account for quite some time (and hence enabling the respective banks to have a good knowledge of their histories) revealed that all (except one) had made requests for credit but 73 per cent were turned down and only one of the successful enterprises received the full amount requested. Aryeetey observes that 'while banks may argue that the remaining 73 per cent had no 'bankable projects', there is also every indication that this signifies the failure of the policy objective of treating small manufacturing enterprises as priority when no appropriate criteria had been developed for assessing the credit-worthiness of applications from such enterprises. In absence of suitable collateral, banks had no other means of striving to attain a policy goal. This occured at times when banks held excess reserves'.

Aryeetey examines two sets of factors. Firstly, the macroeconomic environment and the interest rate policy. Starting with the latter, real interest rates were negative during the greater part of the 1980s. Priority sectors which could borrow at lower rates were therefore even less attractive to the banks, apart from the fact that these sectors have generally been associated with higher risks than non-priority sectors. Low differentiation of interest rates was even more biased against higher-risk demands. The sectoral guidelines did not always take economic trends adequately into account. High priority sectors were not necessarily high performance sectors, while banks clearly focused their lending on the latter ones. The second set of factors concern banking system characteristics and practices. Sectoral guidelines and mandarory targets were often applied without due regard to the specialization within the banking system. Unfamiliarity with priority sectors and with small enterprises led to evasive and even more risk-averse practices, emphasizing the importance of collateral.

If detailed government interventions would not succeed in improving SE access to credit, would the opposite work? This question is examined by Ademola Oyejide for Nigeria. That country has also attempted to set targets for commercial and merchant bank loans to small enterprise and argues that this policy has failed and examines whether liberalization of the Nigerian financial system has led to a better availability of credit to small enterprises. Oyejide finds that the lowering of entry barriers into banking has led to a substantial increase in the number of banks operating in the country. The system of sectoral credit targeting was gradually phased out and interest rates were deregulated, causing a rapid rise and differentiation between interest rates. Notwithstanding there remained a strong commitment in Nigeria for government intervention in favour of small enterprise credit.

Oyejide examined the changing patterns of SE credit allocation between merchant, commercial and development banks, and found that credit from commercial and merchant banks rose much more rapidly than SE credit originating from the development banks. When dividing changes into a credit substitution effect and a credit volume effect he found that the credit substitution effect predominates, indicating that commercial and merchant banks are effectively switching towards small enterprise credit far in excess of old targets. This calls into question the efficacy of the old policies of sectoral targeting and also of the special credit institutions (development banks) and programmes which appear unable to mobilize resources and allocate with a capacity anywhere near that of the merchant and commercial banks.

The experiences from Kenya, analysed by Kirimi Mwarania, do not entirely tally with the ones from Nigeria. Kenya liberalized financial markets in the late seventies and early eighties, leading to a rapid increase in the number of financial institutions, but a credit squeeze in the mid-eighties caused a financial crisis as many new financial institutions collapsed. This led the government of Kenya to strengthen the regulatory framework and by implication create higher entry barriers to the financial industry (e.g. deposit protection funds, higher minimum paid-up capital, limiting deposit mobilization capacity, restrictive shareholdership, collateral lending as the only legal form). These measures indirectly affect the availability of credit to small enterprises. In 1989 Kenya adopted a second round of liberalizing reforms, including interest rate deregulation, monetary policy reforms, restructuring of ailing financial institutions and a restructuring of the two largest DFIs.

Mwarania examines the various potential sources of credit for small enterprises (commercial banks' special and normal lending, near bank financial institutions, DFIs, financial co-operatives, NGOs and government) and comes to the conclusion that only a small percentage of SEs have access to institutional credit. He argues that the future of SE financing in Kenya will depend on how Kenya will choose between two current but mutually inconsistent movements, the one being further financial liberalization and the other maintenance of a segmented financial market with a special financial regime, institutions (DFIs) and programmes aimed at small enterprises. The latter is still prevalent in the government's commitment to a development strategy in which small enterprise development plays a key role.

Mwarania is somewhat sceptical about the view (e.g. that of Oyejide) that liberalization of the financial market will increase the supply of credit to small enterprises. A key issue is to what extent the new entrants are able to withstand market downturns.

The effectiveness of special development finance institutions directed at small enterprises is the subject of the contribution by Roger Teszler. His analysis is restricted to those DFIs in Sub-Saharan Africa which were supported by the Dutch (or more precisely by the Netherlands Development Finance Company). These four DFIs specialized in SEs initially started with credit but many expanded into other support activities (management, technical advice, special microenterprise programmes, industrial estates, wholesale purchasing, etc.). Some of these additional activities have incurred heavy losses and also the credit operations have not done well, with arrears on interest between 10 and 50 per cent and arrears on loan principal between 5 and 25 per cent.

In view of the fact that commercial banks are moving towards (the top segment of) SE financing and that NGOs in Africa are becoming more active at the lower end of the market (microenterprise and minimalist lending), Teszler poses the question of the remaining role for the DFIs. In his view, DFIs should shed their non-loan activities and leave these to other specialized (public, business agencies and NGOs) agencies. Their remaining turnover (and number of clients reached) is extremely small which, apart from the high costs of SE credit applications (compared to large ones), is another important factor explaining the high cost/low profit character of their operations. Various options are discussed such as integrating DFIs into larger financial institutions or expanding the operations of the DFIs to cover all financial operations (including savings mobilization). Finally, Teszler still sees a potential role for the DFIs to form a bridge between formal and informal lending and to promote the formation of groups of SEs for the purpose of credit finance, including ROSCAs.

The latter is object of a study by Dejene Aredo who examines the role and functioning of the *iqqub* in Ethiopia. The *iqqub* is a type of rotating savings association with an element of chance in the awarding of the amount in each cycle. Basic principles and underlying procedures are analysed in general and for a number of specific cases. The *iqqub* is widespread in Ethiopia, in many sectors and for many purposes, and is said to have originated during the reconstruction during the Italian occupation. Its continued spread is explained, among others, by the repressed character of formal institutional credit to the private sector. The *iqqub* may involve fairly small amounts, as in predominantly rural areas for consumptive purposes, but may also involve large amounts, as for example among the big traders in Addis Ababa. Larger *iqqub*s are more institutionalized with elaborate by-laws, employ staff, have sophisticated mechanisms to compensate members for longer waiting times (which indicates non-zero interest rates) and have direct links with the banking system (to deposit receipts and use of cheques). These compensatory mechanisms also reduce the importance of the element of chance in the awarding of the lot in any cycle and therefore make the *iqqub* potentially more appropriate to finance SE credit needs. The design of financial policies and of SE financial assistance programmes should take the potential role of indigenous financial institutions such as the *iqqub* into account.

The final paper in this second part takes a different approach by looking at how financial needs evolve with the cycle of enterprise development. Based on evidence from across developing countries, Carl Liedholm arrives at a number of conclusions: first of all, that SE dynamics are characterized by high birth rates (10 per cent p.a.) and high death-rates. Approximately half of the SEs which close down are not financially profitable, while personal reasons are another important factor motivating closure. Notwithstanding failure, some 50 per cent will start a new enterprise, and only some 20 per cent will accept paid employment. Thus, there is a net addition to the number of entrepreneurs. The life cycle is characterized by a difficult initial period of, on average, three years. While two-thirds of the enterprises will remain the same size, those that do may experience considerable growth spurts which vary by country, sector, gender and location. Few SEs in Africa 'graduate' into larger size groups (fewer than elsewhere) and according to Liedholm, one of the explanatory factors is the finance problem.

Financial needs vary over the life cycle of the enterprise. Initially there is demand for investment capital (provided by own savings or from relatives, and later from suppliers and subcontracting firms). As the firms grows, working capital requirements tend to increase. 'Minimalist' credit programmes may cater to this enterprise expansion. Fixed capital investment for 'graduating' enterprises may be even more difficult to cater for. Technical assistance, credit guarantees and upgrading of special credit institutions (including saving mobilization) are some of the suggested answers, along with interest de-regulation.

The studies presented in this volume provide a good basis for answering the questions raised at the beginning of this section as regards financial policy. The experience with sectoral credit targeting for SSE has not been very successful and it seems reasonable to question the relevance and effectiveness of this instrument. Not only is it difficult to apply it (what percentage?) but also banks are creative enough in their definition of projects to shift portfolio from non-priority to priority sectors without actually changing their real clientele. Experiences show that in the practice of many countries policies are difficult to enforce or sanction.

Also with regard to below-market interest rates there has been a lot of ill-conceived policy. Interest deregulation and greater interest rate differentiation is seen as necessary to ensure an appropriate supply response.

The liberalization of the banking systems in Nigeria, freeing of interest rates and reducing barriers to entry of new banks seems to have improved the accessibility of SSE to commercial banking credit. The experiences in Kenya give reason for caution.

With regard to the financial assistance to SSE a distinction can be made between (1) commercial banks (2) public sector DFIs (3) business-oriented NGOs or private DFIs and (4) indigenous credit systems (ROSCAs).

With regard to commercial banks it can be concluded that they continue to be reluctant for well-known reasons (higher risks and defaults, higher per-unit administration costs). Guarantee schemes have only partially helped to induce the banks to become more active. The opening up of the banking system may actually stimulate banks to differentiate and get into a new niche of SSE lending.

Should donors/NGOs continue their efforts to try to stimulate banks to 'downgrade' lending operations to SME, e.g. by mixed systems where NGOs assume costs of intermediation? This would amount to 'subsidy diversion' which will make lending operations more cost effective and profitable. This would be a possible avenue but would require more investigation and experimentation in African countries on how to link the formal and the informal/NGO systems, whereby one could draw on experiences from other countries (see for example, Seibel and Parkusip, 1990)

With regard to public sector DFIs, there is a growing consensus that they appear to have outlived their original purpose. Several policy options can be considered:

(a) expand the range of DFI activities, thus also extend the range upmarket,
(b) integrate SSE DFI into banks,
(c) broaden the financial base of SSE DFIs, increasing financial autonomy, and/or
(d) find donors to subsidize the SSE DFIs on a longer-term basis.

With regard to private DFIs or business-oriented NGOs the situation is the reverse: they are growing rapidly in Africa. Particularly, single-purpose credit minimalist approaches seem to be working well. However, their clientele is also much smaller and selective. Sometimes, private DFIs have been active in diversifying their activities, including training and consultancy and in that way they are also able to subsidize overhead costs of their lending operation. To what extent this is a desirable strategy may be questioned in the light of experiences from elsewhere (Boomgard, 1989).

With regard to indigenous credit system ROSCAs, the Ethiopean case was of considerable interest as it showed a considerable diversity in arrangements and scale of operations of the *iqqub* system and the possibility of linkages with formal credit systems.

By way of conclusion, it could be stated that various contributions drift towards a reduced differentiation/segmentation in financial assistance programmes in Africa. The liberalization of the financial markets would induce the formal banking system to direct itself to the top scale of the market for SE credit, private DFIs to specialize in providing minimalist credit for enterprise expansion directed at micro and small enterprises, and specific targeted NGO-mediated programmes to concern themselves with survival and enterprise formation situations. Public DFIs would still be justified in those countries which lack a sufficiently-developed financial system.

Policies for sustaining direct assistance programmes

Over the last two decades, substantial experience has been built up with direct assistance programmes to SEs in the fields of technology and technology transfer, entrepreneurship development and training, as well as the promotion of female entrepreneurs. Although at micro-level the case for these programmes and projects is often very strong, evaluations quite frequently express concern about the high costs, limited reach and effectiveness of these programmes. Indeed it is not unusual that as a result, good projects and programmes do not develop beyond the pilot stage. While in some cases internal factors may explain this unintended outcome, in many cases the environment in which these programmes and projects were operating was difficult, indifferent or even hostile in economic and/or socio-political terms.

There is a growing realization that a greater concern for SE specificity (subsector focus) as well as for macro-institutional and policy issues is needed to ensure greater effectiveness and sustainability of these programmes. If public bodies (SMIDAs) are inefficient co-ordinators of support services to SEs, what alternatives can be considered?

Chapters in this volume look at two areas: promotion of women-led enterprises and technology and at the SE membership organization as a provider and co-ordinator of services.

Rudo Gaidzanwa argues that there is a lot of ignorance and misconception surrounding women entrepreneurs and programmes promoting them. She starts by painting, in rather broad strokes, a picture of African post-independence regimes in which 'nation building' and 'state building' took precedence over private entrepreneurship, though in varying degrees depending on the ideological position and international alliances of the élite.

Female entrepreneurship in Africa has specific historical and cultural deliniations. Historical differences in colonial history between West and East Africa explain the much more extended trade, craft and commerce of native peoples in the former. In the Eastern and Southern African settler economies there was much less room for native entrepreneurship. In these countries, non-agricultural enterprise activities are often undertaken by women in marginal positions (childless, divorced, widowed, accused of witchcraft and so on). The deepening economic crisis has stimulated women to venture into trade and craft activities in both conventional and non-conventional areas.

Aid organizations have tried to be 'gender-sensitive' but have failed to understand these dimensions of female entrepreneurship and have, in Zimbabwe, insisted on group-based 'enterprise formation' projects, even in those cases where activities would be barely profitable for one individual woman. Especially rural women were considered homogeneously poor, both in economic and social terms. In many other respects these organizations maintain false assumptions (e.g. about women's motivations) or over emphasize certain areas (e.g. credit and management skill training) and ignore others (e.g. marketing). Many activities undertaken by women are heavily regulated (e.g. food processing, cross-border trade) and women have found it best to operate in an informal manner and hence do not wish to be 'formalized' with credit or other assistance. Finally, many aided projects have ignored problems of sustainability of the enterprise activities arising from procurement of inputs or market fluctuations.

Depending on race, age, marital status, class and life experience, as well as economic conditions and opportunities, women pursue different types of entrepreneurial strategies and aid agencies cannot service these activities with standardized 'credit plus' programmes based on stereotypical conceptions of rural African women.

Marya Buvinic reviews different types of programmes designed to promote women-led enterprises in Latin America. This analysis is considered relevant also for Africa on the grounds that many of the enterprise activities are similar, even though the socio-economic and cultural positions of women are not necessarily the same (and, by Buvinic, seen as more favourable to African women).

Buvinic categorizes assistance programmes into three approaches: enterprise formation, enterprise expansion and enterprise transformation (cf. Boomgard, 1989). The main focus is on the first two of which the enterprise formation approach is the oldest and most persistent, in spite of its widespread dismal failure. Principal reasons as to why these projects 'misbehave' economically are the existence of multiple objectives (social along with economic ones), participatory styles of management, inadequate skill formation, and volunteerism among both project promotors and participants. The direct assistance projects aiming at enterprise expansion normally take the form of minimalist credit programmes with different modalities of implementation. In particular, parallel programmes outside the formal banking system replicate informal sector lending practices and rely on solidarity groups and reduced collateral requirements. In addition, Buvinic argues that programmes that are not gender-specific but take into account credit requirements of distinct activities in which women are active (e.g. commerce as against manufacturing) may have a greater positive gender impact.

Gaidzanwa and Buvinic have a common view on the poor performance of multi-objective, participatory, welfare-oriented women's group projects though they differ as to a preference for minimalist credit programmes. The reason being that African women are thought to have advanced socially less than their Latin American counterparts as evidenced for example by lower participation in post-primary education. They would require direct assistance in areas other than only credit. The two authors share, however, a concern for the wider policy and socio-political environment which tend to trap women in marginal roles and projects.

With regard to technology and technology policy, Samuel Wangwe argues the need to differentiate SEs in terms of their place in the economy, for example a distinction between SSEs operating in final demand sectors with individualized products, SSEs operating on a subcontracting basis to larger firms and SSEs operating in competition with larger firms. New technologies do not necessarily have a large-scale bias, even though they may require considerable initial investment. Much depends on the sector concerned. Experience in some Asian countries has shown that, with appropriate government and other institutional support, small enterprises have been able to play a major role in export-led industrialization in new product areas. In the case of Africa, Wangwe sees prospects for blending new technologies with traditional ones, for example in biotechnology and food processing. New technologies are however knowledge- and skill-intensive and therefore require highly-trained entrepreneurs.

Past technology policies and programmes have tended to emphasize transfer of more or less appropriate (imported) technology without placing emphasis on domestic technological capacity. Wangwe gives several examples of instances of such biases in technology transfer projects as well as other bi- and multilateral projects. New policies would have to emphasize generation of local technologies. Technology acquisition by SSEs themselves should be a prime policy consideration, as there is sufficient evidence that small manufacturing enterprises have the potential for innovation but often lack information and access. The financing of systems supporting technology acquisition is likely to be one of the critical factors.

If government is increasingly seen as an inefficient provider of direct assistance and services to small enterprises, would there be a role for small enterprise associations? Jake Levitsky concerns himself with this matter. Apart from foundations (such as NGOs) there are also membership organizations (associations, trade or business organizations and federations and chambers of commerce). In his review, Levitsky points to the German 'Handwerkskammer' which is a special chamber of small craft enterprises which consists of 65 state-level associations and one federal or central one. The 'Handwerk' system undertakes a wide range of functions, including the vocational training, examinations and certification of trades, insurance, information and advice, promotion, R. & D., finance and savings.

A review of the current status of small enterprise associations in developing countries is undertaken which shows a number of weaknesses which are subsequently discussed (including low membership, poor leadership, inefficient management, non-acceptance by government and inadequate finance). In spite of these, Levitsky remains positive about these organizations and their potential capacity and argues that any transition from a public sector-dominated SSE assistance towards a more pluriform system of services would inevitably be a long and drawn-out process and proposes a transitional phase in which local SE membership associations would play a role as referral points. In his view, donors should support the institutional strengthening of these organizations subject to a number of considerations.

Small enterprise and industrialization policies in Africa: some notes

A.H.J. (BERT) HELMSING

Introduction

Currently a lot of attention is being paid to macro-policy dimensions of SSE and to issues of efficiency of current small-scale enterprises. This debate follows an era in which most attention was paid to researching the quantity dimensions of SEs (how many, how important). Although the current debate has clarified a number of important issues (negative impact of credit, trade and regulatory policies on SSE) and has pinpointed the need for empirical research to verify certain conclusions (e.g. on the impact of trade and exchange rate policies), the debate has not yet paid sufficient attention to the long-term perspective of the role of SSE in the industrialization process.

What is the role of SEs in general or of particular types of SEs in the industrialization process? Since the study of Anderson (1982a) which appeared ten years ago, little attention has been paid to these relationships. Starting from a broad three-type classification of household manufacturing, small workshops and factories, and large factory-type production, the main argument of Anderson is that there is a systematic tendency of household manufacturing to decline while the share of large factories tends to rise regularly. The intermediate category of workshops and small factories would have a low share in an early period, rapidly rising in the intermediate period of change, and tapering off when large factory production would gain predominance (Anderson, 1982a). It should be noted that the database is actually extremely limited, and often on an establishment basis rather than on an enterprise unit basis. Some further work has been done on India and Colombia, but with regard to Africa historical evidence is rather scanty.

A closer examination of industrialization in Africa may throw some different light on this issue. This is not the place to make a detailed analysis, but some notes are offered which emphasize particular aspects. Even these notes should be treated with care, given the considerable heterogeneity of experiences among African countries. I wish to add that the analysis below has a clear bias towards Southern and Eastern Africa given the greater familiarity and affinity with the countries of this region.

These historical notes are followed by a brief look at flexible production systems which are heralded by a number of authors as a new basis (if not paradigm) for small enterprise development. Although one needs to be cautious about the immediate relevance of the concept, case studies point to several important and hitherto under-emphasized dimensions of industrial policy.

The final section of this paper reflects on conclusions in terms of the main themes of this volume.

Small enterprise development and industrialization in Africa

Most studies on African industrialization tend to start and remain preoccupied with factory industrialization. Alongside, there has always existed artisan household production and craft village industries which gained ground in some trades such as metal-working for the making of weapons and agricultural tools, in the making of wood and reed products in construction and building materials and in some parts also in textiles. Freeman and Norcliffe (1985a) give a summary review with regard to Kenya, pointing to the importance of long distance and inter-tribal trade between the interior and the coastal areas.

Certain trades have been associated with particular lineages and have had strong cultural connotations (for blacksmithing, see Fyle, 1987). The importance of lineages facilitated the transfer of technological know-how. It is surprising how little is known about this.

What happened to small enterprises during African industrialization? Three main sets of forces stand out which partly overlap in time and which vary considerably in relative importance across the various countries, namely: (i) effects of colonial policies on crafts and village industries, (ii) effects of import-substituting industrialization, (iii) effects of post-colonial industrialization policies in mixed and state socialist countries. The main arguments in each of these will be given below in the context of Southern and Eastern Africa.

Colonial policies undermined household and village industries in several ways. One important factor, which in Southern African countries played a significant role, has been the direct suppression of independent artisan craft and trade activities in urban areas. Yoshikuni reports on this for Zimbabwe. Early colonial policies were directed at preventing the African population from developing urban roots. Prohibiting independent economic activity and ownership of urban land and property was part of this policy implemented through local councils (Yoshikuni, 1984). In other words, indigenous artisans could not benefit from the growth of urban demand in order to grow in number or to make a transition from purely household-based production towards small urban workshops. The suppression of retail trade meant that small enterprise rural/urban trade linkages did not develop. Since the population in the African locations or townships was meant to provide labour services to the colonial economy, independent economic activity as well as situations conducive to such activities (including unemployment status) was heavily regulated. Much of the current restrictive legislation regulating small enterprise activity in urban areas has colonial origins (Tripp, 1989). Finally, railway construction brought along new trade activity in the areas along the 'line of rail' which tended to be dominated by shopkeepers and tradesmen from among Indian workers who were brought in to build the railways.

A second factor negatively affecting the development of small enterprise was the general discouragement of agricultural surplus production in the 'African Reserves' and the use of discriminatory measures to prevent market participation by peasants (including via state monopsonies and appointed licence traders as well as taxation). Taken together, these constrained local demand in peasant areas for manufactured goods (consumer and agricultural implements). Arrighi (1970) has given historical evidence for Rhodesia indicating that prior to the Land Apportionment Act of 1930 which caused a massive appropriation of land and dislocation of African population, peasants were quite responsive to the economic opportunities generated by the rapid extension and expansion of mining activities which they provided with food products and other consumables.

The land alienation and forced migration to marginal agricultural land in countries where settler economies developed further undermined the productive basis of the black population and with this demand and supply capabilities within existing local industries in rural areas.

Particularly in those countries where labour migration systems emerged (Zimbabwe, Malawi, Zambia), the black rural areas' role in the wider economy was restricted to the export of labour, reducing their own economies to subsistence production in both agricultural and non-agricultural activities.

Together these factors reduced the exposure to technical and product innovations (while the very sparsely-provided education reduced the ability for the adoption and adaptation of these innovations) and to the development of higher levels in the division of labour in both agricultural and non-agricultural activities and enterprise within these African areas. The absence of formation of urban centres and a very selective policy to provide urban and modern physical, economic and social infrastructure prevented the emergence of external economies of scale and a local-level development of the social division of labour and specialization. This was further enhanced by the fact that trade between different 'African Reserves' was subject to several legal restrictions.

The restricted urbanization and indicated discriminatory policies prevented black artisans from migrating to the towns to develop their trade (Yoshikuni, 1984). As a result, local small industries were deadlocked as regards their development in rural areas and there was no alternative urban option from which to develop new small enterprises.

The labour migration system which developed to serve white farming areas and later factories and urban households took away much productive entrepreneurship. Many rural industries were set up, only *after* workers returned from urban wage employment (fired or retired). Thus, at a much older age (40s) and very likely with less disposition to innovate, this self-employment is more likely a form of retirement.

Import-substituting industrialization

What were the effects of the process of import-substituting industrialization (ISI) and its policies of the sixties and seventies on small enterprise development in Africa? The so-called import-substituting industries were generally of a factory mass-production type, even though the scale was much smaller than in Europe or the United States. Current evidence on African manufacturing shows that the process remained primarily in its 'first stage' with consumer goods industries. Only a few countries have realized higher stages of ISI development and have built up some significant intermediate and capital goods industries (Fransman, 1982; Riddell, 1990).

Mass production of consumer goods whether assembly, process technology or large batch production, benefits from economies of scale when in large standardized production runs. Competition is primarily via price. Assembly-type production is inflexible and involves a detailed prescription of labour tasks which are routinized. Apart from production and process control, these industries mainly need semi- and unskilled labour. If continuous assembly and process technology is not possible, one could still operate with large batch production runs which would make these industries suitable for similar labour management situations.

Since the consumer goods industries were already technologically mature in Europe, their 'export' to Africa as ready-made plants and factories could take place relatively easily (following the decentralization propositions of 'product cycle' theories), if and when necessary, and with expatriate process-controllers and plant supervisors. Given the skill gap, local labour was only employed at a semi- or unskilled level. The latter was of significance as it reduced the need for a heavy initial investment and current expenditures in education and vocational or technical training for the black population in order to reduce any skill gap.

Given the relatively small size of the domestic markets, one or two plants could adequately cater for the entire market. Intermediate inputs would continue to be imported from advanced countries and 'embody', as it were, important human and technological progress.

As has been well-documented, import-substitution industrialization in most African countries did not develop into more advanced stages (Riddell, 1990). The principal reason that is normally given is inadequate demand to sustain second and third stage industries but, no doubt, also other factors have played a role, for example, the very absence of an adequately developed techno-institutional support structure. Without that support structure some industries managed to integrate vertically and in this way partially compensate for this lack (for example by manufacturing components and inputs, handling transport and setting up wholesale retail systems).

Given the features described above (mass production in small markets), monopolistic and oligopolistic market structures emerged with a few large enterprises (which were sometimes nationalized after independence). Most foreign investment in these industries during this period was oriented towards local markets and not towards (re-)export. As a result, there was little inducement to encourage local

R. & D. capacity to develop product lines. If it happened, it was basically copied from parent companies in the West (examples are in farm equipment, vehicle assembly, etc.).

Market penetration was inward, relying mostly on domestic internal or external wholesale/retail structures. Since manufacturing production was largely oligopolistic or monopolistic, there were few incentives to develop marketing capacity and skills so as to respond to consumer reactions and requirements, or to refine and adjust product specifications to suit local requirements.

Also, trade systems themselves did not develop that capacity. Product differentiation remained restricted to standardized models and with that the learning ground to experiment with technologies which normally would be the initial step in mastering particular technologies and making them adaptable to local conditions. Thus, apart from well-known problems such as ownership of technology, incremental technological progress was stimulated in this way.

Given the low levels of income, most mass-produced products were in fact either new products or objectively or subjectively superior substitutes to local indigenous makes. The latter meant that local small producers were relegated to marginal market positions and many shifted from manufacturing to repair (e.g in clothing).

Industrialization policies of the period were directed toward protecting domestic factory producers from competing imports through tariffs or quantity restrictions. And, as foreign exchange became more and more scarce, policies followed which increasingly regulated foreign exchange allocation to licensed producers, thereby increasing barriers to entry by small industrialists and traders. The high priority given to industry implied a relative neglect of agriculture, often accentuated by worsening terms of trade for agriculture resulting from price and taxation policies.

One preliminary conclusion would be that if in the colonial period the spread of industrialization to African enterprises was deliberately repressed, the import-substituting industrialization did not stimulate small enterprise development either, as it remained concentrated in a few manufacturing units, heavily dependent on imports and with little inducement to learn and spread economic opportunity.

Colonial and import-substituting industrialization policies reduced local-level demand in African areas. Local/regional exports of existing household and small enterprise production as the second route to an expanded local division of labour, endogenous transformation, and scale enlargement of African small enterprise was foreclosed due to the presence of large import-substituting industries in major urban centres. The latter further delimited the marginal position of small producers.

Not only urban middle and upper classes but also government considered small producers 'unprogressive', and the main priority was given to further development of mass-production manufacturing through import substitution. The very fact that mass-production manufacturing of consumer goods was established 'in short periods', without first requiring a local development of an elaborate social division of labour (agriculture/industry) with the associated requirements in terms of development of public and private techno-institutional support systems gave further support to the belief that a 'faster road to industrialization' was possible (according to the well-known Hirschman adage of the day: namely of 'having the advantage of being a late-comer'). Much of the techno-institutional support systems were either integrated within enterprises or groups of enterprises, and/or were provided by foreign investors/multinational corporations, expatriates and/or local settler/migrant minorities.

Post-independence policies of industrialization

Obviously for some countries these post-independence policies overlapped with the import-substitution industrialization discussed above. Apart from that overlap, one would have to differentiate here between those countries which followed a state socialist road and those countries which adopted a more nationalist mixed economy stance.

Since the industries that were established were monopolist or oligopolist producers, either under foreign or expatriate ownership, and/or with considerable expatriate technical and managerial domination, the newly independent governments often assumed a control-oriented policy (Riddell, 1990). Through administrative measures, foreign exchange allocation, investment regulation and the like, governments gained considerable control. Lack of trust, sometimes combined with politicians' and bureaucrats' lack of familiarity with mass-manufacturing industry, and with political constraints of dealing with minorities, created a restrictive business environment rather than a supportive government industrialization policy.

Government attitudes towards African small enterprise were often quite negative. As so often concluded by observers, almost all African countries have some programmes to promote small enterprises but apart from these programmes, government actions ignore or are even detrimental to small enterprise development. Although nowadays several countries have gone to considerable lengths to develop a comprehensive and systematic policy (e.g. Kenya), there still is considerable truth in this statement — certainly for the seventies and early eighties.

In some African countries the expatriate community left at the time of independence. In some cases this led to a virtual collapse of industries (former Belgian colonies, Mozambique, Angola); in others the departure was not *en masse* and the consequent loss was less complete.

Africanization of economic activity took place to a significant degree in many countries, but often primarily in farming, trade, transport, and real estate (for Kenya, see Leys, 1982). In manufacturing industry, however, this process was much slower and in many countries not very extensive. Kenya appears to be an exception where Kenyan ownership and control has advanced significantly (Kaplinsky, 1982). In Zimbabwe, more than half of the manufacturing sector is foreign-owned while an additional large share is white-owned (see Clark, 1980; UNIDO, 1986). Several countries, such as Nigeria and Kenya, have had 'indigenization of ownership' schemes in order to stimulate an active participation of the black business community.

In countries which pursued a more state socialist development strategy, there were clear discriminatory measures not only against non-indigenous but also against black small enterprise development. Bagachwa (1981) and Tripp (1989) discuss several examples of discriminatory measures. The Basic Industrialization Strategy of Tanzania focused mostly on large-scale state-led industrialization. Further, only certain forms of small enterprise development were permitted, but these would have to fall under the responsibility of the village governments and be run as co-operatives. Individual enterprise was not part of the strategy. It is therefore not surprising that in his study on rural economy, Collier noted the rather low frequency of artisan producers in the Tanzanian countryside (Collier *et al.*, 1986).

In the early post-independence period in Zimbabwe there was a similar bias against small enterprise. Only registered co-operatives could get access to financial support while individually-owned businesses had considerable difficulties qualifying for government-sponsored programmes (Helmsing, 1991b).

In the eyes of many public officials these businessmen/women were technologically backward and had a clear tendency towards trading. Of course, there is some truth in that position but it should be seen in the light of the historical constraints on the development of small black-run enterprise. Moreover, policies towards human resource development continued to be biased, targeting the needs of public administration and public services rather than technical and vocational training. Kenya is a notable exception with its early vocational training efforts (including village polytechnics).

Existing factory industries are an important source of technical expertise for urban SSE in Zimbabwe (Moyo *et al.*, 1984), while in rural areas in Malawi, Zimbabwe, Kenya and Zambia most entrepreneurs are self-taught or have learned from relatives and friends (respectively, Ettema (1984, 1987), Helmsing (1986b), Freeman and Norcliffe (1985), Milimo and Fisseka (1986). Understandably in view of its history, the latter has limited application, implies a slower rate of technical progress and often, though not always, low productivity. In West Africa there is a much wider spread of apprentice system (Berry, 1977). There is no clear explanation as to why this difference exists, but it may be related to an even smaller presence of factory industries and/or longer tradition of indigenous small enterprise.

The limited technological advance does not mean that entrepreneurs are backward, but quite a number of the products are. Kenneth King's well-known study of Kenyan machine-makers is evidence of their considerable ingenuity and capacity (King, 1974). There is also much scope for technological advance, certainly for incremental change in some sectors (e.g. car repair and reconditioning as well as manufacture of vehicle parts and components). But in other sectors products are sometimes displaced inappropriately as exemplified by the well-known example of the automated bread factory in Dar es Salaam. Other examples of substitutes are soap and detergents, hollow-ware and building materials. Similarly, in some product sectors there is simply no tradition of artisan or craft industry existing from which small enterprise could potentially emerge, such as pharmaceutical, electronics, computers, printing and publishing, etc.

Taking these observations together, it may be concluded that the process of industrialization in Southern and Eastern Africa has been distorted both at the top as well as at the bottom of the enterprise structure. The internal division of labour (in terms of work organization and internal division of tasks) within small enterprises is limited (Sverrisson, 1990 on the furniture-making industry). In the absence of the reasonably-advanced external social division of labour (among carpenters and development of specialized inputs, machinery services etc.), it becomes difficult to achieve higher productivity on the basis of poor local demand only.

On the other hand, if demand permitted and conditions were stable, monopolistic/oligopolistic enterprises (be these large by international comparison, or medium to small) located in urban centres would, based on their market strength in one sector, reinvest accumulated profits in other product sectors. Given the limited size of the market and the ISI tariff protection of that market, vertical integration as well as further diversification would take place within manufacturing as well as outside in transport, real estate, commercial agriculture and services. This would lead to the formation of conglomerate groups of enterprises. In many countries of the region a few conglomerates dominate a significant share of the economy (Fransman, 1982). The economic strength of these conglomerates may even have hardened governments' control-oriented attitude towards the manufacturing sector in general.

When the economic situation worsens, firms may reduce their productive investments altogether and move into trade, urban and rural property, etc. This is what happened in the eighties in countries like Malawi, Zambia and Zimbabwe where private sector domestic capital formation came to a virtual standstill (Frischtak, 1990; Green and Kadhani, 1986).

There were few interrelations between these two sides of the industrial structure. Small enterprise is predominantly rural, often of secondary importance in terms of income and employment, with a limited internal division of labour and primarily catering to local demand. Given the discriminatory policies of the past, urban small enterprise expansion is of more recent origin. In the eighties the numerical expansion of the number of small enterprises was, to a large extent, a response to the worsening economic conditions and real wage deterioration (Maliyamkono and Bagachwa, 1990; Tripp, 1989).

In view of the past trends there is a much shorter tradition in small enterprise manufacturing. Enterprises have been predominantly founded by the current owner and the majority have a farming background or are concurrently engaged in agriculture. In contrast, it is interesting to recall that although Berry reported 86 per cent of Colombian metal-working firms to have been bought by the owner; only 14 per cent was founded by the current owner. Even in the case of food processing, characterized by lower initial capital investments, still one-third of the enterprises were purchased (Cortes *et al.*, 1987). None of the entrepreneurs had a direct farming background. The latter is also found to be the case for Indian small manufacturing enterprises (Little *et al.*, 1987).

As a consequence business practices are less routine or standardized, transaction time and costs remain high, and few specialized agents (trade, finance, and training) are involved. Production remains heavily dependent on personal relationships, something which takes a considerable amount of the entrepreneurs' time (Berry, 1984). Conditions for specialization and development of the external and internal division of labour of small enterprises are not very favourable. There is lateral mobility from one product sector to another rather than movement within a particular product sector.

In addition, it is well known that African small enterprises have little, if any, access to credit through the banking system (Liedholm, 1985 and studies in this volume). But at the same time it should be noted that, relatively speaking, few African enterprises have been reported to make use of informal sources of credit. Most finance operates entirely from own and family sources and through customer (rather than supplier) credit. This contrasts with more extensive informal lending by Asian small enterprises. Thus, in spite of the widely-reported demand there may actually be less effective demand than often suggested.

Frischtak (1990) made the point that since marketing is primarily done by small enterprises themselves and directed solely to the localized market area, there is little scope to break out of the local demand constraint. He suggested that rural small enterprises in Malawi need to be connected up to larger markets, something which required the involvement of 'larger or at least more sophisticated traders and producers'. Apart from the question as to whether this suggestion is practicable, the observation does make one ponder whether it is at all realistic to assume that rural small enterprises would form the basis of more elaborate social division of labour in industry.

In other words it is not just a matter of micro-level features of a small enterprise, but equally the external division of labour in which it is operating. Many small enterprise promotional programmes only look at the micro-level dimension and ignore local, regional and sectoral ones.

Will the current wave of structural adjustment be the answer to these problems? Will industrial structures be adjusted and if so in what direction? Are the issues of the industrial basis directly addressed?

Policies aimed at achieving fiscal discipline and the related retrenchment of civil servants and adoption of costs recovery in the basic services it provides will have negative demand effects. The improvements of producer prices in agriculture would be positive in some rural areas but negative in all urban ones. Trade liberalization effects may work one way or the other depending on the characteristics of the sector concerned. The reduced direct intervention by the state in industry, such as the elimination of administrative allocation of foreign exchange, of investment control, of industry licensing as well as of clearly discriminatory policies against small enterprises, will all reduce restrictions and increase competition, but will it induce growth?

In this connection there appear to be two main issues. The first point is the one made recently by Roger Riddell. His main contentions are, among others, that efficient manufacturing production can occur under a far from liberal trade regime, that factors other than price determine the extreme variation in efficiency in various manufacturing sectors, that a sustained export drive also requires far more than a mere cost advantage (see also Stein and Nafziger, 1991); that the development of manufacturing depends critically upon the presence of an adequate base of domestic skills, and that sustained import substitution and development of linkages between subsectors of manufacturing is unlikely to take place without recourse to specific incentives and industrial promotion activities (Riddell, 1990). Putting it in other terms, Riddell is rather doubtful that structural adjustment addresses the long-term issues of industrial development. The latter requires, in his view, a supportive government policy which, one would add, would look quite different from the policies pursued in the 1970s and 1980s. A greater reliance on private sector development, market mechanisms and relationships, while necessary, perhaps ignores the fact that market relationships are weakly developed in the first place. Considerable *initial* investment may be needed to develop the techno-institutional environment for manufacturing industry; this may require substantial public funding (though not necessarily public provisioning).

The rigorous application of liberalization measures may eliminate or bring existing large manufacturing enterprises into severe difficulties. They would lose their monopolistic/oligopolistic character in the face of competing imports. While there may be a favourable effect through reduced pricing of goods, if coming as an economic shock it may precipitate a rapid collapse of these often vertically-integrated enterprises with a consequent loss of organizational capacity for manufacturing. Would a more controlled process of 'vertical disintegration' of the large enterprises and the simultaneous formation of small enterprises be a more attractive option? At least, one should consider the possibility that the disintegration of the large enterprise could become a seedbed for new small enterprises. Similar questions may be asked in relation to privatization of large manufacturing public enterprises.

Given the suppressed indigenous industrial base, is it realistic to leave it to marketforces for dynamic entrepreneurs to emerge by 'natural selection'? Many rural entrepreneurs may decide to hold on to part-time farming and non-farming activities rather than transform themselves into small manufacturing enterprises. The transformation from peasant to farmer has proven to be a complex process. Is there likely to be much difference transforming peasant/artisan into small-scale industrialist? Is the concern for rural industrialization ignoring the fact that historically only few peasants/artisans have become modern industrialists and that new waves of industrialization were carried out by *new generations* of entrepreneurs and business(wo)men, be these descendants of artisan families or unrelated entrepreneurs, or former workers in existing industries? Should the focus move away from peasant/artisans towards potential new, and differently-qualified, entrants into manufacturing?

Should lessons be drawn from the fact that most new industrial development has taken place in towns? The reason being historically that these had sufficient concentration of demand as well as basic supply conditions to start full-time or primary income-generating industrial workshops. I am not suggesting here a new urban bias, but I am considering the mere fact that except for the most intensive farming areas, local demand in any particular area in Africa may simply be too small to sustain a diversified industrial base while high transport costs (plus poor road conditions) may prevent the emergence of local-regional exports.

Should an industrial policy perhaps focus on selected areas and product sectors given the considerable requirements to establish firm roots for industrial development? Do the techno-institutional and infrastructural requirements of industry demand a more selective choice of selected urban centres and of sectors?

Flexible production systems as a new basis for SE industrialization

Although artisan and small enterprise production in Europe had lost ground to large mass production enterprises, during the late seventies and eighties publications appeared which signalled a successful transformation of small enterprises in some areas into flexible production systems (Piore and Sabel, 1984).

Flexible production systems concern 'forms of production characterized by a well developed ability to shift promptly from one process and/or product configuration to another (dynamic flexibility) and to adjust quantities of output rapidly up or down over the short run without any strongly deleterious effects on levels of efficiency (static flexibility)' (Storper, 1990).

Flexible production systems may develop among groups of small firms, though it may also be orchestrated by a large firm (as in Japan) and areas like the 'Third Italy' in the north-eastern part of that country that are claimed to have these characteristics (see Piore and Sabel, 1983; Goodman and Bamford, 1989).

Flexible production systems contrast with mass production systems. Differences at firm level relate to: (a) use of specialized dedicated equipment, (b) the degree of standardization of products and (c) the length of production runs. Flexible production systems are characterized by general purpose equipment that can be quickly adapted, retooled or reprogrammed for new production specifications. Flexibility may be craft based or have a high technology basis (Storper and Scott, 1990). In addition, horizontal and vertical disintegration and fragmentation within large firms has given rise to a new division of labour between firms. The production process as a whole takes place within a network of firms through subcontracting.

The degree of product differentiation is growing in world markets and this could enable producers to tap specific market niches (in style, quality, etc.). Production runs are generally small, which requires a core of highly-skilled labour that can be deployed in a great variety of work situations. At the same time, flexible production systems give rise to a proliferation of forms of labour and work (Storper, 1990).

Flexible production systems require considerable proximity between the firms in order to achieve flexibility in combinations of horizontal and vertical linkages between firms, and to facilitate the intense interaction and communication between firms playing different roles in the network so as to generate the kind of incremental technical change which is so important for maintaining competitiveness (Brusco, 1989). In addition, close location of business services is important in order to be able to respond quickly to market opportunities, both domestically as well as abroad. The proximity of the participating firms has given rise to the close association between the concept of flexible production and of industrial districts (Sengenberger, 1988; Sengenberger and Pyke, 1991)

In their study of experiences of flexible specialization in Europe, Piore and Sabel (1984) point, in particular, to supportive roles of government, not only of central government but in particular of local and regional governments. Flexible production systems may have high social costs in terms of labour requirements (flexible work schedules, flexible employment and turnover of labour) as well as in terms of high rates of firm exits. Flexibility can be sustained if there are mechanisms to compensate for these negative consequences. The existence of traditional social organization facilitated the development and sustainability of flexible production systems. In addition, local government roles were critical in the Italian case not only in easing the absorption of the social costs but also in providing public infrastructure and social services, facilitating tripartite solutions of conflicts, etc. (Brusco 1989; Trigilia, 1989). According to Brusco, governments must be prepared to support services to industry in the fields of market research and monitoring technology developments and of training. Given the initial high costs of developing these services, market-based initiatives are not easily responding to these small enterprise needs (Brusco, 1989).

Given these characteristics it is argued that flexible production systems are suitable for small enterprise development, even though it is not to be ignored that also large firms can also adopt principles of flexible production. Given the globalization of product markets, large firms are increasingly concerned about the efficiency of their material input and service providers. Nowadays, what matters is the overall efficiency and quality of the *entire* production column which has a decisive influence over the position of large firms in world markets.

Schmitz has raised the question whether flexible production systems may be a model on which to base a small enterprise development strategy for Third World countries (Schmitz 1989, 1990). It is not my intention to advocate flexible production systems as a new conceptual answer for the role of small enterprises in African industrialization, but in this connection there are some useful points.

First is the importance of the interrelations between firms (this goes much further than simply sharing tools and equipment) which enable the generation of economies of agglomeration which otherwise would not be available to the firms. Participating firms assume different subcontracting roles (producing inputs, components, or parts of an order); the concentration allows for the emergence of specialized producer services which none of the firms would be able to internalize individually. Participation of producers and repairers of equipment facilitates the process of incremental technical change at the firm level.

Second, the importance of local social organization to facilitate the emergence of flexible production systems of firms is also to be noted. Flexible production points to the fact that success is not just a question of technology or capital but also a matter of social (and political) organization (Trigilia, 1989).

Third, central, and above all local/regional, governments can play a supportive role with regard to industrial development — a mediating role to ease social and class conflicts and absorb the social costs of flexibility.

Fourth, flexible production is not inconsistent with the phenomenon which is found in world markets, namely considerable cross-penetration of markets. It allows penetration in variously defined market segments. The example of Hong Kong shows that small trading companies have played an important role, although definitely not conforming to the postulates of flexible production systems as hubs co-ordinating export demand and small firm producers (Yung W. R. and Soulier, 1989).

The key question is 'who organizes the flexible production system as a whole'? In the European case studies this question is not always clearly answered. For Italy, large firms began to decentralize their production to non-union areas in response to trade union strength in the large industrial centres. In addition, local historical socio-political as well as technological and market demand factors contributed to the emergence of flexible production systems (Goodman and Bamford, 1989).

It is assumed that operating as a network increases the collective capability, as each individual firm can call upon others to produce part of orders, inputs or components on a competitive subcontracting basis. Brusco argues that the existence of large numbers of firms ensures that competitive conditions prevail. Without such market conditions, flexible production may result instead in 'flexible exploitation' and little growth. It should be added though that a system which is 'orchestrated' by larger firms would not necessarily degenerate into such a state as long as government plays a role by preventing restrictive monopolistic practices in subcontracting and implements an appropriate social policy. A similar point is made by Van Meerendonk and Picavet for small enterprise handloom exports (van Meerendonk and Picavet, 1990).

Instead of directly intervening in the economic running of enterprises, governments facilitate their existence and adjustment by providing business/techno-institutional support (because of the high initial costs of these provisions) and by playing an important role in terms of a social policy (cushioning the effects of flexibility).

Some policy questions

After having made a somewhat historical *tour d'horizon* through small enterprise development and industrialization in Southern and Eastern Africa and discussed flexible production in relation to small enterprise development, I will conclude by raising some policy questions in terms of the three main themes of this book.

The pattern of industrialization in Southern and Eastern Africa has been distorted. The development of SSE, through a transformation of indigenous artisan and village industries and by entry of new entrepreneurs, has been severely weakened not only by the colonial urban and industrial policies of the past but also by post-independence industrialization policies, though there are significant differences between countries, particular circumstances and ideologies.

At the same time, by implanting mass production, import-substituting industrialization was seen as a faster road to progress without the apparent necessity of having to make large initial investments over an extended period of time in the techno-institutional environment (human resources, research, technology, economic, and social infrastructure). The vertical integration of large firms together with a continued dependence on import of inputs and the low level of the division of labour within the small firms created a fragmented industrial structure characterized by a low level of external division of labour as evidence by limited linkages between firms (among large, among small, and between both).

Considering structural adjustment in relation to small enterprises, it is relevant to raise the question as to what governments can do, if anything, to restructure industry and what role small enterprises can play in this context. I have argued that structural adjustment policies that would only focus on macroeconomic management and not actively address the problems of industrial restructuring and the issues of the techno-institutional support systems for industries may actually undermine the long-run growth potential.

With regard to the role of small enterprises, several questions are emerging. To what extent should promotion of small enterprises continue to be broad, covering both part-time and full-time enterprises, both rural and urban ones? Should one continue to focus on existing entrepreneurs or on entry of *new* and differently-qualified entrepreneurs and enterprises? These are important policy choices. For example, a programme concentrating on enterprise development at universities among university graduates and technical training institutes and agricultural colleges may reach far fewer would-be entrepreneurs than large low-cost programmes of enterprise development in urban and rural areas, but would the latter achieve better long-run results?

Putting it differently, should direct assistance programmes be 'widened' or 'deepened'? The former would lead to a preference for low-cost minimum package programmes of microenterprise formation and expansion, while the second would imply a selective concentration on much more expensive enterprise transformation programmes and associated development of techno-institutional support systems for particular product sectors and areas.

No doubt the most desirable situation would be a combination of both which would vary from country to country. However, the optimal mix should be the result of a deliberate policy reflection and not the accidental outcome of an unplanned mix of NGOs or of donor agencies operating in any of the countries concerned.

A related policy question concerns the goals of SSE promotion. Is it an instrument to combat rural and/or urban poverty or is it part of a broader strategy of re-industrialization and industrial restructuring? How realistic is the first option in market terms if the basis on which the poor can participate in market relationships is so weak (worsened by declining health and education)? What will the second option do to rural and urban poverty?

The restructuring of African industries may be left entirely to market forces and macroeconomic management but that may, in the short to medium term, result in considerable loss in human resource capacities to run more complex production systems that can potentially achieve high productivity. Can the process of 'vertical disintegration' to which large public and private firms are subjected be stimulated by policy to have a positive result as a seedbed for small enterprises?

Much of the debate on small enterprises in past years has tended to concentrate on micro aspects. Recently, the macro dimensions have come clearly to the fore. I would argue that the debate will reach a more mature stage when meso (sector and local-regional) dimensions are also actively considered. The recent surge in attention to flexible production systems may be helpful in this respect as its conceptualization is localized.

The discussion of flexible production experiences has demonstrated that government continues to play a role, not only at national level but at local and regional levels much closer as it were to the individual firms. For Africa, this means a greater economic concern for decentralization and for the roles of local/regional government in promoting industrialization.

A fundamental issue in industrial policy is the attitude of government to industrialization and towards industrialists, both big and small. The fact that the latter, in a number of countries, include indigenous and non-indigenous minorities further complicates the situation. Notwithstanding, it appears that industrialization for the nineties and beyond requires the active participation of both large and small industrialists, not only in policy formulation but also in the implementation of concrete programmes. High priority must therefore, in my view, be given to questions concerning appropriate domestic mechanisms for public/private policy dialogues, and to how small industrialists can most effectively organize themselves and be represented, taking into account the particularities of the African ethnic and cultural mosaic.

Analysing the policy framework for small enterprise development

WILLIAM F. STEEL

Introduction

The policy environment faced by small enterprises determines in large part their ability to contribute to the process of development through growth in their numbers, size and productivity[1]. A conducive—or at least neutral—policy environment enables programmes of direct assistance to small enterprises and supporting institutions to be effective. An essential step towards a national strategy to enhance the contribution of small enterprises is to analyse ways in which policies can be reformed to encourage rather than retard their growth.

This chapter provides a general framework for such an analysis. It synthesizes a range of experience and views, drawing from the extensive literature without attempting to review it (selected publications are listed in the References). 'Policies' refer to the rules that influence how resources are allocated (whether directly, through markets, or in government budgets) and more broadly to government actions that affect peoples' capabilities and behaviour.

In designing economic growth strategies, special attention to the policy environment for small enterprises is warranted when highly profitable investment opportunities may be lost because:

- policies are biased against small enterprises (for example, import licences that are difficult for small firms to obtain);
- market imperfections constrain small firms' access to resources (for example, the failure of financial intermediation to serve viable small investments);
- social and cultural mores inhibit the participation of certain groups in small business (women, for example).

Policy reform to correct such distortions and create a 'level playing field' would yield a more efficient allocation of resources and, quite likely, generate more employment and a more equal income distribution than a policy regime favouring large-scale capital-intensive investments. In addition, policies that provide positive encouragement to small enterprises may yield dynamic benefits. Experience gained by entrepreneurs and workers in small enterprises may generate future increases in productivity. In some Asian countries, small firms have contributed significantly to technology adaptation and innovation.

From a general policy perspective, small enterprises are those that tend to be excluded from the benefits (and rigours) of official policies and formal institutions. 'Small' is a relative term and its operational definition depends on the particular purpose. The focus here is on understanding how policies may affect different size categories, however they are defined in a particular context. Much of the analysis is relevant to self-employment, although the related issues of income distribution and social welfare are not addressed directly.

Three basic questions should be examined in analysing the context in which small enterprises operate. This chapter investigates how policies affect the factors that determine the answers to these questions:

(i) Are profitable opportunities available?
Incentives: determinants of the profitability of investment, including demand for output, trade policy, taxation and price and distribution controls.

(ii) Are there agents who are able and willing to respond?
Investors: Risk-takers capable of identifying and managing profitable investments.
Environment: Social and political attitudes toward profit-seeking, stability; and the extent and administration of regulatory controls.

(iii) Are resources available to them?
Inputs: Availability of material inputs, sufficiently skilled labour (capital is considered under the financial system) and equipment.
Facilitating institutions:[2] Financial system; markets for capital, labour, and foreign exchange; infrastructure.

Establishing appropriate policies in each of these areas is an essential part of a strategy for small enterprise development—indeed, for private sector development in general. Government policies may operate directly, for example through pricing of inputs, or indirectly, for example by building capabilities through the educational system. Policy reform differs from institutional support and direct firm-level assistance because it affects enterprises generally rather than reaching only individual beneficiaries. According to the UNDP's (1988) survey of donor agencies' experiences, a policy approach has the advantages of 'cost (it is the cheapest way of reaching target groups)' and 'effectiveness (it leaves the entrepreneur free to act as he or she chooses...[with] no outside interference in his or her affairs.' A favourable policy environment can usefully be complemented by institutions responsive to entrepreneurs' demands for technical, marketing and other services that are difficult for small firms to perform internally and by direct assistance to raise the productivity of managers and workers. But an unfavourable policy environment can prevent the expected benefits of direct assistance programmes from being realized.

Incentives

Demand

Macroeconomic policies affect the level and structure of demand for products of different sectors. Low food prices and high wages favour urban consumers, who tend to have a high propensity to consume imports and the standardized products of large-scale industries. An overvalued currency further encourages consumption of imports. Unless the policy environment favours growth of demand for the products and services of small enterprises, supply-side assistance will have little impact on their overall contribution to national income. Yet policies to stimulate demand are frequently omitted from strategies to assist small enterprises.

Structural adjustment policies typically include fiscal and monetary restraints on demand, which may already be depressed by economic crisis. Analysis is needed of the impact of such policies on the lower-income population, who have a relatively high propensity to patronize small enterprises. Compensatory measures can help reverse the downward spiral of declining demand and falling income. For example, Botswana's food security programme minimizes the increase in food expenditure in drought-affected areas and injects badly-needed income.

In many developing countries, a large share of the population remains in rural areas—over 70 per cent in sub-Saharan Africa. In this context, policies to raise rural incomes are essential to stimulate demand for off-farm employment, which in many countries absorbs a majority of the workers engaged in manufacturing. Agricultural development policies generate demand for simple consumer goods and farm implements and increase the agricultural surplus available for processing. Measures to raise rural incomes include restoring agricultural prices to market levels, increasing farmers' access to credit and inputs, encouraging crop diversification, providing marketing services, and investing in rural infrastructure.

In urban areas, an important issue is whether policies can enhance complementarity between small and large firms. In some Asian countries, such as Taiwan, with well-developed urban industrial and financial systems, small enterprises have benefited from subcontracting arrangements with larger firms and relatively easy access to finance. The question is how to make such relationships profitable for both parties, for instance by avoiding policies that favour imported inputs and by ensuring that the tax system does not penalize inter-firm transactions. Direct interventions, such as India's policy of reserving certain products for small enterprises, can prove counterproductive if they protect high-cost, low-quality goods.

In overflowing cities such as those in Latin America, small (especially micro) enterprises provide a large share of the consumption requirements of rural-to-urban migrants. The dilemma is how to make the demand for the goods and services of small producers grow faster than the supply, which is augmented by laid-off workers as well as migrants and new labour force entrants. However, the role of policy in determining migration and urban income levels can only be understood in the context of each country.

Trade policy

Tariffs and quantitative restrictions typically protect import-intensive, import-substitution industries relative to agriculture, especially when combined with a fixed, overvalued exchange rate. Corrective reform of the exchange rate regime may have differential effects by size of enterprise. To the extent that small firms have relatively high domestic input and resource components, they may benefit from exchange rate depreciation that (i) raises agricultural prices and incomes; (ii) increases export opportunities; (iii) raises the price of competing mass-produced manufactures; and (iv) squeezes import-intensive industries (which often tend to be large). Exchange rate reform opened up markets for small enterprises in Indonesia and Turkey, for example.

Trade liberalization decreases protection and increases competition from imports. Small firms may be more flexible in adjusting than larger ones, for example by changing product lines, if they are able to finance investments that may be needed. Import liberalization in Senegal adversely affected most of its overprotected large-scale industries, whereas smaller enterprises were better able to take advantage of market niches by altering their product mix or investing.

The ability of small enterprises to benefit from new opportunities depends crucially on their access to resources and services. Trade liberalization provides easier access to foreign exchange and imports. But a transition period may be needed to build up capabilities and institutions, especially for penetrating export markets. Sri Lanka's textile industry responded successfully to a carefully-sequenced programme of trade liberalization launched in 1977, including complementary measures to provide training and raise quality.

Taxation

The relationship between size and tax burden is an empirical question that varies among countries and, quite likely, among activities within the same countries. Although some observers emphasize the ability of small firms to evade taxes, other evidence indicates that many small firms bear a relatively high burden through indirect taxes, fixed levies unrelated to profits, and the inability to obtain exemptions or rebates available to larger firms. Biases against smaller firms can generally be reduced by avoiding exemptions altogether or incorporating concessions for small enterprises in the tax code rather than granting them only to firms that apply for benefits. Tax systems that impose higher tax assessments for larger firms discourage growth and foster inefficient duplication, for example four-loom weaving units in Pakistan.

Price and distribution controls

Price and distribution controls can likewise work either for or against small enterprises. Smaller firms may be able to evade price controls that are set too low for larger firms to make a profit. In some countries, such as Malawi, lack of access to state-controlled transport and marketing channels constrains effective demand for the products of small firms.

Investors

Entrepreneurship

Entrepreneurs determine the extent of supply response to positive incentives, given a favourable environment. Assessing the availability and abilities of entrepreneurs is one step towards designing an effective strategy for raising investment and productivity.

One issue is how to define 'entrepreneurship'. A restrictive definition would focus on Schumpeterian qualities of risk-taking and innovation or McClelland's 'need for achievement'. At the other extreme, many people are in business for themselves because it is the only means to earn enough money to survive. The two extremes of entrepreneurship are related by the hypothesis that self-employment provides a seedbed from which innovators emerge. The apparent lack of indigenous entrepreneurs in many African countries may be associated more with policy environments that reward rent-seeking and discourage private investment than with an absence of the requisite talents. More evidence is needed on the extent to which a conducive environment accelerates the graduation of small enterprises to greater size and productivity.

A related policy issue is whether entrepreneurship is innate or involves skills that can be taught. If the former is true, the appropriate policy response is to create an environment that rewards entrepreneurial risk-taking and perhaps helps individuals discover and develop their latent entrepreneurial talents. If entrepreneurial skills can be taught, more emphasis should be placed on providing training to the self-employed (or those likely to be) to make them more productive. India has used entrepreneurship development programmes to offset social inhibitions on entering business.

Capabilities

The ability of entrepreneurs to combine resources effectively depends in part on educational policies that emphasize practical business skills such as accounting, finance, and personnel management. Advanced programmes in these areas can enable more sophisticated entrepreneurs to hire specialists. Developing the educational system to provide skills to perform or complement entrepreneurial functions is a long-term effort, however. In the meantime, support institutions may have to fill some of the gaps, for example through specialized training courses, twinning arrangements with larger firms, trade associations, and trade fairs.

Engineering skills are a common denominator among small-scale entrepreneurs who have succeeded, especially through technological adaptation, in countries ranging from Ghana to Taiwan. Early development of light engineering lays an important base for future productivity growth and development of a capital goods industry. A strong polytechnic programme can help build the capabilities for the small-scale sector to play an evolutionary role in the industrialization process.

Industrial entrepreneurs in low-income countries typically lack knowledge about changing technology and markets. To bridge this gap, small entrepreneurs may benefit from association with large firms. These may be firms within the country that are better connected to international markets or foreign partners who act as catalytic agents by demonstrating and applying new methods. This approach requires a policy of openness to foreign markets, entrepreneurs, and managers, which sometimes goes against the desire of indigenous policymakers to protect their nascent industries and nationals.

Environment

Attitudes

The willingness of potential entrepreneurs to respond to profitable opportunities depends in part on the society's attitudes towards business and on the political risks involved. In some societies, women face cultural barriers against undertaking business activities outside the home, whereas in other countries they constitute a major proportion of self-employed people and those in small businesses. Where political ideologies emphasize state control and view private profit as anti social, entrepreneurs may be reluctant to become too visible. On the one hand, a statist approach may inhibit investment generally; on the other hand, entrepreneurs may prefer (or be restricted to) smaller firms in this environment. Where governments are shifting from a state-controlled system to greater private participation, as in Eastern Europe, they must find ways of convincing investors that the change is lasting and that investors will be protected by the legal system.

Stability

The stability of the economy, of government policies towards private business, and of the political regime influence the risks of investing in fixed assets. For economies characterized by high inflation and imbalances in the fiscal and trade accounts, stabilization of the economy is essential to minimize uncertainty and encourage entrepreneurs—especially those outside the country—to take the financial risks inherent in long-term investment. In unstable situations, small investors may prefer commercial and rent-seeking activities with high short-run returns and avoid fixed investments.

Stabilization programmes initially may weaken the incentive to invest by restraining demand and credit. Furthermore, the policy reforms themselves create uncertainty until they are widely perceived to be sustainable. In the transition period, small indigenous investors may be willing to respond sooner than foreign investors who have more alternatives.

From the viewpoint of the investor, political stability means that the fundamental rules of doing business do not shift with changes in the political regime and that the system can resolve different viewpoints, not that power should persist in the hands of one group. An open, resilient system fosters the initiative characteristic of a vigorous small enterprise sector, whereas a centralized system makes access to power essential for small investors.

Regulations

Regulations differ widely in their impact by firm size within as well as among countries. Regulations range from necessary protection of health and the environment to bureaucratic hurdles for which the original purpose is all but forgotten. The smaller the firm, the higher the cost of compliance tends to be relative to profits—especially where size and influence determine access to administrators. However, very small firms may be exempt from, or able to evade, many regulations and taxes. Indeed, small size may be a response to unreasonable or excessively costly regulatory requirements that larger firms cannot avoid. Survey evidence from several African countries suggests that regulations are of less concern to smaller than larger firms, especially relative to demand and credit constraints. Nevertheless, small firms bear costs in the form of harassment for non-compliance and the risk of being summarily put out of business.

In general, more regulations come into play and become binding as firm size increases. One hypothesis is that the cost of complying with regulations has a 'hump'—somewhere between very small firms that operate outside the regulations and large firms that can spread administrative costs over large volumes and also have access to offsetting benefits (especially credit from the formal financial sector). Where valid, this hypothesis may explain low rates of 'graduation' from informal to formal status and the low proportion of firms in the small-to-medium range (e.g., in Africa, compared with Asia). Empirical investigation of this hypothesis can therefore lay the basis for policy reforms to reduce the costs of entry and growth in small enterprises. For instance, a priori approvals can be shifted to automatic registration and the burden placed on the authorities to carry out *ex post* verification, if needed.

One issue is whether 'one-stop' investment centres can effectively bypass burdensome regulations by minimizing bureaucratic requirements. Unless they have full authority to make decisions, however, such centres may add another layer without eliminating the need for authorizations from other agencies. Export processing zones can help bypass burdensome customs and tax rebate procedures, but they require a supportive macroeconomic policy environment and often restrict production for the domestic market. In general, and especially for small firms, it is more effective to correct the underlying regulatory problems than to construct alternatives that benefit only selected firms, usually large ones.

Location restrictions are a controversial issue, especially for the smallest firms. Self-employed sellers and small producers tend to congregate in the dense markets and centres of already overcrowded cities. They often bear the burden of city authorities' efforts to relieve congestion and pollution, whether through harassment for non-compliance with regulations or relocation to less dense, and hence less desirable, areas. The question is how to accommodate the needs of microenterprises within a programme of orderly urban development. Policies that provide a central location where microenterprises can share facilities will stimulate them; dispersing them to remote sites will retard their growth.

The legal system can support small enterprises by giving them legal status without onerous registration requirements and by enforcing contracts. Simple procedures for winding up—as well as launching—a business and transferring assets can facilitate the high death and birth rates characteristic of small businesses.

Administration

Even when regulations are reasonable, their administration may not be. Procedures can be unnecessarily complex, especially for small, less-educated entrepreneurs. Information is often hard to obtain. Underpaid bureaucrats may delay taking action to create an incentive for payments on the side. Potential investors may be discouraged by such an environment. The policy issue is how to create positive attitudes and incentives toward assisting, rather than controlling business.

Inputs

Raw materials

Once in business, success depends on ready access to material inputs. Government marketing policies can directly affect small firms' access to raw materials. Problems commonly arise when local materials, such as cotton and lumber, are marketed through a state monopoly. Import licensing similarly tends to exclude smaller firms from access to imported inputs. Liberalization of these markets is likely to remove biases against smaller firms. Although import liberalization is often accompanied by a devaluation that raises the official cost of inputs, the impact on small firms may be minimal if they were already paying black market rates to obtain inputs.

Small enterprises often use intermediaries rather than wholesalers to purchase inputs, especially imported ones. Bulk purchasing of commonly-used inputs is one approach to lowering production costs for small firms. In Nepal, the carpetmaker's association joined with exporters to create a private trading company that succeeded in lowering the price of wool through direct contracts instead of relying on intermediaries. Such schemes should be cost-effective without subsidies, but they require careful management and a strong association to keep operating costs low and to minimize defaults. The government may also provide support directly through a public agency or indirectly through financial and administrative assistance to small manufacturers' associations.

Labour

A strategy that encourages small enterprises claims the advantages of absorbing relatively more labour for a given investment than larger firms do and of providing training, either on-the-job or through apprenticeship. Restrictive labour laws that require a high minimum wage and make it difficult to dismiss workers may work to the advantage of very small firms that can escape these regulations, but to the disadvantage of firms trying to grow. Policies that subsidize capital work against the employment objective.

A difficult analytical problem is to distinguish between static and dynamic employment effects. Restrictive policies aimed at promoting or protecting employment in the short run are counterproductive if they also discourage investment that would raise the rate of growth of employment over the long run.

Equipment

The productivity of small firms may be constrained by the firms' inability to obtain or afford equipment at an appropriate technological level. In some cases, the source of the problem is import licensing restrictions or inadequate access to finance. Measures that make it easy to import used equipment or to set up leasing companies (and enforce contracts) can ease this problem. Countries such as Pakistan that are trying to develop a local equipment industry are sometimes reluctant to expose it to competing imports. Protection that fosters inefficient local production is counterproductive, however, because it imposes extra costs on downstream industries. Although large firms may be able to obtain countervailing protection or pass on such costs through monopoly pricing, small firms cannot.

Facilitating institutions

Financial systems

A responsive financial system is widely regarded as critical for expansion of the small enterprise sector. In general, the smaller the enterprise the less likely it is to obtain credit from formal financial institutions. If financial policies such as fixed or subsidized interest rates reduce the profitability and thus the incidence of lending to small firms, then policy reforms are clearly in order. Whether policy interventions are otherwise appropriate requires some analysis.

Small enterprises throughout the world have a high risk of failure in their first few years. Lending to them is profitable only if the interest rate spread is sufficient to cover defaults and high administrative costs relative to amounts lent and if mechanisms can be developed to minimize risks and improve recovery. It is difficult to know whether banks avoid lending to small enterprises out of preconceptions or sound business practices. The former case calls for demonstrations that small business loans are less risky than bankers think, for example, through targeted credit programmes and special (but temporary) incentives to entice them into such lending. The latter case calls for measures to improve the environment for small business survival and to strengthen risk-reducing institutions, such as guarantee schemes.

Measures to increase external finance for small business are most clearly warranted for established firms that need working capital to meet current demand or whose needs for expansion exceed what can be generated through profits and family savings. When these firms have bank accounts but cannot obtain credit, investigation into banking practices and ways of adapting criteria and procedures to small enterprises is in order. The ability of small entrepreneurs (especially women) to provide collateral may be inhibited by a legal system that makes property ownership and seizure difficult. The appropriate response may be institutional reforms to deepen financial intermediation. For example, investment at the upper end of the small-scale range may be facilitated by policies to develop capital markets and permit partnerships with foreign entrepreneurs, as is being done in Poland.

A number of programmes have proven that very small loans *can* have high repayment rates, even with low-income clients. These are generally community-based efforts that rely on mutual guarantees to ensure success. Initial loans are typically extremely small, with subsequent loans tied to repayment performance. Only rarely have they been associated with the formal financial system (e.g., Kupedes in Indonesia, a village-based programme administered within an agricultural development bank). It remains unclear how financial policies at the national level can foster such schemes or extend them beyond self-employment, except through legislation that gives community savings and credit schemes a legal status and enables them to interact with the banking system.

Personal or family funds are the predominant source of investment for those in very small firms (including the self-employed). Investing in these small businesses may be the only means of putting savings to work for people who lack access to financial instruments that bear a return. In this case, improving the informal mechanisms through which people accumulate savings may be the most effective means of raising investment in small enterprises. Increasing the delivery of external credit may replace people's own savings and thereby reduce financial resource mobilization. Most of the successful programmes that provide small loans involve a direct link between credit and savings.

Markets

In principle, a market-based system offers firms access to resources on comparable terms without respect to size. When capital, labour, foreign exchange, and input markets are controlled, it is important to analyse how firm size influences allocations and how small firms might benefit from liberalization. Market systems also need to be analysed for monopoly power or other imperfections that restrict small firms' access in practice.

Infrastructure

Provision of infrastructure is an important way for governments to complement private sector development generally. Infrastructural investment, however, may have conflicting effects on small enterprises, particularly in rural areas. On the one hand, it raises low incomes and hence demand, while lowering the costs of production. On the other hand, high transport costs protect local markets from imports and domestic mass-produced goods, while the absence of utilities discourages entry by larger firms. Foot-loose small producers can blossom in these markets, and competition among them may suffice to make them efficient. Public expenditures that raise rural standards of education and health are likely to have unambiguously positive indirect effects on small enterprises and can benefit them directly if the government contracts with small firms to perform the work. Improved transport and electricity will help small firms by boosting agricultural incomes and lowering their costs but will also expose them to greater competition from imports and large-scale producers. Analytical issues are whether infrastructural investments would increase or decrease biases against small firms and whether other strategies would be more cost-effective.

Conclusion

The approach suggested in this chapter focuses on understanding the forces that determine the role and development of small enterprises in a particular context. In designing a strategy or a reform programme, it is useful to assess empirically the extent to which the existing policy regime is biased against smaller enterprises, the likely impact of reforms on small enterprises, both in absolute terms and relative to larger enterprises, and constraints on their ability to respond. Key questions involve what determines the opportunities for small businesses, the supply of investors, and their access to resources. The issues are complex, and actions in one area may have unintended consequences in another. For this reason, policy changes that address fundamental problems are often preferable to direct interventions that introduce new distortions. The analysis should assess where the main constraints lie and what policy changes would generate the greatest complementarity with other factors.

The relative importance of different elements within the wide range of policy-related issues varies by country and activity. An assessment should include interviews with entrepreneurs, consumers, bank officers, NGOs, and other institutions, as well as government officials. In developing a strategy, the capacities of different agents to implement recommended changes must also be considered. Implementation is likely to be more effective when policymakers are involved in developing the strategy and there is a continuing dialogue among donors, government, private entrepreneurs, and NGOs.

Changing from a less to a more favourable policy environment is not without cost. The uncertainty created by policy change tends to make private entrepreneurs postpone new investment until they are confident that the new regime is both profitable and sustainable. The monopoly power of large and state-owned firms is not easy to break. Many small firms that operate on narrow margins may lack the resources to cover increased costs and decreased demand under the new policies intended to benefit them in the longer term. A successful strategy for policy reform must therefore consider how to shift resources towards intended beneficiaries during the transition period, as well as address the policy issues raised in this chapter.

II

Structural Adjustment and Small Enterprises

Impact of structural adjustment on small-scale enterprises in Ghana

BARFOUR OSEI – AMOAH BAAH-NUAKOH –
KWADWO TUTU – NII KWAKU SOWA

Introduction

The purpose of this study is to explore the implications, positive and negative, of the changed economic environment in Ghana, for the development of small-scale enterprises[1]. Small-scale enterprises (SSEs) play an important role in the economy and are increasingly recognized as having a permanent role as a seed-bed for future growth. Their activities span a wide range in both the formal and informal sectors, and they provide a good source of non-public sector employment. Even for some in public sector employment, SSEs provide a substantial supplement to their incomes as second jobs.

Since the inception of the Economic Recovery Programme (ERP) in 1983, within the broad set of structural adjustment programmes, certain policies have affected the activities of SSEs. This chapter will explore the implications, positive and negative, of the changed economic environment in Ghana for the development of small-scale enterprises. The main objectives of this study are twofold: first, to assess the impact of the ERP on SSEs through a sample survey of 1365 enterprises in and around the major municipalities of Accra, Kumasi, Cape Coast and Tamale; and second, to identify measures to promote and develop the sector. From the survey results, it seems the ERP has had a mixed impact on the small-scale enterprises. While output of the enterprises has responded favourably to the recovery programme, the effect of the programme on employment has not been positive.

This chapter provides background information; it defines small-scale enterprise and discusses the characteristics and problems of the small-scale sector. The policies, institutional and financial arrangements which were put in place under the ERP for SSE promotion are then elucidated. The effects of the policies and institutional arrangements are assessed before recommendations and conclusions are enumerated in the final section.

Background

Small-scale enterprises defined

There are several definitions of SSEs. The number of persons employed is the commonly-used definition criterion in Ghana. However, confusion usually arises due to the arbitrariness and inconsistent use of cut-off points employed by various official sources. For example, the Ghana Statistical Service (GSS) in its Industrial Statistics, considers establishments with 10 or more employees as medium- and large-scale. Thus, by implication, small-scale are those that employ less than 10 workers. At the same time, the GSS in the National Accounts classifies companies engaging nine or fewer persons as 'small and medium'.

Other criteria which have been used in defining small-scale enterprises include fixed assets. The National Board for Small Scale Industries (NBSSI) uses multiple criteria of fixed assets and employment size. The Board considers a small enterprise as one employing not more than nine persons with plant and machinery value (excluding land, buildings and vehicles) not exceeding 10 million cedis. The Ghana Enterprise Development Commission (GEDC) also used a definition based on an upper limit of 10 million cedis for plant and machinery.

Confusion also usually arises in the use of the size of plant and equipment to classify firms, since valuation of assets of companies usually presents a problem.

This study uses an employment cut-off of 30 workers to indicate small-scale enterprises. This definition has been used by Steel and Webster (1990) in a recent study of small-scale enterprises in Ghana[2]. Our study further disaggregates the small-scale enterprises into three categories: 'micro', those employing fewer than six workers, 'very small', those employing six to nine, and 'small', between 10 and 29 workers. The following activities were studied:

1. Textiles and garments (including dressmaking/tailoring)
2. Wood products and furniture
3. Food processing (including *kenkey*[3] production, bakeries, grain milling)
4. Motor repairs and welding
5. Leather products (including shoemaking)
6. Metal poducts (including gold/silversmith, blacksmith)
7. Electrical and electronic repairs
8. Watch repairs
9. Printing and publishing
10. Banking and foreign exchange bureaux

Characteristics and problems of small-scale enterprises

There are both urban and rural SSEs in Ghana. In urban SSEs, there are two basic types which may be characterized as 'organized' and 'unorganized'. The organized enterprises typically may engage a number of salaried employees and have fixed production premises. The unorganized firms consist largely of artisans without fixed premises who work in the open air, in mobile 'kiosks', or at home, and employ very few or no salaried workers, relying instead on family members or apprentices for labour. Rural industry is composed largely of family groups, individual artisans, women engaged in producing food from local crops, low-cost soap, fabrics, and village blacksmiths and mechanics.

An important feature of the SSE, whether urban or rural, is the belief that they make better use of scarce factors of production than large-scale enterprises. Data from many countries, including Ghana, show that capital productivity (value added per unit of invested capital) tends to be higher in SSE than in large-scale industry. (Steel, 1977; Child, 1977) This is because the SSE is usually labour intensive and the amount of capital invested is small. The basic conclusion from the phenomenon of high capital productivity is that a viable SSE is an economically sound investment since the tendency is for the country to gain more value added per unit of investment than it would from an equivalent investment in large-scale industry.

A number of problems have been identified with the SSEs in Ghana. These include shortages of capital, raw materials, spare parts and machinery, competition from large-scale industries and complicated procedures which must be followed in order to start or expand a small business (see for example, Checchi *et al.*, 1976). Many SSEs start with only small capital as it has not been easy for them to raise finance elsewhere. Particularly rural enterprises have relied on local savings clubs such as *susu*, where the level of capital a business venture could raise is dependent on what it puts in, and since it usually has barely little to start with, it is unable to obtain substantial finance. Conclusions from other studies have shown that effective linkages of SSEs in Ghana with other sectors of the economy are not well established, leading in particular to loss of sub-contracting from major industries that could alleviate financial constraints of the sector (Aryee, 1976).

Shortage of imported raw materials, spares and machinery has been an added problem mainly due to the difficulty of obtaining import licences for these inputs. This has been a function of the prevailing shortage of foreign exchange. It leaves the entrepreneur with the choice of seeking supplies from local traders at mark-up prices, or doing without.

These problems were sustained by the macroeconomic framework which existed before the ERP. The policy of import-substitution industrialization which was pursued discriminated against the SSEs. The industrial and trade policies as principal determinants of investment were fashioned in such a way that large-scale, capital-intensive enterprises were encouraged. The structure of tariffs also discriminated against SSEs; for the inputs of SSEs were categorized as consumer goods and attracted higher tariff rates than the machinery and equipment imported by LSEs (large-scale enterprises). Also, interest rates policies, the overvalued exchange rates, import licensing and quotas, and controlled prices of inputs all served as disincentives to SSEs by creating barriers to entry into the product market and thus impeding the creation and expansion of SSEs. In addition, institutions set up to promote industrial development discriminated against SSEs. Credit institutions, for example, favoured LSEs, for larger loans are cheaper per cedi to develop, appraise, disburse and collect.

In spite of these problems, SSEs were able, between 1974 and 1983, to partly fill the gap created by the decline of LSEs (Dawson, 1988). And it has been suggested that a relationship exists between the performance of SSEs and the general economic performance. A higher proportion of SSEs tend to enjoy good business when GNP growth rates decline, as SSEs are more flexible and easily able to adjust to declines (Anheier and Seibel, 1987).

The ERP: policies and institutional arrangements for small-scale enterprises

Policies

The macroeconomic framework in Ghana has changed since the inception of the ERP. The ERP, with the subsequent SAPs, are intended to remove distortions through the establishment of various institutions and a policy and incentive framework which involves:

(a) shifting relative prices in favour of tradeables and particular exports;
(b) the restoration of fiscal and monetary discipline;
(c) rehabilitation of the production base and the economic and social infrastructure; and
(d) the encouragement of private investment. Specific policies which have been put in place so far include:
  (i) exchange rate adjustment;
  (ii) fiscal management;
  (iii) trade liberalization; and,
  (iv) divestiture of state enterprises.

These policies could have affected SSEs in a number of ways. The policy of exchange rate management has meant the determination of exchange rates through market forces. The system started first with a series of devaluations followed by an auction system with two windows, and culminating with a system where the rate is freely determined at both the official and the privately established 'forex bureaux'. These adjustments in the exchange rate have moved the rate from ¢30.00 to the US dollar in 1983 to about ¢350.00 to the dollar in 1990. The advantage of the liberalization of the exchange rate is the elimination of administrative allocation of foreign exchange. Import licences have subsequently been withdrawn and importers are at liberty to bring in spare parts and raw materials for production. This policy measure has contributed to the increases in average industrial capacity utilization from 25 per cent in 1983 to about 38 per cent in 1988. On the other hand, the continuous depreciation of the cedi meant that importers have had to pay more for their imports. And with the credit crunch imposed to help check inflation, producers have found it difficult to obtain finance from the banks. Thus, marginal companies have found it difficult to keep production going.

With the policy of trade liberalization, imports of all kinds including consumer goods have been allowed into the country. These imports compete with products of local industries, causing some of them to shut down. In 1988 in response to complaints from the Ghana Manufacturers' Association the government introduced a revised tax structure which provided some protection to some industries. Ghana now has a unified tax structure for imports ranging from 0 to 35 per cent, depending on whether the import is classified as an exempt, concessionary, standard or luxury good. In addition, some form of protection exists for certain import categories including: selected drugs, garments, cosmetics, mineral water, juice, rubber sandals, soaps and some food products. It is estimated that, with special taxes, protection of between 25 per cent and 90 per cent exists for some industries. As part of liberalization, prices and interest rates are also freely determined.

Fiscal management has so far taken the form of rationalization of public expenditure. In an attempt to reduce government expenditure, redeployment or retrenchment of public sector workers has been carried out since 1987. Those targeted for redeployment were mainly without proper qualifications, or those who had reached retirement age. The policy objective was for the retrenched workers to be absorbed into the private workforce, especially into agriculture. It is doubtful however whether the financial compensation paid would set them up in any meaningful self-employment[4].

Institutional arrangements for promotion of SSEs

Since 1970, certain institutional arrangements have been put in place to assist and promote SSEs. The office of Business Promotion (later the Ghana Enterprise Development Commission (GEDC)) was established to assist Ghanaian businessmen to enter fields formerly dominated by foreigners, but which became available to Ghanaians after the 'Alliance Compliance Order' (1970). The GEDC was also charged with helping to strengthen small-scale industry in general, with both financial and technical assistance.

Under the ERP, the institutional base to support SSEs has widened. The National Board for Small-Scale Industries (NBSSI) has been established within the Ministry of Industries, Science and Technology (MIST) to cater for small business affairs[5]. In 1987, the Ghana Appropriate Technology Industrial Service (GRATIS) was established by the MIST to supervise the operations of Intermediate Technology Transfer Units (ITTUs) in the regions. The ultimate objective of GRATIS is to help upgrade small-scale industrial activities by means of the transfer of appropriate technologies to small-scale and informal sector industries from the grassroots levels. The ITTUs are intended to develop engineering capabilities of small-scale manufacturing and service industries in the fields of vehicle and related repair trades. They are also to meet the needs of secondary industries (i.e. non-engineering) by the manufacture and repair of machinery, plant and equipment related to and required by the wide range of small-scale urban and rural industries and agriculture. So far, six ITTUs have been established in Tema, Tamale, Cape Coast, Ho, Sunyani and Kumasi.

Another institutional arrangement is the NBSSI's Entrepreneurship Development Programme, which has been initiated to train and assist persons with entrepreneurial talents to develop them for self-employment.

Financial arrangements

As indicated earlier, credit non-availability has been one of the major constraints to the expansion of businesses in Ghana. Most businesses, especially SSEs, do not have the collateral needed to obtain credit from the banks. In 1970, the Bank of Ghana established a credit guarantee scheme to underwrite loans to small-scale businesses made by the commercial banks. This scheme did not work out. In 1988, the Bank of Ghana obtained a US$28 million credit from the International Development Association (IDA) of the World Bank for the establishment of a Fund for Small and Medium Enterprises Development (FUSMED). FUSMED is to provide financial services through some participating financial institutions to SMEs in all sectors other than primary agriculture, trading and real estate.

Also, under the Programme of Action to Mitigate the Social Cost of Adjustment (PAMSCAD), a revolving credit to the tune of US $2 million has been instituted to assist SSEs.

Impact of ERP on small-scale enterprises

What has been the impact of the policies, institutional and financial arrangements on SSEs? This section is devoted to answering such and related questions. The assessment is based on sample survey results on 1365 enterprises in Accra/Tema, Kumasi, Ho, Sekondi/Takoradi, Cape Coast and Tamale. The basic structure of the enterprises surveyed is depicted in Table 4.1. They are made up of 88.6 per cent of 'micro' firms, 8.6 per cent of 'very small' firms and 2.8 per cent of 'small' firms. By types of product, motor repairs/welding constitutes the largest category, making up 18.5 per cent. This is followed by food processing at 15.8 per cent and then dressmaking/tailoring/hair dressing, 10.2 per cent. The impact of the ERP on SSEs is assessed here on the characteristics, employment, and output.

The effect of the ERP on the characteristics of small-scale enterprises is looked at under three headings: the Enterprise; the Entrepreneur; and the Business/Regulatory Environment. There can not, however, be rigid segmentation since areas under these headings overlap to a large extent.

Enterprises

A useful starting point in assessing the effect of the ERP on the character of the small-scale enterprise is the organizational birth rate of the SSEs. Table 4.2 provides estimates on the year of establishment of the enterprises. The estimates indicate that the greater percentage of all firms in the sample (62 per cent) were established in the relatively short period of time, 1980–90, and a large percentage of the firms (42 per cent) have been established since the inception of the ERP[6].

There are reasons for the large number of SSEs set up under the ERP era. Some of the enterprises, notably forex bureaux, result directly from the ERP. Other reasons include the retrenchment of labour from the civil service and other public organizations, and the general non-hiring of labour in the state sector.

Since 1983 a large percentage of those who have set up small-scale enterprises (20 per cent) have come from the ranks of the retrenched and redeployed. Secondly, those who leave the educational system might previously have liked to work

Table 4.1 Structure of Small-Scale Industries, 1990

	Micro Firms < 6		*Very Small Firms 6–9*		*Small Firms 10–29*		*Total (rounded up)*	
Sector	*No.*	*% of Total*	*No.*	*% of Total*	*No.*	*% of Total*	*No.*	*% of Total*
Garment/Textile	44	3.3	7	0.5	2	0.1	53	3.9
Furniture/Wood processing	113	8.3	18	1.3	4	0.3	135	9.9
Food processing	190	14.0	21	1.5	5	0.3	216	15.8
Motor repair/Welding	210	15.4	29	2.1	13	1.0	252	18.5
Leather processing/Shoemaking	76	5.6	1	0.1	—	—	77	5.6
Metals	79	5.8	2	0.1	—	—	81	5.9
Electric/electronic	116	8.5	6	0.4	2	0.1	124	9.1
Watch repairs	63	4.6	1	0.1	—	—	64	4.7
Printing/Photographs	24	1.8	6	0.4	2	0.1	32	2.3
Non-metallic mineral products	103	7.6	11	0.8	1	0.1	115	8.4
Tailoring/Dressmaking/ Hairdressing	129	9.5	5	0.4	5	0.3	139	10.2
Restaurant/Hotel	4	0.3	4	0.3	—	—	8	0.6
Brick/Tile/Blocks	4	0.3	—	—	3	0.2	7	0.5
Handicraft	15	1.1	2	0.1	1	0.1	18	1.3
Health services	3	0.2	—	—	—	—	3	0.2
Soap making/Cosmetics	27	2.0	4	0.3	—	—	31	2.3
Banking/Forex Bureaux	10	0.7	—	—	—	—	10	0.7
Total	1210	89	117	8.4	38	2.6	1365	100.0

Source: Survey Data (1990).

Table 4.2 Year of Establishment of Small-Scale Enterprises

Period	*Number of Enterprises*	*Per cent of Firms*
Pre-independence (Pre-1957)	36	2.7
Nkrumah Regime (1958–66)	57	4.3
NLC/Busia Regime (1967–72)	136	10.2
NRC/SMC Regime (1973–79)	276	20.6
Linmann/Early PNDC (1980–83)	266	19.9
ERP era of PNDC (1984–90)	566	42.3
	N = 1337	100.0

Source: Survey Results (1990).

in the 'modern' sector. But with job opportunities in the public sector closed to them and with the large-scale private sector trying to adjust to the ERP, the alumni of the school system have now tended to set up small-scale enterprises, especially the micro firms.

The enterprises are owned mostly by Ghanaians (90 per cent), and in the great majority of cases (91 per cent), the present owner established the enterprise himself. All other forms of ownership such as partnership and limited liability are of little significance.

Financial matters present the most acute problem for the establishment of small-scale enterprises. Formal financial institutions provide capital to small-scale entrepreneurs only in the rarest of cases. Our results indicate that 63 per cent of the initial capital for establishing small firms comes from the business founders' own personal resources, 27 per cent from immediate family and other relatives, and 5 per cent from friends. All other forms of capital source, particularly bank loans, are insignificant. Credit availability for expansion and running the enterprises is similarly restricted. Over 74 per cent of entrepreneurs in our sample indicated that they are limited by credit in their operations. Most small-scale enterprises started on a rather small-scale indeed. Because of lack of access to larger amounts of finance, which would allow set-up and operations on a modest scale right from the start, businesses are started with minimal amounts of capital.

The entrepreneur

The ERP measures of labour retrenchment and the 'freeze' on hiring have significantly affected the character of the small-scale entrepreneur. As pointed out, young and well-educated people who otherwise might have sought jobs in the civil service and other public organizations now set up small-scale industries.

The age distribution of entrepreneurs in our sample indicates that owners of SSEs are a young cohort, on average younger than the proportion of the labour force in the civil service. Estimates on the age distribution of owners of SSEs

Table 4.3 Age Distribution of Owners of Small-Scale Enterprises

Age Groups	*Frequency*	*Percentage*
15–25 years	73	5.5
26–35 years	448	33.8
36–45 years	449	33.8
46–55 years	249	18.8
56 and above	108	8.1
	N = 1327	100.0

Source: Survey Data (1990).

(Table 4.3) show that nearly 40 per cent of respondents in our sample are younger than 35 years of age.

Less than every tenth person is older than 55 years. An average of 39 years, a mode of 31 years and a medium of 36 years indicate a fairly even age distribution. In other words, small-scale entrepreneurs represent a population in prime age.

The distribution of educational standards also indicates that, on average owners of SSEs rank higher than the population as a whole. It is clear from Table 4.4 that fewer than every fifth owner of an SSE had never attended school. This reflects the increased education among Ghanaians generally, and also results from more products of the educational system moving into the small-scale sector since 1983. Thus over 80 per cent of entrepreneurs in our sample have been to school.

The higher educational standard of entrepreneurs stands the SSEs in good stead, since as has been suggested elsewhere, entrepreneurs with higher educational training standards are more likely to survive economically in a more 'turbulent' business environment (Anheier and Seibel, 1987).

The level of education is also seen to be positively related to awareness of institutions set up to support the SSEs. Asked whether our entrepreneurs are aware of the existence of these institutions, more educated respondents answered positively than illiterates (see Table 4.5). On the other hand, our results indicate that the impact of the services of the institutions is greater on illiterate than educated entrepreneurs; a higher percentage of illiterate entrepreneurs than educated ones have

Table 4.4 Educational Standard of Owners of SSEs

Educational Level	*Number*	*Percentage*
Primary/Middle	715	55.2
Secondary/Commercial/Technical	300	23.2
College/University	35	2.7
No formal education	239	18.5
Total	N = 1289	100.0

Source: Survey Results (1990).

received financial and technical support from the institutions. Indeed, more illiterate entrepreneurs approach the institutions than their educated counterparts. This situation is beneficial to the small-scale sector. It implies that the more venerable entrepreneurs, in terms of 'survivability' in 'turbulent' economic situations are increasingly receiving technical/financial assistance.

Technical and vocational training of the small-scale entrepreneurs is very limited. Our results on job/occupational training (Table 4.6) indicate that apprenticeship constitutes the main form of training for the small-scale entrepreneur. This result is confirmed by the study of Steel and Webster (1990).

Less than 15 per cent of entrepreneurs in our sample have had formal vocational or technical training. This is a serious limitation which results in lack of proper management, especially in such matters as financial records and bookkeeping, which Aryee (1976), has observed is directly related to the level of vocational/technical training in Ghana.

The picture that emerges then, is of a young and educated small-scale entrepreneur, who lacks vocational/technical training. This picture is indicative of the failure of the educational system to give attention to vocational/technical training and to encourage business skills and attitudes.

The formal sector also unintentionally, provides training for small-scale entrepreneurs. In fact, over 20 per cent of entrepreneurs in our sample had previously worked in either large corporations or in the civil service (Table 4.7).

However, the formal sector seems to have lost its attraction as a job avenue for

Table 4.5 Effect of Education (% of Total)

	Educated *Yes*	*Illiterate* *Yes*
Ever heard of institutions to promote SSEs	42	27
Which institution:		
NBSSI	56	35
GEDC	48	47
TTC	19	6
DRCS	35	17
FUSMED	38	19
GRATIS	25	13
PAMSCAD	70	53
Ever received Financial Support from any of above institutions	9	17
Ever received Technical Support from any of above institutions	19	33
Ever approached any of the institutions	39	48

Source: Survey Data (1990)

Table 4.6 Job/Occupational Training of Owners of SSEs

Type of Training	*Number*	*Percentage*
Formal Vocational/Technical	171	13
Apprenticeship	686	51
Relative*	318	24
Trial and error	82	6
Formal Training/Apprenticeship	29	2
Formal Training/Relative	6	0.4
Apprenticeship/Relative	1	0.1
Trial and error/Relative	40	3
Apprenticeship/Trial and error	7	0.5
	N = 1340	100.0

*Training received informally from a family member.
Source: Survey Data (1990).

the small-scale entrepreneur. Asked if offered paid employment, our entrepreneur would accept it but the great majority (78 per cent) intended to remain in their present jobs. If it is also realized, as our results indicate, that over 90 per cent of our entrepreneurs work full-time in their jobs, then it seems reasonable to suggest that the small-scale sector provides an attractive job avenue.

The survey indicates that there is a dominance of male entrepreneurs in the sector. The results show that the great majority of entrepreneurs (73.7 per cent) in our sample are male. In fact, in certain types of industries such as motor repair, shoemaking, gold/silver/blacksmith, electrical/electronic repair, watch repairs, and forex bureaux the male dominance is total. This finding points to the inadequate attention given to encouraging women to commence in business. The effect, therefore, is that a large group of the population with potential for entrepreneurship is largely being ignored.

Business/regulatory environment

The regulatory environment covers factors that affect the ease and risk of operating a business in Ghana, other than the normal production, sales and profit/loss as-

Table 4.7 Previous Job History of Small-Scale Entrepreneurs

Type of Job	*Number*	*Percentage*
Government (Civil Service)	185	15.2
Large corporation	91	7.5
Small company	139	11.4
None	804	65.9
	N = 1219	100.0

Source: Survey Result (1990).

pects. Regulations are an important aspect of the business environment, since they represent the most direct expression of the government's attitude towards business.

The Manufacturing Industries Act (1971) enjoins all firms to register with the MIST. Other legislation has required firms to register with the Registrar General's Department. Various metropolitan bodies have also required registration and payment of licence and location permits. The Internal Revenue Service has also established procedures by which taxes are paid by SSEs either through their associations on daily, weekly or monthly basis. Those who do not belong to associations have to pay their taxes either quarterly or annually and also to submit annual returns.

The survey indicates that the State (including regulatory bodies) continues to place impediments in the way of small-scale entrepreneurs. Asked whether they have been able to obtain licences easily, nearly one-fifth of respondents answered in the negative. Official bureaucracy is blamed for difficulty in obtaining a licence or permit. As a result, the great majority of entrepreneurs (60 per cent) have not even registered their businesses. Entrepreneurs have to embark on what they consider a complex tour of government departments and agencies which may, on certain occasions, unintentionally offer conflicting information.

Effect on output and sales

What has been the extent of output expansion in the SSEs? Table 4.8 summarizes the survey results on output growth. The results indicate that 52.8 per cent of the sampled firms have experienced expansion in their output while 36.7 per cent of the firms stagnated or experienced decline. In terms of actual percentage change in output part (b) of Table 4.8 indicates that 41 per cent of the enterprises which responded 'yes' or 'no' experienced negative growth rate rates, that is declines in their output, while 12.5 per cent achieved more that 50 per cent growth in output. Those firms that experienced more than 100 per cent growth rates in output were mainly the larger of the SSEs (see Table 4.8, part c). Indeed, output expansion has been hampered most in 'micro' firms. About 70 per cent of 'micro' firms experienced growth rate in output of 10 per cent or less compared with 59.8 per cent and 57.9 per cent of the 'very small' and 'small' firms.

The output pattern is explained by a number of factors:

Competition

The ERP is expected to introduce competition into the economy, and inefficient firms unable to compete would be driven out of business. SSEs face competition from three main sources: (a) imports; (b) large-scale enterprises; (c) other small-scale enterprises.

Liberalization of trade enables importers to bring in goods that undercut the market for goods locally produced by SSEs; that is, competition from imported goods which are of higher quality and relatively lower prices. Although this could encourage healthy competition and help improve the quality of goods produced by SSEs, it could also become a constraint to the development of local small-scale in-

Table 4.8 Changes in Output

(a) *Effect on Output*	*Number of Firms*	*Percentage*
Increase in output	721	52.8
Decline in output	501	36.7
Not applicable	143	10.5
Total	1365	100.0

(b) *Percentage Increases in Firms' Output*

Range	*Number of Firms*	*Percentage*
Less than 0	501	41.0
10 or less	297	24.3
11 – 20	76	6.2
21 – 50	199	16.3
51 – 100	131	10.7
above 100	18	1.5

(c) *Effect on Firm Size*

	Per cent of Respondents in Each Group			
Output Growth	*All firms*	*Micro*	*Very Small*	*Small*
No expansion	41.2	41.2	37.4	46.1
Expansion	52.8	58.8	62.6	53.1
of which percentage increase in output				
10 or less	68.9	70.2	59.8	57.9
11 – 20	5.6	5.5	6.8	5.3
21 – 50	14.6	14.5	15.4	15.8
50 – 100	9.6	8.7	17.1	15.8
100	1.3	1.2	0.9	5.3

Source: Survey Results (1990).

dustry. The survey did support the assertion that imports compete with the products of SSEs. About 34 per cent of enterprises which experienced stagnated output blamed imports as a source of competition. Industries such as garments/textiles have been particularly hard hit. Small-scale garment industries have not been able to withstand competition from imported clothing especially *Oburoni wawu.*[7]

The liberalization of imports and wider availability of foreign exchange has given industrial enterprises access to previously restricted inputs and spares and restored the supply of raw materials. Consequently, capacity utilization in large-scale enterprises has gradually improved and the producer markets have been flooded with consumer items. About 67 per cent of the surveyed enterprises blamed competition from local producers for fallen output. If one takes into account the finding by Dawson (1990) that the large producers have been unable to recapture markets lost to smaller enterprises, local competition to SSEs has come from other small-scale enterprises rather than from the larger producers. Industries which faced stiffer local competition include electrical/electronic, food processing, leather products/shoemaking and furniture/wood processing.

Availability and receipt of financial support

As pointed out earlier, lack of accessibility to capital has always been a constraint to the establishment and operation of SSEs. The survey revealed that credit is a problem for all firms whether expanding or stagnating in output. It is likely that firms that achieved expansion in output could have achieved higher growth rates, while those whose output stagnated could have improved their performance with credit availability. Only 3.4 per cent of firms that expanded their output received financial support from a government agency, while 94.9 per cent of the firms which did not expand output had never received any financial support. Also, 63.5 per cent of those companies whose output expanded received credit with ease, while 81 per cent of those whose output stagnated found it difficult to obtain credit. It thus seems that output expansion in the SSEs is positively related to the receipt of financial support. For the few firms which expanded output and had received financial support, it seems GEDC was the most significant source of financial help. This could be attributed to one main reason. GEDC, unlike other institutions set up to assist SSEs, particularly NBSSI, gives direct credit assistance to enterprises. NBSSI performs more of an indirect intermediation role in recommending firms to financial institutions for help[8]. Many small firms which are recommended by intermediaries or who seek finance on their own are refused credit because of the conventional lending methods which the financial institutions adopt.

Availability of inputs

Lack of inputs is considered to be a problem by the great majority of enterprises (61.2 per cent), although the situation has improved since the inception of the ERP. Most of the SSEs depend on local sources of inputs for their operations, with only 5.9 per cent of enterprises requiring some form of imported inputs. Even then, output expansion or stagnation is not related to the source of input. The ERP has made available inputs and raw materials on a wider scale, as 81.7 per cent of the firms indicated that there is a wider availability of inputs, and as much as 91.4 per cent indicated that this improved situation has had a positive effect on their production.

The ERP attempts at removing foreign exchange controls through devaluations, auction system and foreign exchange bureaux have not affected the output of SSEs. This is due to the fact that most SSEs do not depend upon imported inputs and as such do not require foreign exchange. Only 9.1 per cent of the firms that increased output really needed foreign exchange and only 15.9 per cent of firms with stagnating output needed foreign exchange. For the few that require foreign exchange, the Bank of Ghana was the main source. The foreign exchange bureaux were not significant as a source of foreign exchange for the SSEs.

Demand for SSE products and marketing

Small-scale enterprises in Ghana have traditionally had marketing problems. Most of them, especially the 'micro' firms, produce to serve the poorer end of the market. The larger SSEs compete with the local large and medium enterprises (LMEs). Most SSEs are also producers of final goods and one would expect that their goods would go to final consumers. One would also expect that with the promotion of private enterprise as a mainstay of the ERP, government agencies would be encouraged to support the SSEs, through the patronage of their products, through breaking of public bids into smaller units to enable the SSEs to compete adequately with LMEs.

The survey found that the SSEs do not depend on government agencies for the sale of their products. Thus, the expansion in output is not due to increased demand from government agencies. As little as 9.2 per cent of those enterprises that expanded output relied on some government agency as a market for their products. The dependence of the SSEs on larger-scale enterprises as purchasers of their output either for sale as final goods or to be used as intermediate inputs is very limited in Ghana. Only 13 per cent of the firms produce any item or component for a bigger firm. Also, even interdependence among SSEs is very minimal. Only 17.6 per cent of firms with growing output and 8.4 per cent of those whose output stagnated have other SSEs as clients.

SSEs depend on individuals as their major clients, and the increase in the demand for their products may be due to the expansion in the demand by individuals arising from the substitution effects from higher-priced products of the import-dependent, large-scale firms. Thus, about 57 per cent of the firms experienced increases in the number of customers over the last five years. The importance of individuals in the demand for products of the small-scale sector reinforces the need to adopt policies that will influence the incomes of those who purchase the products of the SSEs, especially the low-income groups.

Although a large number of firms interviewed have no sales growth, they still do not accept that they find it difficult to sell their products (64.3 per cent). The situation has not changed for about 24 per cent of the enterprises.

Only 1.7 per cent of the firms export any of their products. Thus, the sector has been unable to take advantage of the effects of the devaluations on export prices and the bonuses paid to exporters.

Output expansion and types of regimes when established

The survey indicates that older firms experienced greater output expansion than relatively new ones. A greater proportion of firms established during the SMC regime period (69.6 per cent) and early PNDC period (69.8 per cent) (i.e. between 1972 and 1982) expanded output compared with 54.2 per cent of firms established after 1983. These results contradict the findings of Steel and Webster (1990), which indicate that firms established since 1983 have been more successful in expanding output than those established before 1983. This could be due to the experience that those older firms had gained in adjusting to the freer economic environment.

Owners' schooling and output expansion

The survey results suggest that the educational background of the entrepreneur is not related to successful output performance. For example, while 48.1 per cent of university graduates expanded output, 64.8 per cent of the illiterate entrepreneurs achieved growth in output. However, the experience of the secondary/technical graduate highlights the importance of vocational training in the operation of small-scale enterprises. About 68 per cent of those who have had secondary/technical education expanded output.

Location

Only 33.8 per cent of SSEs in Accra expanded output compared with 66.1 per cent of the non-Accra enterprises. This could be due to the fact that with the ERP and a freer business environment, the non-Accra firms have recovered from the stagnation, due to distortions in the economic system which in the 1960s and 1970s favoured Accra enterprises.

Effect on employment

How far has employment in the SSEs expanded? The survey results, as can be seen in Table 4.9, indicate that overall employment in the SSEs has not responded positively to the ERP and its subsequent SAPs. The great majority of firms in our sample (64 per cent) indicated a decrease in employment. The decrease seems more pronounced in firms established during the ERP (26 per cent) than those established before the ERP (24 per cent). Also, firms outside Accra showed a higher decrease (48 per cent) than those in Accra (16 per cent). These results contradict the findings of Steel and Webster (1990) who found that a smaller number of firms in their sample (16 per cent) experienced a decrease in employment.

Why did so many firms experience a decrease in employment? The most critical factor seems to be the availability of finance and credit. The great majority (57 per cent) of firms that showed a decrease in employment had not received financial support. An equally great majority of firms (66 per cent) who experienced a decrease found it difficult to obtain credit. While an even greater majority (72 per cent) indicated that they are limited by a lack of credit in their operations. It was indicated elsewhere that credit and finance non-availability constrains small-scale entrepreneurs from setting up business on even a modest scale. Expansion is also made difficult by this same factor. It is thus to be expected that the non-availability of credit and finance would make it more difficult for entrepreneurs to expand employment.

Conclusion and recommendations

The basic conclusion reached from this exploratory study is that the ERP and its subsequent SAPs have had a mixed impact on SSEs. The freer economic environment appears to have encouraged the establishment of more enterprises, with younger and well-educated entrepreneurs. Output has gone up in a majority of the

Table 4.9 Employment Level and Effect of Adjustment Measures in SSEs (% of Total)

	All Firms	*Micro*	*Very Small*	*Small*
(a) Employment level				
Increase	36	28.2	5.8	1.9
Decrease	64	58.8	4.1	1.9

(b) Effect of adjustment measures on employment decreasing firms:

	%
1. Did you receive financial support	
Yes	10
No	90
2. Is obtaining credit easy	
Easy	34
Difficult	66
3. Input availability needed	
More	76
Less	24
4. Do you need foreign exchange	
Yes	8
No	92
5. Are you limited by lack of credit in your operation	
Yes	72
No	28
6. Regime when established	
Pre-ERP	58
ERP era	42
7. Location	
Accra	22
Other	78

Source: Survey Result (1990).

SSEs. However, employment in the majority of enterprises has not responded positively.

To facilitate the growth and development of SSEs in Ghana the following policy measures are suggested: (i) provision of vocational/technical training to small-scale entrepreneurs; (ii) provision of increased credit and finance to SSEs, and (iii) creation of an enabling business and regulatory environment.

(i) Action towards provision of vocational/technical training to small-scale entrepreneurs

The study has shown that the supply of vocationally and technically-trained entrepreneurs is critical for the success of the small-scale sector. Incorporation of vocational and technical training in school curricula, apprenticeship schemes and practical training programmes for workers and owners of SSEs can all play an essential role in assuring these businesses of a sufficient supply of those manual and management skills necessary for their success. In this regard, the current education reforms in Ghana giving attention in the Junior and Senior Secondary School to vocational/technical and commercial subjects will provide future entrepreneurs with the requisite skills.

(ii) Action toward increasing credit and finance to SSEs

The study has shown that the availability of credit and finance is critical for SSEs. Increasing attention is so far being paid to ways of directing finance and credit to SSEs. However, if the development of the sector is to be self-sustaining, then action is clearly needed to encourage local savings to be directed towards entrepreneurs by means of savings banks and other networks such as credit and savings associations, such as the *susu*. One way by which national development banks, enterprise agencies and other bodies designed to assist the SSEs may reach the very small-scale borrower more effectively is by means of closer forms of co-operation with the local savings organizations.

(iii) Provision of an enabling business/regulatory environment

Small-scale enterprises operate best under sound macro-economic government. The freer economic environment provided under the ERP is desirable. However, attention must be paid to providing an enabling regulatory environment. An example of an innovation in favour of SSEs, that has already been introduced in certain parts of the world, could have lessons for Ghana. This is the 'one-stop office'[9] (or 'Guichet Unique', in French), which enables an entrepreneur of a small business to deal with all, or most, government-generated administrative formalities, connected with his or her business, at a single place and with the benefit of qualified advice. This type of innovation is likely to prove particularly useful in helping small-scale entrepreneurs in dealing with government, and should prove an important factor in encouraging the entry of hitherto undisclosed businesses into the formal sector of the economy.

Impact of structural adjustment on the small enterprise sector: a comparison of the Ghanaian and Tanzanian experiences

JONATHAN DAWSON

Introduction

The structure of most African economies is currently undergoing a period of transformation. Under the aegis of structural adjustment policy packages negotiated with the IMF and the World Bank, governments in all corners of the continent are effecting programmes to alter radically the nature and orientation of their national economies. In most cases this involves a substantial degree of economic liberalization, with the role of the government in the management and regulation of economic activity being much reduced.

Proponents of structural adjustment argue that the heavy involvement of government in the economies of many Sub-Saharan African (SSA) countries since independence has caused major distortions, resulting in a sub-optimal allocation of economic resources, the development of a macro-environment not conducive to economic development, and poor overall performance in consequence. The stated aims of structural adjustment have been to reduce or remove the accumulated distortions, to effect a diminished role for government in the undertaking and regulation of economic activity, and to create a macroeconomic environment conducive to increased activity in the private sector by both domestic and foreign actors.

The potential for enhanced private sector participation is generally seen as being high throughout the economy. In many SSA countries, post-independence governments inhibited the development of private enterprise, often by way of the erection of protective barriers around public enterprises or by guaranteeing their privileged access to productive resources. The performance of these state-owned enterprises has been generally disappointing. Industry has performed particularly poorly, with a negative growth rate of 2.3 per cent in the first half of the 1980s, leaving the sector's share of GDP in Sub-Saharan Africa by the mid-1980s only marginally higher than that prevailing in 1960 (World Bank, 1987). A relaxing of government control over economic activity, argue the proponents of structural adjustment, will permit an expanded role for private enterprise which will be more competitive, more dynamic and more efficient in its allocation of resources.

The small-scale enterprise sector is often considered to have particularly strong growth potential. The scale and operational flexibility of small firms are seen as strengths in environments often characterized by small domestic markets, relatively high transport costs and interruptions in the supply of materials, equipment and parts. It is pointed out that even in the period prior to structural adjustment, when large firms, generally owned at least partly by the state, continued to enjoy substantial protection, small firms – the so-called 'informal sector' – were already experiencing strong growth in many SSAs. Studies from all corners of the continent suggested that the 'informal sector' was accounting for a large and growing share of national output and employment. The removal of discriminatory policies in favour of large industries and the creation of a macro-environment conducive to private sector development, it is argued, should further accelerate these trends.

The aim of this chapter is to analyse the degree to which these projections have proved valid in the case of two of the SSA countries which have embarked upon structural adjustment programmes in the 1980s – Ghana and Tanzania. The next section will provide a description of the findings of studies conducted by the author into the impact of structural adjustment on the small enterprise sector in both countries (Dawson 1991b, Dawson *et al.* 1991). The last section will discuss the theoretical and policy implications arising out of these findings.

The Ghana and Tanzania case studies

Evolution of the small-firm sectors in Ghana and Tanzania

Before looking specifically at the way in which the small-firm sector has been affected by the policies of structural adjustment, it is important to set recent developments within the context of longer-term economic and political developments within the two countries. The small-scale, private, indigenous enterprise sector was frowned upon by the governments which came to power at independence in both Ghana and Tanzania. Nyerere and Nkrumah had similar visions of the societies they were seeking to build, with the state as the principal economic actor and socialism as the underlying ideology. Small, private enterprises were seen at best as irrelevant to the large-scale path of industrialization on which they had embarked and at worst as anti-social and inimical to the development of 'socialist man'.

The overthrow of Nkrumah in 1966, however, saw the beginnings of a sharp divergence in the ideologies and the developmental paths followed by the two countries. In Ghana, the small-firm sector began to play a progressively expanded role in the economy from the early 1970s, though more as a consequence of economic mismanagement than due to a deliberate change in economic strategy. From around this time, the large-scale public and private enterprises which had previously dominated the economy began to experience crisis. Heavily import-dependent, and in many cases having few linkages with other sectors of the economy, they were poorly equipped to adapt to the progressively tighter foreign exchange squeeze experienced by the country. Equipment fell into disrepair and capacity utilization dropped sharply. Meanwhile, spiralling inflation ate into the purchasing power of salaried workers.

As the output of the large workshops began to decline, so the number of small enterprises grew. The trickle of formally trained workers into self-employment, which had always existed, developed into a substantial exodus. Being beyond the control of the state – as well as by virtue of the flexibility of operations afforded by their smallness of scale – these enterprises were able to gain access to the thriving black market in imported components and materials that was developing. Increasingly, those seeking spare parts were directed to the informal industrial areas rather than the large shops and garages.

A large variety of machine tools found their way into the small enterprise sector, both by way of the purchase and renovation of equipment from large domestic factories and in the form of remittances from the many Ghanaians living overseas. There was also a plentiful supply of scrap-metal and timber.

By the early 1980s the Kumasi suburb of Suame, Ghana's largest informal industrial area, was estimated to have grown eightfold over the previous decade and to be playing home to around 40,000 craftsmen operating out of approximately 5000 workshops. Nor was the development of the small-firm sector purely quantitative in nature. In each of the four branches covered by the current author's study – carpentry, vehicle repair, blacksmithing, and light engineering – small firms had conquered new markets and had, to varying degrees, succeeded in diversifying and upgrading production. Small engineering workshops in particular were playing a strong import-substitution function and were manufacturing and maintaining much of the equipment being used by other small firms.

While the private small-firm sector was tolerated – if never officially endorsed or supported – after 1966 in Ghana, in Tanzania until the late 1980s it continued to be officially repressed. At first it appeared that the Arusha Declaration of 1967 would usher in a policy framework in which small firms could flourish. Grounded on the principles of socialism and self-reliance, it acknowledged the role of small-scale enterprise at village level.

The policies pursued in the post-Arusha period, however, proved inimical to the achievement of these goals. Large-scale, mainly state-owned enterprises continued to enjoy huge levels of subsidy and protection as well as privileged access to credit, materials and imported components. Agriculture was starved of investment and producer prices were kept low while parastatal agencies were given a monopoly over the purchase, processing and distribution of most crops. This inhibited the development of backward and forward linkages between the small firm and agricultural sectors. While small private firms were tolerated in the urban areas, in the villages they were effectively outlawed, with the 1975 Ujamaa Villages Act decreeing that all village-based enterprises should be communally owned.

By the late 1970s, the Tanzanian economy was in trouble: its industrial base was highly capital-intensive and import-dependent; low producer prices, along with the poor performance of the state marketing boards, had depressed agricultural output; and the public sector was stretched beyond its managerial, technical and budgetary capacities. A series of exogenous shocks: deteriorating terms of trade for its primary exports; military spending occasioned by the war in Uganda; the break-up of the East African Community; the doubling of oil prices in 1979–80; and the severe droughts experienced in 1981–2 and 1983–4 pushed the economy over the edge.

As in the case of Ghana, the crisis in the formal economy created opportunities for small firms. In several branches, small-scale producers were able to move into markets vacated by larger firms: cobblers increased production of sandals using worn tyres; small soap-making plants proliferated; the production of local tie-and-dye fabrics increased; and the more sophisticated small firms even began to recondition and renovate worn vehicle and machine parts.

For several reasons, however, the response of small enterprises to the emerging opportunities was not as strong as in Ghana. Firstly, as a result of tight government control, no significant black market developed in Tanzania so small firms did not have the same level of access to modern equipment and imported components as their Ghanaian counterparts. This problem was exacerbated by the relative lack of remittances coming back into the country. Secondly, unlike their counterparts in Ghana, state enterprises in Tanzania continued to enjoy an effective monopoly over much economic activity, particularly in the agricultural and food-processing sectors. This greatly limited the scope for private sector activity.

Finally, there was much less of a tradition of artisan production in Tanzania than in Ghana, so the accumulation of experience and techniques in the use of small-scale technologies and local materials had not developed to the same degree. Of particular importance in this respect was the fact that while small-scale entrepreneurs in Ghana had a decade between the beginnings of the foreign exchange squeeze and the adoption of the structural adjustment programme in 1983 in which to develop new techniques and diversify and upgrade the quality of their products, the equivalent period in Tanzania was much shorter – effectively only three or four years. By the time Tanzania embarked on its structural adjustment programme in 1986, its small-firm sector was, in both quantitative and qualitative terms, significantly less developed than its Ghanaian counterpart.

Study areas

Having established in broad outline the state of development of the small-firm sectors in Ghana and Tanzania on the eve of the adoption of structural adjustment programmes, known as the Economic Recovery Programme (ERP) in both countries, it is now time to describe the findings of the above-mentioned studies undertaken by the author. The aim of both studies was in broad terms to understand the different ways in which small firms were being affected by the new conditions ushered in by the ERP and to attempt to identify appropriate policy measures in order to promote the sector's development.

The Ghana study was spatially limited to one area, albeit the densest concentration of small-scale industrial activity in the country – Suame, a northern suburb of Ghana's second city, Kumasi. The study consisted of a questionnaire survey of 672 small firms (in the metalwork, carpentry and vehicle-repair branches), complemented by 45 loosely-structured, in-depth interviews with a representative sample of the 672 entrepreneurs. A similar number of interviews were held with other actors such as small enterprise clients, competitors, suppliers, support agencies and donors, etc.

The Tanzania study was undertaken in early 1991 as part of an ODA consultancy mission. A small sample of small-scale entrepreneurs in a number of branches was interviewed in three areas of the country – Dar es Salaam, Arusha and Dodoma – and interviews were also conducted with a similar range of other actors as in the Ghana study. In both studies, a very general definition of the small enterprise sector was adopted. Firms with a workforce of less than 25 were considered to be small.

Small-firm sector and structural adjustment

The first and most striking conclusion to be drawn from the two studies is that very few generalizations can be made about the impact of the ERP on the small-firm sector. A high degree of heterogeneity was identified, both in terms of the range of policies to be found within structural adjustment programmes and in the different types of small enterprise to be found within the 'small-firm sector'. A complex and multi-dimensional picture emerges in both countries, with small firms of different types – the key variables being the size of the enterprises and the branches or subsectors in which they operate – being quite differently affected by the various policies which go to make up the ERP.

These points can best be illustrated by looking in detail at each of the different areas of policy introduced under the ERP in the two countries and analysing in concrete terms how small firms of different types have been affected. These policies will be discussed under four general headings: external-sector reform; demand-management policies; the liberalization of internal trade and of agricultural marketing and processing; and public-sector restructuring.

External-sector reform

External-sector reform in both countries has been comprised of various measures to enhance the availability of foreign exchange and to liberalize its allocation. The introduction of the 'own funds' scheme in Tanzania and of the unnumbered special licence facility in Ghana has enabled private citizens to mobilize and use foreign exchange without controls. At the same time, the holding of regular foreign exchange auctions in both countries – supported by donor-funded import support schemes – has enabled the private sector to compete for allocations on equal terms with parastatals. Finally, the introduction of private forex bureaus in Ghana (soon to be replicated in Tanzania) has provided another source of foreign exchange to the private sector.

In parallel with policies enhancing the availability of foreign exchange and liberalizing its allocation, both countries have substantially devalued their currency. In Ghana, where the level of distortion of the economy was particularly pronounced, the cedi was devalued by more than 8000 per cent – from 2.75 to 225 cedis to the US dollar – between 1983 and 1988. In Tanzania, the process of currency realignment, which began several years before the launching of the ERP in 1986, has been a little less severe. The Tanzanian shilling has been devalued by 1370 per cent – from 17.84 to 244.42 shillings to the US dollar between March 1984 and June 1992. The currency is estimated to be still overvalued by about 50 per cent compared with the unofficial rate.

An impact of the external sector reform package described above has been a significant increase in the availability of imports. There has also been a large increase in the price of most imports as a result of the devaluations, although it should be remembered that – particularly in the case of Ghana – a large volume of 'unofficial' imports were coming into the private sector via the black market at real (unofficial) exchange rates prior to the adoption of the structural adjustment programme. The price of these goods was unaffected by devaluation. This increase in the availability of (generally more expensive) imports has impacted on small enterprises in Ghana and Tanzania in a number of different ways.

First, a number of small firms have been able to diversify into new product lines due to the availability of certain components. Small firms in both countries were found to be assembling batteries as a result of key parts being available. Access to new imported steel was found to be enabling numerous small enterprises (which had previously been dependent on scrap materials) to make higher quality products. The availability of components such as motors and cutting blades has additionally allowed small firms to increase output in a number of product ranges. The enhanced availability of imported components has proved to be of particular importance to small firms which produce for donors or for large firms, which are often prepared to pay more for products of a higher quality or of a superior appearance. This trend has been particularly evident in Ghana with small firms making sawmilling equipment for local timber companies and animal-feed mills and food-processing equipment for large farms and donors.

The importance to small firms of the improved supply of imports has been confirmed by a more recent study conducted by the World Bank into the impact of structural adjustment on the small-firm sector in Ghana (Steel and Webster, 1990). This study found that while there was a decline in the import content of goods produced by the Ghanaian industrial sector taken as a whole, the use of imports by small firms has increased under the ERP.

The increase in the price of imports as a result of devaluation has enabled small firms in several product markets to outcompete – and in some cases, entirely displace – imported goods. This trend appears to be considerably stronger in Ghana than in Tanzania. Imported goods which have been displaced in Ghana by small-firm products include numerous machine and tool parts, various specialized nuts and bolts, and bulky food-processing equipment. One small firm in Kumasi was commissioned to make gears and sprockets for a local Yugoslav motorcycle assembly plant prior to the adoption of the structural adjustment programme in 1983 due to the scarcity of foreign exchange with which to import the pieces from Europe. Even after foreign exchange became more freely available, however, the plant continued to purchase from the local producer, finding his pieces to be of a similar quality and significantly cheaper than the imports would have been.

A similar, if weaker, trend can also be identified in Tanzania. Bagachwa, in this volume, reports -scale producers introducing new product lines including hand-operated oilpresses, oil expellers, hand-operated waterpumps, water storage tanks and drill presses at least partly in response to the opportunities created by the rise in the price of imports as a result of devaluation.

More commonly, however, the increase in the price of the imports has not been sufficient to protect firms from competition. In both countries, but particularly in Tanzania, enterprises in several branches have lost much of their market in consequence. Standard hexagonal nuts and bolts manufactured in machine shops have been almost entirely displaced by imported pieces. Small-scale producers of soap, of tie-and-dye clothing and of leather sandals have been perhaps the worst affected in both countries as cheap imports of second-hand clothing, plastic sandals, and soap have flooded in. Both Bagachwa and Osei in their chapters in this volume, confirm the devastating impact of imports on firms in certain branches. Thirty-four per cent of the firms in Osei's survey sample (drawn from various locations in Ghana) which have contracted since 1983 cited increased imports as the principal cause.

Artisan soapmakers in Ghana have been further adversely affected by the re-opening of the Lever Brothers plant in the country. However, other than this example, it is interesting that very few cases were identified of enterprises surrendering markets to large domestic firms which had been reactivated by their renewed access to imports. One of the few cases where this was found to have happened was the resumption of the production of plastic beer-crates by a factory in Ghana which had the effect of displacing carpenters from this market.

Increases in the price of imported components have also had a negative impact on firms which had high levels of import dependency. Several firms in Tanzania were found to have sharply contracted – and several others reported to have ceased operations – as a result of sharp increases in the price of inputs and in transport costs – Bagachwa lists a number of such examples in his chapter. This phenomenon was found to be particularly in evidence among the firms located on, or receiving assistance from, the industrial estates in Tanzania, apparently verifying impressions that the privileges accorded these firms acted as a disincentive to efficiency while encouraging high levels of capital- and import-dependence. As mentioned above, firms in Ghana prior to 1983 were largely supplied through the black market at 'real' exchange rates and were thus much less affected by price rises resulting from devaluation.

In summary, the reform of the external sector in both Ghana and Tanzania has impacted on different types of firm in quite different ways. Some firms – those in more traditional micro-enterprise activities such as soapmaking, textiles, tailoring and shoe- and sandalmaking; those competing with large domestic companies which have benefited from investment under the ERP; and those with high import-dependencies – appear to have been relatively adversely affected. Conversely, other types of firms appear to have succeeded in upgrading and diversifying production into product and service niches where they have a relative advantage.

Two key factors can be identified as underlying the ability of certain types of small firm to benefit from external sector reforms. The first is the availability of relatively small, specialist product and service niches into which small firms can move. The second is the level of the firms' technical and technological sophistication and the degree to which this enables them to occupy those niches.

In short, small firms operating in mass markets and lacking either the opportunity or the technological capability to diversify out of those markets have lost out as the economies of scale employed in large-scale production – either domestic or in the form of imports – has proved decisive. Conversely, where small firms have succeeded in occupying specialist niches for products or services for which demand is relatively low and irregular, the flexibility of small firms and their ability to shift production rapidly between various product lines has proved more appropriate than large-scale production. (This is even more so the case with bulky products, since the relatively high transport costs involved make large-scale, centralized production even less viable.)

The nuts and bolts market in Kumasi can be used to illustrate this point. After 1983, imported standard hexagonal bolts, commonly used in all sorts of machinery, flooded onto the local market in large quantities, undercutting small machine shops which had previously been manufacturing them. Many of these workshops, however, successfully diversified into the manufacture of less common and generally more bulky bolts – such as U-bolts and centre bolts – largely succeeding in driving competing imports off the market.

A substantial number of examples of this type of diversification was identified in the case of Ghana both by the current author's study and the later World Bank report cited above (Steel and Webster). These included the increased manufacture of agricultural processing equipment, which also tends to be bulky, of variable sizes and shapes depending on the requirements of the client and characterized by relatively low and sporadic demand; the rebuilding or conversion of vehicles; the building of sawmills (generally in batches of no more than two or three); the manufacture of key components for water-systems equipment run by the national water authorities; the production of various spares for an oil refinery, harbour facilities and for ships etc. The fact that while many of the small firms studied were operating at near-full capacity while their larger competitors were conspicuously idle provides circumstantial evidence that many of the markets for engineered goods in Kumasi are relatively small and specialized.

While some cases of diversification in response to the renewed availability of imports were identified in Tanzania (see Bagachwa's chapter in this volume), this was much less common than in the case of Ghana. This appears to be due primarily to the relative technical and technological weakness of the small-firm sector in Tanzania. This factor will be discussed in greater depth at the end of this section when the various threads of the global impact of the ERP on small firms are pulled together.

Demand management

The second broad area of structural adjustment policies to be considered relates to changes in the pattern of demand within the economy. Structural adjustment programmes have as a general goal the restructuring of demand within the economy. This involves a redirecting of resources away from consumption and towards the productive sectors of the economy. A number of policy instruments have been employed in Ghana and Tanzania in order to achieve this end. On the one hand, policies were introduced to control the growth in the money supply. These included the rationing of credit, a cutback in public sector investment and sharp increases in the prices of public utilities and fees for school and hospital facilities. On the other hand, resources were channelled to those sectors of the economy which were considered to be of the highest economic or strategic importance, particularly cash crop agriculture (by way of improved services and producer prices); infrastructure and transport (strong investment in road and rail construction and maintenance); and manufacturing industry, particularly that with an export orientation (improved investment incentives).

Once again, the impact of these policies on the small enterprise sector is complex and multi-dimensional. At the most general level, it can be said that small firms whose demand comes principally from the general public and particularly low-income groups – predominantly in the form of consumer goods such as furniture, clothes, shoes, etc. – have been adversely affected by the fall in purchasing power among these groups. In addition, small enterprises providing goods and services to the public sector have experienced a drop in demand. This has been the case, for example, with small-scale carpenters in Ghana providing furniture to the civil service and to schools.

On the other hand, small firms which have succeeded in developing significant linkages with the growth sectors of the economy have generally seen demand for their goods and services rise. For the reasons listed above, this trend appears to have been considerably stronger in Ghana than in Tanzania. In the face of the higher technical specifications often demanded by the larger, 'formal sector' operators which often benefited most strongly from the ERP reforms, the superior technological sophistication of many small-scale Ghanaian enterprises has stood them in better stead than their Tanzanian counterparts.

In the field of transport, for example, the increase in repair and renovation work occasioned by the sharp increase in the national vehicle fleet was, in the case of Kumasi, accounted for almost exclusively by small enterprises. Despite investment in the rehabilitation of the large-scale garages in Kumasi, they continued to operate at a small fraction of capacity utilization. The increase in the number of vehicles, together with the rise in the price of imports, also led to a growth in demand for locally-made spare parts, a market dominated by small-scale producers.

Small firms in Ghana also experienced a surge in demand for machine parts, as well as for general engineering maintenance and rehabilitation services, from large manufacturing firms which began to increase their output in response to the renewed availability of foreign exchange. These included operators in the fields of timber, construction, mining and pharmaceuticals. There was a significant increase in the production of agricultural implements such as planters, ridgers, and ploughs as well as of a wide range of food-processing machinery and animal-feed mills.

A final important growing source of demand for small enterprises after the adoption of the structural adjustment programme in Ghana was the small firm sector itself. The more sophisticated small enterprises have played an important function in manufacturing and maintaining the equipment used by other enterprises. Products manufactured and repaired include saw-benches, wood-turning lathes, welding machines and compressors.

This picture of the development of linkages between small enterprises and the growth sectors of the economy in Ghana is in sharp contrast with the situation in Tanzania. Several small Tanzanian enterprises were identified which had received increased orders from economic actors experiencing growth as a result of the ERP. Some of the new product lines manufactured by small enterprises have already been mentioned. In addition, several small machine shops were visited which, like their Ghanaian counterparts, were providing a wide range of services to larger factories – from the manufacture and reconditioning of parts to various repair and maintenance jobs.

The development of linkages was, nonetheless, found to be markedly weaker in Tanzania than in Ghana. The largest constraints on a stronger development of such linkages appears to be the relative lack in the small-firm sector of modern equipment and of human resources with the skills to operate such equipment. Those small enterprises in Tanzania which were found to have developed linkages with growth sectors – producers of food processing equipment, of engineering goods and services, for example – all had uncharacteristically privileged access to modern equipment: several had received long-term assistance from the Small Industries Development Organisation (SIDO); several others were owned by families of Asian extraction, often with relatively good access to foreign exchange; others had managed to accumulate the capital necessary to purchase equipment at auction. Nonetheless, the strong flow of modern equipment and skilled labour from larger to smaller-scale firms which had begun in the early 1970s in Ghana remains no more than a relatively minor trickle in Tanzania, with obvious implications for the relative capabilities of the sectors in the two countries.

Liberalisation of internal trade and of agricultural marketing and processing

Measures to liberalize both trade and the agricultural regime have been introduced in Ghana and Tanzania. In both countries, there existed before structural adjustment a range of price controls as well as parastatal monopolies over the sale of certain goods and over the purchase, distribution and processing of certain crops. This was particularly the case in Tanzania where the state retained effective control over agricultural marketing and distribution, and the activities of private operators were strictly curtailed. In the case of Ghana, while various crop marketing boards were in place prior to 1983 and price controls existed for a range of products, the control of the state over these activities was considerably less complete. A strong black market thrived and the smuggling of a wide range of crops and minerals was commonplace.

It was, thus, understandable that the impact of liberalization and deregulation should have a rather greater impact in Tanzania than in Ghana. So, while the removal of price controls and of the parastatal monopolies opened up great areas of economic space for small retail and processing firms in both countries, the immediate impact of the reforms was particularly pronounced in Tanzania.

Small traders are now active in all parts of the country purchasing surplus crops. A study by the current author into transport and crop marketing in Morogoro Region (Dawson, 1991b) found that while previously there had been significant crop losses due to the failure of the state body – the Regional Cooperative Union – to collect or pay for crops after the harvest, today these are much reduced as a result of the presence of small traders even in relatively isolated villages. Unlike the Cooperative Union, the small traders assume responsibility for the transport of the produce from the farm gate; they pay upon receipt of their purchases; and, on the whole, they also appear to pay superior prices to the farmers. Farmers tend to sell to the Cooperative Union only if no private traders are to hand.

Small-scale traders have also become more active in a number of other fields in recent years. These include the retailing of household and consumer goods, both in the urban and rural areas and the distribution and sale of leather, tanning and shoes. It should be noted that the improved availability of consumer goods in the rural areas as a result of the activities of small traders can be expected in the longer term to contribute to increased agricultural output.

Crop processing is another field in which small firms have become more active in recent years. The best documented case of this is Bagachwa's case study of the grain milling industry (Bagachwa, 1991) – which he discusses in this volume – which identified an explosion in small-scale private enterprise in this sub-sector since deregulation. The National Milling Corporation (NMC), which had previously dominated the milling of grain, appears to have been largely displaced from the market by smaller competitors. It is, however, important to note that while small enterprises in Tanzania have made significant progress in these fields, there is growing evidence that they are unable to exploit fully the opportunities which are currently arising due to a lack of resources – particularly capital. Informal credit markets appear to be only now beginning to develop in Tanzania, while the formal banking system remains in almost every case beyond the reach of small enterprises.

The heavy focus on Tanzania in this section of the paper does not mean that small firms in Ghana are not active in these fields – quite the reverse. The great majority of Ghana's food crops are traded and processed privately on a small scale. Rather, as indicated above, even before 1983, the small-scale private sector dominated these sectors, with the result that the impact of the ERP has not been so dramatic as in the case of Tanzania.

Public-sector restructuring

The final set of structural adjustment policies to be examined here relates to the restructuring of the public sector. The policies employed in this field include the removal of protection, subsidies and long-term support to parastatals; internal restructuring with a view to making them commercially viable; privatization; the closure of parastatals which can neither be restructured nor sold; and retrenchment in the civil service and parastatals. Since this process is only now getting under way in Tanzania, most of the evidence in this section will be drawn from the Ghanaian experience.

Public-sector reforms impact on the small-firm sector in a number of different ways. In the first place, the shrinking of the parastatal sector leaves a considerable amount of economic space which small firms are potentially able to occupy. In the case of Tanzania, the growth of small-scale, grain-milling activity at the expense of the NMC can be seen as an example of this. Similarly, the increase in small-scale activity in a number of the product and service markets in Ghana which have already been discussed – vehicle repair, engineering services, food processing equipment, and animal-feed mills – resulted in some measure from the shrinkage of parastatal actors in these branches.

A second and closely related effect of reforms in this field is the potential for the development of sub-contracting relations between parastatals and small firms, as the former begin to contract out jobs which they previously did in-house. There is some limited evidence of formal subcontracting relationships of this type developing in Ghana, with some parastatals turning to small enterprises for specific and specialist 'one-off' jobs – the manufacture of specific parts, and vehicle and machine repairs, for example – which their own workshops are no longer able to undertake. Several cases were also identified of small construction companies being sub-contracted for public-works programmes by parastatals. The continuing low levels of public sector economic activity since 1983, however, have limited the scope for the development of subcontracting relationships.

The process of parastatal restructuring is too recent in Tanzania to permit the identification of firm trends in this field. Some small firms were reported to have recently won contracts for the provision of curtains and furniture for the civil service. As in the case of Ghana, however, it appears likely that public-sector cutbacks will mean this type of contract is likely to be short-lived.

Third, the shrinking of the public sector stimulates a flow of skilled labour and of modern technology from parastatals to small enterprises. This process, in fact, predates the public sector reform programme in both countries but has intensified as a result of it. The initial impetus for the transfer of skilled labour out of the public sector was the level of salaries which began falling sharply in real terms in both countries some years before the adoption of structural adjustment programmes. Attracted by the much higher salaries to be earned in self-employment, the large movement of skilled workers into small firms which occurred in Ghana from the mid-1970s appears to be well under way in Tanzania today.

This trend rapidly accelerated in Ghana as a result of the retrenchment of public sector employees. Between 1983 and 1989, around 100,000 workers – that is approximately one-fifth of registered salary earners – were made redundant (Economist Intelligence Unit 1987, West Africa 1988). Equivalent figures are not yet available for Tanzania.

The rationalization of the parastatal sector has also stimulated an outflow of modern technology. In the case of Ghana, a certain amount of this equipment found its way into the small-scale sector, most commonly by way of auctions or clearance sales. Many of the machine tools currently operating in small engineering workshops were purchased in this way, with a significant number being bought as scrap and renovated. The incidence of such auctions of machinery in Tanzania is increasing and several of the workshops visited had already equipped themselves by way of purchases at these auctions.

In many respects, the rationalization of the parastatal sector has proved favourable to the small-firm sector. New markets have opened up, while the inflow of modern equipment and skilled labour has enabled many small firms to exploit the opportunities presented. However, the impact of the retrenchment policies has been highly damaging to small enterprises in almost all branches in Ghana – and looks set to have a similar impact in Tanzania. This is because the sharp growth in the ranks of the underemployed has been translated into an avalanche of new entrants into small-scale activities, leading in many cases to an overcrowding of markets.

Despite substantial growth in the 'formal' industrial sector in Ghana after 1983, it proved to have a poor labour absorption capacity and although many of those who were retrenched – as well as new market entrants – moved into agricultural activities, there was a flood of new entrants into small-scale activities. The low barriers of entry into most of these activities offered little protection against this flood. The level of investment required to establish a small retail operation, vehicle-repair workshop or blacksmith shop, for example, is not substantial. Furthermore, the apprenticeship system which exists in both countries guarantees a ready supply of willing and trained prospective new entrants. This trend is mirrored by the findings from Osei's study, cited in his chapter in this volume, that 42 per cent of his sample of small firms were established after the introduction of the ERP, with 20 per cent of these being set up by retrenched workers.

The result has been a proliferation of small firms which compete fiercely among themselves – largely on the basis of the price which they charge for their products. This has driven down remuneration and inhibited innovation. Even in the vehicle-repair branch, where the size of the cake in terms of the total workload undertaken by small garages appears to have grown significantly since 1983, the size of the slices earned by most individual garages has declined. A similar trend is identifiable in most of the subsectors in which small firms are active.

Only small-scale machine shops have to some degree escaped this trend. This is because the barriers to entry into engineering activities – in terms of both the cost of the equipment and of the skill needed to operate it – are sufficiently high to offer it some protection against the overcrowding occurring in other branches. In consequence, this subsector continues to be characterized by a relatively high degree of innovation and product diversification, while cut-throat competition prevails in most of the other small enterprise markets.

Few up-to-date official statistics exist for the growth of employment in the small-firm sector in Tanzania. Nonetheless, a number of recent studies suggest a strong growth in recent years. A study conducted in 1987, for example, found that three-quarters of the enterprises in Arusha and four-fifths of those in Dar es Salaam were established between 1980 and 1987 (Bagachwa and Ndulu, 1988). Similarly, a survey conducted in 1991 in Dar es Salaam found that 58 per cent of recorded firms were less than five years old (Bagachwa, 1991) while recent data from the Bureau of Statistics indicate that the number of small firms established between 1986 and 1990 was about 2500, about three times the total of those established over the previous 20 years which were still in business.

While the small-firm sector tends to be characterized by high turnover rates and a relatively short life of enterprises, these statistics point to a particularly fast growth in the number of firms in recent years. Meanwhile, most of those entrepreneurs interviewed during the current author's study identified the proliferation of other small firms as a significant constraint on demand for their goods and services, suggesting the development of a trend similar to that identified in Ghana.

Overview

It will by now be clear that, as was noted at the outset of this section, few generalizations about the impact of structural adjustment on the small-firm sector are possible. The various reforms have closed some doors while opening others, favoured some types of enterprise while discriminating against others. It is now time to attempt to disentangle the various threads traced above and to present an overview of the global impact of the reform packages on the small-firm sectors in the two countries. Perhaps the best place to begin is by identifying those enterprise characteristics which have proved well suited to the economic environment created by the adjustment process – as well as others that have been penalized by it. These are presented in Table 5.1.

This table pulls together many of the complex, multidimensional and often apparently contradictory trends identified above. What is immediately apparent is the importance of technical and technological modernization as a factor in determining the way in which small firms respond to structural adjustment. The relative sophistication in this respect of numerous small firms in Ghana has enabled them to upgrade their products and services to a level where they have been able to develop linkages with the growth sectors of the economy; to diversify out of product and service markets where the economies of scale attendant on mass production favoured larger-scale competitors; to occupy new niches better suited to their economies of flexibility and serving an import-substitution function; and to protect

Table 5.1 Enterprise Characteristics Favoured and Penalized by SAP

Characteristics Favoured	*Characteristics Penalized*
○ *Low import dependence*	○ *High import dependence*
○ *Development of linkages with growth sectors of the economy*	○ *Few linkages — demand mostly from low-income groups*
○ *Significant technological enhancement*	○ *Little technological enhancement*
○ *High barriers to entry*	○ *Low barriers to entry*
○ *Innovation*	○ *Cut-throat competition*
○ *Serving as import-substitution function*	

themselves against market saturation by raising the barriers of entry – in terms of the cost of the equipment and the skills necessary to operate it – thus permitting continued innovation.

Conversely, enterprises which have experienced little technological enhancement have tended to remain largely dependent on low-income groups as their principal source of demand at a time when the purchasing power of these groups has declined; to have failed to develop significant linkages with the growth sectors of the economy; and to be susceptible to overcrowding of the markets in which they operate and, in consequence, to cut-throat competition and falling income.

While this model must be understood as a rather schematic picture of the development of the small-firm sector under structural adjustment – and while significant variations on the themes presented must be admitted – a polarization of different types of firm along the lines described can be discerned. A similar pattern was, in fact, identified by the World Bank study mentioned above. It talks of 'dynamic, successful adapters with good prospects for the future (mostly found among small- and medium-scale enterprises), and stagnant producers who have not mastered the new environment and who seem unable to change products in the face of mounting competition (found mostly among microenterprises)' (Steel and Webster, 1990).

It is in the context of this analysis that the divergence between the experiences of the small enterprise sectors in Ghana and Tanzania must be located. The stronger performance of the former, in other words, can be understood primarily by reference to its superior access to modern technology and skilled labour. This is not to say that all small firms in Ghana have characteristics favoured by structural adjustment. Far from it. In fact, of the three Ghana surveys discussed here – those of the current author, the World Bank and Osei – only the last records a greater number of small firms reporting a rise in output compared with those reporting a fall since the adoption of the ERP.

Rather, the conclusion of the studies is that there is a significantly greater number of small enterprises in Ghana than in Tanzania which have proved able to adapt successfully to the new conditions. This is important in two respects. Firstly, on a practical level, while many of the small firms in Ghana have failed to adapt to the environment created by the ERP, the presence of a number of more sophisticated firms has had the effect of enhancing the 'collective efficiency' of the small-scale sector as a whole. In other words, the more modern firms have been responsible for the manufacture and maintenance of much of the equipment used by other small firms – including saw-benches, wood-turning lathes, welding and compressing machines, etc. – increasing their technological capabilities accordingly. They also manufacture components – such as grinding plates, shafts and bush-bearings, for example – which have enabled even less sophisticated firms to increase the range of their products. This is an especially important factor where small firms cluster together, as tends to be the case in the urban areas of Ghana.

The second respect in which the presence of a group of small enterprises which have successfully adapted to the environment created by the ERP is important concerns its conceptual and policy implications. On the one hand, it may hold out the possibility of an authentic, small enterprise-led industrial strategy, or one at least in which small enterprise plays a key role. On the other, it points out the need to differentiate between different types of small firm – in crude terms, adapters and non-adapters – rather than perpetuating the current widespread practice of policymakers and planners in assuming the sector to be homogenous, with the problems and needs of all small firms seen as broadly similar. These issues will be explored further in the next section.

Theoretical and policy implications

Two conceptual insights

A number of policy implications can be drawn from the findings of the two case studies. These arise out of, and are informed by, two key conceptual insights afforded by the comparative exercise undertaken above. Firstly, contrary to much of the thinking which has underlain structural adjustment, the creation of an environment which is conducive to the development of the small-scale sector is not sufficient to ensure that optimal results are achieved. In other words, the response of the small-scale sector – as indeed of the private sector as a whole – to the new opportunities which arise as a result of the reforms is conditional on a wide range of factors. These include the stage of development of the sector prior to the adoption of the reforms; the degree to which it has access to the resources – skills, technology, credit, infrastructure, etc. – necessary to enable it to adapt to the new environment; and the level of political and institutional support accorded it.

Where conditions are not generally favourable, small firms are likely to be able to respond only in a limited and imperfect way to the economic opportunities opened up. In Tanzania, for example, despite the immaturity of the small enterprise sector and the poor institutional and policy environment in which it operates, small-firm activity has greatly increased in recent years. This activity has, however, tended to be concentrated in the retail and service branches – petty trading and grain milling, for example – with a much weaker response in strategically more important branches such as metalworking and capital goods. Even in the retail sector, despite the emergence of informal credit markets in recent years (Bagachwa and Ndanshau, 1988), there is some evidence suggesting that traders are unable to raise sufficient capital to exploit fully existing opportunities.

In Ghana, where the small-firm sector was considerably more mature on the eve of the ERP, a higher degree of adaption and successful exploitation of new market niches was in evidence. Crucially, this was particularly the case in the capital goods and metalworking branches where the potential for indigenous technological learning, adaptation and, ultimately, creation are highest. Nonetheless, the lack of institutional support for the sector has seriously inhibited its ability to respond to emerging opportunities. The author's study, supported by that of the World Bank, found that the weak institutional response has been particularly damaging for small firms which have reached a level of technical sophistication and a scale of operations which can no longer be financed from the personal resources of the entrepreneur and his family – generally the most dynamic and innovative firms.

The second central conceptual insight afforded by the studies, once again at variance with much of the conventional wisdom upon which many small enterprise assistance programmes have been built, is a recognition of the great diversity of types of firm, and of the problems they face, to be found within the small firm sector. At the most crude and generalized level, this paper has drawn a dichotomy of two 'types' – adapters and non-adapters. Even if one explores the diversity at no deeper a level than this (due, alas, to pressures of space), it is already clear that to speak of one policy for the small enterprise sector is incompatible with responding in a meaningful and flexible way to the totality of its needs. All too often, this way of approaching the problem has resulted in the small-firm sector being restricted to a form of policy ghetto, managed by a specialist institution at a far remove from the strategic economic and industrial planning ministries.

Having identified the key conceptual conclusions to be drawn from this comparative study, the chapter concludes with some brief remarks on specific areas of policy which they touch upon. The aim is to identify general themes for discussion rather than to make specific policy recommendations.

Institutional framework

To date, small enterprise has been in some measure the Cinderella of economic policy. As a result of the 'formal sector/informal sector' dichotomy, which has dominated so much thinking on the subject since the ILO's seminal study of Kenya in 1972 (ILO, 1972) put the small-scale sector on the intellectual map, mainstream policymaking has tended to view the economy in polarized terms: on the one hand, the formal sector – consisting of urban-based large-and medium-scale industry – is seen as the motor of the economy; on the other, the informal sector – small-scale enterprises of all kinds – is seen as performing the dual function of providing cheap consumer goods to the poor and mopping up the underemployed.

The 'informal sector', in consequence, has generally been conceived of as playing a social welfare role rather than having any potential as a meaningful economic actor. Planning for the sector in Tanzania, for example, is currently being coordinated under the Social Dimensions to Adjustments initiative rather than as part of mainstream economic planning. Its primary importance is seen in terms of redeployment of retrenched workers rather than in terms of any contribution it might be able to make to national economic recovery.

The studies discussed in this chapter suggest that under certain conditions and in certain branches, small-scale production may be more appropriate and dynamic than large-scale production and that small firms may play an important role in developing linkages with other sectors of the economy and in stimulating national economic growth. It is important that the institutional mechanisms established to assist the small-firm sector recognize that certain segments of the sector have the potential to play a significant strategic economic function and merit, in consequence, integration into national economic planning.

Access to productive resources

Small-firm access to productive resources in Tanzania and Ghana is poor. In both countries, the formal banks have failed to develop means for the disbursement of credit which are appropriate to the particular needs of small firms. Securities demanded are generally well beyond the means of most small-scale entrepreneurs, while the large amount of time required for paperwork and the administration of loans acts as a further constraint. While it is true that some NGOs in both countries have succeeded in developing appropriate small-scale loan programmes, these cater for the needs of only a relatively very small number of firms. Only two out of the 672 small enterprises interviewed during the author's study in Kumasi had ever received a loan from a bank. A 1990 study similarly found that in the case of Tanzania, banks and government agencies are a source of only one per cent of the total capital used by small enterprises (Bagachwa, 1990b).

The World Bank study on small enterprise in Ghana referred to above found that access to credit was much the biggest constraint on increased production cited by small-scale entrepreneurs, with 57 per cent citing access to credit for recurrent expenditure and 29 per cent referring to credit for capital expenditure as a major constraint. All of the studies referred to in the course of the author's research in Tanzania identified credit as the largest single constraint identified by small-scale entrepreneurs.

Small-firm access to imports is also weak, particularly in Tanzania. The lower limit of US$5000 on applications for foreign exchange under the Open General Licence scheme effectively disbars small-scale operators.

Furthermore, while in Ghana traders have been supplying small-scale operators with imported components and materials for many years – and communications channels between them are, consequently, well established – this is not the case in Tanzania. A poor flow of market information of this type, together with liquidity shortages on the part of the traders appears to result in small-scale enterprises being starved of required inputs.

Small-firm access to modern technology is extremely weak. Even in Ghana, where the sector is much more technologically sophisticated than is the case in most other SSA economies, the process of technology acquisition has, for the most part, been dictated not by a process of rational technology choice, but rather by buying whatever happened to come onto the market. In many cases, this has comprised old, broken machinery which has been renovated by the entrepreneur. The World Bank report on the small enterprise sector in Ghana found that the poor state of equipment was cited as a major constraint on production by 23 per cent of firms. (The differing needs of different types of enterprise is once again evident when disaggregating this data. The proportion citing poor state of equipment as a constraint ranges from 33 per cent among 'small firms' – between 4 and 29 employees – and only 12 per cent among 'microenterprises' – 1 to 3 employees).

The access of small firms in Tanzania to modern technology is improving as a result of the auctions of public-sector equipment which are increasing in frequency. Nonetheless, there is little hope that Tanzanian entrepreneurs will be able to plan their acquisitions in a more coherent way than was possible in Ghana. As in Ghana, there is little information available to the small-scale entrepreneur on available technologies and sources of supply. Even those sources of investment capital which were available to Ghana's entrepreneurs – among the most important of which were remittances from relatives overseas and the black market – are largely unavailable to their Tanzanian counterparts.

The uneven and generally weak response of the small-firm sector to the opportunities opened up by the ERPs in Ghana and Tanzania must be understood in the context of the failure of the institutions of the state to reorient themselves towards an improved provision of services towards the sector. While the changing environment resulting from ERP reforms has been undercutting much of the long-standing protection of large and generally inefficient enterprises and stimulating increased output from smaller-scale operators, the various support institutions – banks, training institutes, technology research, development and information centres, etc. – have responded only slowly, if at all, to the changing needs of the new economic actors. In many cases, this failure to respond has been a consequence of cutbacks in government funding resulting from the ERP reforms themselves. Strong political and financial support will be necessary in order to persuade and permit these agencies to reorient their services to the needs of the small-scale sector.

Collective efficiency

A final policy implication to arise out of the comparative exercise undertaken here concerns the potential value of measures to promote the collective efficiency of the small-firm sector. This spatial dimension to small-firm dynamics was strongly in evidence in the case of Kumasi: the clustering of different types of small firms fostered a division of labour between them, enabling large jobs to be taken on, with the sub-contracting out of specialist tasks; while, in addition, the presence of small engineering workshops, making and maintaining much of the equipment used by other small firms was found to have contributed substantially to the technological capability of the sector as a whole. These findings concerning the potential importance of collective efficiency as a factor in promoting small enterprise development mirrors those of a number of studies from various countries (for a discussion of these, see Schmitz, 1990).

There appears to be significant scope for policies to foster and promote a creative synergy in the activities of small firms in different branches. Such policies could include the clustering of small firms in industrial areas; providing certain necessary facilities such as electricity, running water and telephones; and perhaps attempting to establish, or promote the establishment of, sectoral associations, and research and development institutes in these areas.

Impact of adjustment policies on the small-scale enterprise sector in Tanzania

MBOYA S.D. BAGACHWA

Overview of recent economic developments in Tanzania

Evolution of policy: 1960s-70s

Tanganyika became independent in 1961. In 1964 it united with Zanzibar to form the United Republic of Tanzania. During the pre-Arusha Declaration period (1961–6) overall development policy was conceived in conventional terms of maximizing growth. In particular, it sought to achieve two major objectives: namely, rapid growth in per capita income and national self-sufficiency in high- and middle-level personnel. This was to be achieved within a mixed but predominantly market economy framework that relied on private (mainly foreign) efforts.

In 1967 the Arusha Declaration was passed. The declaration represented the basic statement on Tanzania's long-term objectives. With the Arusha Declaration, policy for future development was to revolve around four overlapping themes: socialism, rural development, self-reliance and economic growth.

The immediate result of the Arusha Declaration was the nationalization of the strategic activities of the economy in manufacturing industry, commerce, mining, construction, export and import trade and crop marketing. Thereafter, government intervention increasingly assumed the form of promoting new public institutions and the active use of a wide range of economic policy instruments. The most important control mechanisms have included the following: (i) central control of investment planning; (ii) administrative allocation of foreign exchange through import licensing; (iii) price controls administered by the National Price Commission; (iv) credit rationing according to the Annual Finance Plan; (v) wage regulation administered by the Permanent Labour Tribunal; and (vi) confinement policy whereby wholesale trade for some imported and domestic commodities is restricted to specified parastatal organizations. The overall result has been the dramatic proliferation of public sector institutions. For example, the number of public organizations (parastatals) increased from about 43 in 1966 to 380 by 1979 and was about 425 by the mid-1980s. As the World Bank observed, 'Only in countries as large as Brazil (six times the population and 50 times the GDP of Tanzania) and Mexico (3.6 times the population and 35 times the GDP) does one find more than 425 parastatals' (World Bank, 1987a).

Economic performance: 1961 to mid-1980s

Tanzania's development record during the first fifteen years of independence (1961–76) was fairly satisfactory in terms of meeting basic human needs and in achieving economic growth. The country's literacy rate rose from 10 to 60 per cent between 1961 and 1977. Primary school enrolment shot up from 25 per cent in 1961 to over 90 per cent in 1977. Higher education also increased significantly so that for example the number of graduate engineers rose from two at independence (1961) to 18,000 in 1978. Impressive records were also set in health with life expectancy increasing from 43 years at independence to 52 in 1977. During the same period, infant mortality fell from 152 to 103 per thousand births (compared to average decreases from 164 to 130 per thousand in other low-income countries).

As shown in Table 6.1 Tanzania also experienced an impressive average annual growth rate in real GDP of 5.7 per cent between 1965 and 1970; and 5.1 per cent during 1970–76. Between 1965 and 1976 both agriculture and industry grew at rather healthy rates of 5 and 6.5 per cent per annum respectively. Annual inflation rates were generally low and averaged below 10 per cent during the 1965–76 period. As a result of these positive developments, real per capita income grew at an average annual rate of 2.5 and 1.5 per cent between 1965–70 and 1970–76 respectively.

However, during the late 1970s and early 1980s, Tanzania's economic performance weakened substantially, throwing the economy into an economic crisis of unprecedented proportions. The crisis manifested itself in a variety of ways (see Table 6.1):

(i) Real GDP growth declined from an annual average of 5.1 per cent between 1970–76 to 1.2 per cent between 1980–85, when population growth was 2.8 per cent per annum.
(ii) Real per capita income growth declined from 2.5 per cent during 1965–70 to -1.6 per cent during the 1980–85 period.
(iii) Inflation soared from an average rate of less than 10 per cent per annum in the 1970–76 period to 31 per cent between 1980–85.
(iv) The overall budget deficit rose by more than 6 times between 1979 and 1985 reaching an unprecedented 19 per cent for GDP in 1979.
(v) Pressure on the balance of payments intensified as the balance on external account deteriorated abruptly from a surplus of US$137 million in 1977 to a deficit of US$395 million in 1985.

A detailed account of the factors causing the economic crisis is documented elsewhere (see Maliyamkono and Bagachwa, 1990). Briefly, however, they include both external and internal factors. Among the external factors were:

(i) the country's worsening terms of trade; for example in 1985 the purchasing power of Tanzanian exports was just one-third of their purchasing power in 1977;
(ii) sharp increases in the petroleum prices first experienced in 1973–4 and fur-

Table 6.1 Average Annual Real Rates of Growth of GDP and Inflation (Percentage)

	Overall GDP	*Agriculture GDP*	*Manufacturing GDP*	*Public Admin. GDP*	*Real Per Capita Income*	*Inflation Rate (% change in NCPI, 1977 = 100)*
1967–70	5.7	6.7	8.8	7.9	2.5	—
1970–6	5.1	4.5	6.7	13.2	1.9	11.1
1976–9	1.8	1.0	0.6	11.7	1.0	14.9
1980–5	1.2	0.9	-4.3	1.9	1.6	30.6
1986–90	3.7	3.5	2.7	-1.0	0.9	27.6
1977	0.4	1.2	-6.1	6.6	2.4	11.6
1978	2.1	-1.7	3.4	20.0	-0.7	19.8
1979	2.9	0.1	3.3	8.6	0.1	13.3
1980	2.5	1.0	-4.9	-2.1	-0.3	36.0
1981	0.5	1.0	11.2	11.4	-2.3	22.7
1982	0.6	1.1	3.3	-0.1	-2.2	32.6
1983	-2.4	0.8	8.7	-0.2	-5.2	19.2
1984	3.4	0.6	2.7	0.2	0.6	44.0
1985	2.6	0.9	3.9	1.9	-0.2	29.2
1986	3.3	1.1	4.1	-10.8	0.5	33.2
1987	3.9	4.4	4.2	0.6	1.1	29.2
1988	4.2	4.5	7.0	3.1	1.4	28.2
1989	3.3	4.6	7.7	3.9	0.5	25.5
1990	3.6	2.9	7.8	2.2	0.8	20.0

Sources: National Accounts of Tanzania (various); Maliyamkono and Bagachwa (1990); Tanzanian Economic Trends Vol. No. 4.

ther oil price doubling in 1979–80 raised the import bill as a proportion of total export earnings from 26 per cent in 1978 to 56 per cent in 1982;

(iii) military spending occasioned by the war with Amin's Uganda deprived the country of about US$500 million – the equivalent to one year of Tanzania's total export earnings;

(iv) the break-up of the East African Community in 1977 which ended Tanzania's legitimate trade with its neighbouring partners; and

(v) the severe drought experienced in 1973–4, 1981–2 and 1983–4.

Most of the internal factors contributing to the economic crisis revolved around the wrong choice of development policies and strategies and misappropriation of resources. More specifically they included:

(a) neglect of the agricultural sector which received disproportionately low investment; low producer prices; little investment in supportive infrastructure and extension services; poor marketing arrangement for agricultural produce and poor distribution network of agricultural inputs;

(b) emphasis on large-scale industry which were both capital- and import-intensive thus aggravating problems of foreign exchange shortages, undercapacity utilization, technological and managerial dependencies;

(c) excessive rise in public administration which more than doubled its share in GDP between 1971 and 1983;

(d) villagization programme which forced most peasants to move (to unplanned) communal production centres causing immense disruption at least in the short run involving loss of output;

(e) expansion of the public sector beyond its technical and managerial capacities, which has invariably been associated with proliferation of unproductive bureaucracies, financial losses, shortages, and growth of second economy (parallel) markets;

(f) excessive government intervention in the form of quantitative restrictions on all categories of imports, government monopolization of internal trade and distribution and widespread domestic price controls.

Policy developments since the mid-1980s

The sheer magnitude and intensity of the economic crisis, pressure from the IMF, the World Bank and donor community have combined to persuade Tanzania to adopt far-reaching Economic Recovery Programme (ERP) reforms intended to reverse the declining economic trend. The overall objective of the ERP reforms was the gradual attainment of sustained growth in real incomes and output. This called for higher levels of production of food and cash crops through appropriate incentives, improved marketing structures and increasing resources available to agriculture; the carrying out of deferred maintenance to stem the rapid deterioration of the physical infrastructure required to distribute higher output; and a major effort to procure additional imports of raw materials in order to improve the level of capacity utilization in industries. In addition, the ERP aimed at correcting the external imbalance, reducing budget deficit, cutting down inflation and providing incentives to all types of producers. More specifically, the measures undertaken under the ERP have included the following:

Trade sector reforms

(a) Regular adjustments in the Exchange Rate

Exchange rate policy has involved establishment of a crawling peg and shock devaluations. This was intended to improve the country's competitiveness in exports; provide remunerative prices to cash crop producers; improve the balance of payments; correct overvaluation of the shilling; reduce illegal foreign exchange speculation and attract more donor support. Consequently, the shilling depreciated from Tshs8.2 to the US dollar in 1980 to Tshs44.4 in 1986 and then to Tshs145 in 1989. By December 1990, the exchange rate was Tshs195 to the US dollar. According to a recent Government paper, the adjustment of the shilling has led to a cumulative depreciation of the real effective exchange rate of 81 per cent over the 1986–90 period and a premium in the parallel market was substantially reduced from its peak of over 800 per cent in 1985 to about 50 per cent in 1990 (Government of Tanzania, 1991).

(b) Own Funds Imports Scheme

The Own Funds imports scheme was introduced during the 1984–5 budget. The facility functions as an unrestricted import window funded from own sources of foreign exchange i.e. other than that from the official banking system. The facility is open for any goods including capital and intermediate goods, building materials and consumer goods except for a small number of controlled goods for health and security reasons. Just before introduction of the Open General Licence (OGL) in 1988, own funds imports accounted for about 40 per cent of the total imports. For 1990 it accounted for an estimated one-third of total imports. The scheme represents a *de facto* trade liberalization arrangement which has exposed the industrial sector to external competition. It has also resulted in lower levels of effective protection for industry[1].

(c) The Open General Licence Facility

From 1979 until early 1988 all official foreign exchange had been administratively allocated. Starting in February 1988, the Government broadened its liberalization of trade by introducing an OGL facility for imports. The facility is funded by the World Bank and increasingly other donors are coming in. Initially, the OGL was limited to a narrow positive list but it has now broadened to include most items imported in Tanzania except consumer goods. The OGL list of eligible goods has been extensively expanded and the ceiling has been raised from US$200,000 per importer per year in February 1988 to US$1 million in 1989. The co-financing of other donors has increased the resources available in the OGL facility to over US$200 million in a year permitting OGL imports to run at around US$20 million per month. In 1990, imports through OGL accounted for an estimated 10 per cent of total imports. Effective from January 1991, the Government has decided to switch to a negative list of imports ineligible under the OGL thus further improving access to imports. In effect, the OGL represents a significant trade liberalization step for imports financed by official sources of foreign exchange and is especially important for industrialists lacking access to import support.

(d) Specific Export Promotion Policies

A number of export promotion schemes have been implemented during the ERP to complement the exchange rate policy. An export retention scheme was initially introduced in 1982 to allow exporters of traditional exports (coffee, cotton, tea, sisal, cashew nuts, tobacco, pyrethrum and diamonds) to retain 10 per cent of their export proceeds. In 1986, the retention scheme was extended to non-traditional exports with variable retention rates. In 1987 the scheme was rationalized and consolidated by aligning retention rates for a large number of non-traditional exports to 50 per cent and 10 per cent for traditional exports. In 1989, the export retention scheme was limited to non- traditional exports and the retention rate unified at 35 per cent with very few exceptions.

A duty drawback scheme which allows exporters to recover the duty on their imported inputs was introduced for the first time during the 1988–9 budget to correct the anti-export bias for exporters who pay duty on their imported inputs. Another measure for promoting exports introduced during the ERP is the seed capital scheme for pre-financing investment in non-traditional exports.

(e) Tariff Reform

Prior to the ERP, the role of tariffs in influencing the efficiency of resource allocation was negligible as it was overshadowed by the prominence of quantitative restrictions and the administrative centralized allocation of foreign exchange. However, with the introduction of the own funds scheme, the OGL, and the attainment of a more realistic exchange rate in the late 1980s, the role of tariffs in influencing prices and providing protection to local industries has been enhanced.

Until 1988 the tariff structure was very complex involving 18 different rates ranging from 15–200 per cent. Lower rates of 15–50 per cent applied mostly to capital and intermediate goods while the higher 60–200 per cent rates applied mostly to consumer goods. In June 1988 the tariff structure was simplified and specific duties were eliminated. The maximum tariff rate was lowered to 100 per cent while most consumer goods were charged 40 to 60 per cent rates. This was further rationalized by the 1990–91 Finance Bill which reduced the rates to four *ad valorem* rates of 20, 30, 40 and 60 per cent. Similarly, sales tax rates were reduced from 18 to four categories of 0, 20, 30 and 40 per cent (instead of a wide range of 10 to 300 per cent). However, the introduction of an excise tax rate has made the overall sum of tax rates almost equal to the old high tax rates.

(f) Liberalizing Internal Trade

In the early 1980s, about 400 categories of consumer goods were subject to price control by the National Price Commission. Price control amidst shortages resulted in artificial shortages thus fuelling black market sales where pressures of supply and demand and the increased risk of detection dictated a higher price than one set administratively. By 1989 only 10 items remained on the Price Control list. This was reduced further to three (petroleum products, fertilizers and sugar) during the 1991–2 budget. Prices for manufactured imports have been totally liberalized.

Up to 1984 under the system of confinement the wholesale and in some cases the retail trade for essential domestic and imported commodities were restricted to particular parastatal organizations. Producing industries – private and public – had to sell specified goods to specially designated national and regional trading companies and were required to purchase certain inputs (or place their purchase orders through) specific parastatal trading firms. Over 50 broad categories of goods were subject to internal confinement covering mainly consumer goods, building materials and agricultural implements. All imported goods were considered confined unless specifically exempted. By 1990 there were only 10 items still price controlled and confined and another six confined but not price controlled. By July 1991 all items except three had been 'deconfined' and price 'decontrolled'.

Agricultural policy reforms

(a) Producer Prices

In order to increase agricultural output, enhance domestic food security, boost export growth, and improve welfare especially in rural areas, the government has continued to raise producer prices and liberalized agricultural marketing. Although the increase in producer prices has been substantial in nominal terms, in real terms they have not been so. This is explained partly by the implicit taxation of the farmer by the inefficiencies and increased marketing margins of the crop marketing institutions and high rates of inflation. According to estimates by the World Bank (1991) the margins of the marketing boards and co-operatives more than doubled between 1983 and 1987. The producers' share of the export price is estimated to have fallen from over 80 per cent in 1986 to 35 per cent during 1989 and then back to 50 per cent in 1990.

(b) Streamlining Crop Marketing

Prior to the ERP the marketing of agricultural commodities was organized into a single channel system consisting of three layers. At the farm level the primary co-operative societies had a legal monopoly on crop purchasing and input distribution. The regional co-operative unions assembled commodities from the primary societies and had the monopoly of distributing and processing them. The unions were also responsible for channelling credit to the primary societies and providing accounting and audit services. At the top of the marketing chain were the state-owned marketing boards which had a legal monopoly in the official export of cash crops and in the case of grain monopolized its internal distribution to consumers. This system was grossly inefficient and resulted in lower producer prices, untimely delivery of inputs, poor quality of exports due to processing problems and shipping delays. In the case of grain, low prices, restriction on grain transportation across regional boundaries and uniform pricing throughout the country increased shortages resulting in a thriving parallel market[2].

Attempts to streamline agricultural marketing began in 1984 when restrictions were removed on the movement of grain across regional boundaries by individuals in lots of less than 500 kg. Uniform pricing was also abolished. By March 1987 all weight restrictions on grain movement between regions were removed. Minor export crops were deconfined. The National Milling Corporation (NMC) was entrusted with the management of the Strategic Grain Reserve (SGR) with an emergency reserve of 100,000 tons and a variable buffer stock of up to 50,000 tons to stabilize prices. By June 1989, private traders had been allowed to buy grain from regional co-operative unions and primary societies in competition with NMC. As of June 1990 private operators could buy and distribute grain up to the farm level. The management of the SGR was shifted to the Ministry of Agriculture and NMC's access to crop financing credit was cut off because it was in serious financial difficulties thus effectively eliminating it from the market.

By 1991 farmers were free to sell their crops to any buyer including co-operatives[3] and private traders who in turn are legalized to export agricultural commodities including grains. Government still sets prices for the six major cash crops and determines the indicative farm price for maize; but prices for grains have been decontrolled.

Furthermore, the role of the marketing boards is now being streamlined. In effect the role of the marketing boards has been reduced to that of auctioneers or tender administrators; agencies for ensuring quality control and responsible for market intelligence.

(c) Rationalizing Agricultural Input Distribution
The role of private traders has been broadened to include participation in the purchase of some export crops (e.g. cashew nuts and cotton from farmers) and exporting them through a tender system; ownership in the operation of crop processing facilities, for example cotton ginneries and in the distribution of agricultural inputs. Domestic distribution of farm inputs has been opened to the private sector since 1987. The monopoly of the state-owned Tanzania Seed Company is being challenged by the establishment and licensing of private seed companies. In order to improve efficiency of use and to encourage the development of alternative sources of supply and distribution of fertilizers, the Government is gradually reducing subsidies to the state-owned Tanzania Fertilizer Company (TFC).

(d) Restructuring Co-operative Unions
The Government has also embarked on reform to streamline and strengthen co-operative unions which have been plagued with weak management, high operating costs, inefficiency, high indebtedness, and hence a lack of credit-worthiness, and an inability to pay farmers in time. The restructuring is to be undertaken according to international co-operative principles and has already involved adoption of a new Co-operative Act (1991) allowing for voluntary membership and full control of members and requiring equity contributions by members and commercial viability.

Monetary and credit policy reforms

In order to reduce the growing budget deficit, curb inflation, stimulate financial savings, and facilitate more effective utilization and allocation of resources, the ERP sought to check domestic credit growth, limit the rate of money supply growth within the range of 15 to 20 per cent per annum and raise interest rates to positive levels in real terms. Although there was a reduction in credit to the Government, domestic credit growth was always above programme target and broad money grew more rapidly by an average of 33 per cent per annum, far exceeding the anticipated 15 per cent rate. A major cause of excess credit creation has been the continued extension of credit to the agricultural marketing institutions particularly the National Milling Corporation (NMC) which has been unprofitable and unable to pay.

Prior to the ERP, real interest rates were substantially negative. Since 1985 they have been rising periodically, and by 1987 reached near positive levels. Annual interest on savings deposits rose from 7.5 per cent in 1985 to 24 per cent in 1987 while interest on 20-year Government stock rose from 10 to 29 per cent during the same period. Interest on medium-term and long-term lending has risen from 10 to 29.5 per cent per annum. However, the impact of positive interest rates seems to have been diluted by lack of financial infrastructure in terms of geographical coverage and the range of financial instruments.

A financial sector reform is now being implemented following a report by the Presidential Commission of enquiry (July 1990) into the monetary and banking system. The approved strategy seeks to (i) encourage the establishment of domestic and foreign private banks including joint ventures with Tanzanian interests and (ii) restructure the existing financial institutions as well as the financial environment in which they operate.

Performance of the economy since the mid-1980s

The implementation of the initial phase of the ERP (I) lasted between 1986 and 1989. Undoubtedly there have been positive signs of revival in output. Overall production of food and cash crops has recovered significantly after showing a downward trend for more than a decade (Table 6.1). Similarly, a very considerable build-up of imports has been sufficient to ease the veritable goods famine of the early 1980s. Real per capita income has been positive and there has been a substantial decline in parallel market prices of maize. Between 1977 and 1985 the volume of official sales of export crops declined at around 5 per cent per annum whereas between 1984 and 1988 it expanded by 4 per cent per annum. The change in official food crop sales has particularly been more dramatic. As Table 6.2 shows, overall food sales increased by about 100 per cent between 1983–84 and 1987–88.

However, crop marketing problems persist; deterioration in infrastructure is yet to be checked; inflation is still excessive and social services delivery system remain a major source of dissatisfaction.

In order to consolidate the positive achievements of the recovery recorded during the first ERP phase, the Government has prepared an ERP II, or the Economic and Social Action Programme (ESAP), to be implemented during 1989–90/1991–2. Besides taking further steps to consolidate the measures initiated during the ERP I, ESAP gives priority to two other economic recovery-related measures: mitigation of adverse social impact of adjustment and rehabilitation of physical infrastructure.

Government strategy towards the development of small enterprises

Institutional framework

In principle, the Tanzanian Government assigns an important role to the development of the small-scale enterprise sector[4]. Earlier efforts to promote SSEs began in 1966 when the National Small Industries Corporation (NSIC) was formed as a subsidiary of the National Development Corporation (NDC) to develop SSEs. Recognizing the importance of the sector, the ruling political party (then TANU) issued a directive to establish a much more forceful organization – the Small Industries Development Organization (SIDO) in 1973. SIDO was entrusted with a number of tasks including the promotion and development of SSEs; provision of infrastruc-

Table 6.2 Indices of Crop Sales and Corresponding Prices

	1982–3	1983–4	1984–5	1985–6	1986–7	1987–8
Maize sales	100	87	103	149	173	180
Maize prices (Real)	100	150	122	86	76	84
(1)						
Rice sales	100	92	120	195	118	191
Rice prices (Real)	100	143	304	148	111	98
Export crop sales	100	101	102	90	119	121
(2)						
Export producer Prices (Real)	100	101	95	107	106	111
All crops sales	100	94	105	125	139	151
All crops prices	100	125	114	100	93	101

Notes: (1) Price indices based on weighted average of open market and official prices.
(2) All traditional exports produced by small-scale farmers (coffee, cotton, cashew, tea, tobacco, pyrethum, and cardamon).
Source: World Bank (1991).

ture to SSEs; assisting in carrying out market research; provision of financial support, provision of extension services, and assisting in the transfer of technology.

The strategic importance of SSEs is also recognized in the basic industrial strategy (BIS) which was Tanzania's first blueprint of a long-term (1975–90) industrial strategy. The BIS was based on an approach similar to the Mahalanobis model of development for India and the strategy for industrialization pursued by the Soviet Union since the late 1920s. The overriding objective of the BIS was to restructure production in order to achieve self reliance. Five major features distinguish the BIS from past industrial strategies. First was the emphasis on producer goods (iron and steel, metal working and engineering, and industrial chemicals). These were assumed (at least in theory) to have strong intersectoral linkages and hence were capable of facilitating structural transformation. Second, production priorities and the choice of products were to be determined by the basic minimal needs of the majority of consumers rather than market demand. Consequently wage goods (for food, health, education and shelter) were also given priority. Third, in order to achieve self reliance, production of the basic goods had to rely mainly on the use of domestic resources. Fourth, to facilitate decentralization of industry into the countryside, basic industries were to be established at the national level (mainly medium and large-scale), district level (mainly medium and large-scale), and village level (mainly small-scale and handicraft). Lastly, in order to reduce dependence on external markets, production was to cater primarily for the domestic market and secondarily for the international market (only as a vent for surplus).

Although the BIS recognized the need to develop SSEs it was not clear what precise role the SSEs were to play in the industrialization process. Moreover, the BIS was not followed by an explicit technology policy which could have resolved such issues as the type of technology to be employed, the nature of products to be produced and the specific markets to be served. In theory, the institutional framework combined both aspects of centralized and decentralized planning. At the national level there were supposed to be large-scale centralized industries. At the regional and district levels, development authorities could organize and assist medium- and small-scale activities. At the village level, village committees could organize and supervise rural industrial activities. In practice this never happened, and large-scale centralized industries dominated at both regional and district levels while there was almost total neglect in developing village-based SSEs.

Supporting institutions

Role of SIDO

The principal roles of SIDO were to establish, promote and coordinate all policies and programmes for promoting SSEs in the country. Since then SIDO has played five important roles: (a) provision of basic infrastructural facilities like premises, water, and power; (b) provision of financial support to SSEs; (c) provision of extension services to existing SSEs and promotion of new ones; (d) aid in the transfer of technology; and (e) development and provision of training programmes. To operationalize these objectives SIDO has designed and implemented the following major programmes.

Under the industrial estate programme SIDO provides infrastructure such as water, sewerage systems, roads, power and communications to SSEs within the estate. By December 1991 there were 14 industrial estates in 14 out of 20 regions. The industrial estate programme encountered some problems such as intermittent supply of water, power interruptions, lack of raw materials, scarcity of experienced entrepreneurs and low recovery rental incomes (estimated to be 10 per cent).

A World Bank (1987c) review of the programme in Tanga showed that projects in the industrial estate exhibited higher unit costs and lower levels of capacity utilization than those outside the estate. The cost of idle equipment as a percentage of the total cost of equipment was 76 per cent in the industrial estate as opposed to 17 per cent for existing industries. The average unit cost of equipment was about 2.5 times higher in the industrial estate.

There are two other weaknesses of the industrial estate programme. One is that it involves major investments in buildings and machinery. This raises the machine intensity of SSEs located in the estate significantly above those outside it. Secondly, all of the estates are located in large towns (that is, regional headquarters) thus reinforcing the urban bias. It appears unfair to tie the limited funds available for infrastructural investment to the few urban-based SSEs.

The SIDO hire purchase scheme offers financial support to SSEs at concessionary rates. Under the scheme, machinery, equipment and tools are provided to SSEs on a hire purchase basis at a rate of interest of 21 per cent which is below the commercial rate of 31 per cent per annum. The loan carries a 10 per cent down-payment and is repaid between three and seven years. Between 1974 and 1984 loan approvals amounted to Tshs53.3 million for the rural hire purchase programme (RHP) and Tshs256.5 million for the urban hire purchase scheme. In the period between 1985 and 1989 a total of 203 projects worth Tshs287 million were financed under the scheme. The major beneficiaries of the hire purchase scheme have been the urban-based entrepreneurs who received 88 per cent of the total hire purchase fund. In fact, more than half of the number of RHP loans have been channelled to urban areas.

Even in urban areas there is uneven access to SSE credit. As of 30 June 1988, for example, a total of 61 projects worth Tshs342 million had been approved under the urban hire purchase scheme, excluding Dar es Salaam (the largest city). Of these 61 per cent went to two towns – Arusha and Moshi.

There are three major programmes involved in SIDO transfer of technology undertakings.

The Sister Industry Programme (SIP). This entails collaboration between a Swedish (senior sister) firm and a Tanzanian SSE start-up (junior sister) to establish long-term technology transfer. The Swedish International Development Agency (SIDA) provides the investment funds while Swedish companies provide machinery, start-up raw materials and know-how, such as initial training for entrepreneurs, managers and workers. They also assist in plant installation. By 1989, about 142 entrepreneurs and 60 SIDO staff had participated in the programme. It is estimated that between 1976 and 1990 thirty-four ventures at a total investment cost of US$75 million (at constant 1990 prices) employing 1400 people have been established under the SIP.

However, SIP projects have been excessively capital intensive and import dependent. As a result of the foreign exchange shortages they have been operating below capacity levels. In fact, their survival in the mid-1980s was mainly due to heavy import support from SIDA. A recent study has revealed that foreign exchange costs of creating one job in SIP projects is 11 times higher than that incurred in the RHP (Swedish Development Consulting Partners AB, 1991)

The Indian Tanzanian Programme. The programme began in 1978 and involved 48 projects. The Government of India facilitated the transfer of technology by giving a US$4 million loan for machinery, training of project managers and staff in India as well as on the plant level in Tanzania. By 1989, 21 projects were in operation without major problems. Fourteen projects, of which eleven were owned by the District Development Corporations (DDCs), had their equipment repossessed; six projects were working intermittently and six projects were yet to be implemented. It is estimated that the programme employed about 350 persons at an average foreign exchange cost of US$8500. The programme has been beset by incomplete deliveries of machinery, breakdowns, lack of spares and inadequate training. All these stem mainly from poor choice of technology.

Sister-Daughter Programme. The programme motivates the local firms who have gained know-how from senior sister firms from Sweden, to use this know-how to develop local (daughter) firms. Two printing units, one in Kigoma and another in Same, fall in this category.

SIDO provides a myriad of extension services to SSE entrepreneurs. Between 1985 and 1989, SIDO prepared 565 technical profiles, 609 feasibility studies and carried out 82 market surveys. SIDO also gives technical and managerial advice to SSE entrepreneurs on how to set up new units, choose technology, design plant layout, procure machinery and equipment and how to secure markets for their products. However, most of these services are carried out mainly in urban areas. Extension services in rural areas are still constrained by the limited number of staff in regions (about three in number), lack of transport facilities and poor extension network. In Arusha Region, for example, there are three SIDO officials: a head, an economist and a technical officer. They have one old landrover and spend 80 per cent of their time in the regional office.

In terms of entrepreneurial development, SIDO has various programmes for providing basic skills, and upgrading skills of entrepreneurs, managers and workers. Training is carried out in training centres, seminars and workshops, technology transfer programmes and on the job. Between 1985 and 1989, SIDO had trained 1427 entrepreneurs in various operational and management aspects.

Finally, SIDO provides technical, managerial, and economic services, credit for tools and raw materials, and training and marketing assistance to artisans in the handicraft sector. Between 1982 and 1989, about 2385 artisans have been trained in various areas related to handicraft production.

Role of the National Bank of Commerce (NBC)

In 1981 the NBC established a SSE department to deal with the financial needs of this sector. The NBC through its Advances and Term Finance Departments provides medium- and long-term loans to SSEs. Term loans are provided for up to 80 per cent of an investment for a maximum term of ten years at existing commercial rates of interest. Funds for NBC's SSE programme come from its own internally generated funds, KFW of Germany and SIDA of Sweden. As of June 1990, a total of 316 projects worth Tsh904 million (US$4.6m) had been approved for financing SSEs and agricultural production. Of the 316 projects, 116 involved SSEs and received loans worth Tshs508 mn (US$2.6m).

Entrepreneurs generally complain of the high interest rates charged by the NBC (currently 21 per cent for rural term loans and 23 per cent for urban). There are normally long delays — sometimes up to three years between submission of loan applications and disbursement of approved loans. NBC also procures equipment centrally in Dar es Salaam and delivers it to the client. Clients normally complain of inappropriately specified equipment, short loadings and delays.

Co-operative and Rural Development Bank

The Co-operative and Rural Development Bank (CRDB) usually provides medium-term financing to co-operatives and rural (agro-based) SSEs. Other areas to which CRDB extends credit include transportation, trade, tourism and construction. Because the bulk of CRDB's loans goes to seasonal inputs, mainly co-operative unions and agricultural marketing boards, it has a serious loan repayment problem.

Policy impact on SEE development

Overall development strategy

In principle, government can influence the performance and development of SSEs through policies that affect firms' objectives, accessibility to resources, technology availability, and factor and product markets (Stewart, 1987). In the case of Tanzania, the overall development strategy had up to the mid-1980s affected adversely the environment in which SSEs and micro-enterprises operated.

Even the institutional framework of the 1960s and 1970s had revolved around the building of large-scale, centralized and monopolistic parastatals whose emergence and rapid growth pre-empted opportunities for mass production of goods in which there were small-scale alternatives. For example, up to 1984, the state-owned NMC had a monopoly in the procurement, and distribution of raw grains and milled products. This discouraged private investment in small-scale custom mills which had no access to a supply of raw grains and could not serve distant markets because they were not allowed to distribute grain mill products. However, under the ERP, grain marketing and distribution has been liberalized. This has substantially increased accessibility to raw grains for small-scale private (mainly indigenous) mills and permitted expanded markets for these mills which can now distribute milled products to distant customers (Bagachwa, 1991a).

Similarly, the establishment of the large-scale automated SIHA bread factory in Dar es Salaam in the early 1970s threatened the existence of small-scale bakeries, most of which lost markets (Coulson, 1974). Furthermore, the predominance of large integrated parastatals has been inimical to the development of linkages between small- and large-scale enterprises. Most of the large parastatal firms were planned and set up to undertake all operations from raw material processing to manufacture of the end-product. This has discouraged the development of subcontracting arrangements between small and large firms. A glaring example is the World Bank-financed Morogoro Leather and Shoe complex (the largest in Sub-Saharan Africa) which has never promoted small-scale decentralized tanneries nor has ever supplied leather to small-scale footwear manufacturers. The factory has been a total failure operating at 15 per cent of its full tanning capacity and at only 2 per cent of its shoe production capacity (UNDP/UNIDO/ILO/The Netherlands, 1988).

In addition, certain Government Acts and Directives have directly and indirectly discouraged the development of the private sector in general and the micro-enterprise sector in particular. These include the:

(a) Foreign Investment Protection Act of 1963

Up to 1990, foreign investors in Tanzania operated under the Foreign Investment

Protection Act (FIPA) of 1963. This Act, however, has been a major source of dissatisfaction among foreign investors. FIPA provided very limited guarantees with regard to prompt and fair compensation in the event of nationalization and the right to repatriate profits and dividends.

(b) Nationalization Act of 1967
There has been growing uncertainty among private entrepreneurs, especially those of Asian extraction, following the 1967 Nationalization Act and especially after the nationalization of private rented buildings and farm estates in 1972. Paradoxically, the nationalization process was not confined to the commanding heights of the economy but also included the less important retail trading activities, such as small, privately-owned butcheries and rural shops. Because of this and because the role of the private sector was not clearly defined, some private firms shut down their plants while others allowed their capital and farms to deteriorate. New entrants were certainly scared.

(c) Party Leadership Code
The ruling Party Leadership Code (1967), until February 1991, prohibited Government and Party officials from ownership of rentable property, any type of private business, holding shares in business and from holding directorship in private enterprises. It virtually excluded them from engaging in all types of income-generating activities and acted as a disincentive to the promotion of small-scale entrepreneurship. In particular, up to the mid-1980s the Government viewed the micro-enterprise or informal sector as a clandestine sector (Maliyamkono and Bagachwa, 1990).

(d) Ujamaa Villages Act of 1975
The Act stipulated that there should be no place for individual ownership of small industrial enterprises in villages. Such enterprises were to be owned communally by the villages which were henceforth to function as multi-purpose co-operative societies. The Act also abolished the voluntary producer democratic co-operatives, which could be regarded as organizations which cultivated and fostered private enterprise initiative. The CCM Party Programme, which provides a long-term perspective of Tanzania's economic development, regards the role of private capital as useful and acceptable only during the transition to socialism. Even the role of co-operatives is only regarded as politically acceptable during the transition to socialism because it does not facilitate collectivization of production.

Since the mid-1980s, however, the Government has reversed some of these policies. In particular, and as will be shown below, private-sector development is increasingly being seen as an important element in achieving sustainable economic growth in Tanzania. Measures initiated to encourage private-sector development include liberalization of agricultural marketing; adoption of a national investment promotion policy to promote and protect private-sector investment; initial steps to encourage private participation in industrial parastatals; recognition of the microenterprise (informal) sector as a legitimate sector; review of the Party Leadership Code to permit Government and Party officials to earn more than official income; and a recent (1991) decision to allow private banking. These measures are necessary to create an enabling environment for the development of SSEs.

Pre-reform macro-policy environment and its impact on SSEs

In Tanzania, especially up to the mid-1980s, the macro-policy environment discriminated against the development of microenterprises. The major policy impacts can be explained from five perspectives. Firstly, the domestic capital market has been heavily subsidized by the high rates of domestic inflation. The banking sector in Tanzania is exclusively government controlled. Accordingly, interest rates on loans and the structure of loans are controlled by the government through the (central) Bank of Tanzania (BOT). Credit allocation is also carried out quantitatively according to government policy priorities as specified by the Finance and Credit Plan.

Although this arrangement is intended to channel credit to the 'high priority' sectors, it has had two undesirable side effects. One is that credit rationing has led to the bulk of lendable funds being allocated to the large-scale public-sector firms that are both the most politically and economically adept of the eligible recipients. The small-scale sector, which is predominantly privately owned, has thus been discriminated against by the institutional market for obtaining credit on the grounds that they constitute higher risks and incur higher administrative lending costs. These reasons are usually attributed to their wide geographical dispersion and lack of collateral.

This has been the case despite the current policy initiative of the government to redress this bias by creating additional public lending institutions, (e.g., the Co-operative Rural Development Bank (CRDB)), and by reserving a portion of the loan portfolio of the National Bank of Commerce (NBC) for use by small enterprises. A programme of guaranteeing a portion of bank loans to small enterprises by the BOT has also been approved in principle but it has never been implemented. The credit bias is reflected, for example, by the small share of small-scale industry (SSI) loans in total CRDB loans, which averaged 5.7 per cent per year between 1976–7 and 1986–7. Even the share of SSI loans of total NBC-approved loans stood at a relatively insignificant level of 0.57 per cent in 1989–90.

Moreover, to the extent that credit policies have resulted in interest rates that are below the opportunity cost of borrowing domestic capital, they have, as a second side-effect, biased choice of technology toward greater capital intensity. The BOT, which maintains ceilings on deposit rates as well as floors and ceilings on commercial lending rates, maintained fixed nominal interest rates between 1966 and 1984. Thus, for example, the effective lending rate remained fairly constant, increasing from an average of 8.5 per cent in 1966 to about 10.3 per cent in 1982. At the same time, prices as measured by the National Consumer Price Index (NCPI), rose at an average annual rate of about 5 per cent per year up to the mid-1970s but rose four times as much between 1979 and 1985. Thus, the real cost of borrowing for investment has been declining over time.

Similarly, a significant amount of foreign-capital inducement has also been subsidized directly by government policy and indirectly by domestic inflation. For example, interest rates on foreign loans have been extremely low, averaging between 1.1 per cent in 1970 and 2.2 per cent in 1981. These figures are not only far below the domestic rate of inflation but also significantly below the domestic lending rates. The latter aspect may have biased savers toward import-intensive investments. Thus, on the whole, both domestic and foreign loans revealed negative real rates of interest implying that funds for domestic and foreign capital formation were supplied with almost no interest.

Second, distortions have arisen from government intervention in the foreign-trade regime. Up to 1984, the foreign-trade regime in Tanzania employed a rationing system for all essential imports (in conformity with the Foreign Exchange Plan) and were characterized by an overvalued exchange rate. These two policy aspects would tend to favour large-scale public enterprises that can exercise political and economic power (Wangwe and Bagachwa, 1988). Because the direct allocation of import licences tends to favour large-scale firms, the structure of protection provides an implicit subsidy to direct large-scale importers.

The highly devalued Tanzanian shilling, by making imports cheaper, constituted a disincentive for the expansion of domestic markets for SSE producers. In addition, it had a depressive effect on producer prices and hence rural incomes thus compounding the problem of smaller domestic markets for rural non-farm activities.

As a result, SSEs have been negatively affected by the excessive protection of medium and large industries. According to the World Bank (1987b) study, small firms employing less than 25 workers enjoyed a rate of effective protection below 100 per cent and had an economic rate of return of 3 per cent. Conversely, larger firms enjoyed an effective rate of protection exceeding 2000 per cent yet had a high negative economic rate of return.

Third, the Government's regulatory environment has been inimical to the development of the informal or microenterprise sector.

(a) Licensing and registration

Licensing is an important policy instrument which affects the formation and performance of SSEs. According to the Licensing and Registration Licence Act (1967) and the Business Licensing Act (1972), units with investments above Tshs5 million (US$21,740) in buildings and machinery are required to have industrial licences. Units with investments below Tshs5 million (i.e., small-scale units) are required to have a certificate of registration. In addition, the Local Government Act empowers local authorities to charge fees for any business taking place within their areas. This legislation affects the operations of small firms in three important ways. First, they give legality to a business enterprise. Failing to comply with these requirements constitutes illegality, and hence the enterprise can be subjected to official harassment. Thus, although most informal sector activities involve legitimate business transactions such as vegetable selling, shoe repairing and shining, many operators commit offences because they lack licences to operate such business.

Second, legislation may act as a barrier for new small firms to enter the industry. This may be due to either the actual cost of licensing (the amount of fees may be too high for small entrepreneurs to afford) or, because the long and cumbersome procedures for registration or obtaining a licence (ranging between two and twelve months) constitute a serious impediment to the small entrepreneur who generally will have to pay a bribe.

An example of the rampant administrative jungle involved when applying for an industrial licence, is described in detail as follows: 'No licence can be issued unless a company has been registered. The applicant has to take the proposed company name to the Company Registration Office where it is checked whether the proposed name is acceptable. If it is, the articles of association have to be drawn up and taken to the Company Registrar who extracts a variable fee according to whether it is a partnership or a limited liability company. That is only the first step, and having registered the company, an industrial licence has to be applied for from the urban authority, (such as the City Council) on form TFN221. This application has to be approved by (i) the Land Officer (for urban, municipal or city residents); (ii) the health officer for inspecting the proposed premises); (iii) the Ward Development Committee (for political vetting); (iv) the District Council/Ministry/Urban Authority (for planning consent); (v) the Trade Officer (for financial and fiscal scrutiny and the assessment of the licence fee); (vi) the Principal Assessor (for examining income tax for the last three years and collecting outstanding tax liabilities and provisional assessment of tax). The Assessor's tax clearance form, the application form and the registration certificate are taken to the Urban/District authority where the assessed licence fee is paid. The Licence is taken to the Trade Officer where it is lodged and the number related to the Ward where the premises are located is issued, which takes up to three months. Finally the National Provident Office requires registration in relation to employer's liability for national insurance'. (Maliyamkono and Bagachwa, 1990).

Third, in some cases a certificate may impose restrictions on certain product categories. This has been the case for soap and oil processing until recently. Licences for oil-seed processing could not be given unless the processing unit was able to secure its own raw material from its own farm. This discriminated against small units which could not afford to run their own oil-seed farms.

(b) Legislation on standards

There are several legislative Acts which impose standards on the operations of the SSE sector which are generally similar to those pertaining to the large-scale enterprises. Among the important ones are the Factories Act, the Public Health Act, the Local Government Act, the Power Act, and the Penal Code.

The Public Health Act, for example, empowers local authorities to control communicable disease such as cholera. It also sets standards with regard to food, sewerage systems and buildings. Enforcement has generally taken the form of demolition of informal-sector premises and outright banning of such operations. Under a Penal Code amendment in 1983 local authorities were allowed to ban any person involved in 'unproductive' activity. The Destitute Persons Ordinance introduced during British colonial rule (1918–61) and still in force empowers magistrates to detain or send any person to any place if such a person does not have 'visible and sufficient means of subsistence'. The problem is that these codes have sometimes been misused by the local authorities resulting in harassment of informal-sector operators. For example, the Human Resource Deployment Act (1984) required all Tanzanians to be registered and issued labour identification cards. In Dar es Salaam all unlicensed self-employed people including fishsellers, shoe repairmen, tailors etc. were to be removed from the city to the villages because they were considered as 'idle and disorderly loiterers' (Tripp, 1988). This was clearly a misinterpretation of the Act.

(c) Taxation

Sales taxes which are levied on both local and imported final products are a source of complaint among small producers. The 1976 Finance Act exempts the levying of taxes on inputs to be used in processing. Due to lack of proper information, small firms are unaware of this and end up paying taxes on both inputs and output.

There are exemptions from customs and sales tax on machinery and intermediate inputs ordered by SIDO on its behalf for SSEs. But this is not a blanket cover for all SSEs – only those sponsored by or registered with SIDO.

Overall, legislation and regulatory practices in Tanzania work against informal sector enterprises. The problem arises from the failure of public authorities to distinguish the peculiar characteristics of the SSE sector from those of the large-scale sector. The large-scale sector enterprises have the means, ability, and lobbying capacity to work through the required processes and to provide proper documents. SSE-sector firms generally lack such qualifications. In some cases they are ignorant of the relevant legislation and when they are aware of the legal requirements they often do not see the need to comply with them.

Furthermore, the pre-ERP agricultural policies were not in favour of the development of the informal sector. There are two major sources of demand for goods and services produced by SSEs: local demand for consumer goods and services stemming from rising incomes of rural and urban households; and demand arising from forward linkages of processing and adding value to marketed agricultural products, and backward linkages of industrial inputs to agriculture (e.g. farm implements and equipment, transport equipment, building materials etc). In rural areas, the primary demand for goods and services provided by SSEs comes from agriculture – transmitted through both income and production linkages. Consequently, policies designed to increase agricultural output and/or income would tend to stimulate the demand for goods and services provided by SSEs.

Previous agricultural policies resulted in low agricultural output, low incomes and were hence inimical to the development of rural linkages and increased demand for goods and services produced by SSEs.

Lastly, the system of confining the purchase and distribution of goods to large-scale parastatal monopolies was inimical to the development of small private traders.

Impact of recent structural reforms on SSEs

The recent structural reforms implemented since the mid-1980s have shifted the emphasis from direct control and rationed access to market allocation and enhancement of private sector development. Some of the reforms have resulted in a significant reduction of discrimination against SSEs. For example, imports and foreign exchange liberalization schemes (i.e. own funds imports and OGL) have made certain imports freely available. According to a recent World Bank (1991) report, the goods accessible to Tanzanians have increased by 54 per cent between 1983 and 1988. Choice of consumer goods has also improved. Import liberalization especially through own funds import has also resulted in improved supply of intermediate industrial inputs and spare parts. The renewed availability of these inputs has enabled a number of small firms to diversify their production.

Furthermore, imports liberalization has given impetus to some of the small-scale and informal-sector activities by providing them with freely available raw materials, tools and spare parts. This has especially been the case in small retailing enterprises, tailoring, food and woodworking activities. In some cases, however, it has led to excessive competition among small firms which has threatened their existing profit margins and lowered their volume of sales. In other cases it has resulted in plant closures, especially in the less competitive small-scale activities such as soap-making and tie-and-dye cloth making (Maliyamkono and Bagachwa, 1990). The availability of cheap imported shoes has had a detrimental effect on the traditional leather and tyre sandal (*kubazi*) making industry which used to thrive during the pre-import liberalization period. The lift on restrictions to import second-hand clothes, has created expanded employment opportunities for small-scale retail traders but at the same time diminished the work of tailors involved in repairing clothes.

The new reforms have not reversed all elements of the previous policy biases. For example, the more flexible and less administrative OGL system of allocating foreign exchange adopted since February 1988 stipulated the minimum value for each applicant of foreign exchange to be US$5000. Until mid-1990, this was to be secured with 100 per cent local cash cover. Certainly these conditions exclude most of the SSEs from obtaining access to this source of foreign exchange. Although the initial cash cover requirement has recently been reduced from 100 per cent to 25 per cent the new system is still discriminatory if it is realized that many microenterprises neither keep books of accounts nor operate banking accounts which are preconditions for obtaining the required foreign exchange.

Recent devaluation measures have made imports more expensive and raised producer prices creating a sound base for expanding markets for domestic small-scale producers. However, the increase in rural incomes resulting from increased higher agricultural prices has been diluted by the implicit taxation of the farmer by the inefficiencies and increased marketing margins of the crop marketing institutions and the inflation tax. Thus, the full benefits of the large exchange rate movements of recent years may not have been passed on to farmers through real prices increases.

Some small-scale engineering firms that are dependent on imported inputs and do not have the ability to increase significantly the quality of their production have also suffered under import liberalization and devaluation. Themi Farm Implements and CARMATEC are firms in Arusha town which manufacture farm implements. Themi's sales of oxcarts have declined from 2000 in 1985 to 500 in 1990. Similarly CARMATEC's sales of oxcarts have declined from 7000 in 1985 to 800 in 1990. The two firms have also experienced a decline in sales of ploughs. Declining sales are attributed mainly to the influx of imported ploughs under own funds imports and through donor assistance schemes and partly due to high domestic prices of these tools. Higher prices are in turn attributed to high input prices caused by devaluation. For example, according to Themi Farm Implements's officials, the cost of one ton of mild steel was Tshs7000 in 1985. By 1990 it was Tshs200,000 (28.6 times).

Similarly, another small firm, Manik Engineering, has experienced a sharp decline in its sales of grinding machines. Most of its inputs (flat bars, bearings, bolts and screws) use imported materials. Prices for these inputs have shot up dramatically because of devaluation. The price of flat bars, for example, rose by 16.7 times while that of bearings rose by 24 times between 1985 and 1990. The resulting high selling prices have chocked up the demand for these products. Demand problems have been aggravated by the emergence of large-scale own funds importers, like K.J. Motors who imports cheap grinding mills from India. Consequently, employment in the firm declined from 20 in 1985 to just five in 1991.

One positive aspect of the market constraint is that it has stimulated the search for new ways of coping with the problem. Both Themi Implements and CARMATEC have embarked on improvization, adaptation and diversification in the production of new products such as hand-operated oil presses; oil expellers; hand water pumps; water-storage tanks and drill presses. In addition, Themi has also successfully penetrated markets in the neighbouring countries of Uganda, Rwanda, and Burundi. It has also improved its products' delivery services by manufacturing in-house spares to solve the problem of scarcity of spares and by setting up independent satellite units to supply spares to distant customers.

The impact of monetary, credit and financial reforms on the SSE sector is not yet clear. High interest rates would probably aggravate liquidity and repayment difficulties among the few SSE firms who manage to secure formal loans. Perhaps the greatest weakness of the ongoing financial reform is the failure to recognize the need to promote formal and informal credit institutions using new forms of collateral (such as the character of the borrower or the group system as used by the Grameen Bank in Bangladesh) to enable people with few assets to get access to credit.

The new export drive has been particularly successful in promoting non-traditional exports (NTE). The share of NTE in total exports earnings has increased twofold between 1986 and 1989 with exports of timber and timber products accounting for about 30 per cent of the total value of NTE. However, the dramatic rise in the exports of timber logs carries with it unknown environmental hazards associated with deforestation. Such an export drive may therefore deprive small enterprises involved in wood-working and earth-brick making of raw materials on which they depend.

Agricultural reform policies, such as higher producer prices and improved marketing arrangements, have contributed positively to increases in agricultural production and rural incomes thereby boosting prospects for expanded markets of informal sector products.

The reforms have made raw materials more freely available and anecdotal evidence shows a boom in forward-linkage industries such as small-scale grain mills (Bagachwa, 1991a), oil presses, coffee, cashew nut processing and saw mills (UNDP *et al.* 1988). The dismantling of grain trade restrictions has also given rise to a thriving open market trade whose volume is estimated to have increased sevenfold between 1980–81 and 1987–8. The growth in volume has been accompanied by increasing numbers of small traders (both in urban and rural areas), especially in the assembling, wholesaleing and retailing of maize in urban centres. A recent 1989 survey revealed that in the Dar es Salaam wholesale grain markets a new class of informal money-lenders has evolved who provide short-term financing for grain purchasing and financing. They also serve as brokers providing buying and selling services to others for a fee. The number of such traders is estimated to have grown by 6.7 times from 15 in the early 1980s to about 100 in 1989 (Gordon, 1989).

Conclusion

The medium- and long-term effects of the ERP reforms on SSEs are not yet clear. The emerging evidence, however, indicates that the reforms have served as a double-edged sword: threatening some firms' markets through greater imports and domestic competition and revitalizing some others by providing freely available raw materials and spares. The most adversely affected firms have especially been those who have been unable to innovate and those relying on imported inputs – including a number of small engineering firms. For such firms the principal sources of decline in demand have mainly been (i) increased prices of imported raw materials and inputs due to the inflationary effect of devaluation; (ii) falling real incomes and depressed purchasing power among urban and rural households and (iii) increased imports and domestic competition resulting in lower volume of sales.

The beneficiaries of the reforms have been mostly microenterprises using mainly domestic resources and those able to diversify into new product lines. Indeed, the following evidence suggests that the informal or microenterprise sector appears to have grown rapidly over the 1985–90 period:

(a) A recent (1989) survey by the Bureau of Statistics reveals that in Dar es Salaam alone, the number of microenterprises is estimated to be at least three times the level of the mid-1980s.
(b) Evidence gathered by the World Bank during its 1990 survey of 20 informal-sector establishments in Dar es Salaam shows that these microenterprises had, on average, doubled their employment levels between 1984 and 1990. The evidence reveals further that the number of licences issued to establishments in

the informal sector has doubled since 1986. On this basis, one can conclude that informal-sector employment has at least doubled since 1984 (World Bank, 1991).

(c) Results from the 1990 Zanzibar survey of the informal sector show a skewed distribution of firm age towards recent years. About half of the informal sector enterprises had been established within the past five years (Bagachwa 1991b).

(d) A repeat of the industrial survey conducted by the World Bank in late 1989 and covering the same sample as the 1985 survey revealed that output in most larger firms contracted while output in smaller- and medium-sized firms expanded. More specifically 60 per cent of the smaller firms increased production while only 48 per cent of the larger firms managed to do so (World Bank 1991).

(e) A recent (1990) survey of 79 microenterprises that received SIDA support revealed that 33 per cent had experienced substantial increases and 44 per cent some increase in the change in demand over the last few years. Six per cent of the firms stated to have experienced no change and only twelve per cent reported to have experienced decline in demand (Swedish Development Consulting Partners, 1991).

(f) The dismantling of restrictions on grain trade has given rise to a thriving open market trade whose volume is estimated to have increased sevenfold between 1981 and 1988 (Gordon, 1989).

Overall, the recent structural adjustment reforms have reversed some elements of policy biases towards the SSE sector. But some of the new reforms have created some problems for SSEs. Much more specific measures are required to relax the remaining supply constraints and to ensure the development of SSEs. Additional reforms stressing the upgrading of rural and urban infrastructures (feeder roads, telecommunications and cheap and accessible electricity), creation of new forms of credit institutions and decentralization of decisionmaking and resources are certainly required.

Industrial sector in mali: responses to adjustment

JEAN-CLAUDE KESSOUS and GILLES LESSARD

Introduction

Several years ago, Mali set out on a programme of reforms to improve the health of and to deregulate the economy[1]. These reforms concerned all economic sectors and notably the industrial sector which is called upon to play an increasing role as the State gradually withdraws from productive activities in favour of the private sector. In order to assess the response of the industrial sector to these reforms, a survey was carried out with about one hundred firms of all sizes operating in the most representative sectors of activity of the Mali economy. More specifically, the objectives of this survey were to:

(a) obtain as much information as possible on the dynamics of small and medium-sized businesses;
(b) assess the response of industrial units of various sizes to the adjustment measures set up by the Mali authorities since 1988. The underlying hypothesis of this research being that the structural adjustment programmes, by relaxing the constraints inhibiting the development of the private sector, should stimulate the emergence of a new entrepreneurial class by new, more dynamic, and more competitive firms on both the home and international markets;
(c) see whether the new economic environment was favourable to a sustained growth of industrial production and investment and;
(d) determine what the main constraints are which continue to inhibit the capacity of industrialists to respond.

The chapter starts off by giving a brief overview of the socio-economic context of Mali and of the principal reform measures that were taken. This is followed by the presentation, in four parts, of survey results. The first part gives an analysis of the sampled enterprises (stratified by size), their operating conditions and problems, while the second part concentrates on the impact of the reform measures as experienced by these enterprises. The third and fourth parts focus on finance and credit and the regulatory environment respectively. The paper ends with some conclusions and suggestions as to how to further the process of adjustment.

Mali: the socio-economic context

Physical and demographic characteristics

The total surface area of Mali is 1,241,000 km^2. It is a land-locked country, located in the northern part of West Africa. Under the influence of a Sudan-Sahelian climate, the country knew a succession of droughts in the beginning of the 70s which seriously inhibited its growth potential, dependent to a large extent on agricultural activities. From the standpoint of natural resources, Mali has significant geological potential which is little exploited. The country's landlocked state and the weakness of its infrastructure restrict the development of the mining sector considerably. For the time being, mining activities are essentially limited to the production of phosphate, salt, and gold. Gold represents one of the main sources of foreign currency for the country.

In 1990, the population of Mali was more than eight million persons with a density of seven people per km^2. According to the World Bank, the annual rate of demographic growth is about 3 per cent, which will result in a population of 11 million inhabitants by the year 2000. The Mali population is essentially rural (78 per cent of the total), although the repeated droughts have increased migratory flows to urban centres. Again according to the World Bank, in the period between 1980 and 1987 the urban population grew at a rate of 4.2 per cent annually, which is a significantly higher rate than the country's overall population growth.

The Mali population is very young – 45 per cent of the population is under fifteen and more than 50 per cent is under twenty. This strong demographic pressure constitutes one of the main challenges for the Mali economy which is having problems educating a large part of the population and creating jobs for the growing labour force.

Economic structure

With a GNP per capita evaluated at US$270 in 1989 (World Bank, 1990), Mali is considered one of the poorest countries in the world. There is little diversification in the economy making it particularly vulnerable to uncertain weather that causes large variations in agricultural production.

In the twenty years following the independence of the country, the Mali authorities chose a centralized economic approach emphasizing state intervention in all sectors of the economy. At the agricultural level, the interventionist policy of the Mali government resulted in measures to subsidize agricultural inputs and to set prices paid to producers. From the industrial standpoint, this option resulted in the nationalization of most private enterprises and the development of a large number of industrial units under public control. During this period, several state monopolies were created in marketing and distribution channels.

Despite the fundamental changes that the Mali economy has undergone since its independence, the primary sector remains the main area of activity, although its relative weight has fallen considerably in comparison to the 1970s. Currently, the primary sector represents 50 per cent of GDP on average, as is shown in Table 7.1.

Table 7.1 Mali: GDP structure 1976–1990 (per cent)

Sectors of activity	*1976*	*1986*	*1990*
Primary sector	61.0	51.0	49.0
Subsistence agriculture	n.a.	21.5	18.6
Industrial agriculture	n.a.	5.3	5.8
Stockraising	n.a.	13.7	15.7
Fishing	n.a.	3.4	3.4
Forestry	n.a.	7.1	5.5
Secondary sector	9.0	14.0	13.0
Mining	n.a.	2.7	1.6
Crafts	n.a.	1.3	1.3
Modern industry	n.a.	5.6	6.5
Construction and public works	n.a.	4.4	3.6
Tertiary sector	30.0	35.0	38.0
Trade	n.a.	14.2	16.2
Transport and telecommunications	n.a.	4.1	4.9
Other services	n.a.	16.7	16.9
TOTAL	100.0	100.0	100.0

n.a.: not available

Source: Five year plan 1987–1991 quoted by the ILO (GERN report) and the Ministry of the Planning: Flash statistical information 1990.

Agriculture and stockfarming account for 80 per cent of the activities in this sector. In the last thirty years, the agricultural sector was affected by two major droughts, the first in 1968–73 and the second in 1982–4, both of which caused production losses and decimation of livestock. Agricultural production is essentially that of cereals including rice, maize, millet, and sorghum. Mali's main export crop is cotton, which is grown in the southern part of the country. The primary sector accounts for 80 per cent of employment on average, 70 per cent of which is in the agricultural sector alone.

The main changes which have affected Mali's economic structure since the 1980s concern the increased weight of secondary and tertiary activities. The secondary sector includes the mines, crafts, industry, construction and public works, representing nearly 14 per cent of GDP and 9 per cent of total employment on average. The tertiary sector has been growing constantly with a strong contribution from commercial activities. Trade represents the main activity of the private sector. It is practised on the scale of the West African region, the national market representing only a small share in the sales figures of tradesmen. The national network is relatively well structured and financially strong, benefiting from most of the loans granted by banks.

Mali joined the West African Monetary Union (WAMU) in 1984 and, as a country in the French franc (CFA) zone, the convertibility of its currency is guaranteed and the monetary policy is subordinate to the decisions of the Central Bank of the Western Africa states. Mali's membership of the WAMU has introduced rigidities in its monetary policy, in particular with respect to its credit policy and the setting of interest rates.

Industrial sector

As in many African countries south of the Sahara, Mali two industrial sectors exist side by side: a modern industrial sector recognized by the state and an informal sector operating on the margin of legality.

With 6.5 per cent of GDP and 5 per cent of total employment, the modern industrial sector occupied a relatively unimportant place in the Mali economy in 1990. The sector was largely dominated by public enterprises. The contribution of the private sector was relatively small: in 1988, it represented nearly 22 per cent of industrial value-added (IVA); the rest, 78 per cent, coming from public enterprises (35 per cent) or semi-public enterprises (43 per cent). The desire to create the conditions needed for rapid industrial expansion and the option for a socialist ideology were the main reasons which prompted the authorities to intervene on a large scale in manufacturing.

Three industrial subsectors contribute most to the IVA. The largest contribution comes from the food-products subsector which comprised more than 36 per cent of IVA in 1988, followed by the textile-clothing subsector (33 per cent of IVA) and public services (14 per cent of IVA). Other activities are marginal in comparison to these three subsectors except for the chemical and associated industries (8 per cent of IVA).

There is little foreign investment, with the exception of a few subsidiaries of European industrial groups operating in the food products industry. Mali is not a country with a strong industrial vocation; its comparative advantages are limited and subject to the uncertainty of the climate. In addition, the domestic market and purchasing power of the population are too weak to justify the presence of large industrial units.

Performance of the industrial sector as a whole is limited. This is mainly due to: (i) an environment relatively lacking in competition, (ii) poor management of public enterprises under strong control of the State, (iii) errors in the design of industrial plants and (iv) inappropriate economic policies.

Unlike the modern structured industrial sector, the informal sector occupies an important place in the Mali economy, at least in terms of the employment it provides. In urban areas, the majority of the population depends on this sector for a living. The rural exodus caused by the droughts and the economic recession have created a constant influx of labour to the informal sector. This sector also absorbs the people dismissed from the 'deflated' public sector, civil servants on voluntary retirement and young graduates.

A recent survey on the informal sector showed that in 1989, with the exception of primary activities, nearly four active persons out of five were employed in informal secondary and tertiary activities (MPIC, 1989). In addition, the IVA generated by the sector was assessed at nearly CFAfr17 billion, or about 30 per cent of total IVA. The activities related to the textile and clothing sector and to the food products industry were also predominant in the informal sector, closely followed by metal processing activities.

Obstacles to industrial development

In addition to the constraints associated with variations in the weather, the development of the industrial sector in Mali was slowed down by a number of structural obstacles which had a negative effect on the operating conditions of enterprises. These obstacles had undesirable effects on productivity and the capacity of enterprises to be competitive on domestic and export markets. Among these constraints were:

- the limited size of the Mali national market in terms of population and purchasing power. The Mali market has little solvency: about 80 per cent of the population lives in rural zones and has one of the lowest per capita incomes in the world;
- limited integration of the industrial structure which forces most enterprises operating in the modern industrial sector to import their raw materials;
- insufficiency of transport and communications infrastructures. As Mali is a landlocked country and the cost of transport is high, this situation is a great handicap to Mali industrialists;
- a lack of skilled, productive, competitive labour;
- a restrictive legal and regulatory context not suited to the development of the industrial sector;
- a banking sector which is poorly adapted to the needs of the industrial sector and is more geared to the commercial sector;
- corruption and fraud on a large scale which is endemic in the customs administration.

Structural adjustment measures

The deterioration and persistence of macroeconomic disequilibria both from the internal standpoint (budgetary deficit) and the external standpoint (deficit in the balance of payments) led the Mali authorities to set up a medium-term adjustment programme in mid-1988. These efforts were backed by three sectoral adjustment loans granted by the World Bank: one for the public enterprise sector (June 1988), the second for education (June 1989) and the third for the agricultural sector (May 1990). In addition, a medium-term structural adjustment loan agreement (SAL I) was recently signed, which took effect at the beginning of 1991.

The measures taken under these programmes are an attempt to improve the state of public finance and to promote the activities of the private sector in such a manner that it can take over from the public sector as the driving force of economic growth. Among the measures to favour development of the private sector taken since 1988[2], the following should be mentioned:

- simplification of economic regulations to facilitate the private sector's participation in production, trade and employment. The trade code enacted in 1986 is currently being reviewed to further simplify the operating conditions of enterprises;

- establishment of a new investment code in March 1991 to replace the investment code of 1986;
- increased flexibility of operating conditions in the labour market: reforms of the labour code are being studied to promote the creation of job openings and the mobility of labour;
- unilateral elimination of price controls except for a few strategic products;
- reform of foreign trade: abolition of quantitative restrictions, replacement of import licences with a system of automatic registration, suppression of export taxes, replacement of specific taxes and fixed prices for produce with *ad valorem* taxes, harmonization of customs protection, etc.;
- decrease in the tax burden on enterprises;
- privatization of public enterprises.

The adjustment process is still young in Mali and the implementation of reforms too incomplete for a thorough *ex post* assessment. For the time being, the reaction of industrialists is moderate. Certain aspects of the reforms, particularly those concerning fiscal policy and the simplification of regulations with regard to trade, were viewed positively. Opening up the Mali market to international competition, conversely, gave rise to an upsurge of protectionist reactions. The tariff reform was questioned, the industrialists claim that it does not sufficiently protect them, and at the same time there was an increase in fraud. The new investment code is considered to provide little incentive, especially with regard to exemptions for imports of equipment.

Enterprise survey

Methodology of the survey and characteristics of the sample

The survey was conducted during the period between 25 July and 15 August 1991 and covered about 100 formal and informal enterprises in the Bamako district, operating in the most representative subsectors of activity of the Mali industrial structure. A precoded questionnaire drawn up by the World Bank for similar surveys was used after it had been adapted to the Mali context. The sample was predetermined using the quota method. The absence of an industrial census meant that it was not possible to determine a statistically representative sample. An effort was made, however, to obtain a composition of the sample which is in keeping with the industrial structure of the country, at least as concerns the sectors of activity.

Two criteria were taken into account for the processing and analysis of the results: the size of the enterprise and the sector of activity, so as to have an indication of the problems with which industrial units in the various subsectors are confronted in the formal and in the informal sector.

Four enterprise sizes were defined according to the size of the permanent staff:

- microenterprises (Micro): enterprises with a permanent staff of less than four persons;

- very small enterprises (VSE): enterprises with a permanent staff of between four and nine persons inclusive;
- small enterprises (SE): enterprises with a permanent staff of between 10 and 29 persons inclusive;
- medium-sized and large enterprises (MLE): enterprises with a permanent staff of more than 30 persons.

The six subsectors of activity selected were: food products; textile/clothing; wood/furniture; soap/cosmetics, metal-products and construction materials. Enterprises which did not fit into one of these six subsectors were classified as 'miscellaneous industries' (mostly chemical and allied industries as well as printing and publishing).

Table 7.2 shows the characteristics of the sample by size of enterprise, sector of activity and year of creation: had the firms been created before or after 1988, when the first structural adjustment measures were introduced?

Out of a total of 100 firms surveyed, 32 per cent are microenterprises, 31 per cent very small enterprises, 26 per cent small enterprises and 11 per cent medium-sized and large enterprises. The breakdown of the sample by sector of activity is as follows: food products (20 per cent of enterprises); textile/clothing (17 per cent); wood/furniture (16 per cent); soap/cosmetics (11 per cent), construction materials (10 per cent); metal-products (18 per cent) and miscellaneous industries (8 per cent).

The largest industrial units are found in the food-products subsector: five of the medium-sized and large enterprises, or more than 45 per cent of the units of this size, operate in this branch of activity, which is also the subsector in which most of the units of the modern manufacturing industry are concentrated.

The average age of the enterprises is 9.1 years. More than a quarter of the enterprises (28 per cent) were created after 1988, 29 per cent of which were microenterprises, 32.6 per cent of which were very small enterprises and 39 per cent of which were small enterprises. No medium-sized or large enterprise was created during this period. More than 70 per cent of the enterprises established after 1988 were in three subsectors of activity: food products (17.9 per cent), textile/clothing (32.1 per cent) and wood/furniture (21.4 per cent). A more detailed breakdown of the period of establishment shows that about 75 per cent of the enterprises were established after 1980, nearly 46 per cent of which in the period 1980–87, a period corresponding with the introduction of the first measures of liberalization and reform taken with the support of the IMF and the World Bank. The enterprises surveyed employed nearly 2105 people, 64.8 per cent of whom were permanent staff (including the owner and his/her family), 22.7 per cent of which were part-time employees and 12.5 per cent of which were apprentices.

Characteristics of the owners

The youngest entrepreneur was 22 and the oldest 73 years old. The average age of an entrepreneur was 42.2 for the entire sample. As far as formal education is concerned, 61 per cent of the entrepreneurs had gone to a formal school whereas 39 per

Table 7.2 Characteristics of the sample enterprises

Subsectors of activity	*Total*		*Food products*		*Textile/ clothing*		*Wood/ furniture*		*Soap/ cosmetics*		*Building materials*		*Metal products*		*Miscellaneous industries*	
Characteristics	*No.*	*%*	*No.*	*%*	*No.*	*%*	*No.*	*%*	*No.*	*%*	*No.*	*%*	*No.*	*%*	*No.*	*%*
Total number of enterprises	100	100.0	20	20.0	17	17.0	16	16.0	11	11.0	10	10.0	18	18.0	8	8.0
Size:																
Micro	32	32.0	6	30.0	5	29.4	8	50.0	4	36.4	3	30.0	5	27.8	1	12.5
VSE	31	31.0	6	30.0	5	29.4	3	18.8	4	36.4	4	40.0	8	44.4	1	12.5
SM	26	26.0	3	15.0	6	35.3	5	31.2	2	18.2	2	20.0	2	16.7	5	62.5
MLE	11	11.0	5	25.0	1	5.9	0	0.0	1	9.1	1	10.0	2	11.1	1	12.5
Number created:																
Before 1988	72	72.0	15	75.0	8	47.1	10	62.5	8	72.7	8	80.0	17	94.4	6	75.0
After 1988	28	28.0	5	25.0	9	52.9	6	37.5	3	27.3	2	20.0	1	5.6	2	25.0
Number belonging to:																
a man	75	75.0	15	75.0	5	29.4	16	100.0	5	45.5	10	100.0	18	100.0	6	75.0
a woman	25	25.0	5	25.0	12	70.6	0	0.0	6	54.5	0	0.0	0	0.0	2	25.0
Average age (years)	9.1		10.1		6.1		8.0		7.0		9.1		14.2		7.0	
Employment total sample	2105	100.0	717	34.1	381	18.1	141	6.7	183	8.7	106	5.0	385	18.3	192	9.1

Source: Etude Economique Conseil Canada Inc. Survey, July 1991.

cent had not. The average period of education for the entire sample was 10 years. The proportion of entrepreneurs who had gone to school increases with the size of the enterprise.

Three-quarters of the enterprises (75 per cent) belong to a male owner. Female owners of enterprises (25 per cent) are predominant in activities such as textile/clothing (70.6 per cent of enterprises belong to women) and soap/cosmetics (54.5 per cent). The women had received less formal education than the men: 44 per cent of them declared they had never been to school, whereas this applied to only 37.3 per cent of the men. The average age of enterprises belonging to women decreases as the size of the enterprise increases, which means that female entrepreneurs who enter the market are trying to move away from the traditional niche of the microenterprise towards more structured and potentially more dynamic forms of enterprises.

The entrepreneurs who received most schooling are found in the textile/clothing and the food-products subsectors. Conversely, most of the entrepreneurs who were trained as apprentices are found in the wood/furniture and metal-products sectors. In the textile/clothing sector, the number of entrepreneurs with a formal education is equal to the number of entrepreneurs who were trained as apprentices.

Motivation for starting the enterprise

In Table 7.3 the main reasons which motivate the entrepreneurs to set up a business are given: 30 per cent of them state they did so because their parents or members of their families were already in business, 26 per cent to take an opportunity for profit, 22 per cent because they had no other possibility of employment, 8 per cent because they were trained to do business, another 8 per cent due to dismissal and 6 per cent for other reasons.

In general, the distribution of replies did not show a particular predominance with regard to the emergence of a spirit of entrepreneurship or a new class of entrepreneurs if the criterion for entrepreneurship is limited exclusively to profit seeking. The family is still the main channel of access to ownership, although 26 per cent of the entrepreneurs in the sample declared they set up a business in order to seize an opportunity for profit. Among the entrepreneurs who have created their enterprises since 1988, only 10.7 per cent were motivated by profit-seeking, the others created their enterprises as a reaction to the lack of opportunity of employment due to the tight labour market. Most family businesses are found among the microenterprises and the medium-sized and large enterprises, irrespective of the period in which they were established. It is encouraging that the most dynamic entrepreneurs who highly rated either profit-seeking or putting knowledge acquired in a training programme into practice are found in the category of very small and small enterprises of the food products subsector and the textile/clothing subsector: 40 per cent of entrepreneurs in the food-products branch set up a business to take advantage of an opportunity for profit, and nearly 30 per cent of the entrepreneurs in the textile/clothing subsector did so because they were trained to become businessmen. The size of these enterprises is adapted to the Mali market and they are

Table 7.3 The main motivation for starting up in business by size of enterprise, subsector of activity and period of creation in (per cent)

Main motivation	*Parents or relations in business*	*Lack of other possibilities of employment*	*Training for business*	*Taking an opportunity for a profit*	*Dismissed*	*Other*	*Total*
Total sample	30.0	22.0	8.0	26.0	8.0	6.0	100.0
Branches of activity:							
Food products	40.0	10.0	5.0	40.0	5.0	0.0	100.0
Textile clothing	17.6	17.6	29.4	17.6	17.6	0.0	100.0
Wood furniture	0.0	87.5	0.0	6.3	0.0	0.0	100.0
Soap cosmetics	63.6	0.0	9.1	27.3	0.0	0.0	100.0
Building materials	20.0	10.0	0.0	30.0	20.0	20.0	100.0
Metal products	38.9	5.6	5.6	33.3	11.1	5.6	100.0
Miscellaneous industries	37.5	12.5	0.0	25.0	0.0	0.0	100.0
Size of enterprise:							
Micro	46.9	28.1	0.0	15.6	6.3	3.1	100.0
VSE	19.4	16.1	9.7	32.3	16.1	6.5	100.0
SE	15.4	30.8	15.4	23.1	3.8	11.5	100.0
MLE	45.4	0.0	9.0	45.5	0.0	0.0	100.0
Year of creation:							
Before 1988	34.7	16.7	4.2	31.9	4.2	8.3	100.0
After 1988	17.9	35.7	17.9	10.7	17.9	0.0	100.0
Sex of the owner:							
Male	29.3	25.3	6.7	25.3	6.7	6.7	100.0
Female	32.0	12.0	12.0	28.0	12.0	4.0	100.0

Source: Etude Economique Conseil Canada Inc. Survey, July 1991.

well integrated in the national economy, trying to exploit comparative advantages for the country in order to expand. The most dynamic entrepreneurs are found in these categories.

Almost all of the owners of microenterprises operate in the informal sector and declare they set up a business in order to meet the needs of their families and improve their social and economic position. The enterprise is considered a means of survival and the decision to produce in a particular subsector of activity rather than another was not made as a response to new incentives introduced by the adjustment measures. More and more operators have created micro enterprises, limited as they are in their possibility of being active in the labour market and having no means of subsistence. Low entry barriers, however, have increased competition between firms up to saturation of the market: of all of the enterprises established since 1988, it is in the microenterprises that most people declare to have suffered a drop in production. This situation was exacerbated by the fact that the Mali economy is in a transitional phase and that real incomes are still affected by the stabilization measures: nearly half of the microenterprises interviewed mentioned increased competition from other firms as one of their main difficulties and 56 per cent of them have problems in selling their production because 'people don't have enough money'.

When asked to describe the evolution of their production since the structural adjustment measures were taken, all the enterprises declared that they recorded a rise, or in the worst cases a stagnation of their production. Further, a very large majority of the enterprises established since 1988 have experienced growth in their production, especially very small and small enterprises. Several young enterprises, well integrated to meet the needs of the Mali market, have been set up in the last few years. These are small enterprises created by young graduates and persons dismissed from public enterprises, working in the food products or the textile/clothing sectors. This is still a relatively scarce phenomenon on a nation-wide basis: firstly the adjustment process is still young and not enough time has gone by to assess the effects it is likely to have on the development of entrepreneurship and, secondly, the Mali investors have a marked preference for commercial activities and services, as these activities are less risky and offer profit opportunities in a shorter term. As an example, out of 465 projects for the creation of enterprises which are financed and followed up by the European Development Fund[3], only 3 per cent are industrial projects; the rest are split between agriculture, trade and services (transport, tourism, commerce, etc.).

Characteristics of the enterprises

Profile

Most of the enterprises in the sample are owned by a single owner. For 91 per cent of them, the capital is entirely held by private nationals. A large proportion of enterprises operate outside of the regulatory framework: 68 per cent of the firms in the sample declared that they were not registered, in particular the microenterprises (97 per cent) and the very small enterprises (87 per cent). Nearly one quarter of the enterprises have a licence from the Ministry of Industry, Hydraulics and Energy: 46 per cent of the VSC and 91 per cent of the MLC. Two-thirds of the enterprises pay municipal taxes and 56 per cent pay duties and taxes to the State. The micro- and very small enterprises mainly pay taxes in the form of 'licence taxes': on average 63 per cent of them are subject to this kind of tax. Finally, 34 per cent of the enterprises pay customs duties, notably the medium-sized and large enterprises as they import their raw materials directly.

For the sample as a whole, the average use of capacity is 61.3 per cent, with a minimum of 56.6 per cent in the textile/clothing subsector and a maximum of more than 70 per cent in the food products and construction materials subsectors. Only some 29 per cent of the enterprises are members of a chamber of commerce or a professional association. The small enterprises (46.2 per cent) and the medium-sized and large enterprises (81.8 per cent) in particular are members of such associations.

Procurement of raw materials

Over 30 per cent of the enterprises import all of their raw materials, whereas only 18 per cent of them procure these materials entirely on the local market. Enterprises in the wood/furniture subsector rely on imports especially: the absence or scarcity of wood resources forces 80 per cent of enterprises in this branch to import wood from neighbouring countries (notably from the Ivory Coast). The small size of the industrial base makes enterprises very dependent on imports of raw materials. Raw materials represent 92 per cent on average of the total cost of inputs. This proportion is smaller for microenterprises (53 per cent) and grows with the size of the enterprise to reach nearly 95 per cent for small enterprises and medium-sized and large enterprises. Newly-created enterprises (created since 1988) do not make more intensive use of local resources and are as dependent on imported inputs as the older enterprises.

Inter-industrial relations are not very extensive: only 25 per cent of the enterprises declared that they regularly procure their raw materials from large or small Mali enterprises and 5 per cent do so occasionally when their raw materials are not available on the market. The small enterprises (SE) and the medium-sized and large enterprises are the most integrated, since 31 per cent and 45 per cent of them, respectively, acquire inputs from local enterprises. Inter-industrial exchanges take place in the food-products, textile/clothing (cotton) and soap/cosmetics subsectors.

Markets supplied

Table 7.4 gives a summary of the information collected from the enterprises with regard to the marketing of their products, with respect to both the type of client and the markets supplied. For the enterprises in the sample as a whole, the main clientele is made up of (i) high-income populations (30 per cent of the enterprises), (ii) tradesmen (29 per cent of the enterprises) and (iii) low-income urban populations

Table 7.4 Main clientele and main points of sale by subsector of activity and size of enterprise (per cent)

		MAIN CLIENTELE								POINTS OF SALE			
	Total	*Rural populations, peasants villagers*	*Low-income urban populations*	*High-income populations*	*Foreigners*	*Traders*	*Stalls and shops*	*Government*	*Other industries*	*Bamako*	*Markets of neighbouring cities*	*ECOWAS countries*	*Overseas*
Branches of activity:													
Food products	20	0.0	30.0	10.0	0.0	40.0	10.0	0.0	10.0	90.0	5.0	5.0	0.0
Textile/clothing	17	5.9	5.9	47.1	17.6	11.8	5.9	5.9	0.0	82.4	0.0	11.8	5.9
Wood/furniture	16	6.3	12.5	62.5	12.5	6.3	0.0	0.0	0.0	100.0	0.0	0.0	0.0
Soap/cosmetics	11	0.0	54.5	9.1	0.0	18.2	18.2	0.0	0.0	100.0	0.0	0.0	0.0
Building materials	10	0.0	0.0	70.0	0.0	30.0	0.0	0.0	0.0	100.0	0.0	0.0	0.0
Metal products	18	16.7	5.6	5.6	0.0	50.0	5.6	11.1	5.6	100.0	0.0	0.0	0.0
Miscellaneous industries	8	0.0	0.0	12.5	0.0	50.0	12.5	0.0	25.0	100.0	0.0	0.0	0.0
Size of enterprise:													
Microenterprises	32	6.3	31.3	31.3	6.3	12.5	12.5	0.0	0.0	96.9	0.0	3.1	0.0
Very small enterprises	31	6.5	12.9	35.5	3.2	29.0	6.5	0.0	0.0	93.5	0.0	6.5	0.0
Small enterprises	26	3.8	7.7	34.6	7.7	30.8	3.8	3.8	7.7	96.2	0.0	0.0	3.8
Medium-sized and large enterprises	11	0.0	0.0	0.0	0.0	72.7	0.0	18.2	9.1	90.9	9.1	0.0	0.0
Year of creation:													
Before 1988	72	6.9	19.4	23.6	4.2	31.9	6.9	2.8	4.2	94.5	1.4	2.8	1.4
After 1988	28	0.0	7.1	46.4	7.1	21.4	7.1	3.6	7.1	96.4	0.0	3.6	0.0
Total	100	5.0	16.0	30.0	5.0	29.0	7.0	3.0	5.0	95.0	1.0	3.0	1.0

Source: Etude Economique Conseil Canada Inc. Survey, July 1991.

(16 per cent of the enterprises). Very small and small enterprises have a clientele made up mainly of high-income populations and tradesmen. As the size of the business grows, the markets supplied move from low-income populations to more captive markets which are more demanding in terms of the quality of the products (high-income populations, tradesmen, government, other industries). In comparison to older ones, the enterprises created since 1988 address a larger proportion of these markets. None of the very small enterprises sells its products to other enterprises, whereas other enterprises are the main outlet for 7.7 per cent of the small enterprises and 9.1 per cent of the MLE.

As the survey covered the district of Bamako only, most of the businesses included in the survey, irrespective of their size, are trading mainly in that area: 95 per cent declared that they sold a large part of their production in Bamako. Few enterprises export: 4 per cent of the sample – 3 per cent to the Economic Community of West African States (ECOWAS) and 1 per cent to overseas countries. Most of the exporting companies are in the food-products and textile/clothing subsectors, where Mali has comparative advantages. No medium-sized or large enterprise has export sales; they are geared more to import substitution. About the same number of enterprises established before or after 1988 declare that exports are their main source of income. On the other hand, enterprises created since 1988 export more to ECOWAS countries.

Marketing and competition

For 68 per cent of the units surveyed, competition is mainly from other small enterprises (Table 7.5), which confirms the saturation of the market. Thirty-nine per cent of the enterprises questioned declared that there are more than 10 enterprises producing and selling in the same main market. In addition, 87 per cent of microenterprises and more than 74 per cent of small enterprises declared that their main competitors were other small enterprises. Imports represented a source of competition for only 15 per cent of the enterprises and affect small enterprises (15.4 per cent) and particularly the medium-sized and large enterprises (54.4 per cent). Activities sensitive to competition are food-products (25 per cent), building materials (20 per cent), soap/cosmetics (18.2 per cent) and textile/clothing (17.6 per cent).

The larger the enterprise, the more the competition from small units decreases. The markets supplied are not the same: low-income populations for the microenterprises and very small enterprises, higher-income populations and tradesmen for the larger businesses. Competition between small and large enterprises is weak: only 23 per cent of the small enterprises mention large local enterprises as the main source of competition.

Competition is felt most strongly in the soap/cosmetics (63.6 per cent), building materials (70 per cent), metal-products (72.2 per cent) and miscellaneous industries (87.5 per cent) subsectors. In the wood/furniture branch, competition comes both from small enterprises (81.3 per cent) and from large ones (18.8 per cent).

Main problems

In the survey, the entrepreneurs were asked to specify the main difficulties encoun-

Table 7.5 Main competitors by sector of activity and size of enterprise (per cent)

		MAIN COMPETITORS					NUMBER OF COMPETITORS						INCREASE IN NUMBER COMPETITORS SINCE 1988		
	Total	*None*	*Other small enterprises*	*Large local enterprises*	*Both small and large enterprises*	*Imports*	*None*	*1–2*	*3–5*	*6–10*	*More than 10*	*N.C.A.*	*No*	*Yes*	*N.C.A.*
Branches of activity															
Food-products	20	15.0	55.0	5.0	0.0	25.0	15.0	45.0	0.0	20.0	20.0	0.0	30.0	50.0	2
Textile/clothing	17	11.8	58.8	5.9	5.9	17.6	17.6	0.0	11.8	5.9	64.7	0.0	29.4	70.6	
Wood/furniture	16	0.0	81.3	18.8	0.0	0.0	0.0	18.8	0.0	25.0	56.3	0.0	12.5	87.5	
Soap/cosmetics	11	9.1	63.6	0.0	0.0	18.2	18.2	9.1	27.3	0.0	45.5	0.0	27.3	63.6	
Building materials	10	0.0	70.0	0.0	10.0	20.0	10.0	20.0	40.0	10.0	0.0	20.0	40.0	60.0	
Metal products	18	0.0	72.2	11.1	5.6	11.1	5.6	16.7	11.1	0.0	38.9	27.8	11.1	66.7	2
Miscellaneous industries	8	0.0	87.5	0.0	0.0	12.5	12.5	37.5	12.5	0.0	37.5	0.0	12.5	87.5	
Size of enterprise															
Microenterprises	32	6.3	87.5	0.0	0.0	6.3	3.1	21.9	9.4	9.4	50.0	6.3	18.8	71.9	
Very small enterprises	31	3.2	74.2	6.5	6.5	9.7	6.5	16.1	9.7	16.1	41.9	9.7	9.7	77.4	1
Small enterprises	26	7.7	53.8	23.1	0.0	15.4	19.2	19.2	19.2	7.7	30.8	3.8	38.5	57.7	
Medium-sized and large enterprises	11	9.1	27.3	0.0	9.1	54.5	36.4	36.4	9.1	0.0	18.2	9.1	36.4	54.5	
Year of creation															
Before 1988	72	5.6	69.4	5.6	2.8	11.1	11.7	22.2	12.5	9.7	36.1	8.3	22.2	68.1	
After 1988	28	7.1	64.3	14.3	3.6	10.7	10.7	17.9	10.7	10.7	46.4	3.6	25.0	67.9	
Total	100	6.0	68.0	8.0	3.0	15.0	11.0	21.0	12.0	10.0	39.0	7.0	23.0	68.0	

N.C.A.: Not clear or not applicable

Source: Etude Economic Conseil Canada Inc. Survey, July 1991.

Table 7.6 Main difficulties in everyday operations by size of enterprise (per cent)

	Number of answers	*Rank*	*Micro*	*VSE*	*SE*	*MLE*
Business environment						
Taxes and duties	53	1	44	42	65	82
Technology, machines and equipment						
Obsolescence of machines and equipment	51	2	66	48	46	27
Access to new technologies	13	11	16	10	15	9
Finance						
Difficulty in obtaining credit for working capital	42	3	31	48	54	27
Obligation to give clients too much credit	19	8	9	32	23	0
Profits too low to finance purchases of raw materials	12	12	9	16	12	9
Profits too low to finance purchases of new equipment	10	13	13	13	4	9
Demand						
People do not have enough money in general	12	4	56	26	35	27
Too many enterprises operate in the same sector	10	5	47	26	27	27
Too many imports	12	12	0	3	12	73
Procurement of raw materials						
Prices of imported raw materials too high	31	6	31	39	19	36
Price of local materials too high	22	7	31	23	15	9
Procurement of local raw materials	16	9	22	13	19	0
Procurement of imported raw materials	10	13	6	3	15	9
Infrastructures						
High cost of electricity	14	10	29	13	19	9
High cost of transport	14	10	16	19	12	0

Source: Etude Economique Conseil Canada Inc. Survey, July 1991.

tered in the everyday operation of their business. The results are presented in Table 7.6.

For the sample as a whole, the three main operating problems mentioned most often were (i) high taxation (53 per cent of the enterprises), (ii) the obsolescence of machines and equipment (51 per cent) and (iii) the difficulty in obtaining credit for working capital (42 per cent). High taxation comes at the top of the list of the problems mentioned by small enterprises (65 per cent) and medium-sized and large enterprises (88 per cent). The microenterprises and the very small enterprises which operate for the most part outside of the regulatory framework are nevertheless also penalized by the level of taxation which affects them all the more, since it is based on fixed amounts.

The obsolescence of machines and equipment and the need to replace them are mentioned particularly by smaller enterprises (Micro, VSE, SE). For the microenterprises and the very small enterprises, this is the main difficulty.

The main problems listed by the microenterprises give a good indication of the limits of their growth potential, which is restricted by the conjunction of two constraints: a technological constraint (obsolescence of equipment) and a demand constraint (insufficient income of the clientele and very stiff competition from other enterprises). This indicates that they operate in saturated markets.

The medium-sized and large enterprises are also sensitive to difficulties which restrict their demand. However, legal and illegal imports of foreign competitive products constitute their main problem. Nearly three-quarters of the enterprises of this size mentioned this problem, which comes second only to taxation. The dismantling of protectionist barriers undertaken in the context of the structural adjustment measures is a crucial problem for the modern industrial sector, which specializes above all in import substitution and which has only been able to survive sheltered by strong protection.

The difficulties listed by the very small enterprises and the small enterprises show that they have a larger growth potential in so far as the constraints affecting their productive capacity are removed, be they technological (obsolescence of equipment) or financial (difficulties in obtaining credit for working capital). These enterprises are much more limited by the level of demand: between 26 per cent and 25 per cent of VSEs and SEs declared that they had problems due to their clients' purchasing power or competition from other local enterprises.

By subsector of activity, the three main difficulties listed (taxes and duties, obsolescence of equipment, and credit for working capital) are particularly restrictive for the textile/clothing, wood/furniture, soap/cosmetics, building-materials and metal-products sectors.

In the food-products subsector, one of the main difficulties mentioned by the entrepreneurs is the high price of local raw materials. Deregulation of prices for agricultural production resulted in an increase in the price of inputs for certain enterprises. This rise in prices had some induced effects, however, which benefited the industrial sector: several enterprises mentioned that the rise in agricultural incomes as a result of the deregulation was accompanied by a rise in rural demand.

Opening the borders to competing products, which traditionally is one of the main difficulties encountered by the textile sector in adjustment periods, is not mentioned very often by the enterprises of the sample operating in this sector. They were more sensitive to increases in the price of imported inputs and the high price of electricity. Enterprises in the wood/furniture subsector and, to a lesser extent, those in the soap/cosmetics subsector had problems of demand of various types in addition to difficulties in procuring raw materials, so that they are caught in a stranglehold which limits them with regard to both their sales and their production.

In the building-materials subsector, demand is less of a problem than obtaining credit for working capital. The high cost of transportation poses a problem for 90 per cent of operators in this subsector. This is due to many reasons, including: (i) the distance to sources of raw materials, (ii) the poor condition of transport infrastructures and (iii) the weight of both inputs used and products manufactured.

Impact of adjustment

The analysis of the response of the industrial sector to the structural adjustment measures is complex because it is subject to several-often conflicting – forces, the relative importance of which depends on the measures taken. In addition, given the dissimilarity of adjustment policies and the wide variety of enterprises, few generalizations can be made.

An evaluation of the impact of structural adjustment measures was dealt with in this study by asking enterprises of all sizes and all sectors to describe the main changes recorded since 1988 in terms of production, employment, investments, product range, exports and imports. The results are presented below.

Impact on production and employment

Table 7.7 presents side by side the results of the survey on the evolution of production and employment since 1988. As in the previous sections, the firms were subdivided by size and period of creation to better assess their behaviour since the reforms were established. Did they react to the incentive mechanisms set up and if so, did their production and employment grow?

For the sample as a whole, a larger proportion of firms declared that their production had risen (45 per cent as against 18 per cent) since the reforms were effected. Irrespective of the size and the period in which they were established, this rise affected all enterprises unilaterally, except for the medium-sized and large enterprises, which saw their production rise or fall in the same proportion. A second observation is apparent in Table 7.7: the proportion of enterprises which declared to have experienced a rise in production is particularly high for very small enterprises and small enterprises established since 1988, which may indicate that these enterprises reacted positively to the incentive measures taken.

It is possible that these results show the effects of a positive response of supply to the adjustment measures. This consideration must be counterweighted, however, by the fact that the Mali economy is sensitive to changes in weather and that 1988 and 1989 were characterized by a record growth in agriculture which spread to the entire economy. In other words, for lack of more specific indications, the growth phenomenon observed in the sample of enterprises may be due exclusively to the trend of the market.

Table 7.7 Impact of the adjustment on production and employment by size of enterprise and year of creation (per cent)

		Firms created before 1988				*Firms created since 1988*			
	Total	*Micro*	*VSE*	*SE*	*MLE*	*Micro*	*VSE*	*SE*	*MLE*
Production									
increase	45	29	54	33	27	38	77	73	—
decrease	18	21	14	27	28	25	11	0	—
Employment									
increase	70	58	86	73	64	50	89	64	—
decrease	7	4	0	7	22	25	0	9	—
Number of firms	100	24	22	15	11	8	9	11	—

Source: Etude Economique Conseil Canada Inc. Survey, July 1991.

The results of Table 7.7 also show a large disparity between subsectors: the textile/clothing branch is where the largest number of firms recorded an increase in production (82 per cent), followed by building materials (60 per cent) and soap/ cosmetics (55 per cent). Firms in the textile sector increased their growth by diversifying their outlets and seeking export markets; more than half of the firms in this subsector declared that they had exported directly or indirectly. Firms in this sector are also among those which changed their range of products to the greatest extent. By and large, they were producing traditional garments and reviewed the design to adapt it to new fashion trends for export to ECOWAS countries. Unlike the textile branch, in the wood/furniture sector the drop in production was felt most severely: more than 60 per cent of the enterprises in this sector declared that the production had dropped since 1988. This subsector has serious problems in procuring raw materials: first of all, there is little wood available locally and secondly most of the firms import their wood, which makes the cost of their supplies much higher.

The number of firms in which employment grew (70 per cent) is higher than the number of firms which recorded a rise in production (45 per cent). This is true for all firms, irrespective of their size (Table 7.7) and irrespective of the subsector, except as far as firms that operate in the textile/clothing sector are concerned. The small and very small enterprises recorded the largest rise in employment, whereas the microenterprises declared to have experienced the smallest rise in employment, especially since 1988. The shrinking formal labour market increased the flow of jobless who tried to generate an income by establishing small businesses. The enterprises thus created since 1988 show an annual rise in employment of more than 130 per cent, whereas the average for the sector as a whole was only 18 per cent. The very small enterprises were the source of this growth in employment. On the other hand, employment grew the least in microenterprises (2.3 per cent). The weak entry and exit barriers are such that there were as many microenterprises which left the market as new ones which were established, thus causing stagnation of employment.

Impact on investment

More than 43 per cent of the firms questioned declared that they had made new investments in the form of purchases of equipment; the food-products, textile/ clothing, building-materials and metal-production sectors benefited from this capitalization effort (Table 7.8). These investments were made mainly by medium-sized and large enterprises (64 per cent), very small enterprises (50 per cent) and small enterprises (42 per cent) (Table 7.9). Firms created before 1988 were those which for the most part modernized their means of production. Nearly half of them (48 per cent) declared that they had acquired new equipment since 1988, as compared to 31 per cent for those established after that date. As the firms established since 1988 are relatively young, new capitalization efforts were not justified, although the survey shows that 50 per cent of the VSE and 36 per cent of the SE created since 1988 have purchased new equipment. These results suggest that the enterprises reacted to the rise in production by making new investments,

Table 7.8 Impact of the adjustment by subsector of activity (per cent)

	Total %	*Food-products*	*Textile/ clothing*	*Wood/ furniture*	*Soap/ cosmetics*	*Building materials*	*Metal products*	*Miscel-laneous*
Production								
increase	45	40.0	82.0	38.0	55.0	60.0	22.0	25.0
decrease	18	23.0	12.0	62.0	9.0	0.0	17.0	13.0
Employment								
increase	70	70.0	65.0	75.0	64.0	90.0	72.0	50.0
decrease	7	0.0	12.0	13.0	0.0	0.0	17.0	13.0
Change in range of products	22	5.0	41.2	0.0	36.0	50.0	67.0	25.0
Markets penetrated	58	55.0	88.0	50.0	55.0	90.0	28.0	50.0
Share of imported raw materials:								
currently		93.0	98.6	97.0	87.0	85.0	89.0	99.0
increased since 1988	37	5.0	71.0	19.0	27.0	60.0	50.0	37.5
decreased since 1988	17	5.0	6.0	50.0	0.0	0.0	28.0	25.0
Difficulty in obtaining or high price:								
of local raw materials	45	36.0	25.0	47.0	73.0	50.0	40.0	13.0
of imported raw materials	48	20.0	67.0	53.0	27.0	50.0	50.0	87.0
Competition stiffer since 1988	68	50.0	71.0	87.0	64.0	60.0	67.0	88.0
Strongest competition from:								
small firms	68	55.0	59.0	81.0	64.0	70.0	72.0	87.0
imports	15	25.0	18.0	0.0	18.0	20.0	11.0	13.5
Exporting enterprises (directly or indirectly)	15	10.0	53.0	0.0	18.0	0.0	0.0	25.0
Enterprises envisaging exporting	43	35.0	35.0	50.0	46.0	40.0	56.0	37.0
Supply constraints: enterprises able to sell more	35	30.0	65.0	33.0	18.0	60.0	17.0	17.0
Demand constraints:	65	70.0	35.0	67.0	82.0	40.0	83.0	83.0
enterprises able to sell current production but not more	10	10.0	0.0	13.0	0.0	20.0	17.0	16.0
enterprises not able to sell current production	55	60.0	35.0	54.0	82.0	20.0	66.0	67.0

Source: Etude Economique Conseil Canada Inc. Survey, July 1991.

but above all it shows that an effort has been made to adapt to the new economic environment, also by enterprises which formerly benefited from strong protection. No microenterprise established since 1988 has acquired new equipment.

Impact on products and markets

The investment effort made by enterprises did not result in a notable change in the range of products. Only 22 per cent of the enterprises declared that they had modified their range of products (Table 7.8), and these changes were essentially within the metal-products sector (69 per cent), the textile/clothing sector (41 per cent) and the soap/cosmetics sector (27 per cent). The food-products, wood/furniture and building materials subsectors are sectors where the range was modified little or not at all. In fact, the production in these branches is less vulnerable to competition from imported products, either because it is standardized (building materials) or because it corresponds to the specific tastes of the market supplied (food products, wood/furniture). Changes in the range of products were made essentially by very small and small enterprises, and by medium-sized and large enterprises (Table 7.9). In addition, more than one third (37.5 per cent) of the VSEs and half (50 per cent) of the SEs established since 1988 declared that they had modified their range of products, whereas the equivalent percentages for older firms are 24 per cent and 20 per cent, respectively. Young entrepreneurs are looking for captive markets and some are trying to find them not just by diversifying their production, but also by diversifying their outlets. Thus 58 per cent of the enterprises in the sample claimed that they had diversified their market (Table 7.8), notably those operating in the textile/clothing (88 per cent), building materials (90 per cent), food-products (55 per cent) and soap/cosmetics (55 per cent) sectors. These changes were made particularly by the medium-sized and large enterprises as well as small enterprises, especially those established after 1988, 64 per cent of which stated that they had penetrated new markets.

Impact on exports of finished products

Increasing the export of manufactured products is generally one of the objectives sought by structural adjustment programs as the domestic market is too small to support the growth of the industrial sector on its own. Mali is a weak exporter of manufactured products, even to the ECOWAS. This is confirmed by the survey results. Only 15 per cent of enterprises export (Table 7.8) and more specifically, enterprises in the textile/clothing sector. Contrary to what one might think, enterprises in the food-products sector export the least. An encouraging fact is, however, that the number of exporting enterprises is twice as high among enterprises which were established after the adjustment process began. Among these, the small enterprises are those which show the most dynamism in export markets: 80 per cent of exporting SEs in the sample were established after 1988. The interest in exporting is clear for all of the firms surveyed (43 per cent envisage producing for export) and especially for the owners of very small enterprises (45 per cent) and small enterprises (50 per cent) (Table 7.9), more particularly for those established since 1988 (75 per cent and 86 per cent of them, respectively, envisage producing for export). The lack of knowledge of markets and export channels, but above all the difficulty in obtaining credit to produce for export, are the main difficulties noted.

Impact on imports

As Mali is a member of the WAMU, enterprises from the industrial sector generally do not encounter problems in obtaining the necessary currencies to purchase imported inputs. From this standpoint, the adjustment should not have a significant

Table 7.9 Impact of the adjustment by size of enterprise (per cent)

	Total	*Micro*	*VSE*	*SE*	*MLE*
Purchase of new equipment	41	28	45	42	64
Range of products	22	9	26	31	27
Markets penetrated	58	63	45	58	82
Share of imported raw materials:					
current	—	55	84	94	93
increased since 1988	37	22	45	42	46
decreased since 1988	17	25	10	19	9
Difficulty in obtaining or high price:					
of local raw materials	45	57	42	45	11
of imported raw materials	48	40	50	45	78
Difficulty in obtaining credit	54	58	49	59	50
Competition stiffer	68	72	77	58	55
Strongest competition:					
small firms	68	88	74	54	27
imports	15	6	10	15	55
Access to credit					
credit obtained	25	3	23	44	55
tried to obtain	6	4	4	12	9
Exporting enterprises (directly or indirectly)	15	9	13	19	27
Enterprises envisaging exporting	43	41	45	50	27
Supply constraints:					
enterprises able to sell more	35	16	55	50	0
Demand constraints	65	84	45	50	100
able to sell current production but not more	10	10	6	13	18
not able to sell current production	55	74	39	37	82

Source: Etude Economique Conseil Canada Inc. Survey, July 1991

effect on the import capacity of firms. However, the adjustment programmes are accompanied by a liberalization of exports and a realignment of customs duties to reduce differences between the rate on inputs and the rate on finished products. The effect sought is to substitute products of a local origin for imported raw materials.

The customs reform in Mali was undertaken in the framework of SAP 1, and not all of the measures which are stipulated have been implemented yet. The effects of this reform are not yet totally felt by the industrial operators. The survey shows that, since 1988, for 37 per cent of the enterprises the share of imports in their raw materials has grown, whereas for 17 per cent it has fallen. This tendency to increase imports holds for all of the enterprises irrespective of their size and the year of their establishment, except as far as microenterprises established since 1988 are concerned; a larger proportion of the latter entrepreneurs declared that they had reduced the share of imported raw materials (Table 7.9). The textile/clothing subsector has the largest number of enterprises which have experienced a rise in the share of imported raw materials. Only enterprises in the wood/furniture sector declared that they use less imported raw materials; this is due to a fall in activity within that sector rather than to the substitution of imports by local inputs.

For the moment, adjustment does not seem to have given rise to the anticipated effects with regard to a more intensive use of local resources. Apart from the arguments concerning the incomplete carrying-out of the reforms, other explanations can be given as to the interpretation of these results. First of all, the overvaluation of the CFA franc as compared to the currencies of the countries supplying the raw materials has kept the real economic cost of imported inputs relatively less expensive; secondly, it is possible that with the deregulation of domestic prices, the ratio of relative prices did not undergo notable change in favour of local products. In this respect, too high a price of local raw materials constitutes a problem for 45 per cent of the enterprises, which is the same number of enterprises complaining about the high price of imported products (Tables 7.8 and 7.9). Finally, it is possible that the relatively slight reduction in imported inputs originates from the industrial structure in Mali; the price elasticity of domestic demand is limited by the absence of national substitutes for imported products.

Impact on competition

The adjustment is intended to stimulate both national and international competition by deregulating economic activity and liberalizing commercial exchanges. At the beginning of adjustment, imports constituted the main threat to national enterprises, particularly for the large ones in the modern sector which operated in import substitution markets.

This scenario seems to be applicable in Mali taking into account the survey results. Imports are cited by the large enterprises as the main source of competition: nearly 55 per cent of them feel threatened by the entry of competing foreign products (Table 7.9). Small enterprises, for their part, are less sensitive to the intrusion of imported products. They operate on different markets and the competition from other small firms is what threatens their survival. For 68 per cent of the units of the sample, competition from other small enterprises has become stronger since 1988, particularly for the very small enterprises (74 per cent) and small enterprises (53 per cent).

Impact on viability

The impact of adjustment on the viability of enterprises depends on the capacity of entrepreneurs to adjust to the new economic context based on greater competition and better access to external markets. Exporting enterprises are in a better position to take advantage of the new reforms, whereas import substitution firms are affected negatively because their viability is directly threatened by the increased competition as a result of the elimination of quotas and the harmonization of tariff protection. The data in the survey confirm this interpretation. In answer to the question on the viability of their enterprise, 40 per cent of the entrepreneurs declared that their enterprise was more profitable, 43.5 per cent that is was less profitable and 16.3 per cent stated no change. The enterprises which declared that they were more profitable are essentially very small enterprises and small enterprises in the textile/clothing and food-products subsectors.

Enterprises established since 1988 are comparatively more profitable: 56.5 per cent of the enterprises created since that year declared they were more profitable, as compared to 34.8 per cent of those created before that year. The medium-sized and large enterprises seem particularly penalized by the adjustment measures: 73 per cent of them declared that they were less profitable, confirming the vulnerability of import substitution firms to changes in the economic rules of the game. There is a strong correlation between exports and viability, and this correlation is stronger for exporting enterprises created since 1988: 75 per cent of the exporting VSEs and 60 per cent of exporting SEs declared that they were more profitable, and these percentages are 100 per cent and 75 per cent, respectively, for those created since the structural measures were taken.

Constraints with regard to continuation of the adjustment

The evolution of demand for local manufactured products will constitute one of the determining factors in the continuation of the adjustment process which is taking place in the Mali industrial sector, and it will condition its success unless there are new exogenous shocks. Growth in demand will encourage firms to make the required investments to become more efficient and more competitive, which in turn will bring about growth of production and employment. Tables 7.8 and 7.9 give a few indications as to the constraints of supply and demand as perceived by the entrepreneurs interviewed. The data in these tables indicate that the enterprises in the sample are severely restricted by the low level of local demand: 55 per cent of enterprises declared that they could not sell current production and 10 per cent that they could sell current production but not more. The weakness of demand affects microenterprises, and medium-sized and large enterprises most of all. The very small enterprises and small enterprises, on the other hand, have supply-related problems: 50 per cent at least sell their entire production and could sell more (particularly firms in the textile/clothing and building materials branches). The factors which limit supply are mainly the chronic insufficiency of working capital (the reason mentioned by nearly 65 per cent of VSEs and SEs which could produce more)[4]. The other factors which also have a negative effect on production capacity are: (i) the lack of storage infrastructure (damage of production, notably in the rainy season), (ii) fluctuations of prices of agricultural inputs, notably out of season and (iii) deterioration or lack of transportation infrastructures hindering regular supply of raw materials.

Financing enterprises and access to credit

Table 7.10 gives an overview of all of the information obtained from the entrepreneurs with regard to the financing of their enterprises. This data confirms the conservative practice of the banking system both with regard to its willingness to finance industrial operations and with regard to the conditions of access to credit. They also show that despite the reorganization of the banking system undertaken in the context of the structural adjustment programmes, access to financing remains a major constraint for enterprises.

As far as financing at the beginning of activities is concerned, only 10 per cent of the enterprises, mainly small, medium-sized and large enterprises, had the benefit of receiving funds from a bank or a promotional agency. In most cases, however, the main source of financing at the beginning of activities was personal savings (36 per cent of the enterprises), followed by loans or donations from the family (24 per cent) and finally, profits from other businesses (19 per cent).

Banks are less inclined to provide capital to set up a business, but are more willing to finance projects for expansion or working capital. In other words, they tend to support operations which are indicative of more mature enterprises, which have a better structure and have successfully got through the critical beginning phase. This only benefits large-scale industrial units, however. Of the 18 per cent of the enterprises which benefited from loans granted by a bank or promotional agency for their growth or operating needs, 33 per cent are VSEs, 37 per cent are SEs and 80 per cent are MLEs. Other sources of financing continue to be personal savings (22 per cent) and loans and gifts from the family (11 per cent).

Purchases of raw materials are financed directly from profits of the company by 61 per cent of entrepreneurs interviewed, whereas 15 per cent finance them with the help of advances from clients, 13 per cent with credit from suppliers. Very few firms (1 per cent) have a bank overdraft facility, mainly the medium-sized and large enterprises. Since the structural adjustment measures were taken, new equipment was financed to 75 per cent by re-injecting profits of the company or contributions from the family or friends. The breakdown by size of the company does not show major differences, except for small enterprises which benefited in 27 per cent of the cases from loans granted by banks or by a promotional agency.

Since they are operating in increasingly competitive markets and are limited in their growth by the moderate demand in the market, the enterprises have serious difficulty in even finding funds for their working capital to finance their current operations: 78 per cent of the firms interviewed declared that they are in need of funds for their working capital and 80 per cent state that they need funds to expand. The problem of access to bank financing, added to the shortage of own funds, means that enterprises are willing to accept strict conditions in order to obtain credit. Forty-five per cent of the enterprises questioned considered that it would be helpful

Table 7.10 Financing of enterprises and access to credit (per cent)

	Total	*Micro*	*VSE*	*SE*	*MLE*
Financing for establishing an enterprise (main source)					
Profits from other business	19	23	13	19	27
Personal savings	36	29	42	31	45
Loans or gifts from the family	24	42	29	4	9
Bank or promotional agency loan	10	3	3	23	18
Origin of additional funds for growth or operating needs (main source)					
Profits from other business	6	19	10	—	—
Personal savings	22	52	33	21	—
Savings funds or loan company	1	5	—	—	—
Loan from a small tradesman-supplier credit	5	14	—	5	20
Bank or promotional agency loan	18	—	33	37	80
Main source of financing for purchases of raw materials					
Profits of the company, cash reserves	61	70	61	64	45
Client advances	15	17	16	12	18
Supplier credit	13	10	10	12	36
Bank or promotional agency loan	4	—	6	8	—
Main source of financing of new equipment since 1988					
Profits from the business	24	70	67	18	71
Personal savings	2	—	—	18	—
Loans or gifts from the family	6	20	13	18	—
Supplier credit	4	10	7	—	29
Bank or promotional agency loan	4	—	7	27	—
Difficulty of obtaining credit					
Very difficult	55	90	70	71	70
Quite difficult	8	5	25	5	10
Quite easy	4	5	—	10	10
Very easy	5	0	5	14	10

Source: Etude Economique Conseil Canada Inc. Survey, July 1991.

or very helpful to obtain credit at a rate of interest of some 30 per cent, irrespective of whether it is intended for a new investment or to meet the firm's cashflow needs. In addition, 87 per cent of the enterprises interviewed felt that it was difficult to obtain credit from banks, supposing that they have resources available to grant loans to enterprises. Conditions for obtaining loans are so restrictive that nearly 68 per cent of the enterprises considered that it was useless to apply to a bank or a promotional agency, either because their guarantees were insufficient, (40 per cent of the answers) or because of the complexity of bank procedures (8 per cent) or their own ignorance of these procedures (11 per cent).

Although the number of industrial units which obtained loans from a bank or a promotional agency increases with the size of the company, the problem of access to bank credit affects all firms to the same degree. Between 70 and 90 per cent of the enterprises declared that obtaining a loan from a commercial bank was a difficult operation. Similarly, 73 per cent of the enterprises considered that access to credit was a moderate or major problem, and this is notably the case for 88 per cent of microenterprises, 77 per cent of VSEs, 81 per cent of SEs and 64 per cent of MLEs. (Table 7.11). Financing is particularly lacking during the phase in which an enterprise is being set up, when sales are still insufficient to improve the cash-flow position. Unless they have access to a source of credit, enterprises find themselves in an extremely vulnerable position, and this is the stage of their existence in which new financial mechanisms should be developed or the existing mechanisms should be made more flexible to allow for the support of viable investment projects, taking advantage of profit opportunities, and for the creation of jobs and the improvement of the firm's export potential.

Regulatory environment

The regulatory framework for industrial activity in Mali is one of the most rigid and restrictive ones in West Africa. In addition to the lack of transparency, it is characterized among other things by poorly adapted regulations, cumbersome, complex procedures for the creation or closing down of companies and excessive taxation.

In an unequivocal manner, irrespective of the size of the enterprise or the sector of activity in which it operates, the level of taxation and the obtaining of authorizations for land use are mentioned as the main difficulties imposed by the regulatory context. These two factors constitute a moderate or major problem for 65 per cent (Table 7.11) of enterprises and are a restraint on the realization of any investments. The level of taxation uniformly affects all firms, including microenterprises and very small enterprises which operate in the informal sector. Even though most of them operate outside of the legal framework, they have to pay a flat-rate amount on profits and an operating licence tax. The land use problem affects microenterprises first of all (89 per cent), VSEs (70 per cent) and SEs (76 per cent), whereas medium-sized and large enterprises are by and large able to bear the relative cost of starting up business in an industrial zone.

The obtainment of registration and other authorizations from the State constitutes a moderate or major problem for about one-third of the enterprises, mainly for enterprises with a permanent staff of less than 30 employees. Medium-sized and large enterprises are less affected by problems of this kind, since they have sufficient human resources, financial means and the necessary information to go through the formalities. Several operators complained about the difficulty in ob-

Table 7.11 Regulations constraints and investment incentives (per cent)

	Total	*Micro*	*VSE*	*SE*	*MLE*
General business climate					
Uncertainty about the evolution of the economy					
Moderate/major problem	36	47	38	55	82
No problem	22	35	44	29	18
Attitude of the State towards the private sector					
Modernate/major problem	34	40	31	48	54
No problem	41	52	61	43	36
Regulations					
Level of taxation					
Moderate/major problem	64	80	70	91	100
No problem	9	11	15	9	–
Obtaining registration					
Moderate/major problem	28	56	33	44	18
No problem	32	25	50	44	73
Land use authorizations					
Moderate/major problem	65	89	70	76	36
No problem	19	12	26	16	45
Other State authorization					
Moderate/major problem	31	67	53	50	40
No problem	14	20	27	17	40
Finance and credit					
Access to credit					
Moderate/major problem	73	88	77	81	64
No problem	15	8	19	12	36
Cost of credit					
Moderate/major problem	50	72	73	85	82
No problem	9	7	27	5	18
Obtaining funds from the family					
Moderate/major problem	68	77	77	80	40
No problem	18	16	20	20	40
Other problems					
Level of demand					
Moderate/major problem	41	63	29	40	45
No problem	45	33	58	52	45
Transport					
Moderate/major problem	36	41	44	46	55
No problem	37	55	48	36	45
Obtaining water and electricity					
Moderate/major problem	26	40	37	40	30
No problem	36	47	50	50	70
Obtaining technical assistance					
Moderate/major problem	25	29	29	48	10
No problem	46	62	67	43	70
Lack of information on markets					
Moderate/major problem	24	26	29	30	44
No problem	42	52	58	57	33

Source: Etude Economique Conseil Canada Inc. Survey, July 1991.

taining approval under the investment code, and even though the authorities set up a 'one stop' system, the approval procedures are still long and complex.

The attitude of the State with regard to the private sector does not seem to constitute a reassuring element for the small, medium-sized and large enterprises. This perception of the economic environment could hinder the positive supply response, particularly if the relative constraints on credit and demand were abolished. Political stability and a positive attitude towards the private sector are likely to reduce the negative effects arising from uncertainty about the economic environment.

From the information contained in Table 7.11 and, in addition, from the comments made by entrepreneurs, the level of taxation and the difficulties in gaining access to credit are major obstacles to continuing structural adjustment of the industrial sector for the time being. More than 82 per cent of entrepreneurs would like the authorities to relax taxation and use a less coercive policy with regard to overdue payment penalties. Simplifying taxation is also very much desired by certain economic operators who complain about the increasing number of rates and who would prefer that the authorities merge the different taxes into one single tax. Entrepreneurs would also like other measures to be taken to make the current regulations more flexible or to reinforce them in certain cases. The increased flexibility desired by entrepreneurs includes, among other things, (i) easier access to the ownership of land, (ii) access to public markets, (iii) simplification of procedures for the establishment of companies and of import and export formalities. They would like the authorities to adopt measures which reinforce the legislative context with regard to the repression of unfair competition and fraud. They would also like the authorities to give them more protection.

Consequently, even though the Mali authorities have undertaken to remodel and simplify the regulatory framework, these reforms are, in the opinion of several entrepreneurs, still insufficient. Many measures are still needed to establish a degree of confidence which can stimulate production despite the fact that the level of demand in Mali is sensitive to the weather and that bad weather can annul the achievements of the adjustment at any time.

Conclusion

The survey of Mali enterprises proved the existence of a potential base of dynamic enterprises, the creation of which was stimulated by the economic liberalization policies pursued since the beginning of the 1980s. In particular this is the case for very small and small enterprises in the textile/clothing and food products subsectors, which operate in an environment in which competition has intensified because of the increase in the number of enterprises and which are trying, by means of exports, to get around the growth constraints of the narrow local market. The very small enterprises and small enterprises are better integrated in the local economy, where they try to exploit the resource base; they also seem to have responded best to the incentives offered. They are blocked in their expansion, however, by constraints on supply (access to credit, the procurement of raw materials), unlike the microenterprises and the medium-sized and large enterprises, which have demand problems (limited markets, competition from imports).

The adjustment process which began more than three years ago has not led to all of the anticipated structural changes, both with regard to production (little diversified and very much geared toward the domestic market) and with regard to the more intensive use and valorization of local resources. However, several young entrepreneurs owning enterprises created since 1988 seem to diverge from traditional patterns and orient part of their production to export markets. Although much progress has been made, several financial and regulatory rigidities persist, blocking the possibilities of a positive response of supply based on the structural changes which would make Mali's industrial sector less vulnerable to outside impulses. From this point of view, the following measures in particular would be desirable :

- improvement of access to bank credit, either by increasing the flexibility of current conditions or by developing new financial instruments (for guarantees);
- simplification and adjustment of taxation, so that it penalizes business less and can be an incentive to investment;
- facilitation of operating conditions of firms by continuing and reinforcing reforms to simplify regulations;
- promotion of access of small enterprises to public markets, especially markets opened up for projects financed by foreign aid, in order to stimulate the level of domestic demand. Sub-contracting between Mali firms could be encouraged at this point;
- setting up of information mechanisms for markets and export possibilities, especially for the benefit of small enterprises which do not have the financial means nor the human resources to canvas markets;
- setting up of mechanisms for consultation between operators and institutions which are directly or indirectly involved in the dynamics of industrial development in order to improve the organization and operation of the industrial sector, to create a dialogue between operators and public authorities, to identify the specific constraints for each subsector of industry and to find the required solutions on the basis of a mutual agreement.

Structural adjustment and small-scale enterprise development in Zimbabwe

CLEVER MUMBENGEGWI

Introduction

This chapter addresses the implications of the Economic Structural Adjustment Programme (ESAP) on small-scale enterprise development in Zimbabwe. Due to the relative infancy of the programme, which was only launched in January 1991, not much quantitative data exists to sustain an empirical assessment of the magnitudes of these implications. Consequently, this is not an empirical paper but a modest *ex ante* effort to examine the likely impacts of this economic reform package as it takes shape and form.

The chapter is divided into four parts. The first part clarifies some conceptual issues surrounding the debate on the role of small-scale enterprises in economic development. The second part situates the Zimbabwean small-scale enterprise sector within the wider debate on industrialization and economic development strategies after which the principal objective of this paper is addressed. The final part provides the summary, conclusions and suggested areas for further research.

Some conceptual issues in the SSE debate.

A discussion of structural adjustment and small-scale enterprises must be clear as to the conceptual definition of the small-scale enterprise sector. There is little consensus as to the meaning of term 'small-scale enterprise' let alone what a small-scale enterprise development strategy entails. In contemporary Zimbabwean debates on the role of SSEs three definitions seem to emerge. The first is inspired by recent donor-funded surveys of SSEs. These studies tend to focus on the unregistered, non-agricultural, income-generating activities of the poor. As such, no distinction is made between an informal-sector activity and a small-scale enterprise. The use of the term 'microenterprises' to describe such activities does little to clarify the confusion. The second arises from the research interests of academics and other researchers. This tends to focus on unregistered economic activities which are deemed to have the potential to 'graduate' into viable, registered formal-sector enterprises. The third sense of an SSE finds support from the established business community such as the Confederation of Zimbabwean Industries (CZI), Zimbabwe National Chamber of Commerce (ZNCC), the Small Enterprise Development Corporation (SEDCO), commercial banks and other financial institutions.

This refers to registered, formal-sector enterprises, whose size is defined by any of a number of criteria such as number of employees or annual turnover. The CZI claims that 80 per cent of its estimated membership of 1300 businesses falls within the small enterprise category, defined as businesses with an annual turnover of less than Z$0.5 million.[1] While various interest groups are taking positions on this issue, the Zimbabwean government seems undecided as to what it means by 'small-scale enterprises', let alone how to articulate a strategy for their development.

This diversity of conceptual perceptions of SSEs poses a problem from a development-strategy point of view. While it is true that all these types of activities are prevalent in the Zimbabwean economy, from the perspective of articulating a development strategy for SSEs it is essential to have a clear notion of which types of economic activities to promote actively and which to tolerate as an unhappy aspect of the underdeveloped state of the economy.

The second issue pertains to the analyst's perspective as to what an SSE strategy entails. Two perspectives seem to prevail in the debate. The first perceives SSE development as an integral part of an overall industrialization strategy while the second perspective relegates SSE development to aspects of social-welfare concerns with the marginalized condition of the poor. The perspective adopted is important in at least two respects. Firstly, it establishes the threshold of the analyst's expectations in setting targets as to what an SSE-based development strategy could conceivably contribute to the overall development of the economy. Secondly, the policy initiatives motivated under the two perspectives are likely to differ in several fundamental ways. In the former case, an SSE development strategy would be based on some implicit assumptions about the viability of SSEs as individual economic units and the existence of broader intra-sectoral linkages with large-scale enterprises. In the latter case, the threshold of the analyst's expectations is likely to be lower since the intrinsic promotion of SSEs arises from a perceived malfunctioning of the formal economy. It is thus a response to the poor economic growth performance and low labour-absorptive capacity of the large-scale enterprise sector, leading to the familiar problems of unemployment, declining living standards, and abject poverty for a significant proportion of the population. Small-scale enterprise promotion is seen as a convenient solution to a transient problem. Thus, the second perspective fails to see SSEs as an engine of the development process but rather an aspect of the social dimensions of adjustment whose necessity disappears with the success of the economic structural adjustment programme. An assessment of the *ex ante* impacts of structural adjustment in Zimbabwe must be done against the backdrop of the above conceptual issues. In the Zimbabwean case, it is still too early to determine whether the increasing interest in SSEs is due to the need to integrate them into an overall industrialization strategy or simply as an aspect of social-welfare programmes to deal with the malfunctions of the formal sector.

Zimbabwe's manufacturing sector

In order to discuss the impact of ESAP on SSEs, it is essential to situate the SSE sector in the context of the manufacturing sector as a whole. By Sub-Saharan African standards, Zimbabwe's manufacturing sector is fairly advanced and well-diversified in the range of products it manufactures (Riddell, 1988). Several historical factors, such as the formation of the Federation of Rhodesia and Nyasaland (1953–64) and the Unilateral Declaration of Independence (UDI) 1965–79 have accounted for this. The former provided the initial impetus for manufacturing growth by affording the advantages of an enlarged market, an optimistic climate for foreign investment and a larger pool of skilled managerial, technical and professional personnel (Riddell, 1988). But the most notable expansion and diversification took place during the latter period. This was due to a deliberate policy of import substitution pursued by the state through interventionist policies such as:

(a) import restrictions on products that could compete with domestically manufactured goods,
(b) a comprehensive system of foreign exchange controls to encourage the domestic production of import substitutes,
(c) forced savings and investment by use of blocked funds or non-repatriatable profits of foreign companies,
(d) export incentives, and
(e) non-price incentives to foster diversification and strengthen forward and backward linkages with the agricultural sector especially in the food processing industries.

The application of these instruments has left a long-lasting impact on the structure and performance of the manufacturing sector. The need for economic structural adjustment and its associated interest in small-scale enterprises as a development alternative can be attributed to the poor performance of the formal manufacturing sector especially during the post-independence decade, 1980–90. Among its characteristics are the following:

(1) It is an inward-looking sector which utilizes imported inputs, raw materials and technology to satisfy a small domestic market. Its growth prospects seem to be constrained by the exhaustion of import-substitution possibilities. Hence the drive for export orientation as the logical sequel to import substitution.
(2) At the firm level, there is a wide product range necessitated by the import substituting drive for self-sufficiency in basic and luxury consumer goods. This product range seems to be too wide for the size of the domestic market. Thus, efficiency gains from specialization and economies of scale are lost with negative implications for export competitiveness.
(3) The sector relies on imported intermediate inputs and machinery to produce finished consumer goods for the domestic market. Thus, it is highly import-dependent with negative implications for the balance of payments.

The foreign exchange shortages that Zimbabwe is experiencing are in part due to this deep-seated structural problem. It tends to be a net user rather than earner of foreign exchange such that only a healthy foreign exchange earnings performance by primary-producing sectors such as agriculture and mining can compensate for the pressure it imposes on the balance of payments.

Ironically, the industrialization policies of the colonial period were pursued with renewed vigour in the post-independence period. This continuity of policy fails to give recognition to the fact that a system that had been instituted to serve the interests of a tiny minority cannot be stretched too far to include the majority of the population without bursting at the seams. The symptoms of this disintegration have already begun to emerge in the form of chronic shortages of foreign exchange to import raw materials, intermediate inputs, spare parts and new machinery. This necessitated the deepening and widening of foreign exchange price and import controls which further soured the investment climate. The net result is a slowing down in manufacturing growth, rising unemployment, shortages of consumer goods, inflation and declining domestic real incomes. Tax revenues can no longer support the large government expenditure programmes resulting in a huge fiscal deficit.

It is against this background that structural adjustment and its associated interest in small-scale enterprises should be considered. The manufacturing sector seems to have reached the limits of its growth under the import substitution policy regime. Table 8.1 presents a few selected indicators of economic performance of the sector over the 1980–90 decade. The figures for manufacturing employment indicate that the sector contributed on average 16.5 per cent of total wage employment. However, the average rate of growth in employment for the sector was 2.1 per cent for the decade, which translates to nearly 5000 new jobs per annum. When compared with over 200,000 school leavers per year, this underscores the dimensions of the unemployment crisis and the need to look at small-scale enterprises as a source of employment generation. Small-scale enterprises are seen as having the advantage of generating more employment per unit of capital investment. Whereas it is estimated that it takes Z$80,000 to generate a single job in the large-scale manufacturing sector, small-scale enterprises need only Z$20,000 . SSEs are also seen as more efficient as they utilize the more abundant resource (labour) and save on the scarce resource (capital). Evidence as to the capital intensity of the sector is seen from the table, in that manufacturing output grew at a faster rate than employment growth.

The share of manufacturing GDP averages about 24 per cent while employment share is only 16 per cent.

Over the period 1981–5, manufacturing's share of total investment (Gross Fixed Capital Formation) declined. So too did the rate of investment as measured by the proportion of manufacturing GDP attributed to gross fixed capital formation. However, there was a slight improvement in the latter half of the decade. Thus it is the failure of the formal manufacturing sector to generate sustained and meaningful development for the majority of the people that has created interest in small-scale enterprises.

Table 8.1 ZIMBABWE Manufacturing sector, selected indicators

	1980	*1981*	*1982*	*1983*	*1984*	*1985*	*1986*	*1987*	*1988*	*1989*	*1990*
Formal Sector Employment											
All sectors (000's)	1009.9	1037.7	1045.9	1033.4	1036.4	1052.5	1081.1	1085.1	1131.2	1166.7	1192.2
Manufacturing Sector (000's)	159.4	173.2	180.5	173.4	166.3	169.6	176.9	177.4	187.3	195.3	197.1
Manuf. Share in Total Employment (%)	15.8	16.7	17.3	16.8	16.1	16.1	16.4	16.4	16.6	16.7	16.5
Growth in Total Employment (%)	2.5	2.8	0.01	–1.2	0.003	1.6	2.7	0.004	4.2	3.1	2.2
Growth in Manufacturing Employment (%)	10.2	8.7	4.2	–3.9	–4.1	2.0	4.3	0.002	5.6	4.3	0.01
Manufacturing GDP (at 1980 Prices)											
Manufacturing GDP (millions Z$)	802.0	881.0	877.0	852.0	809.0	902.0	933.0	949.0	996.0	1055.0	1101.0
Manufacturing Share of Total GDP (%)	24.8	24.9	24.4	24.6	22.8	23.7	24.1	24.7	24.6	24.4	24.9
Growth in Manufacturing Output (%)	15.2	9.9	–0.005	–2.9	–5.0	11.5	14.5	1.7	5.0	5.9	4.4
Investment (at 1980 Prices)											
All Sectors (millions Z$)	528.0	722.0	788.0	765.0	618.0	505.0	518.0	601.0	692.0	710.0	731.0
Investment as % of GDP	15.3	19.2	20.9	20.0	16.2	12.5	12.6	14.7	15.4	15.1	15.3
Manufacturing	123.0	179.0	135.0	121.0	88.0	74.0	112.0	139.0	135.00	138.00	141.00
Manufacturing Share of Total Investment	0.23	0.25	0.17	0.16	0.14	0.15	0.22	0.23	0.20	0.19	0.19
Manufacturing Invest. as % of Manufacturing GDP	15.3	20.3	15.4	14.2	10.9	8.2	12.0	14.6	13.6	13.1	12.8

Sources: CSO, Census of Manufacturing Industry, Water and Electricity, various years. Harare.

Small-scale enterprise sector in Zimbabwe

The political economy of the development of the manufacturing sector in Zimbabwe has been the neglect of the small-scale enterprise sector. This is as true for the colonial period as it is for the post-independence era. However, there are recent indications of a shift to redress this historical neglect as indicated by the following trends:

(1) In the 'Framework for Economic Reform' (FER 1991) which outlines the structural adjustment programme, the importance of the SSE sector is given explicit recognition. The second Five Year Development Plan (1991–95) elaborates on further policy initiatives for this sector.
(2) In private sector organizations, such as CZI, commercial banks, private and public financial institutions and small-scale enterprise development units, promotional schemes are being formed to complement public sector initiatives. Of significance is the formation of the Indigenous Business Development Centre (IBDC) as the political voice of indigenous entrepreneurs. It has an aggressive agenda for the indigenization of the Zimbabwean economy through development of small- to medium-scale enterprises.
(3) In the donor community, co-ordinated efforts to support SSEs are firmly underway. Donor activity in promoting and supporting SSEs had been going on, although without much co-ordination, long before government policy took specific shape or form. Thus, a strong donor lobby to support as well as influence government policies towards this sector is a reality to such an extent that it appears as though government is responding to donor initiatives rather than having a programme of its own.

As a result of past policy neglect, very little is known about the character, range of economic activities and extent of the small-scale enterprise sector in Zimbabwe. The lack of consensus on the meaning of the term 'small-scale enterprise,' let alone what a small-scale enterprise development strategy entails, compounds the extent of our ignorance of this sector. Post-independence studies are yielding conflicting results as to its magnitude, structure, sectoral composition of output, and employment contribution. Much of the conflict reflects the conceptual confusion mentioned above. The common typology in these studies is the distinction between urban and rural small-scale enterprises. In his 1991 study, McPherson finds little difference between urban and rural SSEs in terms of some of the above aspects. Helmsing (1986b) provides a useful conceptual distinction between different types of SSEs in terms of how they are likely to be affected by processes of institutional change and market incorporation. However, his findings on the magnitude and sectoral composition of output and employment contribution stand in contrast to those of the more recent McPherson study (1991). McPherson estimates that there are some 845,000 SSEs, of which 572,065 (67.7 per cent) are rural and 272,935 (32.3 per cent) are urban. He concludes that Zimbabwe has one of the highest densities of SSEs per 1000 population in the Southern and Eastern African regions. This contrasts with Helmsing's contention that the importance of this sector is 'much lower than in other African countries'. Whereas Helmsing concludes that 'manufacturing is less important than retail trade and commerce', McPherson estimates that 70 per cent are in manufacturing, while 23 per cent and 3.4 per cent are in the trading and service sectors respectively. McPherson explains this discrepancy in terms of the limited coverage of Helmsing's study compared with his which surveyed 5575 primary and 1194 secondary enterprises. However, part of the discrepancy could also be due to McPherson's inclusion of certain non-farm, income-generating activities which Helmsing excludes.

Both the Helmsing and McPherson studies concur on the smallness of SSEs in Zimbabwe. The average SSE is a one-person operation using own and family labour. Only 17 per cent of the labour force is in wage employment (McPherson). Whereas Helmsing contends that most activities are seasonal or part-time, generating a secondary source of income, McPherson finds that most of the activities are almost full-time (11 months per year) with 52 per cent generating over 50 per cent of the owner's income. Rural SSEs tend to service small, fragmented local markets.

An important issue is the nature of the linkages between this sector and the large-scale formal manufacturing sector. Helmsing finds that most SSEs tend to use inputs generated by nature and hence have weak backward linkages with the latter. McPherson on the other hand, estimates that about 55 per cent of such enterprises purchase some inputs for further processing, implying stronger backward linkages. Both concur on the weaknesses of the sector's forward linkages. By the McPherson estimates, 97 per cent of SSEs sell their products directly to the final consumer, indicating the lack of any significant forward linkages with established industry.

In this respect, Helmsing raises a number of pertinent issues on the potential growth and effects of market incorporation of rural areas into the broader macro-economy. His observations apply equally to urban SSEs. He categorizes them into two groups. Type I SSEs, are those that 'tend to decline under the impact of institutional and market incorporation' for a number of reasons. Firstly, such incorporation involves processes of rural-urban migration which transfer purchasing power from rural areas to urban centres. The analogue to this argument for urban SSEs is that market incorporation tends to transfer purchasing power to higher urban income groups which purchase the products of established firms. Also, under rising rural incomes SSE products tend to be displaced by the 'superior' factory-made products of the formal-sector manufacturing firms. Furthermore, changes in consumer preferences associated with rising incomes and market incorporation dampen effective demand for urban and rural SSE products. In the end, these SSEs tend to become marginalized to the extreme fringes of rural and urban informal markets. Type II SSEs tend to increase with market incorporation and institutional change. These are the formal-sector, small-scale enterprises, while Type I SSEs boil down to what we have described earlier as the economic activities of the poor.

The lack of dynamism and linkages with the formal manufacturing sector is related to past colonial policies. 'Decisions related to the establishment of the country's manufacturing base ... and ... its expansion owe very little to the indigenous black people of the country' (Riddell, 1988). The formal manufacturing sector has always been owned by the white settler community or foreign capital interests making use of settler skills. Discrimination against the indigenous black population in education, vocational and technical training and in the labour market created barriers for the acquisition of entrepreneurship and managerial skills. For decades, blacks were barred from establishing manufacturing enterprises in urban areas. They were restricted to limited areas such as rural passenger transport, retailing and distribution activities for white-owned urban manufacturing enterprises. This author concurs with Helmsing in concluding that to date, indigenous entrepreneurship remains concentrated in retail trade and distribution activities. The reasons for their continued dominance are the existence of some managerial experience accumulated in running these types of enterprises during the colonial period, lower initial capital and skills requirements and modest barriers to entry. In the urban areas, the limited size of the informal sector SSEs is due to the restrictive laws on the movement of blacks in urban areas, racial residential segregation, business zoning and other municipal by-laws that have resulted in a much smaller informal manufacturing sector in Zimbabwe than in other comparable African countries (Helmsing, 1986b).

Structural adjustment impacts on SSEs

The issues raised so far make an *ex ante* assessment of the implications of structural adjustment on SSEs an extremely difficult and challenging task. The informational requirements to do justice to the subject matter are beyond the scope of this paper. Justice can only be done if detailed knowledge of the economic activities of the different types of SSEs and specific policy instruments to be applied were available. Impacts and analytical conclusions may be influenced, in a fundamental way, by choices of instruments much more than by the broad structural adjustment objectives. The problem is further compounded by the fact that there may be concurrent policy initiatives to promote SSEs that are not intrinsic aspects of the structural adjustment programme. This makes it difficult to disentangle the 'passive' impacts of structural adjustment on SSEs from those of concurrent policy initiatives.

Notwithstanding these observations, the Zimbabwean SAP has some easily identifiable implications for the development of the small-scale enterprise sector. The programme is based on a very simple underlying assumption that the structural adjustment measures 'will further improve the environment for new investment by small enterprises' (FER, 1991) and thus, the benefits expected from the SAP accrue to small-scale enterprises as well.

Key areas of adjustment and the SSE sector

The central theme of the FER is a statement of faith in the superiority of the market over the inherited system of government controls. The 'Framework for Economic Reform' outlines four key areas of adjustment. These are: (1) domestic deregulation of the economy, (2) trade liberalization, (3) monetary and fiscal reforms and (4) supporting sectoral initiatives.

While the first three are not directly targeted to the SSE sector, their impacts have both a direct and indirect bearing on SSEs.

Domestic deregulation and SSEs

The high levels of unemployment, poor growth performance and declining living standards are attributed to the highly-regulated nature of the economy. A shift away from government regulation of the economy to a more market-based policy regime is seen as creating an 'enabling environment' especially (but not exclusively) for small-scale enterprises. Removal of government controls is supposed to improve the business environment, enable entrepreneurs to respond quickly to emerging market opportunities and to promote competition that improves efficiency and productivity gains. Thus, domestic deregulation of the economic and business environment takes a high profile in the Zimbabwean structural adjustment programme. The key areas of domestic deregulation are:

(1) relaxation of investment approval guidelines,
(2) freeing-up of prices,
(3) relaxation of labour market regulations relating to hiring and firing,
(4) replacement of minimum wage legislation by collective bargaining process with no parameters being set by government,
(5) review of restrictive local government by-laws on small-scale entrepreneurs.

In theory, deregulation may increase the contribution of the small-scale enterprise sector via two processes: (i) productivity gains and (ii) lateral expansion. The short- to medium-term effects of the first four deregulation measures are to improve efficiency within existing enterprises much more than the establishment of new enterprises. The effect of the last measure is more likely to promote new enterprises especially of the informal-sector type.

Productivity gain is the key to a sustainable small-scale enterprise development strategy. Under certain assumptions, a less-regulated business environment might be a positive factor contributing to the achievement of this objective if it promotes free entry and competition among enterprises. In the Zimbabwean context, one needs to make this assumption with some caution in light of the structure of the formal manufacturing sector. This assumption (that deregulation enhances domestic competition) needs to be questioned. The outcome depends on the market structure of the industry being deregulated. In Zimbabwe, formal-sector small-scale enterprises might stand to be negatively impacted given the oligopolistic structure of Zimbabwe's manufacturing sector. A possibility exists that 'unfair trade practices', non-price competition, and various types of collusive behaviour may raise barriers to entry for new firms, thus stifling the entry and/or growth of formal sector SSEs. The IBDC proposal for a monopolies commission underscores the concerns of small, especially indigenous, entrepreneurs, that such strategies of established firms may negatively impact them, given the racial undertones characterizing Zimbabwe's business environment (see IBDC manifesto). White domination of the manufacturing sector is a reality and such fears by indigenous entrepreneurs cannot be easily dismissed as being without economic justification. Standard economic theory demonstrates that markets promote competition, efficiency and equitable development under assumptions of equitable initial endowments and access to resources, entrepreneurial skills, markets and technological information. Thus, deregulation *per se* cannot be assumed to promote intrinsically the growth of small enterprises. Hence the need for sectoral initiatives based on 'infant industry'-type arguments to compensate for the market distortions and imperfections in the manufacturing sector.

These theoretical arguments apart, there are other issues that need to be addressed if deregulation is to benefit small enterprises. Those familiar with the African policymaking environment would be aware that policies on paper and those on the ground are not always identical. Thus, during the deregulation process, especially on price control releases, careful attention has to be given to which prices are being freed up. Given the prevalence of monopolies and oligopolies in the manufacturing sector, deregulation of the prices of products that are vital inputs in the manufacturing processes of small enterprises may be a negative factor in their economic viability and competitiveness. So far, the price releases have been implemented on the products of monopolies whose products are inputs into the retailing and distribution activities of indigenous SSEs.

Furthermore, the reforms implemented to date with respect to price deregulation, government bureaucratic procedures and the labour market environment accrue directly to large enterprises. SSEs benefit if the 'trickle down effects' theory is valid.

Reforms in areas of most tangible promise for informal sector entrepreneurs have yet to occur. This is in the repeal of municipal by-laws regarding zoning, licensing and establishment of manufacturing activities on municipal land. Relaxation of these regulations is bound to lead to lateral expansion of the informal sector to provide a cushion for those people who would be forced out of the formal sector when the initial contractionary impacts of structural adjustment take effect. However, the survival of these low productivity enterprises remains in question if the economy wide positive effects of structural adjustment are realized. Labour would tend to shift back to the formal sector in response to differentials between formal-sector wages and earnings in the informal sector.

Trade liberalization and SSEs

Non tariff trade barriers have always played a prominent role in Zimbabwe's foreign trade regime (Davies, 1988). Foreign exchange allocation and import-licensing regulations were the key instruments used to effect import substitution. In addition to protecting domestic industries, these instruments endowed policymakers with power to direct a scarce resource (foreign exchange) to areas consistent with national (government) objectives. The shift from import substitution to export orientation necessitates a change in the foreign trade policy regime. As such, trade liberalization has assumed the most important place in Zimbabwean debates on structural adjustment. It involves:

(1) gradual dismantling of the foreign exchange allocation system and in its place, expand the open general import licence (OGIL) system;
(2) elimination of import licensing in favour of tariffs and tariff reform as the principal protective devices for domestic manufactures;
(3) exchange-rate adjustment involving the continued depreciation of the Zimbabwean dollar against all hard currencies;
(4) expansion of incentive schemes to promote exports.

These measures are intended to shift resources in favour of the export producing sectors away from those producing for the domestic market. This aspect of the SAP has found much support from the private sector for several reasons. It promises increased access to foreign exchange for the importation of essential raw materials, intermediate inputs, spare parts and new machinery. It simplifies the conduct of foreign trade by eliminating bureaucratic delays and inefficiencies associated with exchange controls and import licensing regulations.

The immediate or short-term effects of trade liberalization are to increase the volume of imports and open up the economy to external competition as more items progressively qualify for OGIL. Raw materials have priority for OGIL treatment in the early stages of the programme, to be followed by intermediate inputs and machinery at later stages of the programme. Consumer goods qualify for OGIL treatment towards the end of the trade liberalization programme in 1995. The increase in imports has immediate adverse balance of payments effects which necessitate balance of payments support from external grants and loans if the SAP is to succeed. Already, only eight months into the programme, the Reserve Bank has had to institute restrictions to curb growth in import demand. The volume of imports is double the resources allocated under the OGIL[2]. The expansion in exports is only anticipated in the medium- to long-term as competition, exchange rate adjustment and export incentives begin to stimulate economic growth and resource allocation efficiency. However, the recently announced monetary policy reforms to curb inflation and the requirement that Zimbabwean exporters quote export prices in terms of hard currencies might act as disincentives to exports.

How these short- to medium-term effects of trade liberalization affect small scale enterprises is by no means obvious. Many of these effects apply as much to SSEs as they do to large-scale enterprises. The problem is that trade liberalization is being implemented without identification of which SSE products have potential to achieve export competitiveness. The often cited export-growth sectors (such as textiles, clothing, furniture etc.) are those already dominated by large-scale enterprises who have an advantage in terms of knowledge of export markets, entrepreneurship and access to foreign trade financing. The lack of these skills among indigenous formal-sector SSEs is indicated by the plethora of import/export firms whose only activity is importing. The export function seems constrained by inadequate knowledge and experience in operating in foreign markets.

If SSEs are in the import-competing sector, i.e. they use imported inputs to produce for the domestic market, they benefit from improved access to foreign exchange to import raw materials etc. but on the other hand, they are exposed to the negative effects of increased competition from imports. The phased nature of the programme over a five-year period is designed to mitigate the adverse effects of the latter and accentuate the positive effects of the former. The magnitude of the competition depends on the products of the SSEs. Competition is likely to be a more serious problem for formal sector SSEs than informal sector. The latter are assumed to produce simple consumer goods for the domestic market which do not come into direct competition with imports.

If SSEs use domestic inputs to produce for the foreign market, growth in world demand, market-penetration strategies and export incentives determine the rate of growth in the sector. In the short term, trade liberalization is more likely to stimulate growth in imports by SSEs in the informal sector than domestic production for external markets. The increased volume of traffic to South Africa and Botswana by women traders bringing in luxury consumer goods for sale on the domestic market where they command higher prices is an indication of this trend. There are relatively low barriers to entry in such cross-border activities and for as long as foreign exchange remains scarce and luxury consumer goods in short supply, these activities will continue to expand because they command higher economic rents per unit of foreign currency than entering into domestic production.

Fiscal and monetary policy reforms and SSEs

Monetary and fiscal policy objectives within the structural adjustment programme involve: (1) curtailment of government spending to reduce the budget deficit; (2) removal of subsidies to parastatals including food subsidies; (3) implementation of cost-recovery measures for government-provided social services especially in health and education sectors; (4) restraint on growth in money supply to curb inflation; (5) market-determined interest rate policies to achieve positive real interest rates.

These measures are intended to achieve and/or maintain external and internal balance. Given that SSEs produce for the domestic market stimulation of domestic incomes is the key to their growth. Unfortunately, in the short run, the effect of the above measures is to reduce domestic demand and incomes which imposes a demand side constraint on the growth of SSEs.

The likelihood of changes in relative prices might also affect the composition of SSEs output. If informal sector SSE products are good substitutes for formal-sector SSEs' output, the fall in real incomes might decrease demand for the former and increase that for the latter through substitution effects. This would be a negative development since it involves movement of factors from high productivity to low productivity sectors of the economy.

Small-scale sectoral initiatives

The 'Framework for Economic Reform' is no substitute for a small enterprise development plan. However, it outlines some sectoral initiatives to promote SSE's. When these measures are taken together with private sector and donor initiatives a basis for a SSE promotional programme can be found. The assumptions underlying these sectoral initiatives are that supply-side factors are more constraining to SSE economic activities than demand-side factors. The FER cites the following supply-side constraints: (1) access to and the cost of finance; (2) a restrictive business and regulatory environment; (3) inadequate managerial and entrepreneurial skills; (4) poor communication and infrastructure.

It gives little or no attention to demand-side issues. This assumption needs to be examined carefully because some factors that manifest themselves as supply-side may in fact be demand-side constraints. For example, up to July 1991, commercial banks and other financial institutions reported that they were 'awash' with surplus funds, yet could not lend to SSEs due to lack of 'bankable' projects from this sector[3]. This apparent contradiction may be the result of lack of effective demand for the products of SSEs manifested as projects with low profitability. On the other hand, it could be the result of imperfections in the financial markets. Thus, it is essential to build a consensus as to what the most critical constraints are in order to develop a plan for the promotion of SSEs.

Another issue that needs careful attention is the trade-off between the sectoral initiatives and other aspects of the structural adjustment programme. For instance, the regime of restrictive monetary and interest rate policies targeted for macroeconomic stabilization simultaneously increases the cost of finance to SSEs and constrains effective demand.

The most comprehensive and articulate programme for SSEs has so far come from the IBDC. It is a programme for promotion as well as indigenization of the small scale enterprise sector. While some of the parallels it draws between the post independence successes in agriculture and the needs of indigenous entrepreneurs in non-agricultural activities can be faulted in a number of respects, it does lay a framework that could form a basis upon which government and donor efforts could be focused. It gives explicit recognition of past policy imbalances against SSEs and especially discrimination against indigenous entrepreneurs. As remedial measures, it calls for 'affirmative action' policies, mobilization of 25 per cent of government contracts for SSEs to boost demand and sectoral devolution of certain aspects of large-scale enterprise operations towards SSEs. These proposals can only be effected through more, rather than less, government intervention in the economy, which may appear inconsistent with the structural adjustment objective of movement towards a market-based economy. But where institutional underdevelopment, market imperfections and/or market failure exist, as appears to be the case, credible economic arguments can justify more rather than less public intervention.

Thus, with the exception of the indigenization aspect of the IBDC programme, most of its action plan are non-contentious issues and consistent with initiatives emanating from government and donor circles. The plan seems to be centred on developing stronger linkages between SSEs and the large-scale enterprise sector.

Government on its part is considering a number of reform measures that may help SSEs move from low-productivity informal sector to higher-productivity formal sector activities. Proposals such as the reform of marketing boards and privatization of some of the functions of parastatals are cases in point. These reforms, if successfully implemented, are likely to open up new areas of economic activities for small enterprises. The notion of large-scale enterprises sub-contracting to SSEs is one that is problematic but if it were feasible it would further strengthen the forward and backward linkages between the two sectors. However, the theoretical assumptions under which all the above measures would be mutually beneficial need to be studied further.

Conclusions

The structural adjustment programme was not conceived with small scale enterprises as its principal target. However, the programme has some direct and indirect implications for this sector. This paper has outlined some of the conceptual difficulties in articulating a small enterprise development strategy, given the history and structure of Zimbabwe's manufacturing sector. It has also indicated some of the likely implications of the structural adjustment programme on the small scale enterprise sector. The diversity of economic activities that come under the rubric of 'small scale enterprise' necessarily means that the impacts are unlikely to be uniform across all SSE categories. On balance, our conclusion seems to be that the short-term impacts are likely to be negative. This is because of the asymmetry between the almost instantaneous impacts of the demand reducing aspects of structural adjustment and the lagged impact of supply-side measures in stimulating enterprise production response. The long-term effects are difficult to determine a priori. This is because they depend, in a much more fundamental way, on the specific combination and sequencing of policy instruments. Since the structural adjustment programme is still in its infancy, these have as yet to be articulated.

The unfortunate aspect of the current policy shift towards SSEs in Zimbabwe is that it is occurring in the absence of both conceptual clarity as to the role of SSEs in the context of the development of the manufacturing sector and without much empirical knowledge as to the dynamics of the sector that would make it succeed where large-scale enterprises fail to alleviate the problems of unemployment, poor growth and declining living standards. Theoretical and empirical research are urgently needed to assist in the process of policy formulation. The urgency is underpinned by the fact that development thinking is prone to 'pander' to fashionable trends — and SSEs are currently in 'vogue', especially in the donor community. Such research can help situate small enterprises within the wider debate on development strategies, and generate empirical knowledge that can inform on the issues of enterprise dynamics and growth within the overall context of the structural adjustment programme. Government and donors alike are cautioned that the search for development success stories should not proceed without the burden of proof being discharged that a small enterprise-based approach to development is likely to succeed. A credible case for SSEs must be made independent of apparent frustrations with the past failures of large-scale enterprises to generate meaningful and sustained development.

Changing policy regimes for small-scale industries in Latin America. Lessons for Africa?

FRANCISCO URIBE-ECHEVARRÍA

Introduction

Social scientists know that drawing general lessons from specific experiences is a hazardous task. Policymakers acknowledge that replicating initiatives in different settings often leads to unintended results. They also know that the risks are greater when transfers take place between two continents with such diverse socio-economic structures as Latin America and Africa. Therefore, this chapter does not contend that Latin American experiences are necessarily a valid source of inspiration for African countries. My intention is far simpler: to discuss the way in which three Latin American countries have been, and are currently, dealing with these issues; leaving the task of extracting eventual lessons, if there are any, to the reader interested in African development.

The transitional character of current policy environments in the three countries (Chile, Colombia and Ecuador) has complicated the presentation. Chile had moved closer to a 'size neutral' policy environment while pursuing a strategy to increase economic competitiveness during the 1970s but is now moving back to a more active role for the state. Colombia and Ecuador have initiated similar, though less drastic, policy reforms. While Colombia is moving faster towards a selective internationalization of its economy, Ecuador, however, is still struggling with stabilization problems.

This chapter is organized into three sections. After this brief introduction, the first section presents a profile of previous small-scale industry policy regimes and instruments, and their ensuing transformations. The main conclusions regarding the performance of these policy regimes are summarized in the second section. Lastly, the third section is an attempt to foresee the likely direction of public policy in response to the impact and challenges posed to small-scale industries by rapidly changing policy environments.

Evolution of policy regimes for small-scale industries in Latin America: cases of Chile, Ecuador, and Colombia

Government preoccupation with the development of small-scale industries emerged in Latin America mostly in the 1960s. However, the initiatives fell at quite different moments of the respective industrialization processes. For instance, the most dynamic period of the import substitution strategy had long passed in Chile, but it predates the fastest expansion of industry in Ecuador. While in Colombia, it coincided with the last expansive phase of the manufacturing sector.

Small-scale manufacturing industry (SSMI) policy regimes were adjusted and updated several times. New instruments were progressively added in response to changing goals, policies, and priorities. Thus, the early, and relatively simple, financial and legal instruments evolved into ever more complex structures in the pursute of solutions to regional poverty, and trade problems. However, they suffered no serious structural changes until the recent stabilization and liberalization reforms when many aspects of the older SSMI regimes were dismantled.

The policy environment in which these regimes evolved was in all cases shaped by import substitution strategies. It entailed very sizeable import premiums and a strong anti-export bias created by high and dispersed protection rates; import quota restrictions, overvalued currencies and import licensing procedures. Despite these similarities, some differences, more of degree than of substance, existed and proved very important for the performance of the policy regimes in each case.

Chile, together with Brazil and Argentina, had the highest levels of protection in Latin America with effective rates ranging from –23 per cent to 1000 per cent (Wogart, 1978; ECLAC, 1990a). In general, manufacturing industries were far more protected than primary products, and typically, SSMI was among the most protected. In 1961, effective protection rates (EPRs) and domestic resource costs (DRCs) for these industries were well above 100. By 1967, the mean level of EPRs increased from 133 per cent to 168 per cent and the standard deviation from 117 to 282 per cent due to higher levels of protection for non-traditional intermediate goods. In the mid-1960s the protection given to traditional consumption industries decreased little but continue to be high (Behrman, 1976)[1].

In Ecuador, typical small-scale industry branches were also far more protected than others within the manufacturing sector. Tariff levels were comparable to those observed in Chile in 1974 but unlike Chile they remained high until the 1980s. The value of the EPRs for food and beverage products was calculated at 136 per cent; for textiles, clothing and leather industries at 185 per cent; for wood, wood products and furniture at 133 per cent; and for paper, paper products and printing at 82 per cent. In 1982 they were still 183 per cent, 183 per cent, 163 per cent, and 92 per cent respectively. During this period, protection levels became more homogeneous between industries as those of non-traditional industries doubled (Fernández, 1990).

Real protection rates for similar industries were much lower in Colombia. All major industries in which small-scale predominated, such as food products, textiles, clothing, paper products, and leather could be considered only modestly protected during the 1960s and 1970s (Wogart, 1978). The rates tended to decrease even further during the 1970s as import duties were reduced and many products transferred to the free import system. On average import duties for consumption goods had fallen sharply from 85 per cent in 1973 to 34 per cent in 1982. Simultaneously the list of products under the free import regime increased from 14 per cent to 70 per cent (Acevedo *et al.*, 1985). Still, despite the shift towards export promotion in 1967, export products (primary and manufactured) were less favoured than capital intensive and import substitution (large-scale) industries.

Significant distortions in factor prices compounded these effects and led to policy environments that: (i) encouraged investment in inefficient but highly protected industries, (ii) discouraged investment in labour-intensive industries; (iii) relieved the pressure for technically-efficient production; (iv) allowed inefficient production organization, (i.e. monopolization of product markets allowed higher than efficient levels of vertical integration); and (vi) transfer large-scale production inefficiencies to small-scale industries via expensive and poor quality intermediate inputs.

Many institutional barriers of the type described by de Soto increased the scale disadvantages suffered by SSMI. Extensive state regulations and discriminatory resource allocation, created a complex decisionmaking environment and high transaction costs (de Soto, 1986). In turn, these difficulties to compete within domestic factors market further crippled the sector's capacity to compete in external product markets.

To stimulate stronger performances the three governments chose to intervene even further creating special policy regimes to counter the negative impact of the general policy environment. These regimes included tax exemptions, increased protection, investment incentives, and organized support systems. *Ad hoc* (concessionary) credit systems and government subsidized individual technical assistance were the backbone of the institutional infrastructure.

Main features of early policy regimes

Actual programmes had started in Chile already in 1961 when the Technical Cooperation Service (SERCOTEC) was created to assist small-scale industry. By the mid-1960s, SERCOTEC had developed the most competent technical assistance programme in Latin America. The programme conducted research and provided advice on production methods, the use of accounting and costing systems, the promotion of sales and marketing, and technological development. To provide technological services, SERCOTEC developed its own mechanical, chemical, and metallurgic specialist teams. The programme also included medium- and long-term loans for small-scale firms and handicrafts.

Further developed by Law Nr. 17.386 of May 1969, the initial strategy relied on two basic instruments (Niccolini, 1988):

Tax exemptions: a fixed scale and a smaller bracket for income and business tax were granted to owners of industrial enterprises and handicraft workshops with capital not exceeding 25 minimum salaries, and employing 15 or fewer persons;
Financial assistance: the Industrial Development Corporation (CORFO) was instructed to provide credit to acquire capital goods and raw materials at concessionary rates for the beneficiaries of the law.

Later extensions of this law (1973 and 1974) defined a higher upper threshold for eligibility, included non-industrial services, and increased tax exemptions. The changes had virtually no impact since the law was abolished shortly after (1974) in the wake of the mid-1970s policy reform.

Financial assistance programmes were initiated in Ecuador in 1961 by the Banco Nacional de Fomento (BNF) and the Corporación Financiera Nacional (CFN). The programme was quite large, granting a total of 11,022 loans for a total of about US$7 million (at 1965 prices). The BNF credit programme was reinforced by technical assistance and training facilities while the CFN programme (Fondo de Promoción y Garantía para la Pequeña Industria) operated through the private banking system (United Nations, 1969).

The law to 'promote handicrafts and small-scale industries' was approved in 1965 and reformulated in 1973. Under this law SSMI received larger benefits than those for industry in general. They included total exemption from payment of import duties for capital goods; partial exemption for raw materials not produced locally; accelerated depreciation; and a variety of other tax exemptions directed to specific types of small firms. A new and more favourable income tax regime was introduced in 1966, and a register to regulate the access to the benefits of the law was created in 1971 and updated in 1973.

Credit terms consistent with their repayment capacity complemented the system. A minimum quota equivalent to ten per cent of the total credit given to large industries was reserved for the sector and was to be lent at the lowest interest rates fixed by the Monetary Authority (RO. 372 20/VIII/73). Financial funds were developed, systems to guarantee credits were created, and technical assistance programmes initiated at the Centro para el Desarrollo (Development Centre, CENDES), Servicio de Capacitación (Industrial Training Service, SECAP), the Centro Nacional para el Desarrollo de la Pequeña Industria y la Artesanía (National Center for Small-Scale and Handicraft Industries, CENAPIA) and the Instituto de Información y Tecnología (Information and Technology Institute, INFOTEC).

This bundle of tax and tariff incentives was supported by a wide range of quota restrictions and their impact vastly increased with a chronic overevaluation of the national currency. In fact, the sucre/dollar exchange rate remained fixed for twelve years in the period 1970–82 despite the high levels of internal inflation.

The Colombian regime was far less institutionalized and less regulated than those of Chile and Ecuador. Policies dealing with credit technical assistance tailored to the needs of small-scale industries had existed since the 1960s but no general law compiling these initiatives was passed until the 1980s. SENA (Servicio Nacional de Aprendizaje), although not explicitly concerned with SSMIs, has provided a valuable contribution in skill development (Cortes *et al.*, 1987). The first, and relatively small, credit programme for small-scale industries was created by the Banco Popular. Additionally, CFP (Corporación Financiera Popular) has played a key role in supplying promotional credit to SSMIs assuming the administration of the World Bank Loan Programme in Colombia.

New objectives, priorities and instruments

By the end of the 1960s the policy objectives of small-scale industries had become far more complex encompassing export promotion, regional and social development goals in all three countries. Specific sets of constraints, incentives, and allocation rules were introduced for regions, industries and types of firms. Along this process clearer differences emerged by country as these changes were adapted to specific development junctures. For instance, Ecuador and Chile paid, until the mid-1970s, special attention to export and regional development promotion while social and regional objectives became far more important in Colombia.

A radical departure from the conventional policies took place in Chile during the second half of the 1970s when a wide-ranging policy reform was implemented by the military government. This reform marked the end of the protectionist period, rolled back state intervention and changed the attitude towards the sector: firm size nearly ceased to be considered a relevant policy issue.

Chile: from boosting import substitution to a competitive open economy.

Chile experienced periodic phases of very low rates of economic growth during the whole period stretching from the 1930s to the 1950s. The exhaustion of the import substitution strategy was one of the root causes since the levels of import substitution of the early 1960s had already been reached before the Second World War but protection once granted proved difficult to dismantle (Behrman, 1976).

Given the anti-export bias of the policy, growth became dependent on the expansion of domestic consumption whose cyclical stimulation by the government led to equally cyclical inflationary pressures. The surge of interest on small-scale industries that led to formal policies is clearly related to these economic problems. Enhancing the efficiency of the traditional sector and reducing the capital costs of generating jobs were key tasks in the domestic demand-led growth strategy to which the import substitution model had become reduced.

Small- and medium-scale industry, given its high labour intensiveness, appeared a promising policy alternative after the failure of the stabilization and liberalization programme of the late 1950s. The intentions to carry out a redistribution of income and political power in the late 1960s strengthened the importance attached to the sector. Regional and trade issues were also of importance as governments strove to reduce inter-regional inequalities and promote exports.

The export promotion incentives were product specific and few small-scale industries benefited despite the initial government intentions (Selowsky 1970). Regional incentives included exemptions from direct taxation, customs duties on imports and raw materials, and prior deposits on capital goods, fuels, and raw materials. Although these benefits were complemented by special credit plans the impact of these regimes was rarely important. Moreover, the demise of many of the industries created under these regimes in the wake of the policy reform of the 1970s proved that they had failed to achieve economic sustainability (Román, 1990).

Impact of policy reforms. Stabilization and liberalization programmes had been tried out three times during the 1955–75 period but ended in failure. The reform that finally succeeded in the second half of the 1970s marked the end of the protectionist period. Paramount to the new approach were: (i) a concern with macroeconomic balances; (ii) reduced state participation in the economy; (iii) non-discriminatory incentive regimes; and (iv) an economy open to external competition.

In this context, drastic legal and institutional reforms were approved in labour legislation, capital markets, property rights, and external commerce. Central to the new doctrine was the idea that a single set of rules for all sectors and firm sizes was essential to allocate resources broadly in line with competitive capacities and comparative advantages. An inevitable consequence of these reforms was the elimination in December 1974 of the special regime for small-scale industries initially created in 1960 and formalized in 1969.

SERCOTEC has retained some non-credit support activities and a guarantee scheme, called the Fondo Nacional de Garantía de la Pequeña Industria (National Guarantee Fund for Small-Scale Industry, FOGAPE) was established to facilitate access to credit (Cárcamo, 1989) but credit programmes were transferred to private financial institutions. Some services have been merged into general programmes or institutions catering for small and large firms while in some cases market solutions have been developed[2]. In the field of training, for instance, the 'Estatuto de Capacitación' approved in 1979 reduced the role of the state-run training system (Instituto Nacional de Capacitación, INACAP) and created a demand-driven market for training. All firms can now deduct up to 1 per cent of their annual wage bill from taxes if it is spent on financing employee training.

Non-government responses have partially compensated for the withdrawal of the public sector promoting exports, diversifying financial services, and providing technical assistance (Cárcamo, 1989). Although unemployment reached 20 per cent of the labour force and real income fell, the government did not resort to employment-oriented credit assistance, preferring to create two 'minimum employment' programmes: PEM (Programme de Empleo Mínimo) which peaked at 350,000 persons in 1983; and POJH (Programme de Ocupación para Jefes de Hogar) which peaked at 190,000 in 1983. In contrast, many NGOs backed by international funding sought to alleviate the growing poverty by creating and supporting small businesses and workshops (Hardy, 1987; SUR, 1988; de Groot, 1989).

New small-scale industries policy regime. A new policy regime is beginning to take shape under the present government. The strategy differs clearly from a purely 'neutral' approach but also stands in contrast to the interventionist and paternalistic styles of the past. A key concern of the new policy is to support the efforts of enterprises to improve their own efficiency, and to create the material conditions for the continued development of new and existing industries.

Under the banner of the 'modernization of small-scale production' it seeks to allow greater accessibility to financial markets; facilitate access to services that cannot be produced within the firms for reasons of scale; and improve technical efficiency and market performance (Ominami, 1991).

Central to these efforts are more flexible guarantee requirements, a credit card system, and a new system of credit guarantees. A Technical Assistance Fund will subsidize some forms of consultancy services starting in 1992, and a competitive fund (PRO-CHILE) will finance services for non-traditional export initiatives by groups of producers.

Support to improve efficiency and performance includes courses on management techniques, and information systems, (SERCOTEC). The Science and Technology programme includes the creation of FONDEF (Fondo de la Investigación Científica y Tecnólogica and FONTEC (Fondo de Desarrollo Tecnólogico y Productivo). And, the new 'Europa Foundation' will provide demonstration and instruction centres to disseminate the use of new technologies.

The approach to poverty alleviation problems has also changed. FOSIS (Fondo de Solidaridad Social), an integrated fund aimed at repaying part of the *social debt* inherited from the application of policy reform is currently reassessing the nature of its microenterprise programme to position it within the realm of economic initiatives.

Ecuador: the oil boom and the small-scale sector

Industrialization began in earnest in the mid-1960s in Ecuador, and much later than in Chile and Colombia. Until 1972 the industrial sector grew slowly based on the internal market and was mostly oriented to meet the demand of higher income segments. The profile of the sector was typical of this model: concentration of ownership, high levels of profit, low rates of job generation, and dependency upon foreign capital and intermediate goods.

Contrary to most other Latin American countries, Ecuador greatly benefited from the oil price hike of the early 1970s and experienced strong economic growth until the early 1980s. However, employment grew barely 0.3 per cent in industry over the boom period while aggregate production increased around 18 per cent in real terms. Average labour productivity grew 16.2 per cent and the average size of firms increased from 46 to 73 employees (FENAPI-INSOTEC, 1986). Within this framework, the employment importance of small- and medium scale- industry decreased from 39 to 31 per cent and most of the reduction took place in small industry. The real role of the incentives granted by the government is still unclear. For instance, FOPINAR, created in 1981 (Fund for the Promotion of Small-Scale and Handicrafts Industries), financed the creation of some 7900 jobs in four years (1981–4).

Regional and trade objectives were also of importance in Ecuador, and a tax rebate mechanism, with incentives similar to the Chilean system was created. As in the Chilean case, industrial products did not benefit much and its participation in exports decreased from 27 per cent (early 1970s) to slightly over 22 per cent (early 1980s). A strong economy during the oil boom encouraged distributive policies along regional lines. Several laws (1973–6) granted benefits to industrialists wanting to locate, or relocate, outside Guayas and Pichincha in designated Regional Promotion Zones. In 1989 the regional focus was sharpened by the concession of 10 year' income-tax holidays and other benefits but this new legislation was short lived since it was cancelled within the same year in the wake of structural adjustment policies (Fernández, 1990).

The measures adopted by the Monetary Authority in 1982 acknowledged the end of the boom period and the onset of the crisis gave more importance to short-term employment creation and poverty alleviation. A number of small microenterprise projects in the private sector and a National Microenterprise Programme (NMP) in the public sector sprang up under the new policy. Modelled after the Colombian experiences, the NMP was co-ordinated by a head organization (Unidad Ejecutora del Programme Nacional de Micro-empresas) and the National Corporation to Support Popular Economic Units (CONAUPE).

Policy reform. Policy reform is still in the process of implementation in Ecuador. Structural policies have included a more realistic valuation of the national currency, tariff reduction bringing down the maximum duty from 335 per cent to 35 per cent, the elimination of surcharges and nearly all non-tariff import barriers. The cancellation of industrial promotion laws, the rationalization of special tax regimes (tax reform)[3]; the liberalization of interest rates and the elimination of special labour regimes applicable to SSMI (May 1990) have created a more scale-neutral policy regime.

Within this context, the Ministry of Industry has proposed new initiatives for SSE (Valarezzo, 1991): (1) improving access to credit; (2) institutional reforms; (3) development of new services; (4) export promotion; (5) research; and (6) training of human resources.

To improve access to credit alternative forms of financing (leasing, factoring) are to be encouraged, creating credit lines for risk capital; and incorporating the SSMI in credit lines dedicated to industrial restructuring. This is complemented by institutional reforms to reduce the costs imposed by regulations (i.e. import and export procedures); and ease local licensing requirements.

Regarding services, emphasis will be placed upon gathering market and technical information, preparing consultants, providing technical assistance and management training, promoting sub-contract exchanges, and strengthening technological development centres. Priority will also be given to those services that (1) promote the role of the small-scale sector in external trade; and (2) direct the desired restructuring process.

Colombia: import substitution and export diversification

During the last thirty years, the Colombian economy has exhibited a considerable dynamism. In spite of a strong growth performance, a structural imbalance between the rapid growth of the labour force and the limited capacity of the urban economy to generate employment became evident after 1961–2 (Employment Mission, 1986). Rates of unemployment surged to 10–11 per cent by the end of the decade, and the real value of wages fell.

The economic performance improved during the early years of the 1970s. Employment creation grew faster than labour supply, (5.9 per cent against 4.7 per cent respectively), and real wages also increased. During this period the small-scale sector experienced a strong expansion. According to DANE, the employment in firms from 5 to 99 workers grew at an annual average of 4.6 per cent and its output rose somewhat faster. This positive development in which employment expansion was compatible with higher levels of efficiency and higher profits continued, though at slower rates, until the recession of the early 1980s.

A fast-growing demand for industrial goods must have played a substantial role in bringing about this boom. A shift to the external markets in the large-scale sector may also have been important in opening new opportunities in the domestic market. In addition, some small-scale industries, specially in the frontiers with Ecuador and Venezuela, also benefited from rising external demand given the oil boom in these countries.

On the supply side, the analysis by Cortes *et al.* suggests that the availability and willingness of capable entrepreneurs, capital and machinery seems to have played the most important role in this performance. In contrast, public policy appears to have been 'neither a major support nor a strong deterrent' (1987). The dynamism of the industrial sector decreased thereafter and by the 1975–80 period the ratio between the rates of growth of gross manufacturing and total domestic product had fallen to 0.86 from 1.28 in the 1960–4 period (Acevedo *et al.*, 1985).

Export promotion and regional issues. The decreasing role of import substitution was evident as its contribution to industrial growth had already fallen to about 4 per cent by the end of the 1960s from the high mark of 38 per cent in 1953–63. At that point in time Colombia introduced a series of measures aimed at modernizing agriculture, reducing unemployment, and diversifying exports that had a strong impact upon the small-scale sector.

In contrast with the Chilean and Ecuadorian cases, the Colombian export-promotion incentive package was not aimed at specific products and certainly not addressed at small-scale industries. Created in 1967 (Decree 444) its main instruments were the 'sliding peg' system for the foreign exchange rate, tax incentives (CAT system), tariff regulations, and credit subsidies. A third major programme, Plan Vallejo, allowed exporters to import raw materials, intermediate inputs, and capital equipment without prior licence, and advance import deposits free of custom duties. The combined impact of these measures was quite large, giving some 60 per cent of additional income in pesos for each dollar of export (Wogart, 1978) and seems to have played a role in the increasing contribution of export diversification to industrial growth, from one per cent in the 1953–63 period to fifteen per cent in the 1968–74 period.

Efforts to promote regional industrialization did not reach a substantial scale until the issuing of special norms to frame the operations of the 'Corporación Financiera Popular' and the 'Fondo Financiero Industrial'. The new norms offered lower rates of interest, longer amortization periods and less stringent guarantees to industrialists willing to locate in intermediate sized cities. The policy also included a special programme to improve basic infrastructure, and to finance the construction of industrial parks.

Employment generation. Two very important characteristics of Colombian small-scale industry (SSI) policies are the early adoption of employment objectives and the surge of non-government institutions. To a large extent, these features can be seen as a response to the alarming situation regarding employment and poverty. The role of SSMI policies expanded beyond industrial development into a whole new set of objectives: employment creation, poverty alleviation, creation of a social sector in the economy, and developing workers production capacity were among the key issues.

However, although Colombia spearheaded the shift, the new approach never crystallized into full national policies. It has been implemented through a stream of independent programmes and projects executed within a top-down supply-driven assistance system that often responded better to concerns of donor institutions rather than national governments. Two methodological approaches may be recognized among the numerous private institutions (NGOs) that sprang up in this environment. The first sought to develop associative forms of production in which the ownership of capital, the management of the firm, and distribution of benefits were all in the hands of the workers. The second approach, linked to an entrepreneurial philosophy, advocated a business approach.

Policy reform. Structural adjustment was not fully in force in Colombia until the early 1980s. Colombia managed to avoid the crisis of the 1970s thanks to a strong performance of the export sector both in traditional products (coffee) and in the non-traditional sector. The recession of 1981–3 was less acute than in most other Latin American countries but halted the progress of the previous period. An important reason is that Colombia entered the eighties with a strong position in the external sector; a positive commercial balance and high levels of net international reserves. The total external debt was only 1.2 times the net reserves and 1.6 times the annual value of exports. The debt service was 14.8 per cent and the interests 11.5 per cent of the value of exports (IDB, 1987; Ocampo and Lora, 1987).

Main factors behind this recession were a series of external shocks: the collapse of the international coffee prices in 1980, the hardening of the conditions in world capital markets, and the devaluation of the Venezuelan currency (IDB, 1987; Ocampo and Lora, 1987; ISSAS, 1989). The slow reaction to adjusting national policies also played an important role.

This crisis helped the microenterprise programme to achieve a national scope. The objective as stated in the 1982 Plan was to 'increase productivity and profitability of microenterprises, create new jobs and improve the welfare of those occupied in those activities'. (DNP-2069-UDS-SENA, 1985). The plan offered financial and technical assistance to microentrepreneurs through local foundations (NGOs) in 23 localities. Financed by the government and Inter American Development Bank (IDB), the first plan (1986–88) concentrated on providing training and technical assistance to firms while the second (1988–90) broadened its activities to include marketing, technical development, technical assistance, organization, credit, and the improvement of labour legislation.

Policies for small-scale industry in an open economy. Adjustment policies helped overcome the recessive cycle, restore economic growth and reduce unemployment. However, they did not create the basis for sustained economic growth as faltering rates in recent years indicate. A second stage of the policy reform has been launched with the aim of improving resource allocation and regaining acceptable economic growth rates. The liberalization of trade was the initial focus but other aspects such as labour legislation, foreign exchange, foreign investment, the financial system, have now been included. Four goals have been set: (1) to promote free trade of goods and services; (2) support and encourage the private sector so that it can operate in a free competitive environment; (3) modernize the economy to increase efficiency; and (4) promote greater international integration.

The law also extends the reduction and homogeneity of tariffs initiated in 1990. The weighted average duty will be reduced from 16.5 per cent to 7 per cent in 1994 with durable consumer products going from 61.3 per cent to 29.3 per cent; non-durable from 26.2 per cent to 11 per cent and other sectors from 37.1 per cent to 11 per cent. The external sector has been reorganized and some of the rigidities in the labour market have been eliminated. A free foreign currency market has been created with resources generated by personal services, tourism, and donations and the capital markets has been liberalized.

The government is conscious of the implications of these changes for the small-scale sector. The Minister of Development committed to the restructuring process (Samper, 1991) has outlined the need for a policy that selectively assigns priorities to those sectors which are closer and more sensitive to international competitive standards. This would include a number of industries (car parts, leather, clothing) in which small and medium scales of production are important.

Performance of SSMI policy regimes

Issues from the experience of Chile, Ecuador and Colombia

Assessing the performance and the outcomes of these three different policy regimes is not an easy task. There are few studies containing relevant material and data is not readily available. However, some conclusions can be extracted from the preceding analysis to formulate at least a series of hypotheses about the performance of special policy regimes within protectionist environments.

Shared features. A general overview of the performance of the initial policy regimes shows a striking resemblance in several areas. In all three cases, the effective outcome was somewhat poor and, at the end, relatively unimportant in aggregate terms. The impact of the legal benefits was very limited in practice while the services offered did not achieve the scale required to make a difference. In addition, the service delivery systems exhibited many shortcomings that made resource allocation inefficient and downgraded the quality of the services. The performance was even poorer whenever more complex policy objectives were attempted.

Limited impact of financial incentives. Most of the few existing studies suggest that small-scale entrepreneurs did not in practice benefit from the special tax and credit regimes. The study in Ecuador showed that 71 per cent of the small-scale entrepreneurs did not use the benefits established in the Promotion Law, and 83 per cent did not receive the tax exemption they were entitled to. They considered the incentives irrelevant and did not take them into account when making production or investment decisions. (Fernández, 1990). In Colombia it took 30 years to approve the general Promotion Law, ten years to create the Industrial ICETEX, and another five years to set the National Programme for Comprehensive Technical Assistance in motion. Consequently, the benefits for the entrepreneurs were rare and dispersed.

Finally, the minor role played by the support system developed under this regime is evidenced by the fact that its abolition in Chile did not produce any major upheaval. In fact, during the critical years of 1978–83 large-scale production decreased faster and more dramatically than in the small-scale sector.

Limited reach of service delivery systems. The intended benefits reached only a small minority of the firms. De Soto (1986) criticizes this and stating: 'special programmes that earmark resources for the small-scale sector only manage to capture a very limited proportion of the resources from the credit institutions'. Furthermore, credit services benefited some specific types of industries but not necessarily those that made the best use of them. Questions regarding access are more serious as reflected in the limited programmes to facilitate access to lenders and prepare credit applications.

A good example of the limited impact of the assistance programmes is provided by the Credit Programme for Micro-enterprises of Colombia. In 1985 the system was among the biggest in Latin America. It had 13 foundations and 21 regional headquarters in 19 cities. Yet, until that date the system had allocated just 3600 credits to 3000 units in a sector comprising 623,000 units in four main cities. The system barely managed to serve 0.5 per cent of the enterprises (López *et al.*, 1991).

Technical assistance was also extremely limited. Training was restricted mostly to entrepreneurs, and served only 10,000 or 1.4 per cent of the existing units in the four main cities of Colombia (López *et al.*, 1991). Other types of technical assistance reached even fewer entrepreneurs. In summary, the mechanisms created by the regimes to compensate for the 'market failures' in the supply of services to the sector, did not succeed in making the services available to the small-scale industries.

Expensive and poor quality assistance. The policy regime relied on a supply-driven system to provide the services the small-scale sector presumably required. Financial resources were allocated to service producers' systems who in turn established programmes to provide the type and the amount of services they considered important. The existing evaluations leave little doubt about the efficiency problems in such a system. The technical assistance of international lending programmes lacked a clear perception of the demand, and an understanding that their quality was very poor (Webster, 1991). The assessments made of non-government programmes are even more devastating.

Failure to achieve specific development objectives. Policy instruments created by the special SSMI policy regimes have at times been directed at specific objectives such as regional development (industrial deconcentration) and employment and poverty alleviation (microenterprises). Indirectly, the pursuit of these objectives had a powerful impact on the sector. All three countries experimented with these regimes but Colombia and Chile did so for a longer period of time.

Regional development. Regional SSMI programmes remained small and did not influence in any significant way the evolution of SSMI nor of the regions. Arica in Chile was one of the most active in industrial development but it remained the home of some of the most inefficient industries in the country until the liberalization killed them in the mid-1970s (Behrman, 1976).

In Colombia, the initial programmes had negligible coverage and are not worth discussing. The more organized programmes of the Industrial Financial Fund were bigger but did not achieve any degree of success. The evaluations carried out show that no aggregate impact was visible and that the policy instruments used did not alter the trends (Garzón, 1979; Uribe-Echevarría, 1983). Specially, no measurable change in the demand for credit took place in the target cities and no deconcentration of previous location patterns occurred.

Employment generation and poverty alleviation. The Colombian microenterprise assistance programme is a good example of this kind of policy. Set up initially by the private sector (Carvajal Foundation in 1976) this programme later received international funding and the support of the state in 1984. The limited magnitude of the activities and the modest impact on the problems it sought to correct have been highlighted in several studies. López *et al.*(1991) have estimated that the various programmes initiated during the mid-1980s created only 5000 additional jobs in 18 cities at a time when urban unemployment affected about 1,100,000 people.

The limited capacity of this programme to meet its employment-generation objectives has become better understood more recently. A series of studies regarding the performance of microenterprises during the economic crisis of the 1980s suggests that at an aggregate level they have a clear pro-cyclical behaviour. An anticyclical behaviour is only observed in self-employment and family businesses and their contribution to employment is obtained at the cost of reducing average income in those activities (López *et al.*, 1982; Uribe-Echevarría, 1989).

Therefore, under a demand restriction the employment expansion observed as a result of the assistance programme could probably have been achieved without it. In summary, with a stable demand function and a low unit-cost/production elasticity, a general increase in the availability of credit would not have a significant impact on the aggregate level of production, employment, or the profit level of the respective sector (Uribe-Echevarría, 1989; 1991).

Export promotion. Export promotion systems were only indirectly linked to SSMI. In Chile, most estimates of comparative advantage gave priority to large-scale processing of raw materials and, as noted by Behrman, export-promotion systems have had a very limited impact on manufacturing in general (1976).

The Colombian export-oriented incentives (late 1960s) provide an opportunity to look into the effectiveness of export promotion in transforming small-scale industries. A study by Echevarría and Perry concludes that the impact of subsidies upon industrial exports was decreasing already during the 1970–74 period (1983). Subsidies, although effective in helping existing industries to export a larger proportion of their production, did not contribute to increased industrial specialization as they had during the late 1960s (Wogart, 1978)[4].

The authors concluded that the subsidies had a one-off effect, causing readjustment at the time they were introduced (1967) but they did not generate continued change in subsequent periods (Echavarría and Perry, 1990). Conversely, the total costs of the subsidies was not small for Colombia. Tejeiro and Elson (1973) estimated that after 1972, the total value of export subsidies reached 50 per cent of the savings for investment in the public sector, and 20 per cent of the total income for central government.

Lastly, Acevedo *et al.*, have also argued convincingly that the export promotion package did not produce structural change in Colombian industry (Acevedo *et al.*, 1985). This is supported by the observation that the branch composition of the Colombian SSMI remained stable, (Castillo and Cortellese, 1989). Therefore, export incentives encouraged existing domestic producers to increase exports but did not create new export industries.

Comparative perspective

Despite the similarities in the policy regimes up until the 1970s, the performance of the small-scale sector shows important differences in each of the three countries. The protection and support given to the Chilean SSI in the early years resulted in higher employment and larger output but it also created performance problems[5]. Strong variations in efficiency by regions and branches were observed in 1978 (Román, 1990) suggesting the presence of large distortions and serious allocation problems. Also, the prevalence of low levels of competitiveness did not allow the development of an export sector.

The Colombian SSI sector though smaller in size, turned out to be more competitive and efficient. From the end of 1960s to the second part of the 1970s, the Colombian small-scale sector exhibits a consistent trend towards higher productivity and an enhanced export performance. According to Cortes, Berry and Ishaq (1987) this strong performance has little, if anything, to do with the policy regime.

Operating in a less protected environment and shielded from some regulations, the sector managed to take advantage of the international trade boom of the early 1970s. Lower real salaries and a 'benign neglect' in enforcing regulations that discriminated against the sector were of importance. However, lesser degrees of protection probably played the most important role, in that they stimulated increases in productivity. By 1966 a study by ECLAC showed that Colombian manufacturing was in a better position to sell typical SSI products at competitive prices than most other Latin American producers (1966).

As a result, an important part of the export growth of manufactured goods during that period took place in industries characterized by medium and small sized plants such as shoe, wood products, clothing, and furniture industries. According to Wogart, only about a quarter of the performance can be accounted for by external factors such as increased demand (1978). Therefore, about three-quarters of the performance must be related to internal factors such as increased competitiveness, better marketing, and government incentives (Plan Vallejo, CAT, PROEXPO).

Although it is difficult to isolate the portion that each factor is responsible for, it is likely that export incentives played a role in strengthening the drive towards exports. Obviously, the relevance of the incentives is related to the size of the productivity gap that needed to be bridged. In this case it seems that the Colombian industrial performance was good enough to make the incentive effective.

The performance of the regime in Ecuador was ambiguous. A highly regulated regime, but with less protection and support than that of Chile, the Ecuadorian SSI sector neither showed the competitiveness of the Colombian nor the over-extension of the Chilean SSI. The extreme overvaluation of the national currency during the oil boom discouraged exports and provided a strong import capacity. Ecuador was, during those years, an important market for Colombian manufactured consumer goods, and SSI industries made a sizeable contribution to this trade.

In summary, despite similar regimes, other factors intervened to produce different outcomes. Differences in the structure of protection; different attitudes towards the enforcement of stifling regulations; the existence of export subsidies; and a favourable conjuncture in neighbouring external markets were the most important. Meanwhile, the variations in the priorities, methodologies and instruments of each country, as well as the differences in the size of the benefits granted and the extension and effectiveness of the assistance provided seem to have had a smaller influence.

Towards a general assessment

There is little doubt that the initial policy regimes did provide valuable services to individual small firms and that they in turn created sources of livelihood for some groups. Yet, in aggregate terms the contribution was very small and did not succeed in modifying the behaviour of the sector. In general, the evolution of the small-scale sector was dominated by the signals generated by the general policy environment and the space left by the set of institutional constraints.

Although not perceived at the time the regimes were put in place, the main reason for their modest impact was very basic. The type and magnitude of the benefits granted and the value of the services rendered could not have countered, and in fact did not, the impact of the heavily-biased policy environment. The result is that these special policy regimes had very limited success in inducing entrepreneurs to invest in improving performance. In fact, the best performer during the 1970s, the

Colombian SSI, was not the most supported but the least protected. It was also favoured by the benign neglect of the government in enforcing stifling institutional regulations.

In Chile, high levels of protection were conducive to problems of efficiency and blunted a more positive attitude towards market competition. Once again, higher levels of support to the sector failed to produce a movement toward greater efficiency.

The relative irrelevance of the regime was aggravated by its incapacity to reach a significant proportion of the firms. A serious error was to ignore the fact that no delivery system works efficiently in the presence of institutional barriers, high transactional costs, and an unfavourable policy environment.

The effectiveness of the programmes was also affected by the flaws of a supply-driven system developed to allocate resources and deliver services. The lack of competition and the patron-client relationships which characterized the system were not very conducive to effective action, efficient and correct resource allocation.

The present characteristics of the small-scale sector in these three countries demonstrate that policy regimes failed, in the end, to attain the desired structural changes. Developed in the context of import substitution policies, the SSMI sector still concentrates essentially on serving the needs of the domestic market. Consumer goods continue to be the main area of specialization. In general, the technology employed in production is relatively simple and productivity lags significantly behind large-scale industry. In spite of all attempts to foster subcontracting and specialization, there is little inter-firm collaboration, either with large-scale industry or other sectors of the economy. Linkages between small-scale units are also rare and inter-firm transactions therefore very scarce.

Small-scale production is still highly informal. Microenterprises account for 40.5 per cent of the industrial employment in Chile (1984), 46.7 per cent in Colombia (1984) and 51.7 per cent in Ecuador (1981). Within the small- and medium-scale (1–99) industrial sector firms with less than 10 workers constitute the great majority : 60 per cent in Chile, 72 per cent in Colombia, and 74 per cent in Ecuador. And the largest proportion of the latter falls in the less than five workers category. In fact, SSMI is still dominated by very small-scale producers.

Product quality has improved but even a cursory look finds it wanting in many respects. Products are mostly generic, quality is low and/or variable, and designs neither keep up with fashions nor demand. There are as many or more problems with the capacity of SSMI to commercialize its production. A significant proportion of the firms only have a very simple sales structure and their marketing strategies are often rudimentary.

Small-scale industry under economic liberalization: responses to a changing policy environment

Current shift in policy orientation

The adoption of 'economic liberalization' policies by these countries has resulted in the elimination of many instruments used in previous SSMI regimes. At the same time, enormous changes in market structures and production technologies world wide have opened up a wide range of new opportunities. Today, in many areas small- and medium-scale industry has strong competitive advantages and as a result has acquired a permanent and dynamic role in the development of industry[6].

With this scenario in mind, the three countries are struggling to redirect their efforts towards the sector. Initially, the main role of the small-scale sector, and more precisely the microenterprise sector, was to soften the serious social impacts brought on by the restructuring process. And although growth benefits were appreciated, short-term job creation and poverty alleviation were conceived as the main contributions of SSI. A closer examination of the role of microenterprises in the process of labour absorption, a re-evaluation of the sector's experience with national programmes, and a view of the role of small scales of production in industrialization processes has changed the manner in which the sector is perceived (López *et al.,* 1982; Uribe-Echevarría, 1983; 1989; 1990; Schmitz, 1990;). The evidence of strong success by small-, some very small, scale production in Europe (especially Italy and Spain, but also Germany) and in the USA has contributed greatly to this re-evaluation. Key authors are Piore and Sabel (1984), and Scott (1988).

In all three countries, small- and medium-scale production is now viewed as a vital component for future industrial development. This perception seems to be increasingly shared by the rest of the Latin American countries. No country within the continent can afford a de-industrialization process. And, to improve the competitive position of industry, small- and medium-scale production must play a dynamic and vital role. Consequently, the new policy directed at SSMI must facilitate changes (restructuring) in the sector and enable the industrialists to implement the process.

However defined, and whichever the policy, the restructuring process will have to deeply alter the existing profile of the small-scale sector in these countries if it is to reach the intended objectives. The next section maps out some of the transformations required to better assess the relevance of the various policy issues and policy proposals. If liberalization of the economy is not to mean de-industrialization, a substantial reorganization of production is necessary to compete in open domestic markets and enter external markets.

At the firm level, many of the problems often found in the small- and medium-scale sector are related to their low capacity to incorporate technical progress. Past performances have been influenced by high degrees of protection from more innovative competitors while, at the same time, constrained by chronic difficulties of access to capital and basic services. Hence, a critical question is whether less or no protection and liberal factor markets would be enough to generate efficient service markets.

As is confirmed by the experience of successful SSMI in more open economies, it is quite likely that: (1) larger average sizes; (2) increased specialization and; (3) more inter-firm collaboration will have to occur in order to transform and modernize the sector. Additionally, to succeed in foreign markets, improved marketing strategies and commercialization channels will be required.

Key policy issues in a changing policy environment

Some proponents of the advantages of economic liberalization seem to imply that restructuring will take place automatically once the reforms are in place. However, the present government of Chile, Ecuador and Colombia seem to disagree with this contention. The dominant view appears to be that to realize the positive impact of these policies on the SSI sector and to maximize its contribution to the 'new economic order', a series of initiatives will be required that help the entrepreneurs to carry out the process. The following discussion reflects some of the emerging issues in an attempt to formulate new policies.

Policy objectives. The three governments share the view that a competitive small- and medium-scale sector capable of retaining domestic markets and expanding into export production is an essential ingredient of the central role industry will have to play in the development of their economies (ECLAC, 1990a). This is a significant shift from the short-term employment creation/poverty alleviation focus of the recent past. However, as the Chilean government has made explicit, the development of the SSMI is also considered a crucial instrument in pursuing long-term equity objectives. In the light of previous policy pronouncements it is reasonable to expect that the Colombian and Ecuadorian position will not be any different.

There is also wide recognition that an extensive restructuring of the sector will be required to meet the challenge of the new policy environment. However, the policy debate about what, if anything, is needed to achieve this restructuring is just taking shape. This is partly because the emphasis on the SSMI sector in Chile is recent and due to the new government, and partly because Colombia and Ecuador are still in the process of implementing general aspects of their policy reform.

Chile, having completed the application of the general Policy Reform, is now keener on establishing the basis for a new stage in the development of the small- and medium-scale sector. Most inefficient firms and industries have already been eliminated and the current objective is clearly set on competitiveness and developing export production. The latter objective includes the promotion of new industries and furthering the links with large-scale industries as well as primary export sectors. The approach seeks to facilitate the efforts of small-scale entrepreneurs by promoting institutional reforms, stimulating the emergence of a wide range of services, and creating a system for Science and Technology development and diffusion.

Colombia is proceeding along a similar track, but is still concentrating on institutional reforms. Colombia, however, has already been making progress in a restructuring strategy for the industrial sector which is already spilling over into the small-scale sector, given the strategic importance of some of its branches. Besides, the Colombian approach favours a more gradual and selective process of economic opening based on the relative competitive strength of different industries. The Colombian government seems also more willing to use a special policy regime for industries subjected to restructuring processes. This includes, but is not restricted to, those industries in which small-scale production is important.

Ecuador is less advanced in the materialization of policy reform as well as in the development of a new policy regime for the small-scale sector. Nevertheless, the institutions associated with the small-scale sector are already actively promoting the preparation of a new policy laid down by the ministry of industry in a recent document. The restructuring of the sector is the main policy target. The removal of obstacles blocking access to services and the lowering of transaction costs are considered prime targets, while the diversification of existing and the promotion of new services would constitute major instruments.

Is a specific policy needed? A 'liberal economy' is one with minimal government restrictions not only on international trade but also in domestic financial, commodities, and labour markets (Taylor, 1991). The question is, therefore, whether economic liberalization policies by themselves would be enough to induce an extensive restructuring of the industrial sector in general and of the small- and medium-scale sector in particular.

The Chilean experience seems to indicate that economic liberalization is in fact effective in eliminating inefficient firms in the small- and medium-scale sector (Román, 1990). There is also convincing evidence that a significant proportion of the large-scale firms have improved their performance and in some cases restructured their operations. However, the situation in the case of the SSMI sector seems to be different. Some improvement in production efficiency and a limited restructuring have taken place. The emergence of new firms, especially those producing intermediate inputs for large-scale enterprises is probably the most well-known phenomenon in this respect. But, on the whole, there is the impression that the SSMI is not heading towards the kind of restructuring required. Export-oriented production is still virtually non-existent, some industries have not been able to recuperate domestic markets, and the modernization of the most traditional (naturally protected) industries is still pending (Ominami, 1991)

A general feeling seems to exist that there is a solid case for intervention to complement the impact of the policy reform on the SSMI sector limited by the presence of externalities, dynamic rigidities, and market failures. But the case for intervention does not stem only from the need to correct misallocations due to market imperfections. As is obvious in the last pronouncement by the Minister of Economics, the Chilean government sees an important role for SSMI in realizing equity objectives.

Very similar approaches are observed in Colombia and Ecuador as well. Furthermore, contrary to historical attitudes, it seems that these two governments are adopting a more interventionist attitude. In the case of Colombia, for instance, in a recent declaration the Minister offered the idea of a new law which would include a package of financial, tax and credit incentives.

Turning to learn, this time, from Asian experience, the successful adjustment performance, export boom, and high rates of economic growth of several South East Asian countries is often presented as an example of liberal policy success. On occasions, this is explicitly contrasted with the disadvantages of the 'pervasive and rapidly expanding role of governments' in Latin America (Balassa *et al.*, 1986). However, not everybody seems to agree with the interpretation that success in the NICs is purely a result of 'liberal policies'. The outcome can equally be interpreted as stemming from an efficient and authoritarian state that pushes resources into selected export industries through a combination of government fiat, subsidies, credit, controls, and export houses (Pack and Westphal, 1986). In fact, some massive investment programmes in support of the restructuring of heavy and chemical industries in South Korea pursued during 1973–9 was criticized at that time after running into a number of problems.

The contention about the need to support infant industries is an additional argument to call for some form of intervention. In fact, a significant expansion into external markets will require the development of new industries. In many of them, the present experience is too thin or non-existent and will require support during the initial experimentation and learning period.

Some of the Chilean experience with the impact of the policy reform in other sectors point towards similar conclusions. Agricultural policy was subordinated, during the initial phase of the reform, to the general policy of macroeconomic adjustment and domestic and external market liberalization. A crisis of large proportions followed and specific sectoral policies had to be introduced. The revision included the establishment of price bands for wheat, sugar beet, dairy products and oil; the raising of tariffs on milk; preferential treatment for domestic suppliers over imports in state purchasing; protection of domestic meat production on sanitary grounds; the provision by the sugar industry of contracts for the planting of sugar beet in order to absorb labour etc. Furthermore, massive renegotiations were carried out to relieve extreme indebtedness, a preferential exchange rate was established for dollar-denominated debts, and special loans were introduced for farmers with difficulties in providing the usual type of guarantees.

The modernization and subsequent export boom of the sector could not have taken place without the policy reform but the adjustments were decisive in nurturing the positive response of the sector. Equally, it is also evident that this response took place precisely in areas in which decades of State efforts (investment in energy and telecommunications, preparation of technicians and engineers, and resource development, i.e. the fruit growing and afforestation promotion plans of CORFO) have created sufficient material conditions.

The concept that the State should not discriminate against or in favour of specific economic activities was, and still is a major tenet of the Chilean economic policy reforms. However, most of the evidence seems so far to point to the need to formulate and implement specific policies if a successful restructuring is going to take place.

What kind of intervention? Another issue is the kind of intervention which may be necessary and effective to accelerate and deepen the SSMI restructuring. The use of discriminatory policies will be, in principle, inconsistent with liberalization policies since it may jeopardize a correct resource allocation. To a large extent this is the position adopted by the Chilean government which has, so far, foregone the use of regional or sectoral selectivity in favour of general competitive systems. Both the Ecuadorian and the Colombian governments seem to give more importance to a regional/sectoral policy framework, accepting the arguments of those defending a more selective approach.

The Chilean government, however, in line with its declared social objectives, has allocated special funds (FOSIS) and is preparing programmes oriented to assist low-income sector activities in a bid to alleviate poverty. The argument about the distortion such programmes introduce in the product markets of SSMI is only one of the objections. In more general terms, these positions revive the old discussion about whether supporting very small (informal) activities is the best, or even an effective, way of repaying the 'social debt' or attending to the needs of low-income groups and other vulnerable groups. In the light of past problems with this type of programme such arguments should not be dismissed without due consideration.

In principle, as the debate progresses, it seems that the position defending an 'enabling role' for the state is gaining support progressively. Under this orientation support programmes would be mostly addressed to release institutional bottlenecks, and promote the development of a system to meet the demand for services by the entrepreneurs themselves. This position assumes that the incentives for restructuring are built in the policy reform and that tampering with them would run the risk of introducing distortion conducive to misallocation.

The importance of institutional environments as a condition for stimulating responses from entrepreneurs and facilitating access to general service systems is increasingly becoming a major focus of attention. Reforms to strengthen property rights, protect innovations, rationalize taxation, diversify credit insurance systems, reduce transaction costs in general, and simplify bureaucratic procedures such as registering and licensing are examples of this approach.

Purpose of intervention: restructuring the small-scale sector. The primary aim of economic liberalization is to correct domestic resource allocation and put it in line with the comparative advantages of the country. It is assumed that international prices represent the true opportunity costs of domestic resource use and that interfering with these prices causes deviations from optimal allocations. A country has, in static comparative terms, a comparative advantage to produce a good if the value of the domestic resource (at 'shadow' prices) employed in earning (export) or saving (substituting imports) one unit of foreign exchange is equal or less to that value. Following this definition, comparative advantages can be revealed by estimating the domestic resource cost per unit of foreign currency earned or saved in different industries or in different firms within an industry.

Traditional and often indiscriminate import substitution encouraged many economic activities that had high domestic resource costs (DRCs). In principle, these type of economies would be more efficient if they transferred resources from high DRC activities to low DRC activities. The success of an economic liberalization programme would be its capacity to restructure the economy by reallocating resources between as well as within industries and forcing efficiency improvements under the impact of external competition.

In this process the development of new industries is vital to avoid de-industrialization. This is a complex problem whose solution may involve more than 'getting the prices right'. Laying the material basis to master new production processes outside the area of current experience becomes an additional component of the restructuring problem. And one that brings considerable strength to the calls for state intervention.

However, production efficiency is not sufficient to ensure success in the market. Effective marketing performances are necessary to survive in highly competitive markets. Price, promotion and commercialization strategies are especially important when domestic markets face new imports. The problem is accentuated when a whole reorientation of production is required to enter foreign markets.

Restructuring is, then, a complex process whose purpose is to increase the efficiency of resource use. This involves: (1) efficient production and, (2) improved market performance. The first process includes the reallocation of resources towards more productive industries and products, and reaching international levels of competition through greater technical efficiency in the SSMI firms.

The process of resource reallocation involves two different aspects. The first is the elimination of firms in industries that cannot survive external competition. The second involves increasing the allocation of resources to existing competitive industries and/or the development of new industries. In the first case expanded export markets are required, while in the second a material base (technology, experience, infrastructure, market information, skills, etc.) must be available.

A specific characteristic of the efficiency problem in the SSMI sector is its dependence on external processes. To be efficient, small-scale businesses need to externalize many functions which are internally performed in large firms. Examples of this type of problem may be commercialization, accounting, maintenance of equipment, buying of inputs, product development etc. Simultaneously, the smaller the firm the more likely that inter-firm collaboration would make a substantial contribution to efficiency.

Certainly, some of these problems can be resolved when the firms grow. If they grow large enough they can efficiently internalize these functions. However, a tendency towards larger firm sizes also means an increased preference for more capital-intensive technologies and higher concentration. And, consequently this may contradict some of the stated social objectives. The alternative, interlocking groups of small, highly specialized firms with a high density of inter-firm transactions and collaboration, has proved to achieve superior levels of efficiency.

There are of course less dramatic examples of internal efficiency being dependent on external transactions. López for instance, reported on small furniture making firms in Medellín. These firms had to develop their own drying and cutting facilities and maintain high inventories of pre-cut raw materials because of the absence of local independent suppliers. This was exacerbated by the unwillingness of existing raw material suppliers to ensure delivery (1986). Uribe-Echevarría reported on the situation of small-scale leather producers in Colombia. These producers did not succeed in entering export markets until the tanneries improved their technology. Thus, a high degree of openness is a major characteristic of the small-scale firm and this means that internal firm efficiency and competitiveness is dependent on an efficient inter-firm division of labour and on the efficiency of processes performed outside and beyond the control of the firm.

For these reasons, small-scale firms must be conceived as a complex production system composed of various collaborating firms rather than exclusive independent firms. The efficiency problems of small-scale firms are very different to those of large-scale firms. The consequence is of course, that restructuring cannot be solely, perhaps not primarily, focused at the firm level. Creating the conditions for increased reliance on external inputs is an essential task.

Innovations at higher levels of production are crucial to the successful restructuring of the SSI sector. Branch and local (regional) clusters appear to be two of these levels at which the problem needs to be analysed in the search for solutions. In summary, access to relevant services is vital for the efficiency of small firms, while instruments to facilitate improvements in the intra/inter-firm division of labour are essential to achieve a meaningful restructuring.

Alternatives institutional infrastructure delivery: systems or markets? There is a growing consensus that the present 'assistance approach' which gave origin to the present supply-driven system is inadequate and must be replaced. A clear priority is attached to a substantial improvement in the quality of the services, increased efficiency in its provision, and to scaling up its reach.

There is still a lack of clarity about exactly what form such systems may take but there is little doubt that the new orientation focuses on some form of market systems. Consensus seems to be building quite rapidly to give the state (or other forms of organized social action) a more fundamental role to play in the generation of inputs for efficient service markets rather than intervening in the markets themselves. This would imply more participation of government initiatives in the science and technology systems, gathering and systematizing information about markets, diffusing technological information, training human resources, and research and development. Programmes sponsoring associative solutions to externalize activities suffering from scale diseconomies fall in the same category.

Access to services. Earlier we established the relatively small influence these special policy regimes had upon the development of the small-scale sector. It is not surprising that their abolition and the retrenchment of the state during the mid-1970s did not produce a great impact on the sector. Moreover, the Chilean experience seems to show that the private sector may be quite responsive provided that an effective demand for services exist. So far, the limited impact of the progressive elimination of the special benefits in Ecuador supports this judgement.

However, Chile's experience also shows that specific access problems may emerge when general solutions are devised. The reform of the human resources training scheme is an interesting example of this problem. As mentioned above, as many as 180 private OTEs rushed to meet the demand for trained labour created by the Training Statute of 1979.

However, small-scale enterprises have not been able to offer training courses to their workers. The maximum quantum of possible discounts (1 per cent of the wage bill) is too small and the refund system (once a year) tends to discourage small entrepreneurs given their permanent financial stringency. The mechanism sought to correct this scale problem has the tried to achieve scale economies by pooling together a number of firms to provide training. This has not provided a solution to the problem but instead has proved efficient for large-scale enterprises that have managed to form an OTIR to improve the quality and efficiency of training for their workers[7].

Some important lessons can be learned from this experience. To succeed in the creation of service markets for small-scale firms requires far more care in the design of the structure. In fact, in the case briefly examined here the funding scheme proved feasible for large but not for small firms. Moreover, the mechanism to correct this problem proved once again very successful for large-scale firms but again unmanageable for the smaller ones. It appears then, that the commonly-held idea that associative solutions can always correct small-scale diseconomies and effectively cater to the service demand of small-scale enterprises is not warranted by everyday experience.

Yet, in other cases, the costs of the services may be too taxing on the small-scale finances. This is especially true in the initial periods when they attempt to enter export markets. This proved to be the case with the commercial services that were directed to expand in export markets. In order to make possible the inclusion of small-scale entrepreneurs in the displays and services, they had to step in with a partial subsidy.

Other barriers to access also need very detailed examination. For instance, in the case of credit, overcoming guarantee and screening cost barriers has proved more difficult than expected. Following the state withdrawal from credit services, some private banks have made efforts to expand in this area using their own funds. However, the results have been unsatisfactory and the new credit system did not improve access to credit for the small-scale industrial sector. The supply conditions for short-term and large loans have been met but a definite lack of sources exists to meet the needs for longer terms and smaller credits (Cárcamo, 1989). Though the solutions existed on paper they did not work in practice and the new government is taking a fresh look at these problems. Lastly, something similar occurs with problems of access to technology. The experience with the single system set up under a non discriminatory philosophy is mixed, and problems of access and specificity of requirements have prompted the new administration to develop a centre to study technology and productivity for the SSI sector.

What role, if any, for subsidies? The debate about the use of subsidies and incentives, though important, seems to be evolving some degree of consensus. New concerns about the distorting effect of using subsidies to sway allocation decisions is developing strongly. Incentives, however, are still accepted as a legitimate part of socially-oriented projects. At the same time, new emerging roles for subsidies/incentives are: (1) facilitating access to services and resources (Chilean reforms); (2) rewarding achievement such as export performance (Colombian case); (3) developing new industries by creating new firms in new industries; (4) supporting vulnerable groups (such as women).

A new issue critically associated with the necessary changes in service provision systems is the increasing criticism of the use of direct subsidies to the production of services. Although still not widespread, some voices hold the view that a shift to pass the incentives directly to the consumer of services (enterprises) would have a series of beneficial impacts such as reorienting the production of services to the real demand, introducing competition and hopefully increasing efficiency and service quality.

III

Financial Policies and Small Enterprise Credit

Sectoral credit allocation policy and credit flow to small enterprises in Ghana

ERNEST ARYEETEY

Introduction

It is generally assumed by policymakers in developing countries, including Ghana, that there is either a high unsatisfied demand or a significant potential demand for credit by small borrowers. It is also assumed that where this does not already exist, it can be created. These assumptions lead to policies that have been described as either 'demand-following finance' or 'supply-leading finance' (cf. Patrick, 1966). In many developing countries where the small-enterprise sector is seen to be active, (at least in terms of numbers in relation to the size of the economy) and where one of the biggest constraints to its further development is perceived to be finance, general governmental policy on the development of the financial system may be regarded to be 'demand-following'.

What is interesting about this type of 'demand-following' finance is that as a result of market imperfections, the financial system's development does not always automatically follow the growth of the real sector of the economy. In fact, 'the increased supply of financial services in response to demand may not be at all automatic, flexible or inexpensive in developing countries. Restrictive banking legislation, religious barriers against interest charges and imperfections in the operation of the market mechanism may dictate an inadequate 'demand-following' response by the financial system' (Patrick, 1966).

In view of these impediments to the 'demand-following' effect, a need is often perceived for intervention in the intermediation process, specifically for the redirection of credit. Intervention entails governments setting up institutions where the private sector is deemed incapable of doing so, pegging deposit and lending rates at levels perceived to be fair to borrowers and savers but not necessarily coinciding with free market levels, rationing credit to different borrower categories at different rates under criteria that underlie mainly government priorities, etc.

Ghana has had a history of influencing the financial system's development since pre-independence days. Indeed, the Ghana Commercial Bank was established in 1953, following what was regarded by government to be the inadequate lending policies of earlier established foreign banks who favoured well-established foreign firms in the dispensation of loans and advances. Government at the time considered banks to be ignoring indigenous farmers and small entrepreneurs. Thus the decision to set up a national bank was deemed to be both politically and economically desirable. Throughout the 1960s and 1970s, various development banks, i.e. the National Investment Bank, Agricultural Development Bank and the Bank for Housing and Construction were set up to meet the financing needs of specific sectors of the economy. Also, as government interest in small borrowers grew in the 1970s, banks such as the Co-operative Bank, the National Savings and Credit Bank, the Social Security Bank and finally the unit rural banks were created. At present, therefore, Ghana's financial system is dominated by what has been described as an 'oligopolistic banking sector' (Aryeetey *et al.*, 1990) made up of the Bank of Ghana (central bank), four commercial banks, three Development Finance Institutions (DFIs), two merchant banks and two smaller banks which grew out of the Post Office Savings Bank and co-operatives as well as 122 unit rural banks.

Dissatisfaction with the pace of financial-sector development and the need for intervention is reflected in the growth in the number of financial institutions in the 1970s. State-owned banks were encouraged to spread their branch networks. As a result, the number of primary commercial bank branches grew by 25 per cent between 1976 and 1984, and that of all other banks more than tripled within the same period. All the existing 122 rural banks were established between 1976 and the present and bank density increased from 1.9 branches per 100,000 inhabitants in 1976 to 3.2 in 1984.

Foreign participation in banking in Ghana is limited to only 40 per cent of bank assets, and this is available in only four institutions. The few well-established foreign banks that operate in Ghana are differentiated from the rest mainly in terms of their market. The market is partially segmented with the foreign banks concentrating on the corporate sector, offering facilities for industry and the export/import trade. Indigenous banks have found it difficult to penetrate this market as a result of the considerable strengths of the foreign banks in this area. Foreign banks achieve this position mainly through their membership of international banking networks, which is of considerable value to their clients which are large foreign-owned corporate entities. They also tend to have better-trained staff.

The foreign-owned banks appear to be less strongly committed to retail banking and mobilization of deposits through branch networks (Aryeetey, 1991).

Notwithstanding the expansion of the network of banks in Ghana, the government and monetary authorities continued to be dissatisfied with the flow of credit to small borrowers throughout the 1970s. Small borrowers were considered to be active and potentially efficient economic agents. Thus, by the end of that period, the monetary authorities had come to the conclusion that intervention in the financial system's sectoral credit allocation mechanism needed to go beyond setting up institutions, to directing the portfolio structure of the banks. The dissatisfaction with the flow of credit is indeed indicated by the Bank of Ghana's (1980) statement on sectoral credit flow to the effect that 'in spite of the high liquidity in the system, the productive and priority sectors in the economy were not receiving adequate institutional credit'. This happened even though the share of domestic credit to the agricultural sector (an activity of small borrowers, mainly) grew dramatically between 1970 and 1975, declined briefly up to 1977 and then continued to grow steadily after that period (see Appendix 10.1). What may have caused concern to the authorities was the fact that the manufacturing sector's share of domestic credit in the 1970s was less stable. At the beginning of the last decade therefore, the credit management policies of the central bank put more emphasis on (a) interest rate policies and (b) selective credit controls and sectoral ceilings than they had done in the previous decade.

It is my view that despite the continuing interest of the government and monetary authorities in directing credit to small borrowers and other priority sectors of the economy, the more direct policy of selective credit controls and sectoral credit ceilings failed to ensure adequate or even significant increases in the shares of domestic credit going to many priority sectors including the small enterprise sector, which incorporates microenterprises here. This chapter is hence intended to show that, following the adoption of selective credit controls and ceilings, the allocation of credit to the priority sector of small enterprises declined significantly, and that this decline illustrated the considerable difficulty of operating a cumbersome policy first within a macroeconomic environment that did not favour it, and secondly, by a financial institutional framework whose orientation was not adequately suited to lending to small enterprises.

The second section of the chapter presents the credit management policies of the monetary authorities with respect to the policy goals, and how the banks were expected to implement these, highlighting the level of interest that the government has shown in the development of small businesses with these policies. The third section of the chapter analyses the allocation of credit by first comparing the planned allocation of credit to various sectors and the actual allocation in some years for which data was readily available, and then focusing on the allocation of credit to the small enterprise sector. This analysis exposes the fact that in the period 1981–8, when these policies were in place, small enterprises received a continuously smaller proportion of total domestic credit destined for the private sector in spite of planned increases. The final part of the paper examines various factors within the economy that may have contributed to the ineffectiveness of the various credit management policies in directing credit to small enterprises and draw conclusions from these. Bearing in mind that these policies have, in the main, been altered since 1988, there is no need to suggest their removal. Indeed, the present research work concentrates on more probable ways of making lending to small enterprises more attractive to the financial system.

Credit Management Policies (1981-8)

Up to the end of the 1970s, the asset management practices of the banking system in Ghana were regarded as having led to an economically inefficient use of credit. To correct this inefficiency in credit allocation, the Bank of Ghana, beginning in 1981, embarked upon various credit management policies. To achieve this end, the selection of as many as eleven borrower categories and sectoral distributions of loans and advances were highlighted. The credit management policies were aimed at eradicating the perceived market imperfections in the banking system's institutional arrangements. Various measures were therefore adopted to channel mobilized financial resources into productive and priority areas. In doing this, the Bank of Ghana directed monetary policy in Ghana between 1981 and 1988 with the following five different control measures:

(a) the liquidity reserve requirements;
(b) interest rates;
(c) mandatory lending to agriculture;
(d) sectoral credit ceilings; and
(e) mandatory cash margins against house ownership loans.

Of direct relevance to credit to small business borrowers were the interest rate controls, mandatory lending to agriculture, and the sectoral ceilings. We concentrate here, however, on the interest rate policies and the sectoral ceilings in view of their importance to small manufacturing enterprises. These are discussed below, in the context of the policy objective of ensuring that priority sectors, regarded as the mainstay of the economy, would receive an increasing share of domestic credit over the period.

It must be borne in mind, however, that the credit management policies of the authorities were part of a more elaborate "Monetary and Credit Plan" which was prepared at the beginning of each year and revised at the beginning of each quarter of the year to reflect various macroeconomic developments within the year. Thus, based on estimated expansion of the money stock, other bank liabilities and net foreign assets, total domestic credit is permitted to rise by a certain expansion coefficient. The total domestic credit is then broken down into the Government's share, the cocoa sector's share, and then the public and private sectors' share in total domestic credit. Government financing needs are usually treated as a priority, leaving credit to the other sectors as a residual element. One factor limiting the amount by which nominal credit in the domestic economy can be expanded since 1983, has been the 'ceiling on net domestic assets' of the banking system as agreed under the IMF adjustment programmes. Thus, within this framework, total expansion of domestic credit to the various economic sectors in the period under review were calibrated, and administered with the above-mentioned control measures to influence quantity and direction.

Application of interest rate policies in directing credit

The practice of applying interest rates differently to different sectors was begun in the 1970s and intensified in the early part of the 1980s. Indeed, for the 1970s, it was noted that:

> In an effort to remove the anomaly, (of limited credit to priority sectors) .... government fixed the lending rate at the maximum of 10% during the 1973/74 financial year.... Interest rates were so adjusted in a downward direction so as to make it easier for institutional funds to flow to the productive and priority sectors with-

out removing the banks' incentive to attract more deposits (Bank of Ghana, 1980).

The policy of applying Preferential Interest Rates to different economic sectors may be regarded as a less direct control mechanism in ensuring that priority sectors gained improved access to credit. This was based on the presumption that the market rate, if universally applied, would exclude some of the priority sectors. Interest rates were perceived by the monetary authorities as the cost of lendable funds, and were subsequently adjusted periodically to promote increases in the level of investment in the different sectors and ensure an inflation-free process of economic growth. The three priority sectors of agriculture, export trade, and manufacturing were specified to benefit from this arrangement. Thus, for example in 1983, commercial banks were directed to charge a preferential interest rate of 8 per cent per annum (instead of the general 9 per cent at the time) on all loans and advances to small-scale farmers whose operations required funds not exceeding ¢50,000. Also, in 1984, at the time when most other loans attracted an interest rate of 21 per cent, credit to the three priority sectors attracted a rate of only 14½ per cent. In 1985, as the rate charged on all other loans and advances climbed to 23 per cent, the rate chargeable on agricultural loans was pegged at 18½ per cent, while credit to the export trade and manufacturing sectors attracted a rate of 20½ per cent. It must be pointed out, however, that between 1985 and 1988, efforts were made to narrow the differential between priority and non-priority rates until these were phased out completely in 1988. With this interest rate structure it was certainly possible for small enterprises to obtain loans and advances from banks at concessionary rates, when banks were prepared to lend. The reaction of commercial banks to lending at such concessionary rates is discussed later.

Application of Sectoral Credit Ceilings in Directing Credit

Until 1988, the Bank of Ghana prescribed sectoral credit ceilings to be applied by all banks in lending to the various sectors. This took the form of permissible percentage increases over each bank's outstanding credit to any sector at the end of the previous year. The aggregation of these sectoral ceilings resulted in a 'global credit ceiling' for each bank. These sectoral ceilings were altered periodically to coincide with government macroeconomic aspirations and needs. Thus, for the purpose of applying these ceilings, a different category of sectors could be designated as 'priority' from those classified as priority for interest rate determination purposes. In 1984, for example, when the economy had been starved of consumer food items following the drought of 1983, the following ceilings were set by the Bank of Ghana for lending to all sectors:

(1) **Priority Sectors**	**Per cent**
(i) Agriculture, Forestry and Fishing	90
(ii) Export Trade	100
(iii) Manufacturing	100
(iv) Transport, Storage and Communications	100

(v)	Mining and Quarrying	60
(vi)	Import Trade	350

(2)	**Non-Priority Sectors**	**Per cent**
(i)	Electricity, Gas and Water	50
(ii)	Construction	60
(iii)	Commerce and Finance	80
(iv)	Services	50
(v)	Miscellaneous	60

For 1985, when the Government's priorities changed, the ceiling for the export trade sector was raised to 300 per cent and that for import trade reduced to 200 per cent.

To encourage compliance with the sectoral credit ceilings, the Bank of Ghana informed all banks that any banks which exceeded any ceilings to non-priority sectors would be required to lodge with the central bank a 'Special Reserve Deposit' amounting to twice the amount of excess lending. Similarly, banks failing to comply with the 'Special Reserve Deposit Requirement' would be liable to the penalty applicable to defaulting banks under the cash reserve requirement.

As mentioned earlier, all sectoral credit ceilings have been removed since 1988. (Indeed the last remaining direct control measure for allocating credit sectorally, namely the 20 per cent mandatory agricultural lending requirement for all banks, was removed in April 1991.) The removal of the ceilings was not surprising, given the fact that throughout the period in which sectoral ceilings were applied, actual bank lending to the priority sectors was often below the ceilings set for them and above that set for the non-priority sectors. For the earlier period ending 1980, the Bank of Ghana noted that,

> lending to most sectors, especially the designated priority sectors, fell far short of permitted limits. In the case of agriculture, for instance, the previous ceiling of 100% increase was lifted completely in September 1981 to encourage the banks to increase lending to the sector. In spite of this encouragement, however, credit to agriculture rose by only 36%. Similarly, lending to the manufacturing sector also increased by only 20% compared with the permissible ceiling of 75%; while credit to the export trade sector even declined (Bank of Ghana, 1982).

As will be seen, the trend of actual credit allocation not conforming to the expectations of the central bank continued until the removal of all ceilings. In 1983, for example, while credit to commerce and finance (non-priority) exceeded the ceiling by 94 per cent, in none of the priority sectors was the ceiling reached. Indeed, between 1981 and 1988, total credit to commerce and finance either exceeded the ceiling or just about reached the ceiling, while credit to manufacturing exceeded it only once in 1984. Also, throughout the period, total credit by the banking system exceeded the total permitted under the credit ceilings, thus suggesting that the application of the ceilings may have constituted a constraint for the banking system.

Sectoral credit policies and lending to small enterprises

As pointed out earlier, a major objective of the credit management policies of the 1980s was to ensure that priority sectors would receive an increasing share of domestic credit. The priority sector of interest in the present context is the small enterprise sector involved mainly in manufacturing. This sector embraces all manufacturing units employing up to 29 persons. It is constituted in the main by the microenterprise sector that has an employment cut-off point of four full-time persons as defined by the National Board for Small-Scale Industries in Ghana. Indeed, the microenterprise sector is estimated to provide 85 per cent of total manufacturing-sector employment in Ghana (Steel and Webster, 1990). Small enterprises in Ghana are usually owner-managed and are rarely incorporated.

In view of the fact that available bank statistics do not differentiate credit to firms of different sizes, credit to the small-enterprise sector is substituted by the credit allocation to indigenous sole proprietorships engaged in manufacturing, and then compared with the credit flow to the entire group of indigenous sole proprietorships and also to the entire manufacturing sector, as well as to the entire private sector from all banks. This is a credible substitution bearing in mind that the operation of small manufacturing enterprises by foreigners was discouraged under the Ghanaian Business Promotion Act 1969 and other later legislation on capital investments. Our earlier description of small manufacturing enterprises as owner-managed and unincorporated also fits most indigenous manufacturing sole proprietorships. Such enterprises may engage in a wide range of manufacturing activity, such as furniture, garments, plastics, construction materials and parts assembly.

Between 1985 and 1990, the share of indigenous manufacturing sole proprietorships in total domestic credit dropped consistently (with the exception of 1986, when the three development banks were recapitalized with external assistance). The share for the manufacturing sector of all loans allocated to indigenous sole proprietorships also dropped, as did indeed the share of indigenous sole proprietorships in total manufacturing sector loans (see Fig. 10.1). What is interesting is the fact that even though lending to small enterprises was categorized as 'priority' under lending to the manufacturing sector, its share of manufacturing credit dropped at a time when lending to the manufacturing sector as a whole had become relatively stable. Indeed the tendency for banks to show a lack of interest in lending to small enterprises is demonstrated in Table 10.1 by the fact that while average loan size to indigenous sole proprietorships was only ¢8000 in 1984, credit to indigenous limited liability companies, which were often larger, averaged ¢596,000. Indigenous sole proprietorships receive on average the smallest amounts and the smallest share of total domestic credit. This is often explained away by banks as being a result of the limited security and assets of indigenous sole proprietorships. Foreign sole proprietorships are limited by law thus also share in total domestic

FIGURE 10.1
CREDIT TO INDIGENOUS MANUFACTURING SOLE PROPRIETORSHIPS
as % of other loans

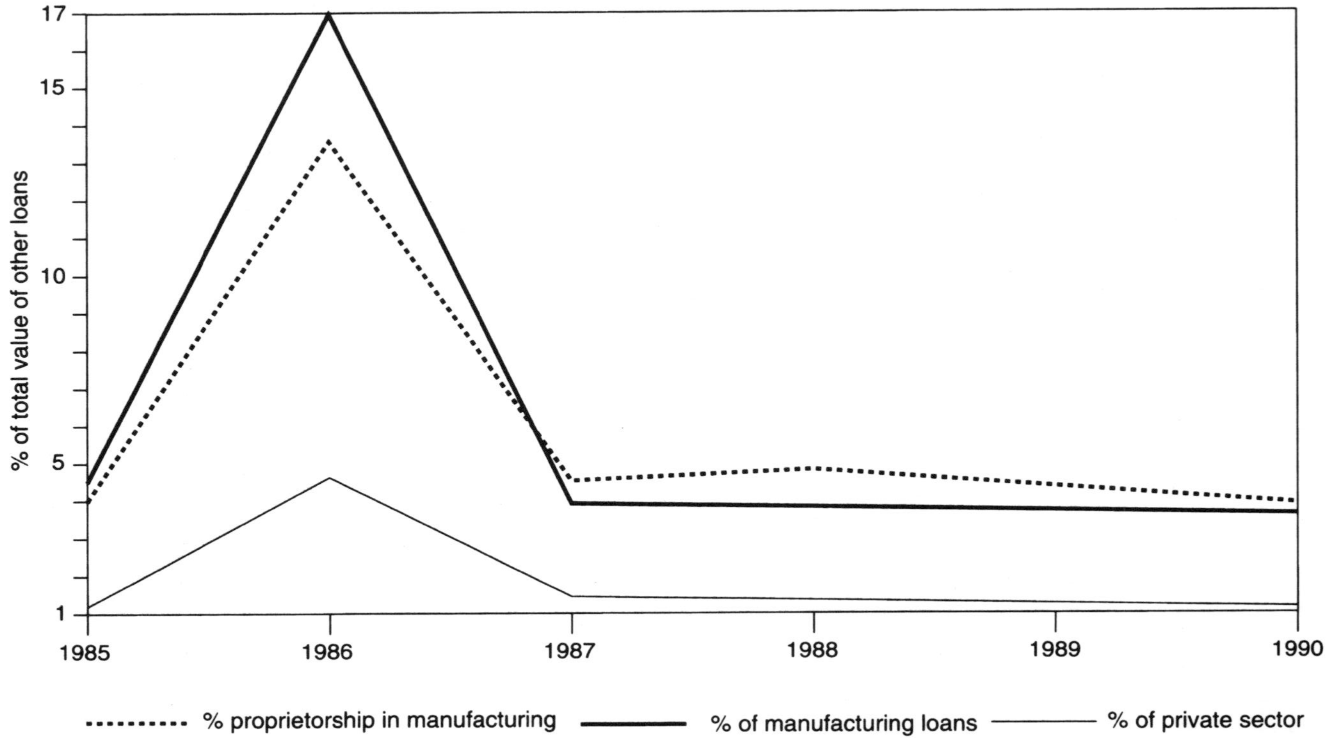

Table 10.1 Distribution of Loans Granted by Commercial Banks, 1984

	Average Amount ¢000	*% of total*	*% of borrowers*	*% of total/ borrowers*
Indigenous sole proprietorship	8	45.0	98.80	0.45
Foreign proprietorship	52	0.04	0.01	0.25
Limited liability				
Indigenous	596	30.0	0.90	33.30
Foreign	2619	9.9	0.70	14.14
Co-operatives	135	0.9	0.12	7.50
Joint state and private	1652	0.7	0.10	7.00
Public institutions	4185	13.8	0.06	23.00

Source: Bank of Ghana, Research Department.

credit. In the early part of the 1980s, public institutions and limited liability companies (both indigenous and foreign) had the largest shares of domestic credit.

Brief case study

To illustrate the dearth of credit to small enterprises, reference is made here to a case study of 100 randomly selected small enterprises (mainly micro-) in the Eastern Region (Aryeetey, 1991). All the 100 entrepreneurs operated bank accounts on behalf of their enterprises. In 52 per cent of these cases, demand deposits alone were run for the enterprises while another 21 per cent operated only savings deposits. The remainder operated both types of accounts (only one enterprise operated a fixed deposit). Most of the accounts of the enterprises had been operated for considerably long periods, (usually starting from the year in which the enterprises were begun), with an average of 7.5 years, thus giving banks ample opportunity to assess the financial position of the enterprises, if not the returns on their projects.

It is interesting that, with one exception, all had applied for bank credit at one time or another since 1985. The average number of applications was two per enterprise. In almost 50 per cent of these cases, long-term credit (more than one year maturity date) was being sought, while the other half sought mainly overdraft facilities. Also, in 49 cases, credit was sought to expand plant size, while 36 wanted credit to purchase raw materials. Only 2 per cent had wanted bank credit to start their businesses. It is significant that only one out of the 100 received the loan applied for in full. In 26 cases, only a part of the original amount applied for was granted while the remaining applications were rejected. In all rejected cases, difficulty in producing adequate collateral was believed by the loan applicants to be the source of their inability to obtain loans.

While banks may argue that the remaining 73 per cent had no 'bankable' projects, there is also every indication that this signifies the failure of the policy objective of treating small manufacturing enterprises as a priority when no appropriate criteria had been developed for assessing the credit-worthiness of applications from such small enterprises. In the absence of suitable collateral, banks had no other means of helping to achieve the policy goal.

Factors affecting bank credit allocation to small enterprises

One feature of the Ghanaian banking system noted by Aryeetey *et al.* (1990) was that banks were lending less than they were capable of doing. For the period under review, all the commercial banks held excess reserves in the form of both cash and government paper. These reserves increased as the problems of public finance diminished and government borrowed less from the system. Thus, by the end of 1988, the commercial banks held about 15 per cent of their total deposit liabilities as excess reserves. The equivalent of about 5 per cent of total deposits was held in excess of the cash reserve requirements earning no returns while about 10 per cent was held in the form of government paper. But why were they not prepared to lend as much as they could? For my purposes, I examine here only those reasons that relate to sectoral allocation policies.

Various factors were considered, first, in terms of how they affected the operation of interest rate policies and credit to small enterprises, and then second, on the operation of the policy of sectoral ceilings. These factors may be classified as those related to the general macroeconomic environment and those resulting from the structures, practices and ideals of the banking system itself.

Macroeconomic environment and the interest rate policy

For the greater part of the 1980s, real interest rates were negative. The fact that inflation in the period remained high (averaging 30 per cent) perhaps indicates a general weakness in monetary policy which made the achievement of other objectives of monetary policy difficult. The negative real interest rates certainly became dysfunctional to the banking system and also in promoting economic growth. A test of the significance of interest rates for resource mobilization and promoting credit allocation by Aryeetey *et al.* (1990) showed them to have had no significant influence. Since the use of lending rates did not discriminate between loans with varying degrees of risk and costs of administration, the real costs of administering credit to the priority sectors became more expensive as they attracted lower rates of interest, same administrative costs for smaller amounts, and yet had greater natural and associated risks. The banks could not lend according to a ranking of risks of return on investment but tended to resort to a rationing of lendable funds among competing borrowers; a practice which led to many other considerations in lending in order to remain profitable. These included such considerations as adequate collateral and other acceptable security, political backing and 'good connections' in loans decisions. In such high risk ventures, even the marginal beneficiaries of credit would be crowded out because the banks became more cautious. It was not surprising therefore that the priority sectors were the main sufferers from the dearth of commercial bank loans and advances. 'Of course no bank would want to give out savings mobilized at an interest rate of 7.5% as credit at a rate of 6% to the risky agricultural sector' (Bank of Ghana, 1980).

Aside from negative real interest rates, the differential rates for different competing demands were not always attractive. Indeed it is apparent that lending to the priority sectors by the banks was not made any more attractive than lending to other sectors. To illustrate this point, one may consider the fact that while the holding of government paper attracted a minimum rate of 13 per cent in 1984 and was considered to be risk-free, the more risky agricultural loans offered only 14½ per cent in an environment of over 50 per cent annual inflation. This may explain why many banks chose to buy treasury bills instead of lending to the priority sectors at a time when they were restrained from lending to the non-priority sectors.

The negative interest rates of the period also affected the term structure of bank lending and therefore its attraction to small enterprises. As a result of interest rate controls, term transformation became a problem as banks were unable to compensate for risk and maturity by varying the interest rates. In 1987 it was estimated that only 15 per cent of commercial bank loans matured over three years. In other words, the contractual maturity distribution of bank lending became dominated by short-term loans, usually up to one year, as banks dealt in very little long-term development finance. For small enterprises that require capital for fixed investments in their attempts to graduate to higher scales, overdraft facilities, which dominated bank lending, were certainly not the most attractive financing option. Banks operate on the short-end of the market largely because of the short-term nature of their liabilities, which are also controlled by interest rates. It may be pointed out that commercial banks mainly calculate and respond to the cost of funds. There is limited inter-bank activity and therefore very little liquidity management. Their main activity is therefore geared towards ensuring that the deposits with the central bank are at the right level and only then investing excess funds.

Macroeconomic environment and sectoral credit ceilings

An appraisal of the credit ceilings and mandating guidelines by Aryeetey *et al* (1990) revealed that they were ineffective. In the early part of the period under review a reduction of credit to the priority sectors was observed. For example, loans and advances to the agricultural sector experienced a 4.4 per cent decline in 1980–81, despite the fact that credit guidelines permitted a 50 per cent increase over the previous year's level. Again, credit to the 'special' export and 'priority' manufacturing sectors recorded in the same period increases of only 7.8 per cent and 0.3 per cent respectively. Credit to the commerce sector, on the other hand, recorded a 53 per cent increase against the permitted 10 per cent.

Basically, the government's macroeconomic objectives that underpinned the sectoral choices (real economic growth within those sectors and abatement of inflation) did not necessarily coincide with the economic considerations of the banking sector. The banks were more interested in resolving the conflict between profitability and liquidity against the background of risks, creditworthiness and investment opportunities. As indicated earlier, directives from Bank of Ghana to the banks to allocate more to the priority sectors were not accompanied by any incentives to the banks, bearing in mind the fact that these sectors were considered by most bankers to be high risk sectors.

The fact that the prevailing macroeconomic environment dictated more how banks structured their portfolios than did the sectoral credit ceilings is illustrated by the way their 'favoured' sectors coincided with 'high-performing' economic sectors. This may be comprehended by looking at the sectoral contribution to GDP and relating this to credit share. The sectoral ceiling 'bindings' on banks were designed so that once a bank had exceeded the ceiling for a sector it could only utilize its lendable funds for sectors where the ceilings had not been reached. If we consider the "most favoured sectors" to be those that banks preferred to lend to once ceilings had been reached, the relationship between the general macroeconomic environment and bank portfolio structures becomes apparent.

Table 10.2 shows that for 1984 and 1988, the commerce sector's credit allocation (the largest) was consistent with its position as a large contributor to GDP. It received about 27 and 30 per cent respectively of domestic credit which was more than its contribution to GDP. It is a very fast-moving sector with high returns and quite appealing to banks. The most favoured sector, (the construction sector), had a credit allocation that far exceeded its contribution to GDP. It received in 1984 10 per cent of total credit, equivalent to 3.8 times its share of GDP. Credit to the construction sector was mainly in the form of advances to local contractors with large working capital needs. They were granted overdraft facilities to undertake mainly government projects. The risk in this sector is lower since profits are higher and the clients are well established construction firms with low default rates. The next favoured sector in 1984 was Mining and Quarrying which enjoyed about 3.6 per cent of total credit which was 3.3 times its share of GDP. The clients here are large corporations involved in mining for export. Such companies require working capital

Table 10.2 Share of Loans and Advances According to Economic Activity, 1984 and 1988

	end-1984			*end-1988*		
Economic Sector	*% of GDP*	*Share total loans %*	*Share total loans/ GDP*	*% of GDP*	*Share total loans %*	*Share total loans/ GDP*
Agriculture	53.9	31.9	0.6	47.2	16.6	0.4
Mining and Quarrying	1.1	3.6	3.3	1.4	3.3	2.4
Manufacturing	7.2	20.8	2.9	9.7	26.1	2.7
Construction	2.6	10.0	3.8	2.5	10.2	4.1
Electricity and Water	0.7	0.2	0.3	1.1	0.2	0.2
Transport	4.2	5.3	1.3	4.8	5.6	1.2
Commerce and Finance	18.7	22.3	1.2	21.5	30.3	1.4
Services	14.4	4.5	0.3	14.6	7.0	0.5

Source: Bank of Ghana, Research Department.

which is repaid once export proceeds come in. Here also the risk is low and the banks are guaranteed repayment from the proceeds of exports. Manufacturing, which enjoyed about 26 per cent of total loans in 1988, took over the second position from Mining and Quarrying in terms of the ratio of loans it received to its contribution to GDP.

The least favoured sectors were Electricity and Water, Services and Agriculture. For Electricity and Water, the main reason was a lack of demand since the sector is largely government-owned, requiring no working capital credit as it received regular subventions until recently. Agriculture, although with a credit share of about 31.9 per cent in 1984, was not a favoured sector because of its risky nature. Its share of credit dropped to 16.6 per cent in 1988 following rising agricultural lending rates and a relaxation of controls. The earlier high level of lending to agriculture was the result of the central bank's requirement for commercial banks to hold at least 20 per cent of their total loan portfolio as credit to that sector. It could be argued then that shifts in the pattern of credit allocations among the respective sectors were more due to changes in the structural composition of the GDP, an indicator of economic strength than to changing government priorities.

Sectoral ceilings and bank structure, specialization and practices

Many banks, especially those set up to function as specialized development finance institutions, found the mandatory lending guidelines unsuited to their areas of "specialization". This was because the sectoral guidelines and mandatory targets were often applied to the banking system without due regard to the individual banks' specialization. For the National Investment Bank and the Bank for Housing and Construction, for example, the requirement that 20 per cent of their lending should go to Agriculture certainly distorted their operational objectives. Similarly, the method of directing an expansion coefficient at domestic credit and the sectoral distribution tended to freeze the institutional structure of loans and advances as it prevailed at the reference date. This caused banks to apply all manner of evasive tactics, such as classifying loans that only had a remote or a very indirect relationship to agriculture as an agro-industrial loan.

It is also apparent that a large amount of the limited disbursement of loans to small enterprises is related to the ability of banks to carry out proper loan processing. A study of the performance of lenders and borrowers under a Small and Micro Enterprise (SME) credit scheme (Duggleby, 1991) suggested that banks generally lacked the capacity to undertake feasibility studies, credit appraisal and loan supervision. Even though most of the state-owned banks have been described under various evaluations as over-staffed, it is suggested that loan officers are usually over-stretched, leading to inadequate appraisal of loan applications. Their task is often not made easier by the absence of important information that ought to have been supplied by loan applicants. With the absence of such information, applications from small enterprises often pile up at banks while being 'processed'.

The perception of risk by bankers in Ghana has been conditioned by many years of high loan default rates and the fear of becoming overexposed. The study by

Aryeetey *et al.* (1990) suggests that the most important concern of bank loan officers is the risk that a borrower might default. Small agricultural loans are reputed to have a 70 per cent default rate. In view of the fact that banks have not had as much experience with lending to small businesses as they have had with agriculture, they tend to classify the two as being similar, thus making banks which are very much risk-averse equally unenthusiastic about small business loans. Subsequently, credit-worthiness criteria employed by banks lay undue emphasis on the provision of collateral, which in many cases would be unavailable.

Conclusion

Ghana's central bank has, since the mid-1970s, applied various interest rate policies as well as sectoral credit ceilings and mandatory lending ratios in the allocation of credit to the real sectors of the economy. Also, until 1988, the central bank prescribed Sectoral Credit Ceilings on lending by banks. In view of the repressed nature of interest rate determination for most of the period, the major allocational tool that guided the actions of commercial banks and development finance institutions in their relations with the real sectors was the variation in sectoral ceilings. Under the policy of setting ceilings each year for various sectors of the economy, the central bank determined permissible percentage increases over previous credit allocations to each sector for each bank, based on the banks' prevailing credit structure.

Bearing in mind that the development of small and micro enterprises had throughout the period (1981 to the present) been a policy goal of the monetary authorities, the resulting distribution of credit signified considerable difficulty in policy implementation and also exhibited the difficulty with which established formal financial institutions can address the credit needs of small and micro enterprises, even under an interventionist approach. It is often argued by banks that lending to indigenous sole proprietorships (small enterprises mainly) is not encouraged by the lack of adequate collateral which increases unduly the degree of risk involved. The need for banks to minimize risk exposure and remain profitable ventures therefore suggests to them the allocation of credit to such 'non-priority' areas as commerce, which has a higher and more rapid turnover in the short-term.

Appendix 10.1 Commercial bank credit 1973–90

	1973	1974	1975	1976	1977	1978	1979	¢ MILLION 1980	1981	1982	1983	1984	1985	1986	1987	1988	1989	1990
Agriculture/Forestry/Fish	21.7	37.9	42.2	139.6	125.4	265.0	307.7	412.4	669.7	1101.9	2012.9	3779.1	7518.1	7476.3	10713.0	9884.6	11476.6	12645.2
Export Trade	18.6	15.7	19.1	22.7	27.3	32.5	43.8	69.4	172.9	67.2	92.0	187.4	490.0	1451.2	2658.6	2595.6	3169.7	3512.1
Manufacturing	77.4	114.2	101.5	165.5	211.8	330.5	395.1	472.0	632.0	635.2	1366.6	3288.4	6046.4	10800.4	15471.0	20901.6	26847.1	23799.4
Transport	19.9	43.4	42.9	58.4	91.8	118.8	160.8	193.5	304.0	201.8	331.3	653.7	1154.3	2021.5	2527.0	5567.4	5810.9	4604.5
Mining and Quarrying	2.2	2.0	6.0	30.0	63.9	88.0	61.0	55.0	145.3	243.0	416.2	497.5	960.2	1437.3	2631.2	1421.7	1927.5	1074.2
Import Trade	36.0	53.1	33.9	41.4	38.2	51.6	33.9	34.4	47.6	42.4	107.4	307.7	990.7	2931.3	3503.8	4416.6	4207.7	4306.1
Construction	29.6	42.0	44.5	105.3	130.5	226.2	289.1	289.1	406.9	511.2	796.9	1273.9	2017.8	3899.3	6267.4	7815.9	8868.4	11012.2
Commerce and Finance (Int. Trade)	36.5	47.0	75.0	109.0	166.1	252.8	216.7	246.1	318.1	293.5	691.1	1175.0	2820.3	5041.9	4317.3	7703.9	9010.2	8806.1
Electricity, Gas and Water	1.0	1.0	1.5	2.2	3.4	15.3	3.2	116.0	26.0	42.2	49.6	21.4	37.8	46.1	169.6	69.0	326.7	297.6
Services	33.3	33.2	27.2	50.2	74.1	75.0	97.4	108.5	181.8	175.0	247.7	533.7	1224.6	2611.5	3137.6	4915.9	5738.6	6563.2
Miscellaneous	7.0	6.9	9.2	27.2	46.4	50.0	52.5	71.5	130.8	96.0	127.2	277.9	451.2	939.0	1088.6	935.0	1632.1	2780.6
Total	283.2	396.4	403.0	751.5	978.9	1505.7	1661.2	2067.9	3035.1	3409.4	6238.9	11995.7	23711.4	38655.8	52485.1	66227.2	79015.5	79401.2

Source: Research Department, Bank of Ghana.

Appendix 10.2 Bank credit to sectors and sectorial ceilings

¢ MILLION

	1980						1981						1982					
	Primary Banks	Second Banks	Total	Abs	Ceiling % of June 79	Total in % of Ceiling	Primary Banks	Second Banks	Total	Abs	Ceiling % of June 80	Total in % of Ceiling	Primary Banks	Second Banks	Total	Abs	Ceiling % of June 81	Total in % of Ceiling
Agriculture, Forestry, Fishing	145.3	267.1	412.4	740.8	100	56	323.1	331.9	655.0	1279.3	120	51	486.7	701.9	688.6	—	—	—
Export Trade	60.8	8.6	69.4	90.8	100	76	80.0	92.9	172.9	194.3	120	89	54.2	13.0	67.2	194.4	120	35
Manufacturing	301.0	171.0	472.0	642.9	50	73	328.3	180.0	508.3	968.1	75	53	357.9	277.3	635.2	968.1	75	66
Transport, Storage, Communications	129.3	64.2	193.5	274.2	50	71	173.6	41.6	215.2	428.0	75	50	176.1	25.7	201.8	428.0	75	47
Mining and Quarrying	43.3	11.7	55.0	74.7	50	74	118.4	18.7	137.1	126.1	100	109	205.8	37.2	243.0	126.1	100	193
Import Trade	29.8	4.6	34.4	34.0	10	101	41.6	6.0	47.6	69.7	100	68	37.0	5.4	42.4	69.7	100	61
Construction	175.8	113.3	289.1	375.8	20	77	247.9	164.0	411.9	460.5	25	89	309.0	202.2	511.2	460.5	25	111
Commerce and Finance	204.0	42.0	246.0	225.7	0	109	263.9	57.2	321.1	333.8	20	96	258.4	35.1	293.5	333.8	20	88
Electricity, Gas and Water	115.2	0.8	116.0	21.3	15	545	41.6	2.6	44.2	54.0	50	82	40.3	1.9	42.2	54.0	50	78
Services	64.9	43.6	108.5	97.0	0	112	93.1	64.0	157.1	201.3	25	78	81.8	93.2	175.0	701.3	25	87
Miscellaneous	22.5	69.0	71.5	59.6	10	120	29.4	102.9	132.3	109.0	15	121	27.4	58.6	96.0	109.0	15	88
Total	1291.9	775.9	2067.8	2636.8		78	1740.9	1061.8	2802.7	4224.1			2034.6	1451.5	2996.1	3444.9		

Source: World Bank, Ghana Financial Sector Review, 1986.

Appendix 10.2 (cont.)

	¢ MILLION															
	1983						1984						1985 Sept. 85			
	Primary Banks	Second Banks	Total	Abs	Ceiling % of Dec. 82	Total in % of Ceiling	Primary Banks	Second Banks	Total	Abs	Ceiling % of Dec. 83	Total in % of Ceiling	Primary Banks	Second Banks	Total	Abs	Total in % of Ceiling
Agriculture/Forestry/Fish	1105.4	907.5	2012.9	—	—	—	2155.0	1624.1	3779.1	3874.6	90	99	2773	1996.1	4719.2	6474.5	71
Export Trade	83.9	8.1	92.0	147.8	120	62	187.0	0.4	187.4	183.9	100	102	429	79.1	508.4	749.2	300
Manufacturing	585.1	781.5	1366.6	1588.0	150	86	1366.8	1921.6	3288.4	2733.1	100	120	1979	3546.5	5576.7	5919.1	80
Transport, Storage, Communication	703.7	127.6	331.3	403.5	100	82	345.7	308.0	653.7	662.7	100	99	508	470.5	978.5	1045.8	60
Mining and Quarrying	732.6	183.7	416.3	486.0	100	86	234.0	263.5	497.5	666.0	60	75	368	405.5	774.3	796.0	60
Import Trade	78.2	29.2	107.4	296.6	600	36	275.4	32.3	307.7	483.2	350	64	628	250.3	879.1	923.1	200
Construction	413.4	383.2	796.6	1022.3	100	78	716.2	557.7	1273.9	1194.9	50	107	1013	915.8	1929.7	2038.2	60
Commerce and Finance	635.7	47.5	683.2	352.2	20	194	954.9	220.1	1175.0	1093.2	60	107	1792	421.4	2213.4	2115.0	80
Electricity, Gas and Water	47.8	1.8	49.6	84.3	100	59	17.8	3.6	21.4	89.3	80	24	79	3.5	32.7	38.7	81
Services	169.2	81.6	250.8	210.0	20	119	306.0	227.7	533.7	376.2	50	142	545	479.6	1024.7	853.9	60
Miscellaneous	38.4	85.7	124.1	110.4	15	112	92.9	185.0	277.9	198.6	60	140	263	255.1	519.0	444.5	60
Total	4593.4	2637.4	6230.8	4701.1			6651.7	5344	11995.7	11555.7			10377	8823.4	19155.7	21348	

Note: This table includes only credit which is subject to sectoral ceilings, except the relatively insignificant credit by RuraBanks.

Financial liberalization under structural adjustment and its implications for financing small-scale and microenterprises in Nigeria

T. ADEMOLA OYEJIDE

Introduction

There is, apparently, a large and influential body of opinion which regards access to credit as a major determinant of the development of small-scale and microenterprises (SSME) in the developing world. According to Elkan (1988), lack of finance on reasonable terms is the most frequently cited deterrent to entrepreneurship, particularly at the small-scale level. This lack of access forces SSMEs to rely more heavily on self-financing than the larger-scale enterprises. In Nigeria, for instance, NISER (1987) shows that as much as 70 per cent of SSMEs obtain most of their investment funds from personal savings.

The lack of access to adequate credit from formal financial institutions is thought to drive SSMEs to high interest charging moneylenders and to hinder their growth and development. This has, in turn, often been used as the justification for establishing special financial agencies and programmes to provide cheaper credit for SSMEs. But, as Liedholm and Mead (1986) note, the number of such institutions is usually out of proportion to the number of SSMEs that could obtain loans from them. Related evidence from Nigeria shows that, between 1981 and 1985, less than 20 per cent of the total number of qualified loan applications could be approved and less than 10 per cent of the total amount applied for was actually approved and disbursed in the SSME Loan Scheme of the Federal Ministry of Industries (NBCI, 1985). It seems clear, therefore, that research and policy must continue to focus on a better understanding of why the formal financial intermediaries are unwilling (or unable) to provide adequate credit to SSMEs with a view to developing incentives to induce a more favourable response.

There are at least two contrasting views and explanations regarding the behaviour of formal financial institutions with respect to the provision of credit to SSMEs. These two views lead to sharply different policy prescriptions. The recent experience of Nigeria provides an opportunity to test, in preliminary and very broad terms, an element of this controversy. The modest objective of this chapter is, thus, to analyse the extent to which the recent experience of financial liberalization in the context of structural adjustment in Nigeria has affected the chances of SSMEs of obtaining credit from the formal financial institutions.

The first section articulates the two contrasting views regarding access to formal credit by SSMEs and the policy implications associated with them; the next section describes the objectives, instruments, processes and effects on the banking system of Nigeria's structural adjustment programme, paying particular attention to the liberalization of the financial system; the broad patterns of credit sourcing by SSMEs from formal financial intermediaries in Nigeria during the 1980–90 period are then discussed, before the last section examines the impact of banking deregulation on the availability of credit to the SSMEs through a simple test of the basic hypothesis of this chapter[1].

Access to formal credit by SSMEs

At the risk of creating analytical caricatures, two broad views regarding access of SSMEs to credit from formal financial intermediaries can be identified in the literature. One may refer to them as 'pro-state' compared with 'pro-market'. Both views stress the importance and significance of the small-scale and microenterprise sector for overall economic development, especially of the less developed countries (LDCs). Both also agree, broadly, that lack of adequate access to credit constitutes one of the major obstacles to the realization of the great potential associated with the dynamic growth of the SSME sector. They diverge sharply, however, with respect to both the alleged cause of this obstacle and the appropriate mechanisms for its elimination or amelioration.

The pro-state view focuses largely on inherent imperfections in the credit market and some institutional behaviour characteristics as the primary sources of the problem. It therefore stresses the role of government intervention as an important and inevitable mechanism for removing the obstacle. In comparison, the pro-market view pays little or no attention to endemic market imperfections; rather it sees government intervention as the primary source of the problem, not a part of its solution.

In more specific terms, the pro-state view emanates from a system in which banks are considered as legitimate instruments for achieving important developmental and social goals. When shortage of investment funds and working capital is diagnosed as holding back the development of the private sector, particularly SSMEs, in such a system, recourse to government intervention in which the credit allocation decisions of banks appears normal. The justification for this intervention can be based on market failure associated with the provision of formal financial support to SSMEs which can be overcome only when government steps in to supplement, enhance or even replace private efforts. It may also be based on the need to overcome the bottleneck created by a combination of conservative bankers and high SSME start-up costs which can inhibit the development of financial intermediation to SSMEs. Finally, the need to provide for a more equitable sharing of the risks and administrative costs of SSME credit between the private and public sectors may provide the justification for special financing schemes (Anderson and Khambata, 1985).

Whatever its justification, the result of government intervention in the credit market for SSMEs is usually to induce formal financial institutions to supply more credit to SSMEs and/or at lower interest rates, through subsidy, offer of guarantees or outright compulsion, than they would otherwise voluntarily provide. Alternatively, separate and special institutions are created and specifically funded to provide more and/or cheaper credit to the SSMEs.

The pro-market view sees government intervention that imposes direct credit allocation to privileged sectors of the economy (such as SSMEs) as distortionary; it not only reduces the freedom of lending by banks, it also damages their profitability. Because such interventions often include low loan rate ceilings and are associated with negative real deposit rates, it is argued that they reduce savings deposits by generating disincentives to financial savings and discourage banks from lending to SSMEs which quickly become unattractive loan candidates, given that they tend to be riskier borrowers, there are high costs of administering numerous small loans and generally low recovery rates traditionally associated with such loans (Callier, 1991). Furthermore, in a market which is financially repressed through negative real interest rates and related credit regulations, the real offer of credit from the formal financial system tends to contract. This necessarily leads to greater self-financing by all private sector enterprises. In this rationed environment, not every enterprise has the same probability of access to credit; in fact, the larger enterprises are more likely to enjoy greater and disproportionate access to credit thus benefiting more from the implicit cost of funds subsidy than the smaller enterprises. The latter are, as a consequence, crowded out of the formal credit system and are forced to rely to a greater extent on self-financing and/or more expensive informal credit.

Hence, the pro-market view comes to the conclusion that it is precisely government intervention which discourages mobilization of financial savings and, as a consequence, restricts the access of private-sector enterprises, particularly the SSMEs, to formal credit. The policy implication emerging from this conclusion is obvious. To ensure improved access of SSMEs to formal credit, the financial system should be allowed to move toward greater reliance on market forces for savings mobilization and credit allocation. This reform, it is suggested, will ensure that the interest rate structure and other regulations do not stand in the way of the development of a competitive financial system.

In general, the pro-state view is concerned about both the cost and adequacy of credit made available to SSMEs while the market view regards credit availability, rather than its cost, as the primary concern. The recent efforts aimed at liberalizing the financial system as an integral part of the structural adjustment programme (SAP) in many African countries provide an opportunity to examine several empirical questions which can be posed in relation to these two contrasting views. What are the consequences of financial liberalization for credit availability and interest rate levels faced by SSMEs? What are the effects of SAP on the banking system itself? Would SSMEs have an equal or better chance of obtaining formal credit from a more competitive banking system? Some tentative answers to these questions are offered below, on the basis of an analysis of the Nigerian experience.

Structural adjustment and liberalization of the Nigerian financial system

Nigeria's structural adjustment programme (SAP) became operational in 1986. Its three major objectives were to (i) restructure and diversify the productive base of the economy so as to reduce dependence on the oil sector and imports, (ii) achieve fiscal and balance of payments viability; and (iii) lay the basis for a reasonable non-inflationary growth (CBN, 1986). With particular regard to the financial system, the primary aim was to enhance financial savings and efficient resource (i.e. credit) allocation through the reduction of complex administrative controls simultaneously with greater reliance on market forces. This was to be achieved in three main directions. First, there was a substantial lowering of prevailing entry barriers into the banking industry. Second, a gradual liberalization of the existing sectoral credit allocation system was embarked upon; while third, a phased de-control of the interest rate structure was implemented.

The lowering of entry barriers into the banking industry had a dramatic effect. The number of banks operating in Nigeria rose dramatically between 1985 and 1990 (see Table 11.1). This number increased by 170 per cent from 40 in 1985 to 108 in 1990. The pace at which new banking institutions came onstream increased continuously during this period while unsatisfied demand for new banking licences (i.e. number of applications for new banking licences) doubled from 1986 to reach 36 in 1987, and increased further to 45 in 1986 and 60 in 1990. It is worth noting that demand for new merchant (i.e. wholesale and investment) banks was much stronger as it accounted for almost 55 per cent of the new banks that opened for business during the 1986–90 period. Overall, the upsurge in the growth of banking institutions in Nigeria during this period has no parallel in the previous three decades or so.

Policy change with respect to government intervention in credit allocation decision of banks was no less dramatic. By the end of 1985, a complex system of administratively-determined credit-sharing targets for the banking system had developed and was delivered to the banks each year through monetary policy circulars and credit guidelines issues by the Central Bank of Nigeria (CBN). At the launching of the SAP, the number of sectors for which targets were specified had risen to 16. This number was gradually reduced, following the policy change, so that by the end of 1990, the number of sectors had been reduced to only two. Thus,

Table 11.1 Number of New Banks in Nigeria, 1986–90

Type	*1986*	*1987*	*1988*	*1989*	*1990*	*Total*
Commercial Banks	1	5	7	7	11	31
Merchant Banks	—	4	9	10	14	37
Total	1	9	16	17	25	68

Source: CBN, Annual Report, various years.

the scope of directed credit and selective credit policies at below-market interest rates was substantially reduced.

Finally, the phased decontrol of interest rates had gone a long way by the end of 1990 from the rigid system prevailing up to 1985 when all rates were administratively determined and communicated to the banks periodically by the CBN. Typically, LDCs are advised that, in liberalizing their interest rates, they should adopt either of two possible strategies (Callier, 1991). One strategy is to set interest ranges for deposit rates and lending rates separately, and allow banks to set rates within these ranges, then widen these ranges over time so as to phase in interest rate liberalization. The second method is to fix the maximum spread between the average cost of funds and their lending rates, and then allow the banks to determine the levels of their interest rates.

The Nigerian interest-rate deregulation process has been characterized by a hybrid of these two strategies. Firstly, the ceiling on bank lending rates was raised from 13 per cent to 15 per cent in 1986. Secondly, subject to the floor deposit rate of 8½ per cent, 'the banks and their customers were given the freedom to negotiate mutually acceptable rates according to the size and maturity of deposits or loans, as well as the forces of supply and demand for funds' (CBN, 1986). In August 1987, banks' prime lending rates became fully negotiable. These changes produced the interest rate structure shown in Table 11.2.

Compared with 1985, most interest rate levels had increased two-to three-fold by 1990. The Central Bank periodically commented approvingly on the result of its interest rate deregulation exercise. In its 1986 report, it declared that 'one significant development during the last quarter of 1986 was the aggressive drive by banks for deposits; in fact, the major banks moved out of their shells and offered attractive savings instruments to the public at competitive rates of interest' (CBN, 1986). Two years later, it was claimed that 'interest rate deregulation has made the financial markets more competitive and stimulated the emergence of new instruments for financing corporate institutions' (CBN, 1988). And, finally, in 1990, the Central Bank concluded that 'the relatively high interest rates had a positive effect on savings deposits generally' (CBN, 1990).

Table 11.2 Selected Interest Rates 1980–90; (per cent)

	1980	*1985*	*1986*	*1987*	*1988*	*1989*	*1990*
Minimum Rediscount Rate	6.0	10.0	10.0	12.75	12.75	18.50	18.50
Treasury Bill Rate	5.0	8.5	8.5	11.75	11.75	16.50	17.50
Savings Deposit	5.0	9.0	9.0	14.0	12.0	16.0	17.50
Time Deposit (6–12 months)	5.0	9.5	9.5	14.0	12.0	16.50	17.8
Time Deposit (over 12 months)	6.25	9.75	10.5	15.0	14.5	17.5	23.0
Prime Lending Rate	7.5	10.5	11.5	17.5	17.0	25.5	29.0

Source: Central Bank of Nigeria, Annual Report, various years.

In spite of (or perhaps, because of) the policy of financial system deregulation and liberalization, commitment to the financing of SSMEs through special arrangements and institutions remained strong in policy circles. Hence, parallel with the financial reform effort was the decision to create additional special institutions and new funding mechanisms specifically targeted at the SSMEs. The People's Bank of Nigeria (PBN) was established in 1990 as a fully government-owned financial institution, intended to have branches all over the country and provide loans to SSMEs at below market rates. Similarly, a new set of financial institutions called Community Banks, was established. In each case, the equity capital of a typical community bank would be contributed by a mixture of individuals and groups in the community and the bank would provide retail banking services only within that community, with the expectation that its activities would focus predominantly on the SSME sector.

Furthermore, steps were taken to establish a number of other institutions charged with the responsibility of channelling funds to the SSME sector. At the apex of these is the Small Business Management Assistance Agency which is meant to oversee three other arrangements. Included in these are (i) the Credit Guarantee Scheme which is to support SSMEs through a variable system of risk sharing; (ii) an SSME Credit Insurance Scheme; and (iii) a Small and Medium Enterprise Loan Facility (SMELF) with a funds base of US $415.8 million sourced partly from the World Bank and the African Development Bank.

Sourcing SSME Credit Through Formal Financial Institutions

With effect from 1979, the Central Bank of Nigeria has directed banks to reserve a certain proportion of their total loans and advances for the SSMEs. These are defined as wholly-owned Nigerian enterprises with annual turnover up to N25 million or whose capital investment does not exceed N10 million. In its most recent survey, NISER (1987) found that in terms of the volume of loans received by SSMEs, commercial, merchant and development banks accounted for almost 80 per cent of loans. Although this constituted only 27 per cent of the funds required by the SSMEs, the actual and potential significance of these formal sources of credit to the SSME sector is not in doubt. But what have been the trend and structure of such credit over time? This is the issue addressed in this section.

Table 11.3 throws some light on this issue by revealing a number of important features of the trend and structure of formal credit. Clearly, total credit (i.e. loans and advances) expanded rapidly over the 1980–90 period. Commercial and merchant banks accounted for the predominant proportion of total credit although their share showed a declining trend, as it fell from 96 per cent to 92 per cent between 1980 and 1990.

Correspondingly, credit to SSME from commercial and merchant banks rose sharply over the same period. In fact, the share of total loans and advances extended to the SSMEs rose from less than two per cent in 1980 to just over seven per cent in 1985 and almost 23 per cent in 1990. The predominance of the commercial

Table 11.3 Loans and Advances of Commercial, Merchant and Development Banks, 1980–90 (₦mil)

	1980	*1985*	*1990*
Commercial Banks	9066.9	12136.8	25764.2
Merchant Banks	400.2	1779.4	7227.1
Sub-Total	9467.1	13916.2	32991.3
Development Banks	367.1	689.3	2958.9
of which:			
NACB	132.5	312.7	1305.4
NIDB	82.3	64.9	642.5
NBCI	152.3	311.7	1011.0
Grand Total	9834.2	14605.5	35950.2
Distribution (%)			
Commercial and Merchant Banks	96.27	95.28	91.77
Development Banks	3.73	4.72	8.23
SSME Credit (₦mil)			
from Commercial and Merchant Banks	106.1	1037.7	7542.0
as % of total commercial and merchant bank credit	1.12	7.46	22.86
as % of total credit of development banks	28.90	150.54	254.89

NACB = Nigerian Agricultural and Co-operative Bank.
NIDB = Nigerian Industrial Development Bank.
NBCI = Nigerian Bank for Commerce and Industry.

Source: CBN, Annual Report, various years.

and merchant banks as the primary source of formal credit to the SSME sector is clearly demonstrated. The table shows that while SSME credit from commercial and merchant banks was less than 30 per cent of total loans and advances of the development banks in 1980, this ratio was over 150 per cent in 1985 and had risen further to almost 255 per cent in 1990. This trend makes it clear that there is more to be gained in terms of access of SSMEs to formal credit by focusing more policy attention on the lending behaviour of commercial and merchant banks.

Impact of banking deregulation on SSME credit

The liberalization of Nigeria's financial system led, as has been shown, to sharp increases in the rates of interest and it involved some phasing out of direct and selective credit-control policies. At the same time, access to credit by the SSMEs seems to have improved, as both the volume and ratio of total loans and advances going to the SSME sector show a marked increase, particularly between 1985 and 1990. To answer the question whether and the extent to which SSME did better or worse, in terms of credit availability, in the new liberalized financial environment, a 'before and after' comparison, using the concept of the counterfactual, seems appropriate.

A model of constant market shares lends itself to this analysis. In this framework, credit to SSMEs as a proportion of total bank (commercial and merchant) credit during two periods is calculated and represented as a_1 and a_2. It is also interesting to calculate the change in the volume of credit to SSMEs over time. This entails a comparison of the absolute figures (i.e. m_1 and m_2) over time as well.

This total change in volume of credit made available to the SSMEs over two periods is measured by $m_2 - m_1$ which can be decomposed into two parts. One of these represents the effects of structural change and is analogous to a substitution effect. The other reflects the impact of change in overall size of total credit available to all sectors and is close to the more familiar concept of income (or wealth) effect. The first effect results from gains or losses in (relative) market share over time; while the second can be ascribed to a general increase or decrease in the share of each recipient sector as a result of the expansion or contraction of total credit. The first effect can be traced to such things as changes in sectoral credit allocation policy and sectoral interest rate and risk differentials. The second effect would reflect overall monetary policy stance and credit ceilings, signalling credit ease or tightness.

Given the percentage share of total credit taken up by the SSMEs in period I (i.e. a_1), the amount of credit for the SSMEs predicted (or regarded as hypothetical) for period II is a_1M_2 if there has been no structural change (i.e $a_1 = a_2$) and M_2 represents the volume of total bank credit to all sectors in period II. A comparison of this hypothetical value of SSME credit (a_1M_2) with the actual value (m_2) in period II yields a measure of the impact of structural change or substitution effect (due to policy and/or perceived sectoral interest rate and risk differentials). Similarly, a comparison of a_1m_2 with m_1 gives the measure of the effect of changes in the overall credit volume. This can be expressed as follows:

$$m_2 - m_1 = (m_2 - a_1M_2) + (a_1M_2 - m_1)$$

where,

$m_2 - m_1$ = total change (TC)

$(m_2 - a_1M_2)$ = substitution effect (SE)

$(a_1M_2 - m_1)$ = credit volume effect (CVE)

Table 11.4 presents estimates of total change and its two component parts for commercial and merchant bank draft to SSMEs during the 1986–90 period. This covers the period of financial liberalization; the base period against which each of the five subsequent years is compared is 1985. In that year, the proportion of total commercial bank loans and advances allocated to the SSMEs was eight per cent (i.e. $a_1 = 0.08$) while the corresponding proportion for merchant banks was 3.4 per cent (yielding $a_1 = 0.034$).

The computations show that for both commercial and merchant banks, credit al-

Table 11.4 Substitution and Credit Volume Effects of Financial Liberalization on SSME Credit, 1986–90 (₦million)

	1986	*1987*	*1988*	*1989*	*1990*
Commercial Banks					
Total change	2669.8	2932.8	3225.0	3561.3	4922.8
Substitution effect	2173.5	2406.2	2601.4	2758.7	3838.9
	(81.4)	(82.0)	(80.7)	(77.5)	(78.0)
Credit volume effect	496.3	526.6	623.6	802.6	1083.9
	(18.6)	(18.0)	(19.3)	(22.5)	(22.0)
Merchant Banks					
Total change	626.5	659.5	922.0	1190.5	1581.5
Substitution effect	565.3	592.7	832.0	1050.4	1396.3
	(90.2)	(89.9)	(90.2)	(88.2)	(88.3)
Credit volume effect	61.2	66.88	90.0	140.1	185.3
	(9.8)	(10.1)	(9.8)	(11.8)	(11.7)

TC = total change (between each year and 1985)
SE = substitution effect
CVE = credit volume effect

Source: author's compulations

located to SSMEs increased progressively from 1986 through 1990 (estimates of TC are uniformly positive and large). This implies that access to credit of the SSMEs actually improved during the period of financial liberalization when interest rates rose rather sharply. How this increase in SSME credit volume was distributed between its two components during this period is, perhaps, even more interesting. In the case of commercial banks, between 78 and 82 per cent of the increased SSME credit was accounted for by movement away from other sectors and in favour of the SSMEs; for the merchant banks, the corresponding ratio was even higher as it ranged from 88 to 90 per cent. Clearly, therefore, most of the large upsurge in commercial and merchant bank credit to the SSMEs did not emanate from a more permissive monetary policy stance during this period.

Concluding Remarks

Before SAP was launched, Nigeria had attempted to provide special access to bank credit for the SSMEs by establishing targets with respect to such credit for commercial and merchant banks. These targets were based on enterprise size as measured by level of capital investment or annual turnover (see section above) rather than loan size, although average loan size for SSMEs was usually smaller than for larger enterprises. Thus, in 1979, banks were directed to extend at least 10 per cent of their lending to indigenous borrowers for small and medium size enterprises. This target was increased to 16 per cent in 1980. Commercial and merchant banks uniformly failed to meet or even satisfy up to 50 per cent of this target between 1979 and 1985. Olashore (1985) cites two important reasons why banks were unable to comply as (a) 'the problem caused by concessionary rate of interest which often encourages diversion of funds to other ventures where such concessionary rates are not available' and (b) 'the loss to the banks who are compelled to lend at interest rates that are often below their cost of funds'. Between 1986 and 1990, however, the share of commercial and merchant bank loans and advances committed to the SSMEs ranged between 20 and 23 per cent; the prescribed target was exceeded when banks had become more liberalized and competitive.

This evidence casts doubt on the need for and efficacy of subsidized credit and the policy of sectoral targeting as these relate to the SSMEs. Special credit institutions and schemes are not likely to be able to mobilize and allocate anything close to the volume of financial savings available to the commercial and merchant banks whose lending behaviour must therefore remain critical to the development of the SSMEs.

Financing small-scale and microenterprises in Kenya under conditions of liberalized financial markets

KIRIMI M. MWARANIA

Introduction

The contribution that small- and micro-scale enterprises (SMEs) can make to employment, production and poverty alleviation is generally recognized. In Kenya, for example, they are expected to provide 75 per cent of all new jobs created in the urban sector and 50 per cent of all rural non-farm employment by the year 2000 (GOK, 1989a) Clearly, therefore, SMEs are expected to be major players in Kenya's economy.

In the past, SMEs in Kenya have been given low priority (GOK, 1989b). This was done not only by policymakers but also by researchers. Despite recent attempts to rectify this situation our knowledge of SMEs is still rudimentary and incomplete. For example, what are the appropriate technology choices for Kenya's SMEs? What market potential exists for their products and services? At what level of efficiency do they operate? What are their financial needs and what is the optimal way of satisfying these needs? What would constitute an enabling environment for their development? At the moment, satisfactory answers to these questions cannot be given.

This chapter addresses one small part of this important area. It attempts to answer the question: who is financing SMEs in Kenya now and what is the likely impact of the ongoing financial liberalization process on this financing?

Policy Environment

Since 1987 Kenya has been implementing a series of economic reform programmes commonly referred to as structural adjustment programmes (SAPs). These programmes have aimed at improving the macroeconomic environment, the incentive structure and the regulatory framework within which economic activity takes place. The overriding aim of these reforms has been to stabilize the economy, reverse economic decline and build a firm foundation for sustainable development.

To date reforms have focused on agriculture, industry, trade and finance. In agriculture, most producer prices have been decontrolled although some further work needs to be done in the areas of input and service supply and output marketing. In the industrial sector the import of raw materials and equipment have been liberalized and certain prices have been decontrolled. However, the major binding constraints in this sector still remain. These are the inadequacy of foreign exchange and the non-competitiveness of Kenya's manufactures in world markets. Financial liberalization began in 1989 and to date interest rates have been decontrolled and the regulatory framework has been strengthened.

While the above reforms are commendable they are not sufficient. There is a need to deepen them. However, at the moment, the government appears reluctant to do this. The reasons for this reluctance are not clear but they may be related to the political costs to the current leaders that are associated with any additional reforms. These costs have recently been increased considerably as a result of the re-introduction of competitive politics. Two areas requiring urgent attention are the parastatal sector and the public sector. These two sectors generate large budget deficits which not only propel inflation and other internal disequilibria but also spill over into the external sector where they cause balance of payments crisis.

Financial sector

Kenya has a diversified financial system, comprising a Central Bank, 28 commercial banks, 57 near-bank financial institutions (NBFI), 33 building societies, 64 hire-purchase companies, 9 development financial institutions (DFIs), over 1300 financial co-operatives, 36 insurance companies, 80 insurance brokers, the Nairobi Stock Exchange and six stock brokerage firms. Despite this range of financial institutions, financialization of savings in Kenya is low. The share of domestic savings held as financial assets is estimated at about 30 per cent which is the same as in the mid-1970s. Financial assets as a share of GDP is about 6 per cent which is higher than elsewhere in Sub-Saharan Africa but much lower than the average level for developing countries. The ratio of broad money (M2) which is used as a measure of monetization of transactions is also relatively low (at 29 per cent).

The structure of Kenya's financial market is characterized by a few strong and dominant institutions in each subsector (commercial banking, NBFI, insurance, building societies, etc.) surrounded by many smaller and financially unstable firms. Many of these weak institutions were formed in the late 1970s and the early 1980s. They were established largely because of low entry barriers and the high liquidity in the economy arising out of the 1976–8 coffee boom.

The new institutions increased competition and used new and innovative approaches in attracting deposits and in lending. They were largely successful in this. For example, their share of deposit rose from 17 per cent in 1978 to 32 per cent in 1987. These achievements, however, were not without cost. On average, the new institutions were poorly managed, invested in riskier assets than the traditional institutions, mismatched asset and liability maturity structures and operated within lower margins than the traditional institutions.

When the government instituted a credit squeeze in 1985–6 the fragile nature of these institutions was exposed. Four indigenous financial groups collapsed and this led to panic withdrawals from the other new institutions. By 1987, illiquidity and insolvency was endemic within the NBFI subsector.

The government's response to this crisis was to strengthen the regulatory framework. Some of the key reforms introduced were:

(a) A Deposit Protection Fund (to cover deposits up to KSh100,000);
(b) an increase in the minimum paid-up capital from Ksh 2 million and KSh10 million to KSh15 million and KSh150 million for locally and foreign incorporated banks respectively;
(c) limiting deposit mobilization capacity of any deposit-taking institution to a maximum of 13⅓ times of paid-up capital and unimpaired reserves;
(d) mandatory provision for bad and doubtful debts to be made annually before appropriating the year's profits;
(e) restriction of the shareholding of an individual to no more than 25 per cent of the equity capital;
(f) making it mandatory for every loan to be adequately covered by collateral and where collateral cover is inadequate making the directors of the institution personally liable for any bad debts arising from the loan.

The above regulations have the potential of reducing lending to SMEs or making any such lending more expensive than it would otherwise have been.

The introduction of a deposit protection fund paid for by the financial institutions means that the costs of these institutions has to rise. They in turn will attempt to recoup all or part of it from the borrowers and lenders. Since some of the borrowers are SMEs they will bear part of this higher cost. The extent to which the financial institutions are able to shift these extra costs to other parties will depend on the relative price elasticities.

An increase in the minimum paid-up capital of a financial institution restricts entry into the industry and leads to greater concentration. As the concentration ratio in Kenya's financial sector is already high (the four largest institutions control the bulk of deposits – over 60 per cent), this increased concentration leads to a quasi-monopoly situation. When small financial institutions were allowed, SMEs benefited because they could deal with firms of their size. Now they have to deal with very large financial firms and they face the danger of being marginalized.

Limiting the deposit mobilization capacity is another form of entry discrimination against small financial institutions and, by extension, against SMEs.

Restricting the shareholders of an individual financial institution may not be a restriction on entry in countries where there are very many wealthy or near-wealthy individuals. However, in an economy like that of Kenya where the savings potential of the majority of the people is very low, restricting shareholders is another form of limitation of entry into the financial sector. It is likely, therefore, to have the same adverse effects on SMEs as the other forms of restriction mentioned above.

Making collateral lending the only legal form of lending affects SMEs very adversely because many of them lack collateral and are therefore automatically excluded from the formal credit markets.

Liberalization: eliminating financial distortions

The efficiency of the financial system in Kenya after 1987 was still reduced by several major constraints:

Differential regulatory structure

Institutions and financial instruments with similar characteristics were subjected to different regulations. For example, commercial banks and NBFIs operated in the same markets, competing for deposits from a common source and lending to the same market segment. Despite these similarities they faced different regulatory requirements. For example, commercial banks were subjected to lower interest rate ceilings, higher capital requirements, greater limits on credit expansion and could not levy non-interest fees and service charges. This discrimination may be the cause of the excessive growth in NBFIs and building societies between 1978 and 1987.

Financial instruments were also regulated differentially. For example, debt financing received preferential tax treatment relative to equity financing. This is because the return on equity (i.e. dividends) was taxed twice (at both corporate and individual levels) whereas the return of debt was taxed only once. This differential treatment may have led to over-reliance on debt financing that is characteristic of most Kenyan firms. This in turn led to unstable capital structures and a stunted capital market (stunted because there is no demand for equity securities).

Prudential supervision

The application and enforcement of laws regarding reporting, audit requirements, and financial contracts was weak. Until recently the regulatory power of the Central Bank was limited and supervision itself was hindered by lack of staff and adequate information.

Financial institutions also faced and still face problems in enforcing financial contracts, especially those involving land used as collateral. It is extremely difficult to realize this collateral in the event of default by the borrowers because courts are sometimes reluctant to enforce the law and at other times the executive wing of the government intervenes on the side of the defaulting borrower.

Monetary control

The main instrument of monetary control in Kenya is the use of ceilings on commercial bank credit to the private sector. These ceilings have been used to offset the effect of the large fiscal deficits on monetary expansion. However, enforcement of these controls has been weak and selective. In particular, government-owned banks appear to have been exempt from these controls because even in periods of tight liquidity they have been able to expand lending.

Development Financial Institutions (DFIs)

DFIs were introduced in the 1960s and 1970s to alleviate market failure in the provision of long-term finance. They have been providing both equity and long-term loans to industrial and commercial enterprises including SMEs. The government owns most DFIs and maintains effective control over those in which it has a minority interest.

Apart from segmenting the financial sector further, DFIs have been characterized by a low capital base, a large portfolio of non-performing loans and heavy reliance on budgetary sources from external sources (i.e. donors). They have also been unprofitable and financially unstable. Instead of helping solve the problems that led to their being formed, they have become problems themselves.

Interest rates policy

For most of the 1960s and 1970s interest rate ceilings were pegged at levels that were too low to allow any positive real return. Naturally, this discouraged savings and attracted investments that would otherwise not have been viable. In the 1980s the government attempted to peg rate ceilings at levels that were above the inflation rate. Success was however hampered by failure to measure inflation accurately, leading to what were probably illusionary positive real interest rates. Inflation in Kenya has been measured using the Nairobi Consumer Price Index (CPI) constructed on the basis of household consumption weights that were last revised in 1974. A new series will be introduced in 1992 which will use household consumption weights derived from the 1981–2 Urban Household Budget Survey. Nobody, therefore, knows for sure what the inflation rate has been and nobody will be able to know it for a quite a while. Until this matter is settled, it is a matter of conjecture whether real interest rates have been positive or negative.

From July 1991 the government removed controls on interest rates. It is too early to determine what the new structure will be but indications are that the base rate is settling in the neighbourhood of 17 per cent with a variable margin of about 6 per cent to cover different classes of risk.

Specific financial reforms

In 1989 the government began implementing a comprehensive financial liberalization programme with a view to removing the above distortions and increasing the efficiency of financial intermediation.

The specific reforms included in this programme are:

Interest rate liberalization

The objective here is to harmonize the interest rate structure across institutions and to allow financial institutions greater flexibility in determining and varying interest rates. Interest rate reforms have been implemented in phases, beginning in April 1989 and the process was completed in July 1991.

Monetary policy reforms

The aim is to shift from credit control to indirect monetary policy instruments including open market operations. Although not much has been achieved in this area yet the government has already started the auctioning of T-bills and T-bonds and is improving the database necessary to use reserve money management and open market operations. In addition auctioning of foreign bearer certificates has began.

Prudential services

Both the technical and legal capacity of the Central Bank has been strengthened. The Banking Act of 1989 increased the role of the Central Bank, reduced the regulatory disparity between commercial banks and NBFIs and brought building societies under the same rules as NBFIs and Commercial Banks.

Staffing of the Central Bank has also been increased and training enhanced so as to cope with the increased supervisory responsibilities.

Restructuring ailing financial institutions

By 1987 it was estimated that 28 financial institutions (four banks and 24 NBFIs) faced solvency and liquidity problems. These institutions accounted for about 15 per cent of the total liabilities of all banks and NBFIs. To avoid a major crisis it was decided to implement an orderly restructuring programme. To date ten trouble-ridden institutions have merged together to form the Consolidated Bank of Kenya. Funds for this restructuring came from the Deposit Protection Fund and the World Bank.

DFIs

A restructuring plan has been drawn up for the two largest DFIs (i.e. Industrial Development Bank and Industrial and Commercial Development Corporation). The plan covers change in their mandate, autonomy, funding, organization and the investment processes. Unfortunately there have been delays in implementing this plan.

At the moment the government is ambivalent about the future of the other DFIs. Some will be perhaps sold, some restructured and others dismantled.

Securities market

Several reforms have been undertaken to remove the bias favouring debt financing. These include the removal of the Capital Issues Committee's role in regulating share issues; elimination of double-taxation of dividend income by conversion of the withholding tax into a final tax, abolition of tax duties on retail-share transactions and tax deductibility of all costs incurred in the issue of shares and bonds.

To strengthen the regulatory and supervisory framework of the securities industry the Capital Markets Act of 1989 was enacted and a Capital Markets Authority was set up to implement it.

The above reforms (and others that have not yet been implemented) are intended to encourage the development of a market-oriented system of financial intermediation. As it currently stands, it is still incomplete because unsustainable public expenditure has not yet been tackled. Yet any financial reform package that does not put a limit on the expansion of public expenditure is unlikely to succeed. However, assuming the financial liberalization programme is fully implemented, what is its likely impact on SMEs funding? We now turn to this issue.

Financing SMEs

Before discussing the financing of SMEs it is worthwhile to first define them. There are no generally accepted definitions of SMEs. Some people use the asset base as the defining rod, some use turnover levels, some use the number of employees, while others use some combination of the three criteria. The Government of Kenya uses the number of employees as the criterion for distinguishing SMEs from non-SMEs and defines a SME as any enterprise with fewer than 50 employees. In Kenya such enterprises are engaged in trade, commerce, distribution, transport, agribusiness, manufacturing and repairs and maintenance.

The SMEs sector may be further classified as follows:

(a) Microenterprises employing 1–5 persons.
(b) Small enterprises employing 6–20 employees.
(c) Medium enterprises employing 21–50 employees.

Needless to say, these classifications are somewhat arbitrary and their only purpose is to enable more focused attention. Furthermore, it is an open question whether (c) above should really be included within the SME sector.

Within the Kenyan context, class (b) above has been referred to as the 'missing middle' because of lack of support. A recent USAID study quoted in GOK (1989a), for example, found that five out of every ten business proposals submitted by enterprises in the missing middle are viable, but only one is funded because of the stringent collateral and equity requirements in existence.

Despite its perceived importance in generating employment and production, the SME sector in Kenya has very inadequate access to credit. Only a very small percentage of SMEs have any access to institutional credit. Most of their financing, therefore, comes from own savings or informal credit markets controlled by NGOs and community welfare groups. A few SMEs have also been able to obtain credit from specialized credit agencies set up by the government and the donor community for this purpose.

The agencies currently engaged in credit delivery to SMEs may be classified as follows:

Commercial banks

As of December 1990, Kenya had 28 commercial banks. These banks had 400 branches, sub-branches, agencies and mobile units and accounted for about 66 per cent of the total deposits in the economy. Nearly all the lending done by commercial banks is short-term (i.e. two years or less) and the bulk of the credit is in the form of bank overdrafts. As the bulk of these overdrafts are rolled over they effectively become term loans.

The commercial banking system is dominated by a few major banks namely: the

Kenya Commercial Bank, Barclays Bank, Standard Bank and the National Bank of Kenya. Together these four banks account for over 60 per cent of the commercial bank deposits and credit volume.

Commercial banks are very conservative in their lending policies and lending to the SME sector does not form a significant part of their portfolio. Exact confirmation of this conjecture is difficult because the reports they file with the Central Bank do not disaggregate lending by size of enterprise. The conjecture is based on the fact that most commercial bank lending has land, buildings and equipment as the main forms of collateral. Commercial banks are exceedingly reluctant to offer collateral-free loans although they are willing to develop functional equivalents to the collateral.

Current commercial lending to the SME sector falls under two broad classes: (a) lending under special programmes and (b) lending in the normal course of business.

Special programme lending. Nearly all the lending in this category is funded by external donors with the government and the commercial banks acting merely as intermediaries. The typical special programme will identify the special business enterprise category to benefit, provide guarantees to the bank to minimize credit risk exposure, provide funds to cover administration costs and subsidized funds for on-lending to the target SMEs. Usually banks are asked to contribute part of the fund to be lent out. The banks that have been mainly involved in this type of lending are the Kenya Commercial Bank and Barclays Bank. The other two banks have also been involved but to a lesser extent.

Some of the special programme lending schemes that have been implemented include line of credit with International Finance Corporation (1977–8); line of credit with United States Agency for International Development (USAID) (1983); the Rural Enterprise Programme funded by USAID; Skills development for Self-Reliance funded by International Labour Organisation (ILO); and the Kenya Women's Finance Trust (1981) funded by Women World Bank.

Broadly speaking, commercial banks are not keen on these types of lending and it is clear that left to themselves (i.e. without government pressure) they would probably not get involved at all. They complain of problems in raising matching funds particularly in times of credit squeeze and also of the long maturity periods involved when loans are advanced to SMEs. With liberalized financial markets the pressure the government is currently exerting on commercial banks to participate in these special lending schemes will be removed. The impact of this on SME development is likely to be adverse unless an alternative credit delivery system is worked out.

Another worrying aspect is the over-dependence on donor funding. It is obvious that if donors withdrew from this funding most special programme lending would cease.

Normal lending. Commercial banks are not required by law to report the extent of their lending to the SME sector. They are also extremely reluctant to disclose this information to third parties making it therefore very difficult to know the extent of their lending to the SME sector.

An indirect method can, however, be used to estimate the total amount of credit flowing to this sector using the aggregated data reported to the Central Bank. By looking at the types of business where SMEs in Kenya are likely to be involved, and by assuming that they borrow within the range up to KSh200,000, the total amount going to SMEs comes to about 4 per cent of the total credit volume. This compares favourably with the worldwide observation that commercial bank credit that goes to the SME sector is in the 2–3 per cent range. This crude 'guestimate' should be taken with care and it probably overstates the actual situation. With an outstanding commercial bank credit of KSh34 billion as of March 1990, the total estimated to be within the SME sector comes to about KSh1.4 billion.

Table 12.1 Loans and Advances by Commercial Banks

End of Year	*Public Sector KSh Million*	*Private Sector KSh Million*	*Total KSh Million*
1982	253.80	6971.43	7225.23
1986	560.17	14072.42	14632.59
1988	3605.62	24253.32	27858.94
1989	3941.11	30075.95	34017.06
1990	4392.24	27418.81	31811.05

Source: Central Bank of Kenya.

Near-Bank Financial Institutions (NBFIs)

The extent of lending by the NBFIs to SMEs is also not known because of non-reporting of this information. However, a similar estimation method to the one used in the case of commercial banks, provides a probable figure of 3.6 per cent for the SME sector. With KSh28 billion as the outstanding NBFIs portfolio of lending as of March 1990, the total credit allocated to SMEs is about KSh1 billion.

NBFIs do not have special lending programmes targeting SMEs. Therefore, all the lending to SMEs is in the normal course of business. Until the onset of the financial crisis in 1985–6, NBFIs were, however, known to be more liberal in granting loans to SMEs. Some observers have argued that the main cause of the crisis was the high percentage of loans and advances that was targeted to non-profitable SMEs (Oyejide in this volume).

Development Finance Institutions

As indicated earlier, DFIs were formed in the 1960s and 1970s to fill in perceived gaps in financial intermediation and in particular the provision of long-term finance. They were sector-specific and one of their major impacts appears to be the increase in financial-sector segmentation.

The Land and Agricultural Bank of Kenya was renamed the Agricultural Finance Corporation in 1963 and restructured to cater for large- and small-scale African farmers in addition to the colonial farmers upon whom it had previously concentrated. The Industrial Development Corporation, which had been formed in 1954, was renamed the Industrial and Commercial Development Corporation (ICDC) in 1964 and reorganized to finance medium- and small-scale businessmen. The Development Finance Company of Kenya (DFCK) was formed in 1968 while the Industrial Development Bank was incorporated in 1973. Both were to provide equity and long-term debt to medium- and large-scale enterprises. In 1965, the Kenya Tourist Development Corporation was formed to finance enterprises engaged in the development of tourism. As the above examples indicate, whenever some need was felt a DFI was launched to meet that need. This was in conformity with the state of economic wisdom then which encouraged an interventionist approach. We appear to have gone full cycle because today the fashion is exactly the opposite. Whenever a DFI exists today the reaction is to restructure it or to dismantle it or better still sell it to the private business.

The DFIs which have special lending programmes for the SME sector include the Kenya Industrial Estates (KIE); the Small Enterprise Finance Company (SEFCO) and the Industrial and Commercial Development Corporation (ICDC). KIE was incorporated in 1967 as a subsidiary of ICDC. Its objectives were threefold, namely: the indigenization of the country's industrial sector, rural industrialization and employment creation. Between 1967 and 1977 it operated as a purely technical and managerial extension services institution mainly assisting clients to prepare bankable proposals to be financed by ICDC. This was done because it was felt that the KIE target group was not capable of preparing project feasibility reports nor could they afford to pay private consultants to do so for them.

From 1977 KIE started lending. Its current lending limits are set at KSh10 million for new projects and KSh15 million for ongoing projects. KIE also has an informal sector credit programme for which the maximum loan limit had been set at KSh35,000 (which has now been increased to KSh100,000 for second-time borrowers).

The future of KIE under the liberalized financial markets is unclear. Suggestions have been made to the effect that with competitive interest rates, commercial banks and NBFIs will be able to take over KIE's current market and therefore the institution should be dismantled or merged with ICDC. Such a rash move may, however, do more harm than good. KIE's success rate has been modest when measured against financial returns. Despite this, it has played a critical role in acting as a nest in which Kenya's budding industrialists have been nurtured. Until the conservatism that currently characterizes commercial banks and NBFIs changes, KIE will still have a role to play in providing project finance and other auxiliary project services. There is, however, a need to reform KIE so that those industrialists who refuse to leave the nest after an appropriate period are thrown out to create room for other more deserving entrepreneurs.

SEFCO was incorporated in 1983 as a subsidiary of the Development Finance Company of Kenya (DFCK). It took over the functions and assets of the Small

Scale Industries Programme (SSIP) set up by the DFCK in 1978. SEFCO finances rural-based enterprises. It has developed various credit programmes designed to access the target beneficiaries. Some of these include the Fully Secured Loan Scheme, the Credit Guarantee Association Scheme, the Individual Guarantee Loan Scheme and the Short-Term Loan Scheme. SEFCO may be said to be the first private-sector company formed specially to finance the SME sector. It has a well-diversified loan portfolio because as a matter of policy it does not invest more than 15 per cent of its lendable funds in any one type of business.

ICDC was inherited from the colonial government and restructured to provide equity and debt finance to small- and medium-scale businesses. It has three loan schemes aimed at the needs of SMEs. These are the Commercial Loans Scheme, the Industrial Loan Scheme and the Property Loan Scheme.

The Commercial Loans Scheme was set up to assist indigenous Kenyans to enter into commerce. At that time (around independence) their attempts were being hampered by lack of start-up capital. These loans were for working capital only and they ranged from KSh50,000 to KSh400,000 and they were repayable over a five-year period. Started in 1964, this scheme had by 1989 disbursed a total of KSh293 million to some 919 traders throughout the country.

The industrial loan scheme was set up to help small-scale manufacturers to set up or expand their industrial enterprises. The loans ranged from KSh20,000 to KSh2 million and covered up to a maximum of 70 per cent of the project cost. Between 1964 and 1990 a total of KSh146 million had been disbursed to over 100 small industrial projects.

The property loan scheme was started in 1969 and was intended to assist in the construction of commercial properties with a special focus on rural market centres. The maximum amount that could be borrowed under this scheme was KSh600,000 and it was repayable within a period of 15 years. By June 1987, a total of KSh165 million had been disbursed. Since then the scheme has been suspended for lack of funds.

It is not easy to assess loan recovery under the above schemes because complete data on recovery rates is non-existent. Discussions with ICDC management indicates that delinquency and default rates have been high.

ICDC is one of the DFIs that has been targeted for restructuring. This restructuring will cover phased divesture and consolidation of assets, emphasis on commercial viability in project selection, explicit budgetary compensation for projects selected on a non-commercial basis and changes intended to improve accountability. It is not clear what the overall impact on SME financing will be. What is clear is that those SMEs that have in the past relied on subsidized credit facilities from ICDC will no longer get it. On the brighter side more funds may be available for genuinely viable SMEs.

Financial co-operatives

There are over 1300 financial co-operatives in Kenya (they are commonly referred to as saving and credit co-operative societies) which accept monthly payment for shares and provide loans to their members. Financial co-operatives are an easy and popular source of loans for both consumption and investment in SMEs. Table 12.2 shows the growth of these co-operatives over the last 20 years.

Most financial co-operatives lend up to three times a member's savings at an interest rate of 1 per cent per month. Repayment is monthly usually over a period of 36 months.

It is difficult to estimate exactly how much of the lending by financial co-operatives goes into SMEs and how much is used in other activities such as consumption, education, and property development (e.g. buying land and building houses for owner occupancy). However, given that over KSh7 billion has been mobilized within the sector, careful targeting could greatly boost what is available to SMEs. A counterweight to this possibility is the fact that financial co-operatives are run on the traditional co-operative principles of service at cost, democratic control and limited interest on capital. With a membership that is largely consumption oriented these principles severely limit the extent to which funds mobilized in these institutions can be channelled to SMEs.

Non Governmental Organizations

There are over 1000 NGOs operating in Kenya. Most of them have strong links with foreign NGOs which are usually the parent organization. Kenyan NGOs are extremely dependent on external donor support and most of them would not survive without this support. Their operations also tend to be area-specific and very few have a nationwide network. Most NGOs begin as community welfare associations although over the years many of them come to include provision of credit in their operations.

NGOs typically employ a few people with one or two very dominant personalities (usually the founder members). Despite this they control considerable budgets sometimes running into millions of shillings.

NGOs run a whole range of credit schemes including Revolving Loan Funds, Seasonal Credit Schemes, Small Enterprise Development Schemes, Gramen Model Schemes, Loan Guarantee Schemes and Individual Credit Schemes. The amounts advanced are usually small (rarely going beyond KSh10,000). NGOs, therefore, are the main sources of extra-household funds used in micro enterprise development. Some NGOs focus exclusively on Women Entrepreneurs while others focus on both men and women.

Table 12.2 Financial Co-operatives

	1972	*1982*	*1987*
Number of societies	101	927	1300
Number of members	35700	600000	730000
Funds mobilized (in Ksh millions)	16	1500	7000
Loans advanced (in Ksh millions)	10	1300	—

Source: Central Bureau of Statistics, Govt of Kenya, various reports.

The future of the role of NGOs as providers of credit to SMEs is tied up with the continued flow of external donor support to them. This is because few of them are financially viable without this support. The financial liberalization programme, however, is unlikely to have a major impact on NGO activities as they currently operate outside the formal financial system and the liberalization programme is aimed specifically at the formal institutions.

Government

The government's direct credit to SMEs has traditionally been limited to the Joint Loan Board Scheme (JLBS) inherited from colonial times and since 1965 managed by the Ministry of Commerce.

The loans under this schemes are approved by a board consisting of representatives from the central government, local authorities and the local business community. The loans now have an upper limit of KSh40,000, and carry an interest rate of 6 per cent. In theory they are repayable within four years although in practice recovery rates are extremely low. Over 35,000 traders have benefited from this scheme. Since its inception in 1955 to December 1987 over KSh200 million were disbursed out of which KSh45 million is still in arrears.

In colonial times, the Joint Loan Board Scheme was one of the few credit openings for native businessmen because financial institutions were prohibited from lending to Africans (if they did so they could not enforce the contract in a court of law). Even then credit was only available to the 'good natives' which in practical terms means petty government spies, chiefs and other cronies of the then political order. With the attainment of independence other credit avenues became available and the status of the JLBs considerably declined. There have been discussions on the wisdom of converting the scheme into a financial institution but to date, no major steps have been taken in this direction.

Recently the government has started the Rural Enterprise Fund. (This should not be mistaken for the Kenya Rural Enterprise Programme which is basically a USAID-financed and private sector-managed fund.) This year's financial allocation to this fund was KSh400 million. However, its continued operation has been cast in doubt with the suspensions of funding by the main donor, the Danish International Development Agency (DANIDA).

Future of SME financing

The future of SME financing in Kenya will depend on the evolution of two current movements which appear to be mutually inconsistent. On the one hand, there is the financial liberalization programme which aims at increasing the efficiency of financial intermediation by removing arbitrary segmentation and by giving market forces a greater influence on credit pricing (i.e. interest rate setting); and savings mobilization and allocation. Implicit in this programme is a strong belief in the superiority of a free market economy over a command economy. This, of course, is the dominant paradigm of our times.

The market economy works best under certain rather idealistic conditions (i.e. perfect and complete markets, full and costless information; rational economic agents, etc.). Where real life markets approach this ideal, as in the economies of the west, market forces can have beneficial effects. In countries like Kenya, where most of economic activities are controlled by monopolists or at best by oligopolists, the belief that market forces can optimally allocate resources (including credit) is rather optimistic (Mwarania, 1988).

The other current movement is towards the formal recognition of the SME sector by the government and in particular recognizing that it is prone to suffer from market failure. This formal recognition began with the publication of Sessional Paper No.1 of 1986. This was further strengthened in the National Development Plan (1989–93) where of the 1.9 million jobs expected to be created, 587,000 are expected to be created within the SME sector. In 1989 the government published a long-term strategy paper for SSE development towards the year 2000.

This year a Sessional Paper is being prepared and tabled in parliament (GOK, 1992). This paper provides a framework for the promotion of SMEs. It is the culmination of the work of a special task force set up in 1987 to work out modalities for promoting the SME sector. With respect to financing, the focus of the paper is on:

(a) Continued reliance on concessionary external loans as a basis of the funding of special credit schemes for SMEs.
(b) A change of policy to allow commercial banks to charge fees for auxiliary services that accompany loan delivery to SMEs (i.e. feasibility studies, and other extension services). Currently banks are not allowed to charge such fees.
(c) Use of the Training Levy Fund by banks and DFIs to train SME clients. Currently only employees of financial institutions can utilize this fund.
(d) Setting up a special training fund for training SME entrepreneurs. Contributions to this fund are expected to come from the government, the donor community and the private sector.
(e) Creating a forum to initiate studies on risks and costs associated with lending to the SME sector. This forum will also review regulations and policies that may from time to time hinder financial flows to the SME sector.
(f) Allowing DFIs to accept deposits in order to generate funds to lend to SME. Currently DFIs cannot solicit deposits from local sources.
(g) Reducing government borrowing from the financial sector so that more resources can be made available to the private sector and hence SMEs.
(h) Continuation by the government to bear foreign exchange risks on any foreign borrowing in order to shield the local business sector from exchange risks that they cannot hedge.
(i) Consider the establishment of an SME Export Credit facility to encourage SMEs to enter the export market.
(j) Relaxing the collateral requirements in the current lending regulations to enable non-collateralized lending to SMEs.

(k) Encouraging the use of credit guarantee schemes in lieu of collateral and exploring the viability of setting up a National Credit Guarantee Corporation.
(l) Training of bankers so that they can have positive attitudes towards SMEs.
(m) Exploring the possibility of setting up a Venture Capital Corporation to provide seed capital and bridging loans to SMEs.

The above thirteen policy proposals suggest a highly interventionist approach in the financial markets in favour of SMEs. They include the continuation of the special credit schemes that commercial banks are already resistant to in addition to setting up an additional three SME-oriented DFIs.

This puts the government in a bit of a paradox. On one hand, it is government policy to integrate and deepen financial markets along a free market economic path. On the other hand, plans are being made to segment financial markets further in favour of SMEs. This difference in perspectives is perhaps symptomatic of the current ideological struggle within the government, with one view coalesced at the Treasury and Central Bank and supported by the IMF and the World Bank clamouring for an open market-oriented economy, and the other view centred around the Ministry of Planning and the expenditure-based Ministries and supported by the UN family of agencies clamouring for an interventionist and expansionary economic regime.

It is not possible at the moment to determine which of the two views will influence government policy in the medium- and long-term. At the moment, however, the Treasury view is in the ascendancy. If this ascendancy is sustained then financial markets (and other markets) will ultimately be liberalized and a broad free market economy will be established.

Conclusion

Eight major factors have been identified as constraining the flow of funds to the SME sector in Kenya. These factors are:

(a) An inadequate pool of lendable funds. This may be the result of the repression in the financial markets arising out of interest rate and other controls. As these controls are removed one would expect more funds to be mobilized as saving becomes more attractive.
(b) The available pool of lendable funds is greatly limited by the tendency of the government to borrow extensively to finance its budget deficits. Most of this borrowing will not stop until the government reforms the public and parastatal sectors. In particular, the public sector payroll burden must be reduced if any meaningful reduction in the budget deficit is to be attained.
(c) Financial liberalization may or may not benefit SMEs. A study in this volume by Oyejide based on the Nigerian experience, suggests that there is an increase in the flow of funds to the SME sector following liberalization. Similar observations were made in Kenya following the implicit liberalization in the late 1970s and the early 1980s. The main cause of this increase may be the larger numbers of suppliers of lendable funds that such liberalization attracts.

However, one must be careful in interpreting this evidence. A sustainable flow of funds depends on the ability of the new financial institutions to survive. In Kenya many of them started failing in 1986. The government responded by introducing financial regulations that appear to have hurt SMEs. In the case of Nigeria one has to wait and see whether the new financial institutions survive and if they fail to survive what the government response is.

(d) The stringent financial regulations introduced in 1987 following the 1985–6 financial crisis are not in the spirit of liberalization. They restricted entry and increased supervision in the financial sector. In the process they may have hurt SMEs seriously, especially with the requirement that all loans must be collateralized. A genuine financial liberalization would have to make major amendments to those regulations.

(e) Sessional Paper No.2 of 1992 on SMEs has already been published and tabled before the parliament. Its main thrust is to propose a strong interventionist policy in aid of SMEs especially in their access to credit. This directly conflicts with the other government policy of liberalizing financial markets. It would appear that the government does not fully believe that free financial markets would serve the SMEs sector adequately. This policy confusion may hurt SMEs considerably as government policy regarding this sector keeps changing from one extreme to another.

(f) Various types of informal credit markets have evolved over the years to serve the SME sector (e.g. financial co-operatives, NGOs, moneylenders, etc.). These institutions appear to have come into existence to fill gaps left by missing formal markets for credit. Because of their nature, it is not possible to determine the total volume of funds mobilized through them and channelled to the SMEs. It is also not possible to determine their long-term survival. All one can say is that a well-designed liberalization programme would have as one of its aims the integration of these informal credit institutions into the formal financial market.

(g) Despite the definite shift worldwide towards free market economic systems there might still be a need for specialized institutions focusing on the needs of SMEs. Even when one accepts the doctrine of free enterprise, it must be realized that SMEs are characterized by information asymmetries and other market deformations that might prevent the price mechanism from performing its functions properly. In other words, market failure may be endemic to SMEs. In such a situation, government intervention cannot be wholly discounted.

(h) Business enterprise development in Kenya (both during the colonial and post-colonial eras) has been heavily protected by the government. This protection may have failed to instill market discipline among the entrepreneurs. Instead there has been a heavy reliance on patronage. This may have led to the current lack of competitiveness of Kenya's produce in world markets. Any design of financial (and other) support packages must avoid a repetition of this negative outcome. This is particularly so now that the world has become a global village.

Dutch experience with SSE Credit: evaluation and policy implications

ROGER TESZLER

Netherlands support to industrialization in developing countries

Except where concessionary exports of Dutch industrial products to developing countries were involved, Netherlands development assistance policies, until fairly recently at least, did not give high priority to industrial development. What was done to provide financial support to the industrialization efforts of developing countries with Dutch official funds was largely the responsibility of FMO (Netherlands Development Finance Company). Some (mainly technical)[1] assistance was made available directly through the government agency responsible for development co-operation: The Directorate General for Development Cooperation of the Netherlands Ministry of Foreign Affairs (DGIS); also, certain PVOs (Private Voluntary Organizations or 'donor NGOs') with financial support from DGIS began working together with NGOs in developing countries to provide support for the development of microenterprises and the informal sector, often as part of a multifaceted development support programme. During the second half of the 1980s DGIS itself began to pay more attention to stimulating local entrepreneurial development. Most of this assistance was aimed at institution building or direct support.

Since the beginning of 1991, FMO has taken over many industrial development support activities from the Ministry of Foreign Affairs, thus, for all practical purposes, becoming the leading institution in the Netherlands for the official support of industrialization in developing countries. At the same time the development co-operation policy of the Netherlands Government has increased its emphasis on stimulating local entrepreneurial activities in developing countries.

Small industry, and to a lesser extent small enterprise in general, has, however, figured high on the agenda of FMO for a much longer period. As early as 1978 FMO decided to broaden the scope of its approach to industrial development and began providing assistance to local entrepreneurship in developing countries by lending its financial support to credit programmes for small enterprise (Harper and de Jong, 1986). In the preceding ten years or so of its existence, FMO had supplied funds only to large industry in developing countries, usually without involving the intermediary services of local financial institutions. Applying the same approach to small enterprise lending would not only have been highly cost-ineffective, but it also would have led to only a very small number of SSEs being reached. For these reasons attempts were made to get local commercial banks in developing countries interested in channelling donor money to small-scale enterprises. Their frequently muted response (for reasons such as the supposedly high risks involved, inadequate collateral, restrictive local banking laws and practices) to these overtures made it necessary to look for other more tailor-made solutions. In due course a number of special Small-Scale Enterprise Development Finance Institutions or SSE DFIs were established to cater to the financial needs of small enterprise. FMO has participated in a number of these SSE DFIs as a minority shareholder and by providing technical and long-term capital assistance. By the end of 1990 a total of sixteen such participations had been established of which fourteen were still operational at the time of writing[2].

Dutch experiences with SSE DFIs in sub-Saharan Africa

Of all developing regions in the world, sub-Saharan Africa poses the biggest challenge to the development community. In 1989, 27 of the world's 41 low-income economies were located in sub-Saharan Africa, i.e. three-quarters of all countries in that region with a population of 1 million or more (World Bank, 1989b; Mead, 1989). Agriculture still accounted for 37 per cent of GDP; and because a high share of personal income still must be spent on food the size of the market for non-food products remained limited. Urbanization was still as low as 28 per cent, a rough indication of the low productivity of agriculture. However, existing intra-regional differences in terms of per capita income (Mozambique US$80 and Botswana US$1600), urbanization (Burundi 5 per cent and Malawi 12 per cent as against Benin 37 per cent and Zambia 49 per cent) and density of rural population (high in countries such as Rwanda and Malawi; low in countries such as Côte d'Ivoire and Zambia), together with relatively less reliable statistical information makes generalizations even more hazardous than usual. Infrastructure is poorly developed, in particular in rural areas. Declining agricultual production for the region as a whole (1979–81:100; 1987–89:95) only increases the problems caused by the rapid growth of population (Côte d'Ivoire for example has an annual population growth rate of 4.1 per cent and Kenya of 3.9 per cent; the region averages 3.2 per cent) and secondary school enrolment percentages are among the world's lowest (in 11 countries this figure is below 10 per cent and for the region as a whole it is below 20 per cent).

While recognizing the existence of important intra regional differences as factors limiting generalization possibilities, a pattern does emerge for sub-Saharan Africa of extremely low levels of development with few of the characteristics that make industrial development sustainable, especially in the short run.

At the time, the majority of the countries of the region gained political independence, there was a great lack of institutions to support the development process, and parastatal institutions to remedy this were set up in quick succession. For small enterprise, the Indian broad spectrum SIDO (Small Industry Development Organization) model was 'imported' in countries such as Kenya (Kenya Industrial

Estates, or KIE), Tanzania (SIDO), Zambia (SIDO) and Senegal (Société Nationale d'Etudes et de Promotions Industrielles, or SONEPI) which aimed at providing all a small entrepreneur could ever need. A more limited approach was adopted in the SSE DFI, initially as an SSE window in the World Bank inspired parastatal Development Finance Institutions (DFIs) (Levitsky, 1988), but which later expanded to departments or even separate agencies. In these SSE DFIs the local DFI would attract expatriate donor agencies or PVOs (the latter not necessarily specialized in financial operations) as minority shareholders and providers of long-term funding.

These new development finance institutions deployed considerable activity in providing long-term finance for SSEs (far more than in supplying short-term funds for working capital) as well as business advice (often not related to the loan extended) and in some cases even infrastructural amenities (industrial estates or sites). In this manner they were gradually being turned into 'one-stop-shops' for SSEs, rather like SMIDAs (all-purpose Small Industry Development Agency).

FMO and SSE DFIs in sub-Saharan Africa

FMO has participated in five SSE DFIs in sub-Saharan Africa: SEFCO (Small Enterprise Finance Corporation) in Kenya, SEFO (Small Enterprise Finance Organization) in Liberia (discontinued), SEP (Small Enterprise Promotion) in Zambia, Indefund in Malawi and Tswelelo in Botswana. These institutions were established in the beginning of the 1980s in order to cater for the long-term financial needs of indigenous SSEs in particular. In due course, new financing activities have been taken up such as loans for working capital as well as leasing and hire purchasing activities. By the middle of 1990, the aggregate portfolio of the four had reached a total of 870 loans, of which roughly one-third was used for the establishment of new enterprises and approximately 20 per cent had been taken up by woman entrepreneurs, especially as the owners of microenterprises. However, only about 10 per cent of the loan applications eventually resulted in loan approvals. This points to a combination of a significant (but maybe not well thought out) interest of potential clients and cumbersome procedures at the SSE DFI. Nevertheless, annual portfolio growth rates are quite high, averaging above 20 per cent.

All four have become involved in other activities which are not always directly related to SSE financing and which would not appear to have improved their financial solvency. These 'sidelines' include management and technical advisory services, special programmes for small loans or micro-entrepreneurs, industrial estates and wholesale purchasing services for SSEs. Some of these activities have been discontinued because of the high losses incurred.

However, the core activities of the SSE DFIs also cause considerable problems. Arrears on the collection of interest (10–50 per cent) and principal (5–25 per cent) are too high. The percentage of loans in arrears is very high in three of the four institutions (67 per cent and more).

Whereas the four institutions continue to make a profit on their lending operations, this is not the case any more if all costs are taken into consideration. High operational costs (also for non-core activities) and low collection rates are offset insufficiently by the rapid growth of the portfolios. Outright grants (for fixed assets and technical assistance) as well as the stepped-up disbursement of concessional loans (interest-bearing deposits) by the donor board members of the SSE DFIs have contributed substantially to the income of these institutions.

Finally, it should be borne in mind that the 1980s have seen the beginnings of an important change in the attitudes of the big commercial banks, which have started to develop SSE lending programmes (e.g. Barclays in Kenya and Botswana), often for SSE clients with good current account histories. This change is illustrative of the increasing moves towards the conscious insertion of small enterprise in national development processes. At the same time it undermines the *raison d'etre* of special DFIs for small-scale enterprise.

Clients' opinion of the SSE DFIs

The accompanying table (13.1) summarizes the response by 180 clients of the four SSE DFIs (25 per cent of the combined portfolios). It indicates that whereas relatively few clients are entirely satisfied (especially in Zambia and Malawi), the majority are satisfied ('efficient and acceptable'). Nevertheless, nearly half the clients in Malawi and Zambia want some change in the existing relationship. These changes refer to the desirability of the SSE DFI also to provide other services. Practically all clients are willing to pay for this. In Kenya and Zambia, technology was considered to be the most important issue for such additional assistance; in Malawi and Botswana, marketing. Although in all four countries assistance in business management was considered important it was never seen as the most serious problem.

A closer look at the figures, however, suggests that there are some problems of a more hidden nature. Thus, in Botswana, among the additional services requested from the SSE DFI, monitoring and *ad hoc* business advice were mentioned as 'other fields' by 19 of the 20 firms interviewed. These activities are within the mandate of the SSE DFI concerned. Similar complaints are voiced about SEP in Zambia, but mainly by SSEs in the copper belt, where SEP at that time had not yet set up its proposed branch office. On the other hand, Tswelelo was praised for the speed with which it processed loan requests while SEP was chided for its slowness. Speed in itself is not necessarily only a virtue. Clients have reported that SSE DFIs on occasion process a loan so quickly that the import of equipment for which it is destined has not yet materialized. This can lead to situations where the entrepreneur has to start debt servicing before he or she has had time to make some money, or even before the equipment has arrived.

Other complaints express the need for the SSE DFIs to do much more than merely provide credit to SSEs. For the intended objectives of promoting SSE to be achieved, a development bank should offer a wide range of services including business advice on all aspects of business management, technology transfer, raw materials, training seminars, and regular monitoring of projects. Credit facilities without other essential services will fail to ensure the sustainability and profitability of projects. The entrepreneurs feel that even if the SSE DFI itself cannot provide all these services, it must be able to point to organizations which offer them, and liaise with these organizations to ensure that its clients are assisted. For example, on the issue of technology advice it is recognized that the SSE DFI should not necessarily help them, but it must, however, ensure that they know about organizations which can assist them. One client suggested vehemently that all the assistance should go through the SSE DFI to avoid confusion on the part of the SSEs. Very few are aware of consultancy services operated by the SSE DFI and how they can benefit from them. The few who know about them feel that they are very expensive. Some clients even suggested the government should foot the bill for technical and business advice to small manufacturing enterprises.

On the subject of regular monitoring of projects some entrepreneurs had strong opinions, accusing the SSE DFI of only being interested in getting their money back. Apparently clients are only visited regularly when they are in arrears.

In Malawi, serious concerns were voiced about shortages of funding for SSEs, especially for working capital. None of the interviewed suggested, however, that Indefund should do something about this. Where change was suggested this referred to an additional financing facility of technical assistance and advisory services. Similar points were raised in Kenya, where much equipment being used is in need of a major overhaul for which the firm lacks easy access to funding.

It would appear that many clients of the SSE DFIs have become used to the concessionary treatment meted out to them over the years and are reluctant to make the switch to a more market-determined socio-economic environment (Keddie *et al.*, 1989). This in turn can give rise to doubts to the viability of such firms in the first place, given the high rates of arrears and even defaults observed among the clients.

Viability of SSE DFIs

Because they are not considered as banks in the formal sense of the word, SSE DFIs have no way of becoming involved in current banking operations such as checking accounts, savings deposits etc. The non-bank nature of SSE DFIs is emphasized by the not uncommon practice of providing long-term finance to clients by a cheque drawn from a commercial bank or even by paying the supplier of equipment to the SSE directly.

Even at high recovery rates and with full-cost charging for all the services which they provide these SSE DFIs would have been hard put to make financial ends meet but for repeated fresh funding by the founding partners of the SSE DFI concerned. Two reasons stand out for this lack of sustainability:

(a) the limited outreach of the financial institutions most of which only have a small number of clients (mainly in the city where the SSE DFI is located); and,
(b) the limited range of banking operations undertaken by the SSE DFIs.

To sum up, as non bank financial intermediaries, the SSE DFIs are involved in costly and high-risk, long-term financing operations on the one hand, and SSE non-financial supporting activities for which concessionary fees (or even no fees at all!) are charged on the other. They are therefore extremely hard put to survive as viable financial institutions. This state of affairs was aggravated further as the result of commercial banks beginning to take an interest in SSE operations and the emergence of leasing companies as suppliers of equipment to SSEs. Without drastic changes in the *modus operandi* of the SSE DFIs they cannot survive as such.

On the other hand, where SSE financing institutions have been established as independent financial institutions from the start, success appears to have been less elusive for these institutions, although it is questionable, whether – if at all – this success is the result of advantageous SSE operations[3].

Can this viability be increased?

Spreading high costs over a few clients will either make the charges per client pro-

Table 13.1 Questionnaire completed by SSEs examining the Relationship between SSE and SSE DFI (More than one answer possible)

	Kenya	*Zambia*	*Malawi*	*Botswana*
Could not be better	26.2	4	10.0	40
Efficient	38.8	40	38.3	45
Acceptable	34.1	54	43.3	15
Sub standard	1.7	2	8.3	5
Change in relationship desirable	—	—	48.8	20
Assistance for obtaining loans	70.0	50	46.3	75
from SSE DFI?	68.0	26	25.0	40
from NGO?	1.0	2	10.3	0
from others	1.0	10*	12.8	35**
Free assistance	2.0	98	69.7	80
Not free assistance	68.0	2	30.3	20
Should other assistance be provided by SSE-DFI?; positive response	86.2	82	71.4	80
technology?	62.1	44	33.3	35
business management?	56.9	38	58.3	13
marketing?	62.1	44	61.1	55
other?	53.4	44	35.3	95
SSEs willing to pay for this:	90.0	84	73.5	85
Summing up the relationship:				
just right	—	66	60.0	55
could be better	—	24	45.0	55
too intrusive	—	6	2.7	0
should provide other services	—	48	45.0	45

*Friedrich Ebert Foundation and SIDO.
**Business consultants
Source: Keddie *et al.*, 1988.

hibitive (and thus counterproductive by frightening them away), or can only be recovered by subsidizing the lending activities in some way or other. Subsidized credit has become increasingly frowned upon in this age of market-led economic restructuring and development and seen as a factor contributing to financial distress (World Bank, 1989b). A number of half-way solutions have been attempted, such as: loan appraisals by third parties (often NGOs), guarantee funds (financed by others, such as donors), subsidizing the non-loan activities of the SSE DFI (e.g. special staff training), or even hiving them off as independent activities with outside funding.

But these in turn all involve subsidy diversion rather than subsidy elimination. As many of these activities individually are loss-making they will fail to become self sustainable. In other words their cost must be compensated by other activities which are profit making and for that they must be incorporated in a more comprehensive institutional configuration. At the same time certain apparently successful and entirely local initiatives, of which the Grameen Bank in Bangladesh is perhaps the best known, have raised serious doubts about the SSE DFI approach itself. Finally, doubts are even raised whether there is a need for special SSE credit programmes, with arguments such as:

- existing SSE DFI credit programmes are limited, costly and slow;
- informal credit is a very important source of credit;
- informal interest is not subsidized;
- informal technical assistance is non-existent.

That would perhaps be going a bit too far, especially for growing small firms in the formal sector. It is precisely for this category that the formal SSE credit programmes which are implemented by SSE DFIs are intended.

Average SSE DFIs are only involved in the business of extending loans, receiving interest payments and recovering the principal. As a result they lack the money-making opportunities of commercial banks. The expectation that loan schemes once funded would develop into some kind of *perpetuum mobile*, with hindsight seems somewhat naive, for a number of reasons, such as:

(a) the high costs of assessing and monitoring loans, especially in cases where SSE clients operate in remote rural areas (sub-Saharan Africa, in particular, is still characterized by relatively low levels of urbanization and poor rural communication amenities.);
(b) the high costs of the SSE advisory services as well as the administration and control of any other amenities for SSE development;
(c) the lack of a modern banking tradition to make clients used to regular repayment habits has contributed to high rates of default (and high losses for the SSE DFIs).

Because the SSE DFIs only capture a segment of the financial transactions of their clients for which they are not even able to charge rates based on recovering full costs (the market cannot bear it and major shareholders, not excluding donors, are often opposed to any supposedly harsh treatment of small entrepreneurs whatsoever) their prospects of becoming self sustainable are not very bright, not even for efficiently operating SSE DFIs. For this state of affairs to change, one (or preferably more) of the following changes will have to be given serious consideration:

(1) Expand the range of the SSE DFI activities to cover all the financial transaction requirements of its clients.
(2) Integrate the SSE DFI in a larger financial organization.
(3) Broaden the financial base of the SSE DFI, for example by inducing it to tap traditional local sources of finance; thus increasing its financial autonomy (bridging financial dualism).
(4) Find donors who are willing to subsidize the SSE DFI concerned over long periods of time (Kleiterp, 1991).

The first two underline the necessity of integrating SSE DFIs with some type of larger financial organization which can cater in particular to the needs of large and small modern enterprises. The third option points towards strengthening the links of the SSE DFIs with traditional and microentrepreneurial activities and hence will tend to emphasize services for microenterprise and small traditional firms. The fourth option, while perhaps the most feasible in the short run, is more in the nature of a palliative than a real solution.

Any link-up between traditional sources of finance and the development of modern enterprises would appear to be somewhat complex, because it involves two entirely different groups of clients (traditional small savers and more modern small entrepreneurs), each requiring a highly specific approach. For small savers, modern financial institutions will only be attractive if the savings which they deposit form the basis for a credit line on which they can draw (Seibel, 1989; Jackelen, 1989). Using small savings to finance non-related business will not be acceptable, especially for those small savers who with great difficulty and at long last have managed to gain access to the bank via self-help groups or ROSCAS (rotating savings and credit associations) where the link between savings and loans is evident. If this existing financial dualism is to be overcome it will have to be tackled, not only by removing the inefficiencies within the formal financial system, but also by bridging the gaps between formal and informal or modern and traditional sectors in developing countries[4]; a process which will require certain transformations of both the modern and the traditional sectors.

Institutional support and enabling environment: two blades of a pair of scissors

Up to this point the argument by and large has concentrated on the potential and problems of SSE DFIs *as institutions for providing credit*. In recent years, however, the attention of development policymakers and practitioners has started to shift from this supply side approach, i.e. from emphasizing the effectiveness of specific instruments or institutions in providing technical support for improving the capacities of the target group. It is now being replaced more and more by a demand-side approach, that is, by measures and interventions that help to create a socio-economic environment enabling private (small-scale) enterprise to find its way. This move has gained some added strength from the widely-felt necessity to cut back government expenditure in the wake of structural adjustment programmes and from the combined findings that disappointing results have been obtained with subsidized credit programmes and that apparently even micro entrepreneurs are willing and able to pay full market rates for credit (Meyer, 1988). On the other hand, such changes are resisted by those entrepreneurs who have benefited most from past concessionary support.

By focusing on such demand-side policies it is hoped to increase the domestic market for locally manufactured products. Whereas the objective of supply-side intervention is to increase the knowledge and/or the facilities available to the entrepreneur, the demand-side approach stresses the significance of an expanding market for business growth and development, i.e. the importance of a favourable socio-economic environment with supportive government policies and effectively guaranteed equality of access to institutions.

Although each of these approaches as such is not without its merits, an enabling socio-economic environment would appear to be the seed bed on which supply-side support flourishes best. The latter should not, however, be seen as a substitute for sound development policies; as such it is often not even a second-best solution (Carr, 1989), especially when the product of the institution concerned is provided at concessionary rates or even given away free[5].

For SSE credit schemes to stimulate small enterprise development effectively, two conditions must be met:

(1) there must be a market for SSE output and the entrepreneurs must know how to work it; and
(2) the entrepreneurs cannot meet their credit needs in a satisfactory manner by other means (personal savings, loans from family and friends, effective informal credit markets, but also commercial banks).

The SSE DFIs were conceived and set up in order to provide credit to small enterprise in the belief that this was the major bottleneck to their development. When credit alone proved insufficient, supporting technical and even infrastructural assistance was added. Concessionary rates were thought to make the product or the message more attractive to the target group. This type of approach was considered necessary, either because other and more effective strategies were deemed to be unfeasible or because they simply did not occur to the institutions involved. These latter refer to measures such as redressing government-imposed price distortions, foreign exchange availability and credit schemes which all tend to favour modern large enterprise. On the other hand, reservation schemes limiting the government purchase of certain items to small producers have failed to improve the development performance of this sub-sector; not only because many larger firms have availed themselves of this opportunity by legalistic subterfuge (regrouping as qualified smaller firms), but also because the small firms benefiting from this arrangement fail to develop further.

Finally, it is worth dwelling for a moment upon the way that the pre-eminence of demand-side policies at present tends to be taken for granted. Contrary to underlying assumptions of demand-led policies, markets are far from perfect and efficient supportive activities as well as government intervention will be needed to compensate for distortions and excesses. Whereas development, in principle at least, should be market led, the same cannot be said for survival!

A too eager condemnation of institutional assistance on the basis of past failures may well create an institutional vacuum rather than redress the balance between government and market[6], with the former providing the macroeconomic and legal environment in which the latter can develop. In such an approach the kind of institutional assistance for which there is an effective demand will be provided at market rates.

Specific credit requirements

Different categories of SSEs will have different credit requirements. Thus, the approach embodied in the SSE DFIs is aimed specifically at modern small enterprise (preferably manufacturing). At the insistence of certain boardmembers (shareholders or partners) a number of these have become involved in support programmes for informal and microenterprise. Such new ventures have not yielded promising results; costs were high and outreach was extremely limited. Moreover, the SSE DFIs involved are already so hard pressed to manage their existing operations and to meet their own costs that they are in no position to absorb the losses incurred by this new line of credit which requires an entirely different approach involving efforts, such as:

- group formation;
- good and intensive local outreach;
- intensive monitoring, training and extension;
- specific assistance with legal problems and bureaucracy.

Present bank staff may not be up to this task (they will certainly not have been trained for it) and it is open to question whether such attempts at microenterprise development will yield promising results. Perhaps entirely different approaches are required in order to insert the target groups in the development process, for which other institutions are better qualified. In certain developing countries the formal banking system has failed to meet the financial needs of private enterprise, forcing the latter to look for and use other and more informal sources. This argument, however, fails to convince as grounds for opening up formal sector financial institutions for informal credit requirements. Instead, inventive solutions should be considered such as:

(a) Providing credit to the entrepreneur as an individual person rather than to her or his informal firm (as exemplified by the CCC (Central de Credito Cooperativo) in Peru);

(b) Using the estimated returns of a business venture as collateral (as is the case with a UNDP sponsored SSE credit programme with the BICGUI (Banque Internationale pour le Commerce et l'Industrie) in Guinée);
(c) Building bridges between the formal and the informal sector, e.g. by forming joint liability groups (Bank for Agriculture and Agricultural Co-operatives or BAAC in Thailand).

SSEs, a mixed bag

Manufacturing is a far from homogeneous sector; the same is also true for SSE as a sub-sector (if indeed it is a sub-sector at all). For policy analysis and formulation a certain type of classification of SSEs may therefore be required, if only in order to permit the fine-tuning of policies and programmes to different types of entrepreneurial activity, as well as for allowing policy makers to recognize that not all SSEs will benefit equally from policy and programme interventions. Similarly, the effective promotion of different types of SSE will require different institutions.

There is sufficient evidence that SSEs form a far from homogeneous sub-sector. This is not the place to go into details of SSE classification (Farbman and Lessik, 1989; Teszler, 1989). Here it should be sufficient to point to the extreme cases of the survivalist informal 'pre-entrepreneur' who has (and is aware of) entirely different business necessities than the registered modern small manufacturer. Whereas all industry undoubtedly will benefit from an increase in effective demand, such benefits will not be distributed equally among all producers because of existing market segmentation. Initial increases in income will begin by changing volume and frequency of purchases rather than types and qualities of the goods in demand. Thus, low-income groups initially will continue to buy simple low-quality goods made by local micro and small producers. But if the increase in effective demand succeeds in becoming more durable, it may lead to changing patterns of consumption and as a result to less demand for the output of the small producer, unless the entrepreneurs concerned can keep up with these upward shifts in effective demand. Furthermore, such changes will tend to affect small producers of consumer goods differently than small producers of components or semi-finished goods. The former may run the risk of seeing their market disappear as increasing incomes make consumers aware of better quality goods produced by larger modern manufacturers, whereas the latter may see their market grow in the wake of increasing industrial and construction activity.

There was a tendency at one time to group together many differing forms of economic activity which only had in common that they were evidently not large scale under a single SSE banner.

A closer examination, however, brings to light important differences in terms of business organization, location, type of output produced and so forth. Here the significance of these differences will only be considered from the point of view of credit and a link-up or bridge with formal institutions.

In this line of thought, individual pre-entrepreneurs (Farbman and Lessik, 1989), whose business is survival in practice, will at best have recourse only to family and friends, money lenders, suppliers and customers (all sources of informal finance). In this case no link-up with formal finance seems possible. By bringing individual microentrepreneurs together in co-operative or associative groups (such as ROSCAs) with common production or retailing interests it is possible for such groups to gather sufficient momentum for their collective credit needs to be formalized as the amounts required become tangible for banking authorities and group members serve as mutual guarantors. Maintaining the viability of such groups, however, requires intensive support for which formal financial institutions are ill-equipped (and which are out of the question when it comes to sources of informal finance). Finally, established formal small enterprise will often be turned away by commercial banks (except for deposits and current payment accounts) and will then attempt to find long-term financing in SSE DFIs.

Similarly, small manufacturers involved in the production of components for larger industry or construction may find that an economic upswing is leading to increased demand for a better quality product. The cost of the ensuing necessary shift in technology can be financed informally via the large client, or formally via a commercial bank or a SSE DFI. The informal approach has the disadvantage of increasing the dependence of the SSE; the formal one will probably take longer to arrange. A dilemma of this type would appear to be a good case for financial integration and linkage.

Different credits for different SSEs

Start-up capital in the case of the SSE entrepreneur will usually be obtained from personal savings or loans provided by family and friends. It will cover initial outlay for fixed investments and working capital. Only modern small entrepreneurs can aspire to external funding for their start-up (venture capital, leasing or hire purchase). Experiences with this approach in Africa are limited and do not hold out much promise. Thus, the Swedish International Development Authority (SIDA) supported urban and rural hire purchase schemes in Tanzania that were not a success because they became bogged down in bureaucratic delays and were insufficiently monitored (Keddie *et al.*, 1988).

Capital for expansion or equipment replacement is one of the major areas in which SSE DFIs operate. It is also an area in which, in a number of countries at least, commercial banks and leasing companies have become active – as far as SSEs are concerned this interest is still subdued. Nevertheless, there are increasingly occurring cases of small entrepreneurs with good cheque account records successfully applying for loans to purchase machinery and transport equipment. Working capital requirements would appear to be met mainly from personal savings and from suppliers or customers; larger formalized SSEs have recourse to the formal banking circuit from which they can obtain working capital advances on booked orders (Liedholm, in this volume; Meghir, 1991).

The biggest problems would appear to occur in finding start-up capital in general as well as working capital for very small enterprises (VSEs).

Additional supportive measures

The SSE DFIs were established at a time when, especially in sub-Saharan Africa, institutional development was virtually non existent. Most local banks were overseas branches of English, French and Portuguese banks, catering mainly to non-indigenous banking needs. Limited postal savings account systems were in existence in Kenya and Nigeria, but these were not involved in providing credit to small business. Large business was controlled by overseas enterprises and smaller activities were dominated by Indians and Pakistanis (Eastern and Southern Africa) and Lebanese (West Africa) with strong ties among each other and with their countries of origin. Indigenous African enterprise was practically non-existent and could not fall back on any formal training institutions to try and catch up, for the simple reason that such facilities did not exist.

In such conditions it was not surprising that the state was looked to for a solution; as a result, large manufacturing and marketing establishments were set up in the public sector and parastatal facilities were created to stimulate African (synonym for small) business. These SIDOs or SMIDAs (small industry development agency), set up with large amounts of government and donor funding and aiming to provide a comprehensive range of support services ('the supermarket approach') often at concessionary rates, have managed to reach small numbers of SSEs at great expense per client who in turn often fails to develop her or his enterprise beyond the incubation stage.

The active interventionist policies adopted by the vast majority of the economies in sub-Saharan Africa since the 1960s, instead of getting development moving, had only made these economies – already heavily hit by droughts and declining commodity prices – even more dependent on external assistance for their mere survival. As a result these SMIDAs became increasingly donor-dependent not only for their development, but even for their mere survival[7].

Beginning with Ghana, which according to the World Bank has the most distorted price system of all LDCs, the World Bank, the IMF and certain large donors such as USAID embarked on a series of structural adjustment programmes in 36 countries of sub-Saharan Africa involving a total outlay of US$30 billion (Wolgin, 1990). Since then, adjusting countries at least have outperformed non-adjusting economies (such as Zambia) in terms of the growth of overall production, agriculture, exports and imports. A definite breakthrough, however, has not yet been achieved. Because the costly government services (SMIDAs, but also health and education services) failed to reach large segments of the population, expenditure reductions in these fields did not have an overly negative effect.

This does point to the necessity of a radical change in institutional support. In the first place, it is important to distinguish between those entrepreneurs that have or will have the potential to pay for training, extension and equipment and those who do not. The latter (often referred to by terms such as survivalists or pre-entrepreneurs) will often lack the basic skills and training to become independent creators of income and hence require assistance in terms of basic education etc.; the former, however, are either in a position to pay (and hence can exert effective demand for what they require) or could well be so in the near future, in which case the cost of technical assistance can be incorporated in a loan to the entrepreneur concerned[8]. This should be done without burdening the SSE DFI with this activity, but rather by establishing a working relationship between financial and technical support institutions.

To sum up, in a changing policy environment of the type brought about by structural adjustment, institutional supporting measures for SSE development could be thought of along the following lines:

(1) Survivalist pre-entrepreneurs: improving the effectiveness of basic education and vocational training (basic human capital development); this is basically a government task (cf World Development Report 1991).
(2) Microentrepreneurs who are willing to form credit unions or ROSCAs in this manner have made a decisive step towards bridging financial dualism; they should be able to contribute to the cost of supporting technical assistance (e.g. via NGOs).
(3) Established SSEs should be able to pay for the technical assistance which they require (the cost of it could be included in a loan); this assistance should be provided by separate institutions having a working relationship with the SSE DFI concerned. By paying for services rendered the entrepreneur has the right to pick and choose, thus making institutional support demand-side oriented.

Concluding remarks

SSE DFIs were established in the wake of parastatal Development Finance Institutions for the purpose of providing long-term finance to SSEs which otherwise would not have had access to formal credit lines. These new non-bank financial intermediaries were only allowed to carry out a limited range of financial activities (often at concessionary rates, although this was later changed in most cases) as well as certain non-related activities, the latter often at the behest of certain minority shareholders (microenterprise finance and support, technical advisory services, industrial estates etc.) These SSE DFIs failed to achieve economic and financial self sustainability. The portfolios remained small, operational costs were high, and arrears and even defaults on the payment of interest and even the repayment of the principal reached alarming proportions. Commercial banks, who were not interested in providing long-term credit to SSEs in the early 1980s, did keep open their doors for profitable SSE cheque accounts and towards the end of the decade started to branch out into long-term SSE financing.

The process of structural adjustment has made it difficult to keep on funding the loss-making SSE DFIs, except for external donor financing. But even there, changes are taking place and the concept of subsidized credit is becoming less and less acceptable. In view of the changing attitudes of commercial banks ways and means have to be sought to integrate the activities of SSE DFIs and commercial banks, improving the accessibility of the latter for SSEs. Non-financial assistance will have to be put on a more commercial footing with the effective demand of the client as the determining factor.

A second major development is the recognition of the economic importance of informal microenterprise and informal sources of finance. These activities have tended to be self reliant (by default) or received some assistance from NGOs. Via credit groups (such as ROSCAs) it is possible to bridge existing financial dualism, thus bringing microentrepreneurs into contact with formal financial institutions. Initially, the funds thus banked will have to be used for microenterprise funding; once a relationship of mutual confidence is established, this earmarking can be discontinued.

Finally, it should be observed that the mixed bag of SSEs makes a strong case for a differentiated approach. Different types of SSEs have different financial and non-financial needs which cannot all be well serviced from one single SSE DFI or SMIDA. It would appear desirable, however, to arrive at a series of working arrangements between financial and non-financial institutions involved in the stimulation of SSE development which would lead to 'two-stop-shopping' (one stop for credit and one stop for technical assistance) for SSEs as well as potential access to a network for more specialist assistance.

To round off this review of the lessons learned from Dutch assistance to SSE DFIs in sub-Saharan Africa an attempt is made in Table 13.2 to provide financial and non-financial assistance for a broad classification of SSEs.

Table 13.2 Types of SSEs and types of assistance

Type of SSE	*Financial assistance*	*Other assistance*
Individual pre-entrepreneurs	informal credit NGO support	basic education and vocational training (government and NGOs)
Groups of micro-entrepreneurs	ROSCAs as a bridge to DFIs or banks	financed as a part of market rate loan and provided e.g. by NGOs
Well-established	SSE DFIs or commercial banks	as part of market rate loan

The *iqqub* and its potential as an indigenous institution financing small enterprises in Ethiopia

DEJENE AREDO

Ethiopian economy: an overview

With a population of over 50 million and a land area of 1.2 million square kilometres, Ethiopia is quite a large country. It is perhaps well-known that Ethiopia, with a GNP per capita of US$120 in 1988, is among the poorest countries in the world.

The main characteristics of the Ethiopian economy, besides the persistence of recurrent drought and famine, are the insignificance of commercially-exploitable minerals, a low level of incorporation in the global economy, inability to absorb private foreign investment, heavy dependence on official financial sources for capital investment, growing dependence on food aid as the agricultural sector fails to feed the population, heavy-handed policing of the economy by the State, and the growing importance of the public sector.

The Ethiopian economy is dominated by peasant agriculture which constitutes 42 per cent of the GDP, 90 per cent of total exports, and more than 80 per cent of the total labour force. In recent years, this sector has exhibited noticeable trends including declining per capita food production and a fall in the relative contribution to GDP, an increasing concentration of surplus grain in a few administrative regions, and escalating food prices. The disappointing performance of the agricultural sector, coupled with external shocks and other problems, has severely retarded the growth of the whole economy. The recurrent drought and famine, in particular, have had devastating effects on the other sectors. As the average annual growth rate of agriculture declined from 1.2 per cent during the period 1965–80 to -1.1 per cent during the 1980–88 period, the growth rate of GDP dropped from 2.7 per cent to 1.4 per cent over the same period. Cereal food imports rose from 118,000 tonnes in 1974 to 1157,000 tonnes in 1988, making the country one of the biggest food importers in Africa. The gross domestic saving dropped from 12 per cent of the GDP in 1965 to a mere 4 per cent in 1988, while the deficit in the resource balance increased from 1 per cent of the GDP to 11 per cent during the same period. On the other hand, total central government expenditure rose from 13.7 per cent of GDP in 1972 to 35.2 per cent in 1988. Expenditure on defence and security alone, as recently admitted by the former Head of State, accounted for as much as 50 per cent of the total central government expenditure while the share of social services declined considerably. The overall budget deficit rose from 1.4 per cent of GDP in 1972 to 6.8 per cent in 1988.

The performance of the external sector, too, is disappointing. Merchandise exports declined by 0.7 per cent annually during the 1980–88 period while imports rose by 7.2 per cent annually during the same period. The current account deficit, after official transfer, jumped from US$32 million in 1972 to US$389 million in 1988. The debt service ratio, as a percentage of export of goods and services, soared from 11.4 per cent in 1970 to 37.4 per cent in 1988.

The ever-worsening food security situation in the country has adversely affected the nutritional status of the population. The per capita daily calorie supply had dropped from 1824 calories in 1965 to 1749 calories in 1988 (McNamara, 1990).

The Declaration on Economic Policy of Socialist Ethiopia (1975) stated that it was 'necessary to allow and encourage the private sector to participate in certain defined fields of activity'. However, subsequent government policies were such that the private sector was neither encouraged nor assigned 'defined fields of activity'. In fact, the private sector was considered as a transitory economic appendix that should be discouraged and eventually eliminated in favour of big enterprises, in line with the government's declared objective of socializing the economy. Accordingly, different policy instruments, including credit, taxation and pricing policies, were employed to discourage the expansion of private enterprises. Different types of restrictions were imposed on the operation and business diversification of the private sector. For example, small-scale enterprises could only be proprietors or partners with unlimited liability and a maximum investment ceiling of 0.5 million Birr (official exchange rate: 1 Birr = US$0.48; with a parallel rate around US$0.125) was imposed on them until the policy revision of July 1989.

However, the government did not succeed in reducing the importance of the private sector in some branches of the economy, as can be seen from Table 14.1. Private enterprises remained dominant in the agricultural sector (95 per cent of output) retail trade (91 per cent), passenger transport (95 per cent) and imports (83 per cent). With the new government this is likely to continue.

Formal Financial Market

Credits during the pre-revolution period in Ethiopia were characterized by concentration of bank operations in few urban centres (for example, Addis Ababa alone accounted for 64 per cent of the bank branches), high collateral and minimum loan requirements which favoured big businessmen over small ones, and virtual neglect of the agricultural sector which, by 1974, had received not more than 10 per cent of the total bank credit in spite of the fact that the sector had accounted for more than 50 per cent of GDP (National Bank of Ethiopia, 1975; Haimanot Asmerew, 1990).

The post-1974 period saw the nationalization and consolidation of various types of banks into specialized banks consisting of the National Bank of Ethiopia (NBE), the Commercial Bank of Ethiopia (CBE), the Agricultural and Industrial Development Bank (AIDB), and the Housing and Saving Bank (HSB). The NBE, being the

Table 14.1 Share of the Private Sector in Selected Branches of the Economy

	Per cent
Consumption on GDP (1988)	72.0
Savings in aggregate national saving (1988)	77.0
Coffee exports (1984)	32.0
Total exports (1984)	30.0
Paid-up capital in manufacturing industries (1988)	3.6
Freight transport (dry) (1984)	88.0
Freight transport (liquid) (1984)	75.0
Passenger transport (1984)	95.0
Agriculture-area cultivated (1988)	95.0
Agriculture-total output (1988)	94.0
Retail trade (1984)	91.0
Imports (1984)	83.0
Grain marketing (1984)	70.0

Sources: CSO 1982; ONCCP 1984/85; CSO 1985; World Bank (1990a); World Bank (1990b).

central bank of the country, is responsible for issuing currency, planning and coordinating all banking activities, formulating monetary policies and acting as a financial arm of the government, etc. The CBE, the biggest bank in the country, is primarily responsible for the mobilization of domestic savings and for extending loans to all commercial activities. The AIDB extends short-, medium-, and long-term loans to the agricultural and industrial sectors, particularly to the former sector. The HSB concentrates on activities related to buildings, including private dwellings. A detailed description of the banking system in Ethiopia is given in (Mauri, 1987; Yeshitla Yehualawork, 1989; Haimanot Asmerew, 1990; Assefa Admassie, 1987; Mahtsentu Felleke, 1989). In addition to the banking system, the Insurance Corporation and pension contributions can be mentioned as organized financial intermediaries in the country.

The financial intermediaries in Ethiopia are highly biased in favour of the socialist sector of the economy. For example, the loan interest rate is seven per cent for individual farmers and private enterprises, and six per cent for state and collective farms (NBE Credit Regulation: NBC/CR 1). Shortage credit has been identified as the major problem of small enterprises (Zewdie Shibirie, 1986). Most of the agricultural loans of the AIDB (which are as high as 89 per cent) go to state farms which account for not more than 5 per cent of the total agricultural output. The private peasant sector receives an insignificant amount of loans (less than 1 per cent) from the AIDB (Haimanot Asmerew, 1990). That is, existing credit policies of the government have contributed to limitations in the farm household's access to formal sources of credit.

In recent years, the CBE has attempted to reach the rural population by increasing the number of bank branches from 86 in 1974 to 147 in 1986 (NBE, 1975;

Yeshitla Yehualawork, 1989, Mahtsentu Felleke, 1989). However, in a country where three-fourths of the rural population live a day's walk from the nearest all-weather road, it can be said that the 'savings in Ethiopia are only mobilized from urban population and organizations' (Yeshitla Yehualawrok, 1989).

The total deposits of the banking system (NBE, CBE, AIDB and HSB), in 1986–7 amounted to 4.3 billion Birr (of which demand deposit was 60 per cent) (NBE 1986–7).

The major sources of credit for the bulk of the rural population are friends and relatives. According to the 1983–4 Agricultural Survey of the Ministry of Agriculture (1984), friends and relatives had accounted for as much as 78 per cent of the total credit extended to the peasant sector during the survey period and the rest of the credit had originated from the formal sector through peasant service co-operatives (19 per cent) and 'local merchants' i.e. money-lenders (3 per cent). In a study undertaken in North Showa, it was shown that as much as 96 per cent of rural credit originates from the non-institutional sector (i.e. friends and relatives).

Rural credits, averaging 20 Birr per household, were put to both productive uses (29 per cent) and non-productive uses (71 per cent). The proportion of farmers using credits ranged from 21 per cent in Illubabor province to 41 per cent in Arsi province. These credits were used, in order of importance, for agricultural inputs (27 per cent), food (24.8 per cent), clothing (12.4 per cent), social/religious purposes (9.8 per cent) (Ministry of Agriculture, 1984).

The *iqqub*

Small-and micro-scale enterprises, which are subjected to repressive government policies, are denied access to credit from the formal sector. They meet their credit requirements largely from the informal sector of which the *iqqub* a voluntary, rotating savings association of individuals, is an important part. The general purpose of this study is to generate empirical information on the nature and operations of the *iqqub*. In so doing, it is possible to explore possibilities for promoting the *iqqub* as an alternative source of finance for small- and micro-scale enterprises in Ethiopia. The specific objective of the study is to identify and characterize the different types of *iqqub*, to characterize *iqqub* in rural areas and to identify the linkage between *iqqub* and other financial institutions. Moreover, the economic importance of the *iqqub* should be established on the basis of empirical evidence. This is important because some people doubt the economic importance of the *iqqub*. For example, Comhaire (1966) asserted that 'On economic grounds, the *iqqub* can hardly be regarded as a productive institution. It satisfies a spirit of gambling, rather than that of true saving'.

This paper focuses on the following specific questions: Does the *iqqub* involve genuine savings? How are the relative and absolute size of contributions to the *iqqub* related to the characteristics of the participant? Are there distinct types of *iqqub* with respect to the purpose of savings, size of the kitty (the pool), and linkage with the banking system, etc.? Do all participants equally benefit from involvement in the *iqqub*? Is *iqqub* money used for productive purposes? and, how can we characterize the *iqqub* in rural areas?

Two basic approaches are followed in generating the data required for this study. First, the *iqqub* is studied as an institution. For this purpose, questionnaires were used. In addition, interviews were conducted and documents investigated. The same procedure was followed in both urban and rural areas. Second, household surveys were undertaken to study the characteristics and opinions of the participants. In addition, the participant-observation method was used to generate additional information. The case-study approach is taken as the basic method for generating the required data. The other major sources of data are documents and publications. The researcher has also gained from his personal experience as a long-time member of an *iqqub* until recently. The survey was undertaken between November 1990 and April 1991.

The *iqqub*, an institution which has remained the preserve of anthropologists and sociologists (e.g. Asfaw Damte, 1958; Comhaire, 1966; Baker, 1986), has received little attention from economists. The only serious economic analysis of the *iqqub* that is available is from Mauri (1987).

In the literature, the *iqqub* is conceived as a form of traditional savings institution:

- The *iqqub* is a form of saving association in which weekly or monthly payments of a fixed sum are exchanged for the privilege of receiving a large sum at some point in the life of the group (Levine, 1972).
- The *iqqub* belongs to the type of traditional financial institutions which are included under the savings associations (ROSCAs) (Mauri, 1987)
- The *iqqub* was a saving club combining a bank and lottery (Baker, 1986).

The above definitions suggest that the *iqqub* is a savings association where each member agrees to pay periodically into a common pool a small sum so that each, in rotation, can receive one large sum. And all savings and loan associations with a rotating fund 'have savings as a core feature', according to Miracle *et al.* (1980).

What is the economic logic underlying the widespread use of the *iqqub*? This question can be approached in two ways: (1) the traditional approach which analyses the *iqqub* in the framework of financial intermediation as is the case with similar rotating savings and credit associations (ROSCAs), and (2) a new approach which analyses ROSCAs (and hence the *iqqub*) in terms of 'the logic of collective action' (Callier, 1990).

According to the first approach, a financial transaction is undertaken implicitly through the borrowing and lending activities of the participants. With the exception of the last recipient, all others borrow from each other for a varying period of time but borrow at zero interest rate (a negative interest rate if there is inflation). Opportunity cost is involved for those participants having opportunities for investment. The essence of this approach is as follows: 'all members switch at some point in the cycle from a position of net saver to a position of net debtor, except the first person to collect the kitty (who is a net debtor throughout the cycle) and the last one (who is a net creditor throughout)' (Callier, 1990). This approach is common in the literature (for example see Miracle *et al.*, 1980). Although logically valid, the approach does not fully explain the emergence and specific features of ROSCAs in general and of the *iqqub* in particular.

According to the second approach, which is developed by Callier, 'to the participants, the ROSCA is more like a pooling of resources needed to gain the benefits of some kind of collective action.... than like a combination of contracts involving mutual loans and debt service payments: the logic of the ROSCAs is the logic of collective action, not the logic of the market—hence the idea that interest rate considerations are a secondary aspect of the arrangement, absent from the original concept of the classical ROSCAs'.

Focusing on the '*tontine*s' (the term for ROSCAs in francophone Africa), Callier argued that 'The creation of a *tontine* is one of the most obvious Pareto improvements that people who save in order to purchase a bulky asset can create for themselves in a society with fragmented capital market'. The Pareto improvements are seen in terms of the reduction of the waiting time required to purchase a bulky asset: 'The pooling of resources reduces the time of 'waiting' before the purchase for all participants except the one who is last collecting the kitty (who nevertheless does not have to wait more than if he had saved alone)'[1].

The implications of this interpretation, according to Callier, are the following. First, the incentive to participate is directly related to the adequacy of the kitty relative to the contemplated purchase. Second, there is little incentive to participate in more than one cycle of the same *tontine*. Callier elaborates this point as follows: 'the alternative to the participation in several *tontine*s simultaneously in case of insufficient kitty is to participate in several cycles of the same *tontine* until the necessary amount has been accumulated. However, this strategy would defeat the main purpose of the exercise as the waiting time cannot be expected to be reduced significantly in this case. This may explain the allegedly high mortality rate among *tontines*, as *tontine*s disband or reorganize after one cycle. This mortality is therefore not a symptom of financial distress or of failure to satisfy the needs of the public. Lastly, the *tontine* loses its *raison d'être* when capital market segmentation vanishes.'

Origins of the *iqqub* in Ethiopia

The origins of the *iqqub* can be traced to the period of the Italian occupation, 1936–41 (Pankhurst and Endreas Eshete, 1958; Comhaire, 1966; Alemayehu Seifu, 1969; Levine, 1972)[2]. The two major factors behind its emergence during that particular period of the country's history were a state of insecurity created by the war and relative expansion of urbanization as was noted by Pankhurst and Endreas Eshete (1958):

> When many houses were burnt, cattle killed and families rendered destitute ... a method was in consequence required to accumulate lump sums of money for capital expenditure in rebuilding homes, purchasing livestock, etc. The steady

growth of the market economy and of government and other employment in more recent years has moreover produced a rapid expansion of *iqqub*.

Here, it should be noted that the *iqqub* emerged only about 20 years after the first bank notes were issued in the country to replace the numerous media of exchange that had until then been in use[3]. This point may suggest that the dual financial market emerged during the first half of the twentieth century, perhaps resulting from the inability of the formal sector to meet the growing demand for an appropriate financial intermediary.

The organizational set-up and procedures of the *iqqub* are described in detail in Mauri (1987), Asfaw Damte (1958), Pankhurst and Endreas Eshete (1958), Aspen (1989) and Comhaire (1966). Here I shall note a few points only.

First, the basis of an *iqqub* is established social ties. The *iqqub* is made up of homogeneous groups: people from the same work-place, the same ethnic background, the same trade, the same schooling background, or the same neighbourhood. Homogeneity may help to reduce the problem of default. Secondly, people from all walks of life, ranging from the rural poor to the urban rich, from shoeshine boys to high-level government officials, participate in the *iqqub*, and the per-head contributions vary according to the purpose of the *iqqub* and the economic status of its members (for example, see Baker, 1986; Landuber Araya, 1983). In a sample survey undertaken in 1960, it was estimated that 60 per cent of the respondents belonged to one or more *iqqub* (Comhaire 1966). Thirdly, in some cases, *iqqub* may be paid either in kind or in labour as in the case of women's mutual support networks in Wollaita (Dessalegn Rahmato, 1989; Wibaux, 1986; Altaye Alaro, 1991).

Advantages of *iqqub* over the banking system

Both the *iqqub* and the modern banking system emerged concurrently with the emergence of commodity production, urbanization and modernization of Ethiopia during the first half of the twentieth century as indicated above. However, further growth of the modern sector during the second half of the century did not reduce the importance of the informal financial sector, the *iqqub*. Both sectors have been developing along parallel lines. The recent attempt by the Insurance Corporation to sell policies to *iqqub*s has utterly failed. An interesting question here is why people prefer *iqqub* to the formal financial sector? According to Mauri (1987), the major reasons are the following: (1) the intimate integration between the financial services offered by the *iqqub* and the strengthening of the ties of solidarity and friendship in the group, (2) the forced savings of a contractual nature, (3) the provision of credit services particularly suited to the needs of the participants and the flexibility and adaptability of the *iqqub* to various situations and needs, (4) the low risk of default, (5) the low or practically non-existent costs of administration and transactions, (6) the absence of minimum investment threshold, (7) the probable tendency to gamble on the part of the members and the consequent attraction which the lottery holds for them and (8) the secrecy which surrounds the *iqqub* and the member's involvement in it.

Big traders' *iqqub*: three cases

Big traders' *iqqub* is often fraught with secrecy. The present author has encountered difficulties in collecting information about this type of *iqqub*. Three of the prospective informants that the author approached through friends not only declined to co-operate but were also furious at the idea. It was with great difficulty that the author gathered data on the following three case studies.

The specific features of the big traders' *iqqub* are as follows. The total collection (the kitty) is very large. There are cases where the kitty amounts to a quarter of a million Birr. The number of participants is high and the life of a cycle is very long. Membership is limited to a certain section of society, businessmen in particular. It is believed that most of the big traders' *iqqub*s are located in the market centre of Addis Ababa, the Mercato area. The lives of such types of *iqqub*s are quite long; they have a low degree of mortality. All members may not know each other; it is enough for a new comer to be known by only five to six participants who provide information regarding his creditworthiness and also act as guarantors for him. The system of determining the order of rotation takes into account one of the basic economic principles, viz., the principle of opportunity costs of using a resource. They make extensive use of the banking system. The costs of transactions involving remuneration of officials and miscellaneous expenses are relatively high. Though basically business-oriented, the social interactions among members are strong. Compared to other types of *iqqub*, the big traders' *iqqub* are relatively institutionalized, complex and well-organized in terms of their procedures and their lives. They operate on the basis of elaborate written by-laws. The following case studies illustrate the propositions given above.

First case

This is perhaps the oldest *iqqub* in Ethiopia: the first cycle was initiated 45 years ago by a certain Memhirie Wolde-Mariam, a clergyman from the Guragie ethnic group. Membership during the formative years of this *iqqub* was limited to 25 to 30 persons contributing from 1 to 3 Birr each per week. Every time one cycle is terminated, another will start afresh. The present cycle, which was initiated in September 1989, consists of 170 members contributing 500 Birr each per week. The total collections (the kitty) per week amounted to 85, 000 Birr per winner. In addition to the 500 Birr, members contribute 10 Birr each every week. This fund is used for two purposes. Eighty-five per cent of it is deposited in the bank as reserve in the account of the president of this *iqqub*. The reserve fund is used as a supplementary fund required to cover shortfalls arising from possible defaults by members. In case there is money remaining from the reserve fund after meeting emergency requirements, it is distributed among members at the end of a cycle. The remaining portion of the special fund (i.e. 15 per cent of the 10 Birr each collected from members each week) is spent on drinks served to members' weekly meetings. Members also contribute 10 Birr each at the beginning of each cycle for the purchase of stationery required for the *iqqub*.

A new member is admitted into this *iqqub* after proving that he is known by at least five persons among the members. These persons are expected to be his guarantors. A member collects drawings (the kitty) upon presenting six guarantors. One reason behind presenting such a large number of guarantors is to spread the burden of covering defaults over as many persons as possible. Cases of defaults are, of course, brought to court. It is the duty of the president and the secretary to undertake the necessary litigation. The *iqqub* officials are paid salaries amounting to 500 Birr each per month. This sum is roughly equal to the monthly salary of a recent university graduate. Money required for salaries is raised by 'selling' lots, on a monthly basis, to a needy member. The 'price' of a lot is directly related to the length of the remaining life of the *iqqub* in a cycle, or to the expected waiting time. The 'price' ranges from 10 to 5 per cent of the total collection. For example, a member who wants to 'buy' a lot at the beginning of the cycle pays 8500 Birr (10 per cent of 85,000) while a member who wants to 'buy' it at the end of the cycle 'pays' 4250 Birr (5 per cent of 85,000). It is also interesting to note that those members who collect the kitty late in the life of the *iqqub* are compensated; all members, except the first ten, are entitled to a premium of 500 Birr each (in addition to the 85,000 Birr). The premium is covered by collections from the 'sales' of *iqqub*. It should also be noted that a member winning a lot can 'sell' his lot to a needy participant.

This *iqqub* has also a sort of rudimentary insurance scheme in the form of *iddir*. In the event of the death of a member, all other members raise special funds and provide financial assistance to the family members of the deceased. A member whose business enterprise is destroyed by fire is entitled to immediate collection of the kitty free of charge.

The money collected from this *iqqub* is used either for the establishment of a new business enterprise or for the expansion of existing ones. The kitty is often paid through the banking system; the president gives a cheque to the beneficiary.

Second Case

There are 120 members of this *iqqub* contributing 404 Birr every weekend. The total (kitty) per week amounts to 48,480 Birr. The four *iqqub* officials are paid a sum of 400 Birr per week as a whole. The salary of the officials is raised by making deductions from the total collections of members. A participant in need of money may 'buy' a lot. The 'price' of a lot is again directly related to the length of the remaining waiting time. They ranged from 10 per cent at the beginning of the cycle to 3 per cent at the end of the cycle. The kitty is deposited in the bank until winners cash the cheques they have received from the president.

This *iqqub* has encountered some problems of default. A member may fail to pay his dues as a result of business failure or other reasons. In that case, guarantors are obliged to cover the default. However, the winner can collect the kitty on time as the shortfalls are reimbursed from the funds accumulated from the 'sales' of lots. The kitty could be kept in the banks for quite a long time in cases where a winner is unable to present the required number of guarantors.

Third case

The third big traders' *iqqub* consists of 41 members contributing 2000 Birr per month. The life of a cycle is thus 41 months. The total collection per month amounts to 82,000 Birr per winner. But, about 61 Birr is deducted from the total collection and is used to cover expenses on drinks served to members attending the monthly meetings. In addition to the 2000 Birr, members also contribute 50 Birr each per month. This special fund is used to cover miscellaneous expenses. One such expense is the premium granted to the last person collecting the kitty. This person is not lending money to others at a zero interest rate; he is compensated consistent with the simple economic principle that money has opportunity costs. However, a considerable portion of that special fund (50 Birr collected from each member) is paid to the president and the secretary in the form of salaries.

The kitty is often deposited in the bank and the winner is given cheques. The two major reasons behind this practice are: (1) a winner may not get a guarantor on the day of collection of the *iqqub* and (2) it is safe to keep such a large some of money in the banks. Cases of robbery of *iqqub* funds are common. There are also cases of winners being paid in cash in lieu of cheques. The major reasons are that: (1) the president of the *iqqub* may not have a cheque in his hand at the time of drawing lots and (2) some winners may not have confidence in cheques.

Needy members may 'buy' the pool (kitty) every third month. During the first half period in the life of the *iqqub*, the selling price (payments required for transferring the pool to another participant) is 8 per cent of the total collection. Then, the rate is progressively reduced until it is the turn of the last person who obviously gets his collection without payment and without a guarantor. It is interesting to note that the rate at which a participant 'buys' a lot is presumably less than the rate of returns on investment to which the kitty is put. A portion of earning from 'sales' of a lot is used to cover shortfalls arising from defaults. Any remaining funds from this money are distributed among all members at the end of the cycle. Until then, the money is deposited in the bank in the personal account of the president.

The screening process, (i.e. the admission requirements) is strict. A necessary condition to be admitted to this *iqqub* is ownership of big property or especially the ownership of a business enterprise. A winner collects the kitty upon presentation of three to five guarantors. A winner who is unable to present guarantors could collect the kitty only at the end of the cycle. Guarantors covering defaults are granted priority in 'buying' the pool (kitty).

The first cycle of the present *iqqub* was initiated around 1977. The termination of one cycle is followed by the beginning of another cycle. There is often a lapse of time between the initial collection of contributions by the president and the drawing of the first lot; it takes time to reach the required membership size and until all members pay their first contributions. In the meantime, the collections are deposited in the bank in the personal account of the president.

The officials of the *iqqub* are interested in the re-start of another cycle. Therefore, they try to promote a good image of 'their own' *iqqub* among the participants. For example, at the end of each cycle they hold a great feast for all the participants and distribute all residual funds available. This point suggests that a sort of competition exists among *iqqub*s in attracting new members or retaining old ones.

Members appreciate the relative advantages of big traders' *iqqub*. For example, a member of this *iqqub* told the present writer that he was able to buy a truck and later a bungalow with *iqqub* money. He also said that *iqqub*, unlike banks, imposes self-discipline in saving a large sum of money.

The case of small traders' *iqqub*

A small traders' *iqqub* is set up by people engaged in small-scale business. This type of *iqqub* is common among people working in the informal sector. Membership is also open to salary and wage earners. The kitty is of a small size. Unlike the big traders' *iqqub*, membership is often limited to people living in a neighbourhood. The following is a case study briefly illustrating this type of *iqqub*.

The *iqqub* is located in the midst of an area dominated by weavers. It was established more than nine years ago by neighbouring dwellers. Initially, the contribution per participant was 2 Birr per week. Membership is not fixed; it rises and falls from cycle to cycle. Presently, there are 52 participants contributing 12 Birr each per week. Those who lack the means to contribute 12 Birr per week can pool resources and pay the full sum jointly. The kitty amounts to 624 Birr. Every time one cycle is terminated, another one starts by more or less the same people participating as in the previous one. The president and the secretary are paid 6 Birr each per week. During the last eight years, they have taken two cases of default to court. For the last five years, the office of secretary has been held by a certain school teacher. It is with money he got from this *iqqub* that he built a kitchen for his house. This *iqqub*, like big traders' *iqqub*, operates on the basis of a written by-law.

Iqqub in the rural areas

National survey

The *iqqub* is not limited to urban areas; it is also common in the rural areas though perhaps to a lesser degree. A national rural household survey of the Central Statistical Office (CSO) shows that the annual contributions to *iqqub* per household is 18.9 Birr (Table 14.2). The per-person annual contribution is 3.75 Birr. The proportion of the annual household income allocated to the *iqqub* is 0.96 per cent. On the other hand, the proportion of bank deposit in the annual household income is reported to be 2.04 per cent. No clear-cut pattern has been observed regarding the relationship between household income and contributions to the *iqqub* ($R^2 = 0.2$). This may be due to defects in the data basis of the CSO survey. On the other hand, the survey suggests that the bank savings rates rise with higher income categories (see Table 14.2).

Case of a village

One shortcoming of the CSO survey is that it did not take into account the relationship between the *iqqub* and household socio-economic characteristics. The following case study of a village addresses this and related problems.

Table 14.2 Contributions to *Iqqub*, bank deposits and income in rural areas

Income group (Birr/Year)	Iqqub *per household (Birr/year)*	Iqqub *per person (Birr/Year)*	Iqqub *as per cent of income*	*Bank deposit as per cent of income*
199 and below	1.02	0.34	0.28	0.04
200–299	5.79	2.21	1.87	0.25
300–399	1.18	0.37	0.15	0.45
400–499	5.71	1.55	0.99	0.73
500–599	4.23	1.05	0.61	0.95
600–699	5.77	1.47	0.61	0.70
700–799	4.51	1.11	0.49	1.90
800–899	6.87	1.59	0.71	1.50
900–1099	9.96	2.19	0.75	0.99
1100–1299	9.68	2.03	0.61	1.23
1300–1499	11.57	2.26	0.57	1.24
1500–1699	15.48	2.85	0.73	1.10
1700–1899	18.74	3.40	0.89	1.70
1900–2299	18.64	3.22	0.78	1.83
2300–2699	21.93	3.59	0.76	2.92
2700–3499	97.01	15.73	2.63	2.83
3500–4299	28.31	4.30	0.70	3.10
4300–5099	15.37	2.33	0.38	2.94
5100–5899	21.92	3.63	0.58	1.50
5900–6699	8.85	1.20	0.20	4.82
6700–7499	48.88	5.51	0.98	8.90
7500 and above	39.46	5.56	0.48	4.65
Average	18.92	3.75	0.96	2.04

Source: CSO, 1988. National Rural Household Survey, Addis Ababa.

Sina-Debre-Sina Village (Peasant Association) is located along the Addis Ababa-Dessie highway in Mafoud Woreda. The total number of member households of the Peasant Association was about 168 in 1989. About 48 of them belonged to a co-operative farm named Gelila Agricultural Producers' Co-operative. Of the total land area, amounting to 800 hectares, 131 hectares (most of which consisted of high-quality land and forest land) is controlled by a co-operative farm.

The villagization scheme, to concentrate dispersed households into nucleated villages, was partially implemented in the peasant association. Some households, for one reason or another, did not move to the new village sites.

The major crops grown in this rugged and degraded terrain, in order of importance, are horse beans, teff, field peas, wheat, barley and maize. Crop yield is extremely low. The village is a typically poor area in North Shoa.

The data for the present study was generated through a household survey covering about 50 per cent (144) of the active (i.e. grain-selling) farm households of the village. The reference period of the study was the agricultural year 1988–9.

During the survey period, there were three separate *iqqubs* in the Sina-Debre-

Sina Peasant Association. The weekly contributions per participant were 2 Birr in each case. It was possible for a participant to get his (her) name registered as a member more than once depending upon his (her) ability to save. It was also possible that a person who could afford only 1 Birr would join with another person to register as one member.

Of the three *iqqub*s found in the area, the biggest one has 205 'members' of which 79 per cent was from the Sina-Debre-Sina Peasant Association. The length of one cycle was about four years. The pool per week was 410 Birr. The second *iqqub* has 74 'members' of which 39 per cent was from the same peasant association. The kitty amounted to 148 Birr per week. The third *iqqub* has 60 'members' of which 50 per cent was from the same peasant association. The kitty amounted to 120 Birr per week. It is interesting to note here that three separate *iqqub*s, with total weekly funds of 678 Birr, operate in a poor village consisting of not more than 160 households living in a mountainous area of less than 800 hectares.

All the three *iqqub*s have written by-laws which define the procedure of the *iqqub*s and the duties of the participants. The by-laws of one of the *iqqub*s mentioned above has the following provisions: A winner should bring two guarantors upon receipt of the pool. Any participant failing to present guarantors is bound to collect his share at the end of the cycle. Similarly, a participant with any defaults should collect the pool at the end of the cycle. Deductions amounting to 5 Birr per week, are made from the pool as payment to the secretary and the president. Priority in collecting the pool is given to these officials. A participant in need of money could get the pool by paying 3 Birr. This is possible only once a month. But, a participant with serious financial difficulties (for example, difficulties arising from the death of an ox) is entitled to the collection of the pool free of charge. This point suggests that *iqqub* involves not only business (money) relations but mutual assistance in time of difficulties like *iddir* (see below).

The household survey revealed that 50 per cent of the sample households participate in *iqqub*. The weekly contributions amounted to an average of 2 Birr per household. The two major purposes for joining an *iqqub* are consumption and investment objectives (see Table 14.3). The latter was mentioned by the respondents 35 per cent of the time. Does this suggest that even very poor people save and invest?

It was also reported that *iqqub* is sometimes used for a totally different but interesting purpose. *Iqqub* itself is pledged as security to a non-member creditor who has a claim on a member. This involves a written agreement by the president of the *iqqub* to the effect that he would reimburse the creditor from the kitty accruing to the member in the event of default.

The relationships between the types of peasant organizations and household characteristics, on the one hand, and the *iqqub*, on the other hand, are indicated in Tables 14.4 and 14.5.

The degree of participation in *iqqub* is the same for both villagized and non-villagized households. However, contrary to the theoretical expectation that households with higher economic status have higher average propensity to save, the villagized households, in spite of their higher economic status, contribute a

Table 14.3 Purpose for joining *iqqub* in the study village, 1988–9

Purpose	*Number of times purpose is mentioned*	*Per cent*
Consumption	39	54.4
Purchase clothes	21	30.8
Purchase food	7	10.3
Miscellaneous	11	16.2
Investment	24	35.3
Crop production	16	23.5
Purchase livestock	5	7.4
Education of children	3	4.4
Payment of compulsory contributions	5	7.4

Source: Village Household Survey, by the author.

smaller sum (1.90 Birr per household) to *iqqub* than the non-villagized ones (2.20 Birr per household).

Two of the major indicators of the household economic status are volume of crop output (331kg for villagized versus 262 kg per household for non-villagized households) and number of livestock (4.2 Tropical Bovine Units (TBU) for villagized versus 3.8 TBU for non-villagized households) in Table 14.5. Interestingly enough, the same pattern of savings behaviour is reported with respect to the other categories of household (i.e. members and non-members of the co-operative farm and male-headed and female-headed households). Members of the co-operative farm, despite their high participation in the *iqqub* (52.4 per cent versus 48.6 per cent for non-members), contributed only Birr 1.5 per household per week against Birr 2.60 for the non-members. On the other hand, members of the co-operative farm, with 1.34 hectares of land per head (non-member = 0.96 ha), 380kg of food

Table 14.4 Relationship between the extent of participation in *iqqub* and type of peasant organization in the study village, 1988–9

Peasant organization *Type of household*	*Total in sample*	*Number participating in* iqqub	*Per cent in* iqqub	*Average contribution to* iqqub *(Birr/hh/week)*
Villagized	65	33	50.7	1.90
Non-villagized	12	6	50.0	2.20
Member of co-op. farm	42	22	52.4	1.50
Non-member of co-op. farm	35	17	48.6	2.60
Male-headed	67	32	47.8	1.90
Female-headed	10	7	70.0	2.10

Source: Village Household Survey, by the author.

Table 14.5 Contributions to *Iqqub* and household characteristics in the study village, 1988–9

Peasant organization and Types of households	*Average household size*	*Average age of the household head*	*Average total land holding (ha/hh)*	*Average annual crop output (kg/hh)*	*Value of annual crop output (Birr/hh)*	*No. of livestock TBU/hh*	*Average contributions to iqqub (Birr/hh/week)*
Villagized	6.0	53.0	1.17	331	115.2	4.2	1.9
Non-villagized	6.3	52.0	1.15	262	91.4	3.8	2.2
Member of co-op. farm	6.4	56.0	1.34	380	132.6	4.7	1.5
Non-member of co-op. farm	5.5	49.7	0.96	249	86.2	3.4	2.6
Male-headed	6.2	54.1	1.21	327	114.3	4.4	1.9
Female-headed	5.2	47.0	0.93	276	92.5	2.7	2.1

Note: Value of output was estimated by using the Agricultural Marketing Corporation's purchase prices for 1988–9.

Source: Village Household Survey, by the author.

grains (non-members = 24kg), 4.7 TBU of livestock (non-members = 3.4 TBU), appear to be 'richer' than the non-member (private) peasant households. Similarly, female-headed households, though invariably poorer than the male-headed households, save more in the form of *iqqub*. In fact, the highest level of participation (70 per cent vs. an average of 50 per cent) is reported among women. Women do not have enough land and labour to depend wholly on farming activities. They resort to the preparation and sales of local spirits and beer for survival. They tend to save a portion of their meagre incomes in the form of *iqqub*.

Implications for the promotion of small and micro-scale enterprises

In this study we have attempted to identify and characterize the distinct types of *iqqub* in Ethiopia. Each type of *iqqub* has its own specific features. The big traders' *iqqub*, for example, is different from other types of *iqqub* in many ways. First, it has a strong linkage with the banks. Secondly, its operations are based largely upon the logic of the market; it is business-oriented. Thirdly, it has developed sophisticated mechanisms for compensating those members with longer waiting time for collecting the pool. Fourthly, its costs of transactions are considerable. Fifthly, its operations are quite complex, formalized and institutionalized. However, it still maintains its culture appropriateness. This type of *iqqub*, therefore, may be an important source of credit for small-scale enterprises and is perhaps capable of funding medium-size enterprises.

The *iqqub* is not limited to urban areas only. Even the rural poor have savings potentials. The *iqqub* could be used as a launching pad for savings mobilizations schemes (such as savings and credit co-operatives) in the rural areas. Such savings may help the promotion of small- and microenterprises in rural areas where banks are not available. Moreover, the existence of large numbers of *iqqubs* in rural areas suggests that there is a demand for savings and lending services and some degree of excess liquidity.

The study has revealed that a person can participate in more than one cycle of a given *iqqub*. In other words, there may be incentives to participate in more than one cycle of the same *iqqub*. It is also possible that a person participate in more than one *iqqub* at a given point of time. This point suggests that, contrary to what many people think, the *iqqub* is not a one-off act; it has continuity. The *iqqub* can be a reliable source of funds for businessmen.

The study suggests that an increase in the size of the *iqqub* is associated with an increase in the costs of transactions, strengthening of the linkage with the banking system, improvement in economic rationality and business-orientation of the *iqqub*, and formalization and institutionalization of its procedures and operations. Therefore, is it not possible to help the *iqqub* develop into a sort of Grameen Bank?

Contrary to conventional thinking, this study has revealed that: (1) all members more or less equally benefit from an *iqqub*; (2) the *iqqub* is not meant for a short period; it has quite long cycles and low mortality rates; (3) the pool from the *iqqub* kitty is used for consumption as well as investment purposes; (4) gambling is a marginal aspect of *iqqub*; (5) members do not necessarily borrow from each other at zero interest rate; and, (6) there is an incentive to participate in more than one cycle of the same *iqqub*.

The *iqqub* in Ethiopia has evolved, through trial and error and without government assistance, into a complex and well-organized financial institution capable of developing self-adjusting mechanisms in the face of changing circumstances. The resilience and apparent expansion of the *iqqub*, however, should perhaps not be ascribed to the growth in the economy but rather to the ever-growing economic and social difficulties prevailing in the country.

With appropriate government policies it may be possible to gradually transform existing 'traditional' financial institutions into modern ones. An increase in the deposit interest rate, for example, may encourage people to keep *iqqub* money in the bank. The big traders' *iqqub*, also has the potential for developing into a sort of banking system.

The realization of the potential of existing informal (and semi-formal) financial institutions depends, to a great extent, on the degree of appropriateness and effectiveness of government policies. Existing policy constraints need to be removed. More government support should be given to the *iqqub*. The *iqqub* needs legal protection from embezzlement and mismanagement by swindlers. The by-laws and book-keeping systems of this institution should be updated and systemized.

This chapter has attempted to throw some light on the efficiency and dynamism of a component of Ethiopia's hidden economy, the informal financial sector. Policymakers should create the enabling environment towards realization rather than stifling of the energies and creativities of people participating in this indigenous and culture-appropriate financial institution.

Small- and microenterprise dynamics and the evolving role of finance

CARL LIEDHOLM

Introduction

This chapter examines the dynamics of small and micro manufacturing enterprises in developing countries, particularly in Africa, and the evolving role of finance in that process[1]. Topics that fall within the purview of firm dynamics include the creation, evolution, and disappearance of firms and how these patterns vary by country, stage of development, industrial sector, and policy environment[2].

Studies of small-firm dynamics are important because they provide insights into the feasible and desirable patterns of growth in manufacturing output and employment. Since small firms dominate the industrial scene in most developing countries, a deeper understanding of how these firms evolve may make it possible to pursue an industrialization path that builds on these enterprises, thereby leading to results that are potentially both more equitable and efficient than alternatives stressing only large-scale firms. Such studies can also uncover ways that policies and programmes can facilitate, or at least not impede, this evolutionary process. There is increasing evidence that finance plays an important role in this process (World Bank, 1989b; Adams and Fitchett, 1991). Yet, most scholars have not placed finance in a dynamic context. McCleod (1986) is a conspicuous exception.

The dynamic themes for both small enterprises and finance will be brought together in this chapter. The next section reviews the macro and micro evidence on small-firm dynamics. This is followed by an examination of the evolving demand for finance on the part of these firms and of the evolving sources of this finance, particularly informal ones. The policy implications of these findings are then examined.

Small Enterprise Dynamics

The limited number of dynamic analyses on small enterprises in developing countries can usefully classified as either *macro* studies, which examine aggregate changes in the size, location, and sector of such firms, or *micro* studies, which focus on the birth, growth, and disappearance (death) of individual firms. The salient findings from the dynamic studies are briefly reviewed below. (Liedholm and Parker, 1989; Liedholm and Mead, 1991).

The macro studies indicate that the absolute number of micro- and small enterprises is increasing in virtually all developing countries. Growth in numbers of firms appears to be highest in enterprises with 2–9 and 10–49 workers, and lowest in one-person enterprises. In some countries, in fact, the number of one-person firms is declining in absolute terms. In over one-half of the countries for which data are available, employment in small and micro-firms is growing more slowly than medium- and large-firm employment, shifting the relative balance of employment toward somewhat larger enterprises. This is one facet of the structural transformation that normally accompanies rises in per capita income. In particular, there is a secular shift toward somewhat larger firms, based in larger localities, producing more modern products.

Micro-level studies provide important additional insights into the process through which this transformation is taking place as well as the paths of individual enterprises over time. Such information has been relatively rare, however, several recent studies, particularly in Africa, have begun to shed light on enterprise dynamics at the firm level[3].

One of the striking findings is that the aggregate figures understate the magnitude of the changes taking place at the individual enterprise level. Not only are existing firms expanding and contracting, but many new firms are being created (births) while others are disappearing (deaths or closures). This great churning among firms is masked by the macro-level data. The vast majority of new firms are microenterprises (10 workers or fewer), and preliminary evidence from Africa indicates that the annual birth rate of such firms is typically close to 10 per cent (Liedholm and Parker, 1989).

Disappearance (death or closure) rates are also high for micro firms. Recent findings from studies in Kenya (Parker and Aleke Dondo, 1991) and Swaziland (Fisseha and McPherson, 1991) are providing new insights on this neglected aspect of enterprise dynamics. Only approximately one-half of the micro-enterprise deaths in those countries, for example, occur because the activity is not financially profitable (business failure) ; other prominent causes of closure include personal reasons (for example, the entrepreneur may be in ill health or die), government intervention, and better economic options.

Approximately one-half of the entrepreneurs of closed firms eventually started new enterprises, while less than 20 per cent accepted paid employment elsewhere. These closure rates are highest in the initial three years; indeed, over half the enterprise deaths in Kenya and Swaziland took place during this period. After three years, however, the enterprises' chances of surviving increase markedly.

The growth rates for the surviving manufacturing microenterprises are extremely high. Recent findings from studies in six African countries reveal that the average per firm growth rate of such enterprises in the urban areas of these countries is about 15 per cent per year (see Table 15.1). Although there are variations by country (from 4.5 per cent in Lesotho to 24.8 per cent in Kenya), by location within each country (urban growth rates are often twice the rural ones), by gender of entrepreneur (male-headed enterprises grow approximately twice as fast as female-

Table 15.1 Annual micro-manufacturing enterprise growth rates per firm:[1] for African countries

Country	*Annual Growth Rates (per cent)* Urban	Rural	All Areas
South Africa	21.1	—	—
Swaziland	15.6	4.6	6.6
Lesotho[2]	4.5	2.8	4.1
Kenya	24.8	—	—
Nigeria	15.6	—	—
Ghana	11.9	—	—
Africa – urban – overall	15.5		

Notes:
[1]Average annual growth rate is in terms of employment and is defined as follows: (A-B/B) / C where: A = number of workers now; B = number of workers when enterprise started; and C = number of years firm has been in existence;
[2]Includes non-manufacturing microenterprises.

Sources: South Africa – Liedholm and McPherson, 1991; Swaziland – Fisseha and McPherson, 1991; Lesotho – Fisseha, 1991; Kenya – Parker and Aleke Dondo, 1991; Nigeria – Chuta, 1989; Ghana – Steel and Webster, 1990.

headed ones), and by subsector, the contribution of microenterprises to the growth process in these countries cannot be overlooked. What is particularly striking is that these rapid growth rates are found even though the majority of surviving enterprises in most countries do not grow at all. In Swaziland (Fisseha and McPherson, 1991), for example, about two-thirds of the surviving firms remained the same size. If firms expand, however, they tend to do so in growth spurts, which tend to occur after the third or fourth year of the firm's life.

The following picture of the life cycle of a typical microenterprise thus begins to emerge. The firm originates as a tiny enterprise – typically a one-person operation – with three years of struggle, a high probability of failure, and little growth. If it survives these first three years, however, it is likely to experience a sudden spurt of growth, that will typically project it into one of the larger size categories of micro enterprises.

Relatively few of these microenterprise, however, ultimately graduate or transform themselves into more complex 'modern' small and medium enterprises. Approached from the other end of the process, one may ask how many of the existing 'modern' small and medium firms originated as larger firms rather than emerging out of the huge pool of even smaller microenterprises? A summary of the empirical evidence is presented in Table 15.2.

One important finding is that, in six of the seven countries, the majority of modern small and medium manufacturing firms did not 'graduate' from the micro 'seedbed', but rather started with more than ten employees. Moreover, the graduation rates in African countries are found to be substantially smaller than those found in Asia and Latin America. In Asia and Latin America, one-half or more of

Table 15.2 Origins of modern small and medium private manufacturing firms (with 11 employees or more)

Region/Country	*Year*	*No. of Firms*	*No. of workers per firm*	*per cent with Micro Origin – graduated*[1]	*per cent with no Micro Origins*[2]
Africa					
Nigeria	1965	64	11–200	43.7	56.3
Northern Nigeria	1989	59	11–200	42.0	58.0
Sierra Leone	1975	42	11–200	30.1	69.9
Botswana	1982	20	11–200	20.0	80.0
Rwanda	1987	28	30–870	10.7	89.3
Asia					
India	1979	244	11–200	65.6	34.4
Philippines	1978	47	11–200	48.9	51.1
Latin America					
Colombia[3]	1978	76	11–200	50.0	50.0

Notes:
[1]Started with fewer than 11 employees.
[2]Started with 11 employees or more.
[3]Includes metal-working establishments only.

Sources: Botswana – computed from data compiled by Government of Botswana, 1984; Nigeria – computed from data generated by Harris, 1967; Northern Nigeria – computed from data generated by Chuta, 1989; Rwanda – computed from data compiled by Ngirabatware, Murembya and Mead, 1988; Sierra Leone – computed from data compiled by Chuta and Liedholm, 1982; India – computed from data in Little *et al.*, 1987; Philippines – computed from data in Anderson and Khambata, 1981; Colombia – computed from data generated by Cortes *et al.*, 1987.

the modern small and medium firms had expanded through the size structure, while in no African country did even half graduate. The percentage of small and medium firms that originated as micro firms, however, is higher in West than East/Central Africa. An important issue is to what extent inadequate access to finance, informal or formal, may have impeded this graduation process.

Evolving demand for finance

The magnitude and composition of the small and microenterprises' effective demand for finance will typically vary as they evolve. In particular, the relative importance of fixed and working capital as well as the overall magnitude of each will change as the firms age and grow.

Most new firms are microenterprises. At their inception, the overall capital needs of microenterprises would seem, at first glance, to be quite modest. This is reflected in the initial capital requirements reported in most studies of small manufacturing enterprises, with figures ranging from US$63 in Sierra Leone (Chuta and Liedholm, 1985), US$480 in Haiti, (Haggblade *et al.*, 1979), US$792 in Jamaica (Fisseha and Davies, 1981) and US$839 in Bangladesh (Bangladesh Institute of

Development Studies, 1981). Yet, in relation to average income, the significance of the initial capital barrier looms somewhat larger. In Bangladesh, the overall initial capital requirement amounted to almost six times the country's per capita income. Moreover, most surveys report the proprietors themselves typically perceive lack of capital to be their most pressing initial constraint in establishing a small enterprise (Liedholm and Mead, 1987).

The majority of this initial investment is typically used for fixed rather than working capital. In Jamaica, for example, approximately two-thirds of the initial investment of microenterprises went to fixed assets (primarily machinery and tools), while one-third was for working capital (Fisseha and Davies, 1981). A similar pattern is reported in Colombia (Cortes *et al.*, 1987). These proportions varied somewhat by size, type, and location of enterprise, but in most instances, the relative significance of fixed capital was maintained. This result does not obviate, however, the important complementary need for working capital, which particularly tends to be underestimated at the firm's birth.

Once the micro-firm begins to produce and eventually expand production, however, the demand for working capital typically increases both absolutely as well as relative to fixed capital. This follows because these initial output increases are accomplished primarily by adding variable inputs, which are largely financed by working capital; there is thus an increased utilization rather than an expansion of the initial fixed capital.

Available empirical evidence indicating that a substantial amount of 'excess capacity' exists among small enterprises provides support for this view. Excess capacity measures are difficult to quantify precisely and studies in developing countries are particularly sparse[4]. Surveys of small manufacturing firms conducted by Michigan State University and host country researchers in five countries, however, have generated some information on many facets of their operation including excess capacity (Liedholm and Mead, 1987). On the basis of the responses of entrepreneurs to the question of how many additional hours they would operate their existing firms if there were no demand or materials constraints, the estimates of overall excess capacity ranged from 18 per cent in Egypt, 24 per cent in Honduras, 35 per cent in Jamaica, 37 per cent in Sierra Leone and 42 per cent for rural manufacturing firms in Bangladesh (Liedholm and Mead, 1987). In Ghana, Steel and Webster (1990) estimated that 86 per cent of the enterprises were operating at 50 per cent or less of capacity. Excess capacity did vary somewhat between industries and by location in each country, but rarely did it decline below 10 per cent; virtually no small firms in these countries operated on more than a single shift.

Additional evidence of the relative importance of working capital for microenterprises can be found in recent studies that have asked entrepreneurs what they perceived as their most pressing constraints during their initial periods of growth[5]. In South Africa (Liedholm and McPherson, 1991), for example, 'lack of operating funds' was the most frequently cited primary business problem that microenterprises experienced when they expanded. In Swaziland (Fisseha and McPherson, 1991), 'lack of operating funds', along with 'bad debts of customers', another working capital component, were the two most frequently cited business problems faced by microenterprises at the time they were growing.

Lack of working capital would appear to be a relatively more important constraint for growing microenterprises than for the larger, growing 'modern' small firms (with more than 10 workers). An important finding from Chuta's study of 300 micro- and small firms in Northern Nigeria (Chuta, 1989), for example, was that 'obtaining adequate working capital' was more frequently cited as a problem for rapidly growing *micro-* firms (41 per cent), than for rapidly growing 'modern' *small* firms with from 11–50 workers (23 per cent). Indeed, for firms growing with just one or two persons, working capital shortages were the most frequently cited constraint to growth. Steel and Webster (1990) also report that in Ghana 'lack of credit for raw materials' was the most frequently cited constraint on expansion for enterprises with from four to nine workers (64 per cent), but was only the second most frequently cited expansion constraint for those enterprises with from 10–29 workers (54 per cent).[6]

Why should this demand for working capital be expected to increase as microfirms expand? Firstly, the quantity of working capital demanded would be expected to vary directly with output or sales, since the principal use of working capital is to finance labour, raw materials, and other purchased inputs that go into goods produced for sale. Strong support for this hypothesis comes from an inventory demand study that used data on small enterprises in Sierra Leone (Kilby *et al.*, 1984). This study found that the relationship between the level of sales – indeed the square root of sales – and inventory was positive and significant at the one per cent level.

Secondly, the quantity of working capital would be expected to increase with the lengthening of the production and marketing period for raw materials and finished goods that frequently accompanies the 'transformation' of micro- into 'modern' small- and medium-scale enterprises. Microenterprises in several industry subsectors, for example, produce to order and thus operate much like a job-shop, where customers may even provide the raw materials. This institutional arrangement keeps the marketing and production periods relatively short, the inventory-sales ratio small, and the corresponding demand for working capital relatively low. If these microenterprises not only expand but transform themselves into modern small- and medium-scale enterprises, however, these periods frequently lengthen as one facet of that transformation. Tailors and carpenters, for example, would no longer produce custom orders, but would begin to operate like a factory in which inventories of finished clothing or furniture would be maintained.

Evidence from enterprise surveys in Honduras and Sierra Leone provide support for the differing production and marketing periods between micro- and modern small enterprises in at least some industry subsectors. (see Table 15.3) In both countries, the inventory-sales ratio of small-scale clothing and furniture enterprises were significantly higher than those of their microenterprise counterparts. Thus, as firms in these industries grew, the demand for working capital increased not just with sales, but grew even more because of the increased inventory-sales ra-

Table 15.3 Inventory-sales ratios for micro- and Small scale enterprises

	Sierra Leone	*Honduras*
Clothing		
Micro**	.02	.04
Small Scale	.10*	.10*
Furniture		
Micro	.05	.04
Small-scale	.15*	.10*
Bread		
Micro	.02	.01
Small-scale	.02	.01

Notes:
*Significant difference at 1% level (Chi Square).
**Micro – up to 10 persons; Small – more than 10 persons

Sources: Sierra Leone: data from Chuta and Liedholm, 1985; Honduras: data collected during 1980 survey at 485 rural micro and small scale industries (Stallmann, 1984).

tio. The constancy of the ratio for micro- and small baking establishments, however, reminds one that this increase is not ubiquitous and must be examined on an industrial subsector basis[7].

Other characteristics associated with this enterprise transformation, however, might be expected to reduce somewhat the demand for working capital. Firstly, small and medium firms may be able to realize some economies of material bulk purchases, particularly since the transaction cost of placing a raw material order is fixed irrespective of size (see Kilby *et al.*, 1984).

Secondly, there is evidence that the capital intensity of 'modern' small- and medium-scale enterprises typically exceeds those of microenterprises. (Liedholm and Mead, 1987). Since the proportion of working capital demand will vary inversely with the capital intensity of production, this should tend to reduce the relative demand for working capital. These two countervailing factors may help explain why working capital shortages appear to become a less severe constraint for expanding modern small- and medium-scale enterprises, when compared with their micro-counterparts. An abundance of other inputs including fixed capital is also required when a microenterprise is transformed into a more complex, modern small-scale enterprise (Liedholm, 1990; Boomgard, 1989). Indeed, there is typically a sharp, discontinuous jump in the demand for fixed relative to working capital when the firm reaches this stage in its evolution. Unfortunately, data on the precise magnitude and mix of this demand for most countries are still rather limited[8]. In Ghana, however, Steel and Webster (1990) report that 'lack of credit for equipment' is the most frequently cited future expansion constraint for firms with from 10–20 workers.

Evolving supply of finance

The sources of finance available to a micro- or small-scale enterprise also change as it evolves. This evolution affects not only the relative importance of informal and formal sources of finance, but also the relative contribution of various types of informal finance.

Indeed, at the inception of the micro-firm, neither formal nor informal sources of finance play any significant role. Rather, the initial investment of such a firm is overwhelmingly obtained from internal family sources, primarily personal savings and gifts from relatives or friends. The empirical evidence from Africa, for example, indicates that these sources consistently accounted for over 95 per cent of the original capitalization of microenterprises, ranging from 98 per cent in Nigeria (Aluko, 1972), to 97 per cent in both Tanzania (Schadler, 1968) and Sierra Leone (Chuta and Liedholm, 1985). A remarkably similar pattern emerges from the evidence generated in other parts of the world. Personal financial sources represented 94 per cent of the original capitalization of microenterprises in Jamaica (Fisseha and Davies, 1981), 91 per cent in Haiti (Haggblade *et al.*, 1979), and 89 per cent in the Philippines (Anderson and Khambata, 1981). The paucity of funds obtained from either formal or informal external sources at start-up is striking.

The micro-firm's access to outside sources of finance, however, begins to widen as it ages and evolves over time. McCleod (1986) argues that these widened opportunities are directly linked to increases in the reputation and assets of the firm.

What pattern of financial evolution might be expected from our knowledge of microenterprise dynamics? During the typical microenterprise's first few years of struggle and initial growth, its assets and reputation would both be limited and its outside sources of funds meagre. Consequently, the firm's internal free cash flow from depreciation and retained profits provides the major source of capital during this period in its life-cycle. Internal sources of finance thus continue to dominate. In Sierra Leone and Bangladesh, for example, 89 per cent of the capital for expanding units came from this source, while in Haiti the figure was 81 per cent (Liedholm and Mead, 1987).

Nevertheless, even during this early period a few external sources of informal finance begin to emerge. One of the first, and most overlooked of these, is credit from the customer. Retail customers frequently supply the entrepreneur with either the raw materials or a cash down-payment to purchase the raw materials (Kilby *et al.*, 1984)[9]. In rural Egypt (Davies *et al.*, 1984), for example, 80 per cent of the firms indicated that customers made advance payments, either in cash or in kind. The relative importance of this form of credit varied by subsector, ranging from 100 per cent for mat-making to 43 per cent for metal shops. The extent of this practice is often directly related to the reputation of the producer; consequently, as the product quality and delivery performance of the entrepreneur become better known to the consumers over time and as the firm's reputation in their eyes grows, customer prepayment should increase. Advance payments by customers represent a creative response to the obstacles arising in low-income countries with limited financial intermediation. The customer provides resources and in return frequently receives implicit interest in the form of a price discount, which may range from one to ten per cent depending on the subsector concerned (McCleod, 1986).

Another form of informal consumer credit that also grows as the firm ages is the sub-contracting mechanism, in which the customer – typically, a much larger firm – supplies the micro-firm with the raw materials required to produce the ordered goods. Sub-contracting tends to be limited to a few subsectors, such as clothing, wood, and fabricated metal, and is more widespread in Asia than in Africa (Mead, 1985).

An additional external source of informal finance that becomes increasingly available as the firm evolves is trade credit from or accounts payable to suppliers of inputs. This source of credit tends to be less important than credit from final customers for most industries in low-income countries; in Egypt, for example, less than 10 per cent of the micro-firms obtained inputs on credit. Accounts payable to input suppliers tend to grow in importance, however, as the firm evolves and improves its reputation. In Egypt, for example, it was the somewhat larger and older of the microenterprises that have the greatest amount of input credit (Davies *et al.*, 1984).

Professional money-lenders are another source of informal finance for microenterprises. Microenterprises, however, typically do not make extensive use of this part of the informal financial market in most low-income countries (Kilby *et al.*, 1984; Anderson, 1982). In most cases recourse to money-lenders occurs at infrequent intervals, primarily for small working capital loans, for a few days, at interest rates not infrequently exceeding 100 per cent; yet the loans are extended quickly and few transaction costs are involved. The access to money-lenders, however, grows as firms age and evolve. In both Haiti and Jamaica, for example, less than one per cent of the microenterprises used money-lenders at start-up, but the percentage rose to 1.7 per cent in Haiti and 3.9 per cent in Sierra Leone when they expanded (Kilby *et al.*, 1984). Once the reputation of the firm is established, it typically remains the client of that money-lender for a long period.

An expanding array of informal sources of finance thus become available to the microenterprise as it evolves. Most of these sources initially provide short-term working capital, for which the microenterprise's effective demand initially tends to be relatively high. It is also this type of finance which the informal market is particularly well suited to provide.

Some fixed capital, however, is also supplied to micro-firms by the informal financial market. Since the perceived risks of longer-term lending to microenterprises are deemed to be relatively high, not much term finance is provided by the informal sector (World Bank, 1989b). The importance of establishing a reputation on the part of the microenterprise becomes even more crucial in this case and the availability of informally supplied fixed capital thus may come at a somewhat later stage in the typical firm's evolution.

There are two major informal sources of fixed capital: supplier credit and sub-contracting. Supplier credit for fixed capital typically becomes available when a micro-firm becomes well-established and develops a good payment record (Kilby *et al.*, 1984). The supplier has some incentive to offer such credit in order to boost sales and can use the equipment as security. Fixed capital is also sometimes provided to microenterprises by the larger parent firm as part of a sub-contracting arrangement (Mead, 1985).

Finally, at a later stage in their evolution, microenterprises may begin to have access to the formal financial market. This frequently occurs once they have transformed themselves – graduated – into modern small and medium enterprises, although a few microenterprises have been able to obtain credit from regular financial institutions (Liedholm and Mead, 1987). Evidence that institutional or formal finance plays a bigger role as firms grow is revealed in enterprise surveys in Colombia (Cortes *et al.*, 1987) and the Philippines (Anderson and Khambata, 1981). Unfortunately, for most countries, data on the graduation or even the evolution of firms from informal to formal financial sources are sparse and this phenomenon has rarely been examined (Meyer, 1988).

The following picture of the financial evolution of a typical microenterprise begins to emerge from these findings on the demand for and supply of finance. At its inception, the microenterprise's primary financial need is for fixed capital, which is almost entirely obtained from internal family sources, mainly personal savings. Once operations begin, the working capital needs typically predominate, and most of this is financed from the firm's internal free cash flow. As the firm matures and its reputation grows, external sources of informal finance begin to emerge. Credit from customers is frequently the first source to appear, followed by credit from various suppliers, professional money-lenders and others. These are primarily short-term sources of funds that are used to meet the working capital needs of the microenterprises. If the microenterprise grows larger and transforms itself into a modern small or medium enterprise, however, its need for both fixed and working capital greatly expands. At that point, the firm may now begin to have increased access to the formal financial market.

Implications for financial policy

What financial policy implications emerge from this dynamic perspective on small enterprise? Specifically, what are some of the lessons learned that might lead to improvements in the way that both the formal and informal systems provide financial services to micro- and small enterprises?

One important lesson emerging from the findings is that the magnitude and composition of the microenterprise's demand for finance as well as its access to the sources of that finance typically vary significantly over its life cycle. Consequently, one must take careful cognizance of these systematic variations when determining the appropriate volume and types of financial resources that might be provided to such enterprises.

Although a surprisingly wide variety of informal sources are available to meet many of the evolving needs of microenterprises, there are several limitations with these informal financial arrangements. Firstly, these informal sources are independent and generally segregated from one another. Consequently, there is little or no integration of disparate sources and uses of funds either between the informal institutions themselves or between them and the formal financial institutions. There is also relatively little integration within individual units of the needed multiple financial services, such as savings, deposit, and cheque account activities. When these services are integrated, additional information is generated for lenders on the entrepreneur's evolving financial management ability – one element that contributes to the entrepreneur's growing reputation.

Second, the success of several innovative microenterprise pure financial service (often referred to as 'minimalist credit') programmes, such as the Grameen Bank in Bangladesh, the Badan Kredit Kecamatan (BKK) in Indonesia or the Get Ahead Foundation in South Africa, provides an indication that even the effective working capital needs of evolving micro- and small enterprises in these countries have not been adequately met by the existing financial system. (Boomgard, 1989; Biggs *et al.* 1990). Increased attention needs to be focused on how even these 'successful' schemes can be scaled up to reach larger numbers of micro- and modern small-scale enterprises in these countries. One promising path is a financial systems approach that aims for financial viability of the lending institutions and stresses the importance of savings (Rhyne and Otero, 1991). Among the institutional variations of such an approach are options that would link microenterprise programmes to formal sources of finance (such as directly with commercial banks or through so-called second-level institutions) or that would transform microenterprise programmes into specialized financial institutions themselves capable of providing both savings and credit services. Moreover, if such schemes are to be developed in other countries with similar financial gaps, they should take cognizance of the new lending technologies, many of which were borrowed from the informal financial system, that have been developed to keep transaction costs and risks of default low. Elements of this new approach include character-based lending, group dynamics, and the prospect of repeat working capital loans to motivate repayment, a savings component, and the charging of market (cost-covering) interest rates (Meyer and Cuevas, 1990; Rhyne and Otero, 1991).

Third, informal financial sources are not particularly well suited to meeting the evolving fixed capital needs of micro-firms. As firms grow and perhaps attempt to transform themselves into modern small-scale enterprises informal lenders become less able or inclined to provide the larger sums for the longer time periods that are now required (World Bank, 1989b).

Enabling the firm to have access to formal sources of finance as it grows provides one viable alternative for increased funds. The transition, however, is not usually a simple or smooth one as usually an entirely new set of procedures and requirements, such as strict collateral, for obtaining loans must be mastered. Moreover, commercial banks and other formal financial sources are frequently reluctant to deal with unfamiliar small enterprises, because of the higher transaction costs and greater perceived risks of lending to them.

Several approaches have been proposed for facilitating this transition. One is to provide technical assistance to the firms themselves to teach them how to obtain loans from formal financial institutions (Meyer, 1988). A second approach is to provide technical assistance instead to the commercial banks and similar financial institutions on how they could lend more effectively to small and microenterprises (Kilby *et al.*, 1984). So far, only a small number of commercial banks, such as the Bank Rakyat Indonesia (BRI), have been interested in making loans to microenterprises. With lenders' accumulation of experience and improved information, the risks of lending to these enterprises should decline. Loan appraisers' and loan officers' judgments will improve with an increase in knowledge of specific trades and with the experience they gain by lending to this sector. Lending institutions, however, are not going to willingly engage in this 'learning-by-doing' process unless these initial high costs can be reduced. A loan-guarantee scheme is one such cost-absorbing mechanism, although the track record of such schemes to date has generally been poor (Levitsky and Prasad, 1987). Commercial banks would be more willing to provide unsecured short-term loans to such enterprises if the guaranteed portion of the loan were reasonably high and if all screening costs above those incurred for standard loans could be shifted to the guarantor. To help ensure that the guarantee subsidy is confined to learning, the banks should be given an incentive, such as a declining guarantee over time, to move new borrowers into a normal commercial relationship. A third approach would be to graduate or convert an entire microenterprise lending programme or scheme into a financially self-sufficient institution providing a complete array of financial services to a larger and broader group of micro- as well as modern small-scale enterprises (Meyer, 1988, and Rhyne and Otero, 1991). These three approaches are not mutually exclusive, however, and indeed all may be needed to ensure that the financial system does not impede the evolution of small and micro-firms in developing countries.

Several general financial policy implications stem from these considerations. Firstly, interest rate deregulation looms as a high priority. If microenterprise lending programmes are to be financially self-sufficient, they must be able to charge 'market' (cost-covering) interest rates. Secondly, regulations concerning acceptance of deposits should be reviewed to permit, under certain conditions, microenterprise schemes to offer the savings services that have been shown to be so important to their viability. Finally, policies that contribute to a general extending of the formal financial system and the strengthening of its links with the informal system will be needed if the evolving financial requirements of micro- and small-scale enterprises are going to be adequately satisfied.

Conclusions

This examination of small and microenterprise dynamics has focused attention on the evolving role of finance in that process. At different stages in the life cycle of the typical microenterprise, the needs of the firm, including its effective demand for finance, vary in a rather systematic fashion. A surprisingly large array of formal and informal sources of finance is available to the firm, but their relative contributions vary as the firm evolves.

Informal financial arrangements, in particular, have been shown to be quite responsive to this evolutionary pattern. Yet, the lack of integration of these diverse informal sources and services as well as the gaps in the availability of both short- and long-term funds at certain stages in the firm's evolution point to deficiencies in the existing financial system. It is only when the informal and formal financial markets become better integrated and more unfettered that the evolving financial requirements of small enterprise will be more completely met.

IV

Policies for sustaining direct assistance for small enterprises

Women entrepreneurs, donor promotion and domestic policies

RUDO BARBRA GAIDZANWA

Introduction

Donor agencies have routinely mapped out priority areas for development in developing countries on the basis of their perceptions and definitions of what the problem areas are and what the best solutions should be for the 'problems of the Third World'. Historically, in Africa, the majority of the donor agencies have been from the West and this has resulted in the suggested and preferred solutions to the problems of poverty and underdevelopment in Africa being defined in terms of the West's experiences with economic and social intervention. Most of the Western countries have espoused liberal, capitalist approaches to the running of economies and politics. On the basis of their experiences in development, they have tended to favour these approaches in their dealings with developing economies, polities and societies.

The attainment of political independence from colonial governments by the majority of African countries in the 1960s took place during the height of the modernization approach to development in the poorer countries of the world. Modernization implied doing the same things that the colonial capitalist countries had done in order to duplicate the process of development in the poorer countries. Thus, there was a strong emphasis on supporting entrepreneurship among the more 'progressive' sections of the populations in the developing world. This entailed the commercialization of their operations in trade, commerce, agriculture and manufacturing. However, the need to implement social democratic welfarist measures in order to meet the needs of the bulk of the population, hitherto ignored or poorly served by colonial governments, the poor managerial base and lack of diverse skills necessary for the running of these economies that were expected to service expanding numbers of claimants brought about crises in most economies. The poorest people did not benefit much from these measures and after the first decade of independence, most of the African countries had developed structural problems in their economies.

The decline in economic growth and the resultant political instabilities that became evident in some countries such as Ghana and Nigeria brought about a rethinking of the strategies for achieving economic growth and political stability at levels that would bring a net result of broad-based development. The role of the state was redefined in such a way that state direction and management of development became a priority. This resulted in the expansion of state bureaucracies and other bodies that were closely linked to the state for the purposes of nation-building and economic growth. The market mechanism became less favoured as a means of bringing about significant development as long as it was not directed by the state. This was a result of the disappointing experiences with the market with regard to equity in the distribution of wealth in most African countries.

The role of civil society was also altered to make room for a more directive state. Thus, individual liberties, interests and endeavours were supposed to be subservient to the task of nation-building – which was expected to benefit the majority of the African populations. It is in this phase of Africa's development that ideologies stressing community, sharing and sacrifice held sway in countries such as Tanzania, Ghana, Zambia.

It is important to mention that the move towards a more pronounced statism was continuous with the economic and political policies that had been espoused and implemented by the colonial governments in their bids to exclude the colonized majorities from power and to direct the form and content of their participation in social, economic and political processes. In fact, in a lot of countries, the post-independence regimes utilized the social, economic and political tools that were bequeathed to them by their colonial predecessors and these tools in the form of legislation and state bureaucracies proved quite handy in maintaining state primacy in different kinds of initiatives that are related to the creation of wealth. In countries such as Zimbabwe, Zambia, Kenya and Nigeria, the British-based labour relations machineries in industrial relations were carried over to post-independence periods.

The ways in which different African regimes went about implementing these ideologies of community, sharing and sacrifice differed depending on whether they believed in the free market or in state direction of market forces. The states that tried to implement the socialist models of different hues were influenced by the problems that they encountered with balance of payments after their welfarist, distributionist policies began to deplete their earnings alarmingly. This was the case with Tanzania. Others such as Zimbabwe were influenced by their dependence on countries such as China, Ethiopia and the Eastern bloc countries that had given them aid during their struggles for national liberation. Yet others such as Kenya, the Ivory Coast and Botswana chose the market route as the most suitable for development.

What is clear is that in most of these countries, despite different choices in their economic policies, there was a common factor which emerged, namely, poor economic growth, balance of payments problems, declines in overall productivity, authoritarianism in their political systems and narrowly-based classes of local entrepreneurs. This was the case in countries such as Kenya, Zaire, Nigeria and Zambia, to mention but a few. In these and other African countries, entrepreneurs tended to be closely related and beholden to the cliques that monopolized political power. The advent of independence and the creation of bureaucracies which administered the distributive services of the state attracted vast numbers of qualified people particularly in the public sector.

The emphasis on nation-building ensured that criticism of state initiatives, no matter how wasteful and costly, was muted. Thus, it was relatively easy for state bureaucrats to utilize their entrepreneurial skills within the state machinery in order to create wealth for themselves without the necessity of setting up their own enterprises and financing the costs of starting and running these enterprises. During this period, very little attention was paid to the people who were not able to find niches within state bureaucracies. It was only in the mid-1970s that attention started to focus on small-scale, labour-intensive enterprises as it became clear that state-led enterprises could not generate enough growth for development in those countries that had opted for distributionist policies. Among those that had adopted market solutions to development problems such as Kenya and Ivory Coast, some growth was experienced in tandem with deepening poverty.

Donor agencies also reacted with unease when faced with the intransigence of poverty in most parts of Africa. Their funding of technical experts in the context of benevolent and not so benevolent 'nation-building' regimes had produced poor results, particularly in the public sectors of countries such as Tanzania, Zambia and Kenya. The private sectors in the majority of countries were subjected, at best, to benign neglect especially in those countries which had espoused ideologies and interpretations of ideologies in ways that stigmatized private enterprise. The general paralysis of aid agencies was compounded by their interests which were governed by cold war imperatives.

These considerations made it difficult for the aid agencies to vary their aid programmes or to switch them to those sectors and countries that could best utilize them. Thus, Western aid agencies investing in African countries with market economies had to support these countries' programmes even if it was clear that the policies would not lead to significant development. By the same token, countries in the Eastern bloc supported regimes which implemented unworkable policies of attempted collectivization and nationalization in Ethiopia and Tanzania which were not sustainable. Thus, African economies became more concerned with soliciting, utilizing and administering aid programmes rather than with supporting indigenous entrepreneurship. The fact that substantial proportions of the aid given was siphoned off by the ruling party and state bureaucrats led to the search for alternative or rather, supplementary, funding channels given the levels of poverty, unemployment, famine and general economic decline in most of Africa.

The small-scale enterprise thrust gained ground in this context and became popular in the 1970s with the 'small is beautiful' movement that was championed by Schumacher. In Africa, the move away from state-led development was a result of the growing authoritarianism of significant numbers of regimes in the climate of economic decline. Those sections of populations that had not been accommodated by post-independence states had begun to operate increasingly outside the areas circumscribed by these states. The state machineries themselves were increasingly unable to 'capture' large proportions of their populations whose skills were increasingly devoted to survival and evading the machineries of the states that were attempting to squeeze resources from them through taxation and other forms of appropriation. Thus, in Zaire, Zimbabwe, Zambia, Uganda and Ghana, state machineries became more coercive as the African people began to withhold as much as they could from governments that were unable to provide the basic necessities for dignified human existence.

The quest for jobs and employment for the poor in Africa generated research into their survival strategies. The informal sector was duly 'discovered' and documented while labour-intensive methods of production began to be seen as the answer to Africa's problems. Small scale enterprises were seen as more 'fundable' given the failures with the funding of large-scale industrial, agricultural and infrastructural projects in the 1960s and early 1970s. Thus studies by scholars such as King on Kenya (1977) and Hart (1973) on Ghana became important and they provided donors with another funding channel which they hoped would generate incomes for the poorest in Africa.

Small scale enterprises can be formal or informal and both have attracted donor and academic interest, holding out as they do, the prospect of absorbing relatively large numbers of workers at lower costs than large, high-capital and high-technology enterprises in public and private sectors. With respect to the informal sector studies, research and debates, the motives of the participants were and still are mixed. In the first instance, the small-scale enterprises were viewed in an instrumental manner. Some governments were interested in promoting their activities in this area in order to increase and broaden their declining tax bases. In fact, employees and workers in different types of enterprises were disappearing into small-scale enterprise activities in order to evade the state which tries to extract taxes from them. This has been the case in Zimbabwe where the high rates of personal tax acted as a disincentive for people who were in waged or salaried jobs to remain in those jobs. Thus, states cannot be assumed to be interested in the welfare of small-scale entrepreneurs simply because the entrepreneurs are rhetorically encouraged to help themselves by starting their own ventures.

The encouragement of small-scale enterprises in Africa was partly a result of state fatigue with respect to the provision of social and other services. Self-reliance was heavily advocated in the 1970s in Kenya, Tanzania, Zambia, Ghana, Nigeria and Uganda precisely because the governments could not live up to their promises to provide the basics for their populations. The small-scale enterprise approach provided a way out for those states that were interested in shedding their responsibilities to their people. Within this discourse, people who expressed sentiments of entitlement directed at the state were then stigmatized as dependent, lacking in initiative, lazy and unpatriotic.

From the point of view of the donors, small-scale enterprises were a relatively safe area for investment given that their fingers had been burnt in the process of funding large, disastrous projects. With small-scale enterprises, the risks were much lower and the donors were less likely to be drawn into discussions of equity and development nationally and continentally. In any case, there were few alternatives given the failure of land reforms, industrialization and development in most African countries. This, then is the context within which small-scale enterprises were introduced into the development policy debate in Africa.

Historical context of entrepreneurship in Africa

Entrepreneurship was already developed in some parts of Africa where societies had become complex and functional differentiation in activities was already intense prior to colonization. This was true for the ancient empires in West and Southern Africa. Trade and commerce were intensified by the encounters and interactions with traders and travellers from Europe, the Arab world and from neighbouring nations prior to the colonization of Africa. The focus and direction of entrepreneurship changed as armed conflicts with and interventions by colonial powers became more intense at the end of the nineteenth century.

Colonialism impacted on Africa in different ways depending on the specialization in and priorities established for these countries with respect to participation in the colonial economic enterprises. In West Africa, there was a strong emphasis on trading in cocoa, palm oil, rubber and other crops that were needed for the industrial enterprises in the colonial countries. Plantations existed in tandem with the small landholdings of the native peoples who also grew the export crops to earn cash. In West Africa, colonial settlers were not able to establish themselves permanently because of climatic problems and the fact that export crops could be extracted through trade with the native peoples without necessitating permanent settlement by large numbers of Europeans.

In contrast, settlers in East and Southern Africa were able to maintain a more permanent and enduring presence because of the more tolerable climate and the nature of the products and commodities and also the organization of work that they needed to implement if they were to extract these products successfully over a long period of time. In East and Southern Africa, mining and privatized, individually organized agriculture were the major activities of the colonial project and this necessitated the recruitment and control of land and labour, extracted from the native peoples.

As a result of this variation in colonial activities, there was a different pattern to the organization of entrepreneurial activities amongst the native peoples in Africa. There was often a need to find niches in economic activities that were not occupied and monopolized by the colonials. In West Africa, the native peoples went into the local trade of cash and food crops, cattle and other commodities. Women were active in trade, crafts and commerce. The absence of large settler populations meant that there was more space for entrepreneurship by the native peoples in order to satisfy their everyday needs as well as for earning incomes from trade and commerce with the colonial entrepreneurs.

In East and Southern Africa, the relatively large settler presence had a deleterious effect on entrepreneurship especially in urban areas because trade, mining and commercial agriculture were monopolized by the settlers who used racist and segregatory legislation to regulate the economies in favour of the white settlers. Thus, blacks and Asians were left to organize and exercise their entrepreneurship in the provision of services for themselves. Thus black entrepreneurs were active in retail trade, transport and small crafts and commodity production for the poorer black populations in those urban and rural areas designated for blacks. This effectively cordoned off large sectors of the economy from the reach of blacks. It must be noted that in all parts of colonial Africa the state was an important agency for organizing enterprises through the granting of inputs, credit and other support to colonial ventures in the public and private sectors and this was instrumental in marginalizing the native populations very effectively in most of the lucrative areas of the colonial economies.

The effect on black women in East and Southern Africa was to confine them almost entirely to the peasant agricultural sector because many black women were not initially engaged in wage labour and could not, therefore, legally establish themselves in business in urban areas. Those who managed to establish themselves in urban areas were often marginalized, independent women who had little family support and encouragement. They fitted themselves into fringe activities such as food selling, beer brewing and prostitution, frequently illegally, and therefore were subject to harassment by state, municipal and community agencies which did not approve of their presence and activities in the towns. In rural areas, most married women only had access to land through usufructuary rights within marriage and they could not mobilize resources to establish themselves in trade unless they were involved with their husbands as unpaid family workers in small enterprises such as shops. Thus, they were almost entirely involved in small craft production and trade and they serviced the poorest population groups in the country.

Studies conducted on the participation of women in business enterprise at various levels suggest that most women have been and still are active in the unwaged sector of the economy where they retail petty commodities such as knitwear, baskets, pots as well as fruit, vegetables and other foodstuffs. Studies by Moyo *et al.*, 1984; Gaidzanwa, 1984; ILO 1986, Mutambirwa, 1989; ENDA, 1990 and in Zimbabwe found that women tend to be employed in small, home-based low-capitalised enterprises that supply goods and commodities for low-income consumer communities particularly in the urban areas. The limited demand for the goods of the women effectively placed a barrier to their expansion. These enterprises were not able to absorb labour beyond the household and they relied on credit from their own savings, friends, parents and children in wage work. Most of the entrepreneurs used labour-intensive methods of production in activities such as bread making, tailoring and uniform-making, agricultural production and processing.

Thus, entrepreneurship amongst women has developed along the contours imposed on it by capitalism in Zimbabwe until the post-independence period. The post-independence period heralded an intensified level of statist intervention and involvement in productive enterprises. Those enterprises that were not nationalized were subjected to control through legislation on wages, conditions of service retrenchment of labour and the general conduct of the tripartite relationship between state, labour and capital. It became important to pour resources into the running of the state since the state was becoming increasingly involved in production and regulation of the enterprise relationships. Private entrepreneurs were necessarily affected by these developments. Very little help in terms of financial support was given to them in countries such as Zambia and Zimbabwe. Other countries such as Kenya were more helpful and supportive to private entrepreneurs because the state had not denounced private enterprise as exploitative. During this period, the entrepreneurs who had been discriminated against during colonialism had to continue their uphill struggles for existence and progress with minimal state support.

The crises that beset African economies in the 1970s and the 1980s have been instrumental in bringing private entrepreneurship into respectability once more. Growth of African economies is expected to result from unregulated private enterprise which is supposed to motivate individuals who have hitherto been suffocated by state regulation of enterprise.

Cultural components of entrepreneurship

It is necessary to understand that entrepreneurship, like other human endeavours, is culturally mediated. For example, in Europe, it was quite disgraceful to be involved in trade if one was an aristocrat. It was the emerging bourgeoisie who were able to gain a foothold in trade together with the impoverished members of the aristocracy who found the imperatives of social respectability difficult to realize with dwindling incomes and resources. Similarly, in the Southern African region, warrior societies valued military conquest rather than trade as a more acceptable mode of entrepreneurship. Within classes and strata in different societies, it might be more respectable to be non-labourers in spite of the fact that trade and commerce may be more materially lucrative though socially disdained. For that reason, the motivations for entrepreneurship may differ at different historical periods between and within societies depending on which classes are in the ascendant at specific moments.

If we examine the history of entrepreneurship in Africa, it was frequently the prerogative of chiefs and other ruling people to establish trade and commercial links with strangers. Thus, the established, politically powerful clans and lineages were in a better position to consolidate their wealth which could trickle down to the subjects in instances of drought and famine. The changes in power configurations within African societies after colonialism were a result of the demotion and defeat of some nationalities and classes and the emergence of others in the colonized societies. The religious converts, the literate and the state functionaries were, in most cases, drawn from the powerless and the marginalized within communities and households and they sought to use the colonial system as a refuge as well as a basis for a new status system within which they could excel.

The new classes that were created by colonialism obviously co-existed with the old ones that struggled to survive in their old or revised forms. It was possible for the new classes to use their literacy and numeracy in obtaining jobs, in buying the best property that was available to blacks as well as in establishing new business ventures along the lines of those of the settlers. On the other hand, members of the established classes, whether traditional or new, could also combine literacy and traditional forms of prestige and status to become entrepreneurs. The formerly deprived could use the colonial system to create new bases for wealth accumulation through their new skills as teachers and state functionaries who could buy shops, farms, transport vehicles and other means for creating and increasing their incomes. Thus, in countries such as Zimbabwe, there were different types of entrepreneurs depending on how they had fitted, failed to fit or resisted fitting into the colonial system.

In the towns, the people who were prominent in the private sector open to blacks were frequently uneducated people who had not been able to obtain jobs as clerks, teachers and policemen in the colonial state apparatus. Among the women, the entrepreneurs were usually women who had been marginalized in rural areas by divorce, childlessness, witchcraft accusations or widowhood and thus had to fend for themselves and their children in situations where their education and skills were not valued in the colonial economy. The wives of the high-income earners amongst the population also found it more challenging to become entrepreneurs because it was more logical for them to work outside the wage sector since their incomes, combined with those of their husbands, were highly taxed. These were the women who explored other possibilities outside wage labour.

Entrepreneurship development was heavily influenced by political, cultural and other considerations which propelled different types of women into extra-wage sector pursuits for various reasons. It is important to bear in mind this differentiation in motivation and commitment to participation in entrepreneurial activities by women all over Africa. During the colonial period, many people were motivated to advance themselves through formal education because this was the basis for obtaining relatively well-paid jobs in the colonial economy. During that historical period, it became less prestigious to be involved in trade, commerce and other types of industry that were not premised on high literacy and numeracy. This requirement channelled people's aspirations accordingly and was instrumental in justifying statism with its emphasis on large organizations and bureaucracy that necessitated the development of cadres who were skilled in managing state enterprises which often failed to generate surpluses and support themselves.

Changes in entrepreneurial patterns after the economic recessions

Entrepreneurial patterns have changed quite markedly as economic crises have beset African economies. The recessions of the 1970s and 1980s have eroded the living standards of the poorest, as well as the middle classes, particularly those who have been employed in state and parastatal bureaucracies. Inflation and the devaluation of African currencies on world markets has had the effect of pushing the populations into intensified income-generating activities, both legal and illegal. In the heavily-regulated economies which have poor capacities for policing the regulations, the red tape has become a source of frustration and has held back the efforts of those people wishing to engage in income-earning opportunities. Effectively, the bureaucratization of the civil services and the attempts at economic control by the state during times of economic stagnation or contraction have led to the criminalization of certain forms of entrepreneurship.

Economic recession has led to crises in production and consumption in Africa and created openings for people to engage in the provision of basic goods and commodities which they had previously taken for granted. For example, in Uganda, Zambia and other countries, salaried people have penetrated the market gardening niche in order to provide meat, vegetables and other products which are no longer available or affordable on the open market. Similarly, those people in public and private sectors who have opportunities for travel overseas in the course of their work have been able to engage in import-export trade in electronic goods that are not locally available or affordable.

Gender and entrepreneurship in the 1980s

Economic recession has had more specific effects and implications on a gender basis in Africa. The shortages of goods and services that are consumed regularly have created some opportunities for those women who have been engaged in food production and distribution. This has been particularly so in parts of West Africa where women have been active in this area for a long time. The major constraints have been related to access to land to grow food for those women who are not involved in distribution. The hostility that has been directed at market women in Ghana, Nigeria and Zaire points to the strengthening of the control that women have been able to exercise in the provision of goods and services for everyday consumption. The governments in these countries have periodically attacked women who are involved in marketing and distributing consumer goods for 'profiteering', for being unpatriotic and against the national interest. This has happened when women have seized the economic opportunities available to them in supposedly free market environments.

In Central and Southern Africa, the opportunities for women have not been in food production and consumption because of the erosion in women's land-use rights and of control over the proceeds of agriculture in their households. Thus, women have tended to venture into relatively new areas such as import-export trade across regional borders. In mineral-rich countries such as Zimbabwe, Zaire and Zambia, women have also been involved in some aspects of trade in gold, diamonds and emeralds. However, it is necessary to point out that women tend to be involved in the more peripheral and less lucrative sides of these operations such as gold panning on river banks in Zimbabwe or courier functions for those people who actually realize the highest profits when the minerals are illegally marketed.

Recession has created the conditions necessary for mobilizing women's entrepreneurship outside the contours habitually delineated by the accepted divisions of labour. The mobility of women has increased in most African countries. For example, women from Ghana and Nigeria travel extensively within their own countries as well as outside them to the Middle East, Hong Kong and Singapore in order to purchase electronic goods cheaply. In Zambia and Zimbabwe, some women who have access to cheap airline fares travel to Mauritius regularly in order to procure cheap electronic products for resale in their countries of origin. At the lower end of the market, women from Zimbabwe travel regularly to Botswana and South Africa to purchase cheap consumer goods which are not available or affordable in the local market for resale to high-income consumers in Zimbabwe.

These activities have had the effect of forcing African governments to reconsider their economic policies as it becomes more obvious that state control over all kinds of economic activities is neither possible nor desirable. The rash of programmes for supporting small-scale entrepreneurship is a reflection of the realization by governments that they need to do more to generate local manufacturing capacities in order to satisfy the demands and needs of their populations for goods, commodities and services that are necessary for a decent standard of living.

Responses of Aid organizations

Overseas non-governmental donor agencies have been at the forefront of developing and funding women's entrepreneurship in Africa. This has been due to the fact that new micro-projects are visible, organizable and manageable and easily amenable, requiring small infusions of capital, low-level personnel. These projects such as those of Oxfam-America in Zimbabwe have tended to have multiple goals and objectives, some of which contradict each other. Gaidzanwa (1985) and Sibanda (1986) have written evaluations of these projects that show that the projects assumed that women could effectively incorporate more work in gardening, goat production and agricultural work without impacting negatively on their domestic and agricultural work within individual households. Women tended to be 'organized' in groups for tasks that are normally performed by individual women with the assistance of their children and/or husbands.

The results of these projects were dismal to say the least because the government personnel responsible for helping the women with technical and other advice were already overworked and as a result, they resented the assumption by NGO personnel from Oxfam-America that extra work with the women was possible. On the other hand, the government personnel could not verbalize their resentment lest they be perceived as hostile to 'development'. In the end, they passively resisted the work by giving minimal time and input to the NGO- funded project for producing vegetables in Chivi. In that particular project, the person deciding on funding had a religious welfare assistance background which was critical in determining the ways of conceptualizing projects. The income-generation capacity of the project was poor and it was unable to sustain itself.

Aid organizations and agencies have tried to help governments in Africa to divert their attentions from large and unviable projects to small-scale industries and enterprises that are run by individuals or small numbers of entrepreneurs. Strong emphasis has been placed on reaching women who have been identified as comprising a large proportion of the poorest in Africa. Laudable as this objective might be, it was also clear that a lot of the funding was carried out on the basis of very little knowledge of the form and content of the entrepreneurial activities that men and women were involved in throughout Africa.

In the 1970s and 1980s, donors 'discovered' rural women in the Third World and they went about developing programmes and staffs for funding women's projects. For example, in Zimbabwe, European and American non-governmental organizations built on the experiences of religious organizations that had mobilized women into savings clubs on a group basis. The group ethic was then assumed to be the critical factor which, when combined with funding of inputs, was expected to help women to earn incomes for themselves. This resulted in women being grouped to perform a variety of activities some of which were not amenable to that type of organization if they were to function effectively and profitably. Women were organized to bake bread, manufacture soap and raise chickens. What was ignored was the fact that, depending on the scale of production, certain activities such as soap-making on a small scale were only profitable if carried out by a few women. In one area which was serviced by the Manicaland Development Association with the help of NOVIB, a Dutch non-governmental organization, groups of up to twenty women could be found manufacturing relatively small quantities of soap and earning miniscule incomes after the profits had been distributed amongst the women. The same applied to bread-making groups (NOVIB, 1989).

With respect to pig and chicken rearing, women's work was increased because the activities are water intensive and large numbers of women had to walk long distances in rural areas in order to get to the pens and perform their share of the work for very little profit. These types of projects demotivated large numbers of women who found them unprofitable. This approach was quite extreme and it was partly a reaction to the state-led large-scale approaches of the 1960s and 1970s. There was a swing to the other extreme where production and manufacturing were supposed to benefit more people than was feasible. Thus, the attempt to spread the benefits to wide sections of communities resulted in the development and implementation of projects that were not funded adequately but were expected to benefit too wide a population (Gaidzanwa, 1985).

There were other assumptions implicit in these approaches that were supposedly gender-sensitive. Rural women were taken to be undifferentiated in their poverty and disadvantaged state. Issues of age, marital status and life experience were subsumed under the veil of poverty. This resulted in the similar treatment of women who had dependent, adult or no children. Those with small children had a heavier childcare burden than those with relatively grown-up children or none at all. Similarly, older women have more status, power and mobility, especially if they have married sons and daughters. They bring these status differences into whatever activities they engage in and these differences have to be recognized since they affect the labour, time and effort that women can mobilize in their entrepreneurial activities.

In urban areas, the funding of projects for women has been similarly undifferentiated with government, non-governmental organizations and international aid agencies giving help to co-operatives of women who are involved in group activities in the area of craft production and the provision of services. The urban-based group projects appear to be more lucrative than their rural counterparts but the point still remains that other types of individually-based entrepreneurial activities have not been sufficiently explored for funding. Most of the entrepreneurs who have 'emerged' and established themselves are those who have gone through the formal channels such as banks and finance companies, small enterprise development agencies and other similar bodies. These bodies do not and cannot reach small entrepreneurs who cannot or prefer not to go through formal channels for various reasons.

It must be recognized that many female entrepreneurs are forced to operate illegally in many countries because of the regulatory mechanisms that exist for public health, licensing and other purposes. If we bear in mind that the states in most African countries are constantly looking for means of extracting income from private consumers through different forms of taxation, duties and levies, we can understand that most small entrepreneurs have a reason for remaining 'submerged' as a way of evading 'capture' by the state, local government and other regulatory agencies that depend on private citizens' rates and taxes for their survival. Thus, the different types of entrepreneurs operate in different ways in order to maximize incomes for themselves.

In most African countries, funding for the small entrepreneurs in the co-operative sector is contingent on registration and other procedures that are not appealing to most women. These procedures rely on and assume literacy and numeracy, conditions which cannot be fulfilled by large numbers of women in developing countries. These requirements force illiterate and innumerate women to stay out of these co-operative groups or to join them on terms of subordination and dependence on the more literate members of their communities and groups. These factors build in a lot of potential problems such as inequality, mixed motivation and multiple agendas in women's activities in the small-scale sector. Thus, the agencies that have tried to aid women in small-scale enterprises have tended to reach the most accessible and regulated types of entrepreneurship while leaving the unregulated and potentially more needy sections of the entrepreneurial communities unreached.

There has also been a bias towards aiding and funding relatively new groups of entrepreneurs without paying attention to the history and transformation of entrepreneurial activities over time. The older, more established entrepreneurs may face adversity due to economic and social changes that might restrict their output, inputs and clientele. Very little attention is paid to the stage issues in the life-cycle of small-scale enterprises and quite a large number of entrepreneurs are quietly submerged when the conditions that generated and supported their existence change. In Zimbabwe, for example, the contraction of people's wage incomes, the flooding of markets by similar types of goods and along with the lack of yarn, this has forced many women out of the production of different types of apparel. The tailors and dressmakers who have been able to survive are those serving the upper-income categories of the population with fixed premises, wage workers, machines and distribution outlets all over the towns. The smaller tailors and dressmakers have to work in their homes, serving their immmediate neighbourhoods. This restricts their possibilities for growth and outreach.

In terms of prioritizing skill areas, most aid agencies have tended to assume that the biggest hurdle that women entrepreneurs face is that of obtaining credit and inputs. This has resulted in the provision of start-up capital and very little training in marketing, packaging and other processes necessary for sustaining an enterprise. Thus, rural and urban women's groups have produced masses of goods, services and commodities which lack markets and this has demotivated women further. The skills necessary for reading changes in market trends are very important and it has been the individual operators and networks which have been able to change the direction and emphases of entrepreneurial activities as trends change. In Zimbabwe, the women who initially produced crochet goods for the local and tourist markets quickly veered towards production for the markets in Botswana and South Africa as soon as a glut developed in their home market. They also diversified the arrangements for payment in those countries so that they could maximize their earnings in foreign currencies. It is imperative that, in the context of changes brought about by the policies for restructuring economies hit by recession, aid agencies must focus on helping existing individuals and networks to maximize their market opportunities rather than opting for the bureaucratically convenient and easy option of supporting groups whose productivity and incomes are lowered by the use of an inappropriate form of organizing work and enterprise.

The sustainability of the programmes for entrepreneurship is important. In many African countries, programmes for small-scale industries are often embarked on in response to consumer shortages. Very little attention is paid to the possibilities for survival or diversification of these programmes where the shortages are sporadic and unpredictable rather than regular. In Zimbabwe, for example, many bread-making, poultry and piggery projects were started as a response to bread shortages due to rising nationwide demand for bread and meat. The deterioration in the transport infrastructure contributed to the unavailability of bread, particularly in rural areas. In 1991, there have been problems with the supplies of wheat for bread and these bakery projects are in deep production trouble because they cannot compete with the larger bakeries for the wheat supplies that are now scarce. Most of these small groups will probably fold up unless they diversify their bread ingredients to include maize flour or other grains. This could have other implications such as the need to develop and market other types of bread which will be attractive, palatable and as convenient to store as bread from wheat. Whether these groups will be able to meet this challenge is another question.

It is also important to note that the conditions in Africa are conducive to speculative types of entrepreneurship which might not be desirable or likely to lead to sustained growth with development. This point has been made earlier in this paper and it is quite clear that women also get involved in speculative ventures that are not sustainable or beneficial to wide ranges of population groups in Africa. The bourgeoisie in different parts of Africa tend to be consumption-oriented partly because they acquire their wealth through speculation, embezzlement and other ways that are conducive to the development of large income disparities, growth with poverty and a devaluation of productive entrepreneurship.

Differentiation of women entrepreneurs and donor support

Given the discussion above, it is necessary for donor support to differentiate women's enterprises by type, input, skill and need. This will enable support to be more varied. For example, in Zimbabwe, women who produce apparel for the local market could be helped by linking them with manufacturers of cloth so that they can buy it more cheaply. They could also benefit from exposure to design and fashion trends locally and regionally so that they can respond quickly to the changes in taste and trends in the different age, ethnic and gender markets for clothes in Zimbabwe.

Those entrepreneurs designing and manufacturing clothes for the high-income consumers whose reference groups are Western need up-to-date knowledge in fashion trends outside the country and the region and they will need skills to research markets for their goods in a market that is characterized by stiff competition from manufacturers based in Europe and the South-East Asia region. They will need knowledge on international arrangements that might allow them to contact solidarity groups that help to market goods from the South. They will also need to target particular niches for specific types of clothes which they can produce at lower costs and better quality levels than other potential competitors rather than producing a wide range of clothes *per se*. Thus, clothing producers are differentiated by market, scale and volume of production and they need different skills.

Similarly, women who are producers and/or traders need different types of skills depending on whether they trade petty commodities within their localities, nationally or internationally. In Zimbabwe, some women trade foodstuffs which they grow themselves while others trade foodstuffs produced by others. Those who trade commodities produced by others may have enough capital and knowledge of markets in major towns but their constraint may be affordable and reliable transport rather than credit for purchasing commodities. Those who retail their small surpluses after satisfying their own consumption may benefit from a broadening and strengthening of the local consumer base rather than credit to buy more seed, fertilizer and implements since they may have enough capital if they manage to sell all their surplus locally at reasonable prices.

Professional women are increasingly getting involved in retail and trade in Zambia, Zimbabwe, Botswana and other countries in Africa because they want to *main-*

tain and if possible to increase their consumption levels. Thus, they are less likely to go into small-scale retail of foodstuffs and other small commodities. Instead, they may start off in small-scale activities that bring in an income that comprises at least 30–40 per cent of their salaries per three months or so. This may be in the form of baking high-priced wedding cakes, making wedding dresses, arranging flowers for companies that can place large, regular orders with them or importing electronic goods for friends and relatives. They usually build on traditional 'feminine' skills which they commercialize and repackage so that they can be sold to high-income individuals and organizations. These women need public relations and social skills that will expose them to high-income people and organizations. They also need some inputs that have to be imported. Thus, they need clients who can afford to buy high-priced cloth, cake decorations or alternatively, they should have sources of foreign exchange which can allow them to add more value and uniqueness to their services and commodities than is locally available.

Such women need different types of skills which are more personalized than women in the business of selling bread and other foodstuffs for which there is a steady market. They will need to know how to get information on forthcoming social events such as weddings, conferences, funerals and christenings of people they are not linked or related to socially. They usually try to work as unregistered entrepreneurs so as to avoid high income tax on a personal level. They do not necessarily have any ambition to become formal businesses with overheads such as offices, telephone and personnel bills, given that the activities that help to generate incomes for them are not regular or predictable. They also use personally accumulated funds and donor agencies dismiss them as middle-class or privileged women.

Women entering 'non-traditional' (for women) areas of enterprise in different countries also need sustained and more varied types of support. For example, women who run consulting, legal, management and other companies that provide services may find it difficult to break into the established areas of their specialization because of the male-dominated networks and relationships. They may need sustained support to equip their libraries and information systems if they are running law firms. They may need loans to help them hire good quality staff and to retain their staff. They will also need to know which organizations support women's enterprises by giving them custom. The information pertaining to the possible ways of entering business in an area where they are a minority is crucial since they will need to be more creative and imaginative that their male counterparts who might be in the same position.

Women who have already been in business and might want to diversify or change their area of emphasis will start off from a different base and level from that of women with no business experience. The former may have more knowledge about the demands of entrepreneurship, the sacrifices in terms of time, leisure and other socially desirable pleasures that need to be foregone until the business or venture is fully established. Since they need transformative skills to turn their businesses towards production for more lucrative markets locally and regionally, they need skills and business knowledge about the age, sex and income structures of their potential markets and the consumer strength and possibilities for satisfying demand for their goods in the long term.

Women who are single, divorced or widowed with male and/or female children will also tend to organize their businesses differently from those women who have their spouses to account to or to help them. The single women may create wider and functionally differentiated businesses to give their various children different and discrete areas of control and to bequeath their children with an inheritance that will not lead to disputes after the death of the mother. On the other hand men, in patrilineal societies, may prefer to bequeath their businesses to their eldest sons or to their sons and not their daughters so they may organize their enterprises in a centralized way to facilitate control and inheritance by one person. This will depend on the lineal customs and traditions of the women and the ways in which they incorporate their male and female children into their different businesses. It is very important to analyse enterprises over time in order to learn how businesses survive, are inherited and how they operate in the second or subsequent generations. This affects women's willingness to become entrepreneurs particularly in countries such as Lesotho where women's incomes and property are still legally controlled by fathers, husbands and brothers and women are legally subordinated to men. All these factors have to be taken into account when supporting women's entrepreneurial activities in Africa.

In policy terms, it is important for donor agencies wishing to support women to understand which women's projects are most viable and why. As Buvinic has suggested in this volume, direct assistance programmes need to be task-focused. She also draws attention to the poor performance of multiple-objective projects which are organized around female-oriented tasks and run by women's and religious organizations on a welfare basis. In countries such as Zimbabwe, where government and municipal regulations are of colonial origin and were designed to exclude Africans, it is important to reform or repeal legislation on the size, location and staffing of enterprises in the small-scale sector. As it is, in Zimbabwe women who want to hawk, vend or be active in trade and commercial activities require all manner of licences, registration and regulation so it is very difficult to make their enterprises profitable and stable because of the onerous regulatory framework within which they have to operate legally. It is no wonder that most of them operate illegally and cannot therefore make use of any formal and institutionalized credit facility, marketing arrangement or organization that requires registration.

Conclusion

If donor support is to have a significant and beneficial impact in the area of small-scale enterprises and entrepreneurship, attention must be paid to the issues that have been outlined in this chapter. These are the history and cultural contexts of entrepreneurship among women, the differentiation of women entrepreneurs by race, age, marital status, class and life experience. It is erroneous to treat women as a homogeneous category that can be reached with credit policies for group-based micro-activities. The changes in the economic, social and political climates in different countries are important because they steer entrepreneurial efforts in specific directions at given points in time. Donor policies need to recognize existing types and likely directions in entrepreneurship so that they can help to develop and sustain efficient and sustainable enterprises that can meet the needs of the populations of Africa more effectively.

Promoting women's enterprises: what Africa can learn from Latin America

MAYRA BUVINIC

Introduction

Any attempt to derive lessons from development projects has to first recognize the many differences between countries and cultures that limit the applicability for Africa of experiences that have unfolded in Latin America. The ability to generalize is constrained by the diversity of economic situations and policy environments within each region as well as across them, the heterogeneity of firms in the informal sector in both Latin America and Africa, and differences in the condition of women that can affect their responses to enterprise promotion interventions. The latter differences are explored briefly below.

Latin American women have a number of advantages over African women that are important for successful entrepreneurship. These advantages result from the region's comparatively higher rates of urbanization and modernization. Latin American women have, on average, substantially more schooling and lower fertility rates than African women, and thus are better equipped to have access to productive resources and have more time to devote to the enterprise. A majority of the Latin American women also live in large cities, where population density and the concentration of interdependent markets and economic agents facilitates operating businesses and implementing enterprise promotion programmes (Tokeshi, 1989).

Most African women, on the other hand, still reside in rural areas where enterprise promotion activities are more difficult to implement because of lower population densities, less demand for local products, and more difficult access to markets. Partly because of these features and the work burden, the time constraints of the average woman in Africa against participating in enterprise promotion programmes are higher than those of her counterpart in Latin America.

On the other hand, there are cultural differences between women in the two continents that give an upper hand to African women in enterprise activities. The economic activities of African women are better recognized by society, and they have relatively more physical and economic independence than women in Latin America. In many African countries, women have their own plots of land to cultivate, inherit land through matrilineal descent, and control their own purses within the farm-household (Bruce and Dwyer, 1988). These women's rights are mostly unheard of in Spanish-speaking Latin America.

In addition, in Africa the coexistence of tribal rights with legal rights, and the relatively lower importance or lack of enforcement of the latter, is a potential advantage to women in forming enterprises, as is the higher cultural acceptability of women's organizations and women's groups. The more developed legal and regulatory frameworks in Latin America exclude women and can pose serious barriers to their independent participation in economic activities.

For instance, married women in Peru need the husband's co-signature for a business loan application. A female participant in a credit line for microentrepreneurs in Comas, a poor neighbourhood on the outskirts of Lima, confessed to us that she had to lie about her marital status in order to have access to the loan.

While women's groups are an integral part of African daily life, in Spanish-speaking Latin America, men have traditionally opposed women's participation in women's or, even more so, mixed groups, constraining women's access to resources, such as credit, that use groups or associations (i.e., co-operatives) as delivery channels.

But there are also important similarities between women and between their enterprises in the two continents which justify the utility of this exercise, despite the heterogeneity of the enterprise environments and the differences between the women. The similarities that women share cross-regionally are that they are subject to the universal sexual division of labour that defines women as having dual responsibilities for home and subsistence/market production; restricts women's work in the marketplace to female occupations with lower productivity and earnings; creates a gender gap in earnings and access to formal credit, modern technology, land and other assets; and results in the greater poverty of women relative to men.

The similarities that their enterprises share are that they are the smallest in size, number of workers and income; use informal credit and traditional technology; fall mostly into trade and services; and are the object of highly similar assistance programmes by overseas donors, the state and NGOs.

These similar features provide a common ground for deriving lessons which, nevertheless, should be taken as broad guidelines to be assessed and adapted to the specific environments in which women operate their enterprises in African countries.

Project experiences in Latin American countries

Projects to promote female entrepreneurs have emerged in Latin America (LA) only in the last ten to fifteen years. Overall, they have been small in concept and in financial resources, have been funded largely by overseas development assistance, and have been implemented by NGOs. They can be classified into four groups or approaches, with different objectives, features and results, although bearing in mind that there are exceptions in all approaches and that some projects may share features of different approaches.

The approaches are (i) the enterprise formation approach; (ii) a variant of the enterprise formation approach reflected in the survival activities of women's groups in response to economic crises and adjustment programmes; (iii) the enterprise expansion approach, and the (iv) enterprise transformation approach.

Enterprise formation approach

This is the oldest and most widely-used approach for promoting female entrepreneurs through projects in the LA countries, despite its dismal success in fulfilling its objectives. The approach is best exemplified by income generation projects for poor women with the multiple objectives of integrating women into market production, reducing gender inequalities, and/or providing welfare assistance to them. These projects deliver a number of services or promote different activities in response to the multiple goals they embrace and, while they target poor women directly, often include all women indirectly in the target population (especially when reducing gender inequalities which is a major project objective).

The characteristic features of these income generation projects for women include group organization and group production; a participatory style; group training in awareness raising and gender solidarity; skills development in what are perceived as 'female appropriate' tasks; subsidized credit or other inputs; and attempts at marketing the group product. The underlying premises are that group functioning and participatory styles are effective vehicles for women's enterprises and have the added benefits of developing gender awareness and solidarity.

Projects are frequently implemented by women-only organizations, and participants and implementors are volunteers. Many of the women-only implementing agencies have emerged from organizations providing relief and have developed institutional competence in welfare assistance rather than in the implementation of development projects. This institutional capacity goes back to the creation of the separate functions of development and relief after the Second World War, and the use by international relief agencies of women's clubs and women's organizations throughout the Third World to distribute free goods. This welfare history is shared by women's organizations in Africa, Asia, and Latin America and is critical in understanding the constraints of the enterprise formation approach.

The results of these projects are dismal in terms of enterprise development and income generation for poor women. But despite their well-known and generalized failure rate, they persist as a preferred project strategy, a preference that is manifested in a recent ILO unpublished analysis of social development projects in the region (Villarreal, 1991).

Elsewhere I have analysed in detail the 'misbehaviour' of these projects, and have tried to explain the persistence of this project approach for women (Buvinic, 1986). Below I summarize the main reasons that account both for their economic failure and their ability to survive.

These projects share with a majority of other development interventions directed at poor women, over-ambitious project objectives including social as well as economic aims. These ambitious aims cloud performance evaluation measures and serve to justify project continuation despite failure in the project's economic achievements.

One of the principal features of six UNIFEM funded projects in different countries recently reviewed by ECLAC (1989) was that they shared multiple objectives: economic/production objectives, gender-related individual objectives, social and family welfare objectives, and organizational ones. While responding to the many problems that poor women actually face, this plethora of goals makes project implementation difficult and justifies project continuation when social aims are achieved, even if the economic activities fail.

In a recent evaluation of microenterprise projects and artisan workshops for poor men and women in Santiago, Chile, Raczynski (1989) concludes that, while the enterprise formation approach with the urban poor is neither an effective nor a viable policy to create stable employment and adequate incomes, it nevertheless has positive psycho-social outcomes, especially for the *women* participants, that are couched in terms of increased self-esteem and assertiveness.

Raczynski further states that the psycho-social achievements are more likely when the projects follow a participatory style. And this is the second major reason for the economic failure of the enterprise formation project approach. It is well known that participatory management is not conducive to effective economic performance (Tendler, 1982). But despite this knowledge, when women in particular are the beneficiaries of enterprise-formation interventions, and because projects and implementors have multiple aims, participation is the preferred project style. The conflict with the economic performance objectives is perhaps most clearly stated by a woman who, for 15 years, has participated in an artisan workshop in the district of Conchali, in Santiago, Chile:

> I often ask myself, how is it that these workshops continue to exist, because with this (practice) of having everybody participate in all decisions, this does not benefit the enterprise economically. (translated from Raczynski, 1989)

The multiple objectives and the participatory style are two basic reasons why enterprise formation projects with poor women 'misbehave'; that is, they survive failure in the economic objectives by achieving social goals that, at least in the short term, are sufficient to ensure continued beneficiary participation and funding from donors.

A third contributing reason for economic failure can be found in the choice of income-generating skills to be taught. Most often, enterprise development focuses on areas appropriate to women and the development of skills that implementors perceive are familiar to women. However, these skills are frequently really not at all familiar to women, are difficult to teach, require background knowledge that most poor women do not have, and usually result in products that have no or low market demand.

A large, rural development project in the highlands of Bolivia in the 1980s tried to teach Aymara women, who have exclusive responsibility for sheep herding and shearing, the very unfamiliar skills involved in papier-maché flowermaking! Sewing classes, as the one observed in San Jose, Costa Rica, often require basic mathematics, including the notion of fractions, and are beyond the reach of most poor women. Because market analyses are seldom a component of these projects, an all-too-frequent sight in income-generating women's groups is the stockpile of crafts, clothes, or knitted items that go unsold.

A last reason for the failure of this approach is the 'volunteerism' required of both participants and implementors. It is often assumed that poor women have time on their hands or, in other words, that the opportunity cost of their time is zero or close to zero (because they do not earn cash incomes). This is obviously not the case and causes both participant desertion when the women cannot afford to continue volunteering time and self-selection in the sense that the less poor stay on.

The volunteerism of female implementors, while cost-saving in the short term, does not work either. The lack of technically-competent personnel is a significant element in project failure. Female volunteers often come from a welfare tradition, or may have technical skills in social rather than economic issues, which rationally leads them to steering these multiple-objective projects to the fulfilment of social goals, to the detriment of the economic ones.

High-profile women activists from the welfare as well as financial sectors, who volunteer their time to lead these projects, usually have general political agendas for themselves and their gender that can also interfere with project execution. In this case, enterprise promotion activities for poor women become secondary to or a vehicle for the larger aims of achieving power in the male-dominated financial worlds and redressing gender inequalities in society.

The choice of women activists as project leaders can create a vicious circle of exclusion where they volunteer to help other less well-off women but end up, because of broader issues associated with the gender struggle, contributing to the failure of income generation projects for poor women.

Survival activities of poor women

The survival activities of women's groups in response to the region's widespread economic crisis in the 1980s and the income losses resulting both from recession and structural adjustment measures can be classified as a variant of the enterprise-formation approach. The main differences with the income-generation projects described above are that groups form spontaneously as a result of economic need, and that the main goals of the agencies that assist these groups are to help the poor weather the economic crisis, rather than helping women increase their economic participation. The implementing organizations are often church groups, who also come from a relief or welfare orientation, and have little or no technical expertise in running enterprise formation activities.

The projects include other 'survival' activities as well as enterprise development, such as communal kitchens (*ollas comunes*), which are more successful than the forming of viable enterprises, for essentially the same reasons already mentioned. During the 1980s, in Santiago, Chile, 99 per cent of the participants in grassroots economic organizations or 'solidarity workshops' were women. In

1986 about one-fourth of these workshops generated no income, and 57 per cent of them generated income that was lower than the minimum government subsidy provided through an emergency employment programme (Hardy, 1987).

Enterprise expansion approach

This approach is characterized by the delivery of credit, and sometimes training and/or technical assistance, to women who already operate/own microenterprises in the informal sector, mostly in commerce and services. The objectives of projects operating with this approach are largely economic: to improve the economic performance of microenterprises, generate employment, and 'graduate' informal-sector producers to the formal sector. Some projects include a gender-specific objective (to increase women's incomes), but all projects using this approach have a far narrower set of goals compared with enterprise formation activities, and thus have a far easier time fulfilling these goals.

One can roughly distinguish three different modalities in the delivery of credit to women's microenterprises that are associated with different success rates. There is the credit line for microenterprises, both male- and female-owned, directly through a development bank or through an intermediary dealing with a bank with the characteristic features of formal-sector lending; parallel programmes outside the formal banking system delivering minimalist credit that replicate features of informal-sector lending and include solidarity groups for male and female microentrepreneurs; and credit lines for women only, operated by intermediaries dealing with banks or by parallel institutions.

An example of the first modality is the credit line that the Industrial Bank of Peru (BIP), a government owned development bank, established in the 1980s for urban microenterprises in Lima and secondary cities. While one of the explicit policies of the credit line was to reach female clients, by the end of the second year of operations, only 16 per cent of the loan portfolio had been disbursed to women.

Our evaluation of the credit line at that time revealed that the characteristic features of formal sector lending discouraged women clients from applying for loans. These features included a preference for fixed over working capital loans (and therefore, for longer grace and loan periods and larger loan amounts) and for manufacturing over commerce and petty trading, and tough collateral and documentation requirements, which were much more restrictive in practice than on paper. The average collateral registered in 1984 was double the minimum required by the BIP and single loan-application files that we reviewed were around 100 pages long! (Buvinic and Berger, 1990).

One of the principal reasons for women not applying for the BIP loans was that the majority of women-operated enterprises in Peru, as elsewhere in Latin America, are in petty trading and other commercial activities, where the main need is for working rather than fixed capital loans.

A minimalist credit programme in Santiago, Chile, run by a parallel agency (Propesa), demonstrates the importance of targeting trade activities to reach female enterprises. The programme started by excluding these, which resulted in a heavily male-dominated loan portfolio, with fewer than 20 per cent of the loans going to women. Last year, Propesa changed their regulations and began working with street and market vendors through solidarity groups. Currently, more than half of Propesa's clients are women.

In summary, the results for women of bank credit lines for microenterprises are dismal since commercial activities where women predominate are excluded, and women who apply have a tough time competing with men given the formal sector lending structure and its priorities.

Most agencies in the region affiliated to the NGO Action International use the modality of minimalist credit that replicates the characteristics of informal sector lending and includes solidarity groups for micro-vendors. They are set up as parallel programmes outside the formal banking system, include three types of graduated lending, market interest rates, segmentation of the market into micro-producers and micro-vendors, solidarity groups for micro-vendors, reduced collateral requirements, a low amount of paperwork, and an entrepreneurial philosophy with faith in the capacity and rationality of informal sector producers. They make no explicit distinction between male-operated and female-operated microenterprises.

The affiliates are often set up specifically to run the credit programme, and have no other commitments or lines of work. They have technically-qualified, paid staff, and expatriate assistance and leadership, especially at the start, which is more conducive to a specific task orientation as it has no ulterior political motives, except those of ensuring successful project performance for the donor agencies. A largely male leadership, expatriate as well as in-country, has easier access to the financial and political resources needed to set up these programmes.

The results are viable projects for male- and female-run microenterprises, at least in the short term. The focus on micro-vendors and on solidarity groups shifts the transaction costs of lending to the borrower and increases women's access to credit, both because of the focus on commercial activities and the elimination of real guarantees. The minimalist orientation facilitates project performance and mitigates against having a mix of social and economic objectives that are difficult to attain through one project. The fact that a majority of the programme leaders are men helps to break the disadvantage of powerless women leaders helping poor women.

Women constitute more than 50 per cent of the recipients of loans to commercial activities in these programmes, with excellent repayment rates. Women, however, are less well represented in the portfolios for micro-producers and borrow, on average, smaller amounts than men.

Prodem, in Quito, Ecuador, overcame the pattern of having low female representation among micro-producers by targeting female clients from the outset. With funds from USAID, Prodem set up a special earmarked fund of US$50,000 to be disbursed to women during the first two years of operations and obtained technical assistance. As a result, Prodem records disaggregated information by sex of borrower from project start-up, and both the management team and the credit analysts embraced the objective of reaching women clients not as an 'add on' but as an integral part of the programme. And this investment paid off well beyond the end of the technical assistance.

Prodem was launched in 1984 and two years later, women accounted for a full 65 per cent of micro-vendor group borrowers and 35 per cent of individual borrowers in micro-production. In 1988, Prodem signed an agreement with the IDB to expand the programme's size and reach. The programme was reoriented to emphasize very small manufacturers, and graduated loans were given for fixed and working capital. In August 1989, about 1200 new loans had been granted. The majority of loans were very small, under $120; the cumulative rate of arrears was 1.8 per cent, and about 79 per cent of the overall costs had been covered by project-generated income. Almost all the loans went to individuals rather than to solidarity groups. Despite this fact, women were 58 per cent of the loan recipients for the period (Buvinic 1990).

This unusually high percentage of women in the loan portfolio for micro-producers can be attributed to Prodem's explicit targeting and the initial women-oriented investments, the commitment of managers and loan officers, the crucial programme ability to report on the loan portfolio performance by the sex of the borrower, and the structure of the loans that encouraged applications from very small operators.

These programmes show that women's microenterprises can be reached as long as there are critical modifications in the structure of loans or the supply of credit. Loans that require personal group guarantees rather than real collateral, that minimize paperwork, and that lend small graduated loan amounts over time can both charge market interest rates and be successful in attracting a female clientele with reliable repayment records.

The problems with these minimalist credit programmes are their moderate coverage, their questionable long-term financial viability, since they do not function entirely as banks and do not have deposits, and their limited capacity to graduate clients into the formal banking sector and to transform their enterprises, especially the women's enterprises, which are the smallest and least productive.

Our evaluation of the impact of Prodem credit on women and men borrowers showed that, over a year, the credit granted maintained rather than increased or transformed production. The credit did not solve the problems that the micro-enterprises had with the demand for products and did not change the level of technology.

But the credit had indirect benefits that were sex-specific and suggest that, especially in the case of women, the indirect benefits of these programmes may be larger than direct ones. The Prodem loans helped women build a credit history and increased the efficiency of women's (but not men's) operations, reducing significantly the daily hours that women spent on the business (Buvinic *et al.*, 1989). It is likely that increased business efficiency enabled women to substitute home time for work time and translated into increased child welfare.

The third kind of enterprise expansion programmes are credit programmes exclusively targeted at women, through a parallel programme or through a women-owned intermediary that deals with the banks. The implementing agencies are run by women; the programme objectives may be restricted to providing credit and technical assistance to poor women microentrepreneurs or may include a larger target group of women-run businesses of different sizes and incomes. The objectives may also include gender equality advocacy aims that are beyond the credit programme *per se*. The credit structure can be minimalist or credit plus other forms of assistance, and it can follow the features of formal or informal sector lending.

The short-term results of these programmes have been mixed. As may be expected, the better performers are the programmes that target poor women and follow a minimalist approach with features of informal sector lending. A concern of these programmes is how frequently women borrowers become a 'front' for men who really use the credit. Furthermore, a risk of the more successful programmes is that their success attracts men who then want to 'take over' the programme.

Enterprise transformation approach

This approach, which entails changing the nature of entrepreneurial activities to make them competitive in international markets, has been emerging with the transformation of the LA economies in recent years from an import-substitution to an export-oriented development model, and the resulting devaluation, opening of markets, diversification of production, privatization and strong export orientation that guides economic policy (ECLAC, 1990b). This approach has had two opposite consequences for the promotion of female-operated enterprises.

On one hand, the opening of labour and product markets and the promotion of export-oriented industrial growth, either by setting up export-processing zones or by providing incentives to domestic and multinational export firms, has resulted in cascade (linked) sub-contracting, with forward (selling to) and often also backward links to the informal sector which produces for export firms in the formal sector, especially in manufacturing. Cascade sub-contracting has significantly expanded the demand for female workers and, in theory at least, the economic opportunities of women workers who produce for these firms (based either at home or in workshops).

Cascade sub-contracting, however, is predicated on low wages, no benefits, and seasonal or intermittent demand for work, and this is one of the reasons why it has attracted so many women, who are more willing than men to work under these conditions. The outcome of this type of work for women can be severe exploitation of women micro-producers, especially by less affluent national firms (Joekes and Roxana 1987).

A solution to this problem of potential exploitation that has worked, without displacing women workers, is the establishment of non-profit, intermediary agencies whose main function is to bridge the gap between export firms and low-income women producers, as well as between the latter and credit and training institutions. These intermediaries ensure that the contractors get quality and timely products, and give women producers access to credit, technical assistance and organizational skills to operate efficient contracting arrangements with large firms.

In Santiago, Chile, Cideme, a non-profit agency, worked out a contract between home-based micro-producers from low-income neighbourhoods and a large supermarket chain, for the production of cleaning supplies for the national market. Cideme obtained credit for the women from the local affiliate of Women's World Banking (Finam) to purchase sewing machines and to give the women a steady minimum wage, and it oversees production to ensure timely and quality product delivery. The project has been operating successfully for over two years.

On the other hand, the opening of economies to international markets has had adverse effects for women in the agricultural sector. These effects occur when agribusiness firms, unaware of women's productive activities in the agricultural sector, draw up contracts with male farmers, individually or through farmers' associations. The farmers turn to their wives or daughters to furnish the additional farm labour required, increasing women's already heavy unpaid workload, with the result that women have to give up their own income-generating activities and/or subsistence agriculture, with negative implications for women's enterprises and local food production.

Von Braun (1989), for instance, found that women's farm work increased by 78 per cent in a non-traditional, export-oriented vegetable production project in Guatemala. Women had to substitute farm work for off-farm income-generating work, losing control over economic resources, since men were paid and controlled the income from the highly profitable farm work.

Rating of the different approaches

In brief, the project experience summarized points to the viability of projects that follow the enterprise expansion approach and provide minimalist credit to women's microenterprises, and suggests that the indirect benefits to women from these projects may be greater than the direct effects on their enterprises. It also indicates that cascade subcontracting arrangements can promote female-operated enterprises provided that they are mediated by intermediary organizations that ensure against exploitation of female workers.

The analysis argues against enterprise formation approaches, projects with multiple objectives and 'credit plus' interventions, and warns of the potential problems of female-activist leadership for political as well as productive agendas, and women-only projects, that tend to have multiple objectives and have less access to economic resources.

Finally, the analysis questions the long-term viability of all projects, including the more successful minimalist interventions, and points to these projects' limited coverage and incapacity to transform women's enterprises. A major reason for the incapacity of these projects to do more is the policy environment in which they operate.

Policy environment

The policy environment in which all project approaches have operated in the region has been, with no exception, indifferent or hostile to the promotion of women's economic activities, including enterprise formation and expansion.

Aside from allowing or encouraging outside donors to fund the projects already mentioned, no government in the region has formulated and implemented direct, specific policies to promote women's enterprises. The 1980s has been termed the 'lost decade' in terms of investments in human resources, and this is especially true for women. The few significant investments that governments, with weak financial resources, have made on women have been exclusively in their roles as mothers and nurturers, through maternal health and nutrition programmes.

The main reasons for this lack of attention from governments include contraction in government resources and fiscal spending, policy choices that encourage the development of large (read male-owned) firms that can readily compete in international markets, and a still deeply-held belief that developing the economic activities of women may have a negative impact on both child welfare and the very existence of the family.

The sustainability of any project intervention requires local funding and commitment, features which are lacking in the region in terms of the promotion of female enterprises.

In addition, indirect policies in the region have often been openly hostile to the growth of women's enterprises. The legal and regulatory frameworks, already mentioned, work against micro-producers in general and women micro-producers in particular, who in many countries are legal minors if they are married and who cannot afford the high transaction costs required to set up and operate an enterprise. Police harassment of street and market vendors without permits is well known, and affects women who predominate in the sector.

The only exception to these negative indirect policies has been the change many countries are implementing from inward- to outward-oriented development strategies. This change has in some cases unintentionally increased the demand for female-operated enterprises in subcontracting arrangements.

It is important to note, however, that the opening of economies to international markets and competition may be a necessary condition but does not suffice for the development of women's enterprises in the small and microenterprise sectors, as the case of Chile reveals. The opening of the Chilean economy in the last fifteen or so years to international markets coincided with welfare-oriented policies towards women and with no direct policies to promote the small and microenterprise sectors, resulting in no significant growth of women's enterprises.

Technological choices and educational policies have also worked against women entrepreneurs. Governments have preferred capital-intensive technologies that are beyond women's reach; investments in technological research and development have been meagre and have excluded women. This is especially the case in agricultural research institutes that have ignored women's work in agriculture in their technological R. & D. and, therefore, have not developed appropriate technologies in food processing. The few resources that governments have invested in non-traditional, technical education and training have benefited men over women.

Given this policy context, in a sense it is remarkable that some projects benefiting women entrepreneurs have performed as well as they have.

By way of conclusion: lessons for Africa

From the Latin American experience reviewed in this chapter the following general guidelines and research needs emerge for the promotion of viable and, hopefully sustainable, female-led enterprises in African countries:

(i) In *direct assistance programmes* the best performing and most viable projects are those that seek to expand women's enterprises by the delivery of minimalist credit that replicates features of informal sector lending to women micro-producers and micro-vendors. These projects are run by parallel lending agencies that are set up for the purpose, are task-focused, and reach men and women clients but include both the capacity to disaggregate the loan portfolio by the sex of the borrower and specific incentives to reach women clients, included in the programme design.

The worst performers are multiple-objective projects that seek to form group-run women's enterprises in 'female-appropriate' tasks and include personal and social development objectives or family welfare ones; they should be avoided at all costs. Their style is group-oriented, participatory and volunteer based. These projects are usually implemented by women-only organizations or church groups with a welfare orientation and/or a larger political agenda that conflicts with project performance.

Since the best performing projects are often run by male leaders with access to economic and political resources, funders need to be cognizant that female leaders may need an extra 'helping hand' (in terms of financial and technical resources) to set up these projects and have to make sure that larger political agendas do not interfere with project performance. The choice and development of implementing agencies and actors is delicate and critical.

The promotion of subcontracting arrangements between women's enterprises in the informal sector with formal sector industries geared to national or international markets can also be a viable project strategy with the intervention of intermediary agencies that protect women workers.

Given the Latin American experience, projects should be aware of and watch for the following negative effects :

- the constraints on women's time, especially in rural areas, and the substitution effects that may occur with project interventions that increase the demand for women's labour;
- the loss of women's income-earning activities with the modernization of agricultural sector activities, especially in food processing;
- female leadership styles, resource constraints, and political agendas of high-profile women activist leaders;
- exploitation of women operators through subcontracting, especially by local firms;

○ men taking over successful women-only projects.

(ii) In *the policy environment* directly and indirectly friendly policies are needed to foster women's enterprises and ensure long-term project viability. Especially in Africa, directly positive policies to promote female entrepreneurship should include gender-informed and gender-targeted R.& D. in agricultural production and processing, emphasizing technology development for small-scale operations. Similarly, there would be a need for gender-informed and gender-targeted programmes for the transfer of rural technologies. Most importantly, directly positive policies should include donor and national commitment to financing start-up costs of direct assistance programmes for women's microenterprises.

Indirectly friendly policies should include: (a) revising regulatory and legal frameworks with special emphasis on removing the constraints that female microentrepreneurs face in setting up business and having access to productive resources; (b) devising agricultural sector policies that favour the development of small-scale rural industries; (c) strengthening institutional development of female NGOs and of government agencies; and (d) investing in female education and technical training/apprenticeship programmes for females.

(iii) In *policy-oriented research* there is a dearth of empirical data in African countries on the informal sector, and on women's participation in the sector, which means that most of the topics dealt with in this chapter would require empirical studies to inform policy and programme design. Topics suggested for study include:

○ the characteristics and determinants of women's participation in the informal sector, and the relationship between this participation and women's poverty;
○ the characteristics and constraints of women's microenterprises, differentiating those of micro-producers and micro-vendors and distinguishing survival from microenterprise activities;
○ the time women spend in subsistence production and processing and gender-appropriate technological solutions to shift this production to the market;
○ indirect effects of macro- and sectoral policies and regulatory and legal environments on the promotion of women's enterprises;
○ situation-specific demand studies to establish women's need for credit and the structure of credit programmes;
○ the situation of women operators that work under contracting agreements and identification of measures that ensure good working conditions for, but do not displace, these workers;
○ institutional development needs and diagnoses of a variety of institutions in the public and private sectors, emphasizing female-based agencies in the government and non-governmental sectors, that can assist female entrepreneurs.

Small and microenterprise promotion and technological policy implications

SAMUEL WANGWE

Introduction

The experience of development in Africa has shown that macro- and sectoral policies and the institutional framework induce responses (negative or positive, intended or unintended) at enterprise level. To that extent, enterprise level development requires careful formulation of supportive macro- and sectoral policies and an appropriate institutional framework.

Development experience in the last two decades, and more so in the last decade, has led to changing perceptions of balance between a number of categories: the balance between markets and administrative controls; various agents of development in society (e.g. between public enterprises and private enterprises, large and small enterprises); technology imports and local technologies, between old and new technologies; and the balance between internal and external factors influencing development. Critics of the post-independence approaches to development in Africa have highlighted various aspects, many of them reflecting their theoretical and/or ideological orientations. For instance, the neo-classical school stresses the neglect of the role of prices and markets in resource allocation while the radical perspective stresses the inability to analyse the role of class formation in these countries and the constraints posed by the external economic environment (Weiss, 1988). Even in these debates, it is increasingly being recognized that many generalizations based on ideological positions are not tenable. In view of such changing perceptions on development, it is timely to re-examine the place of small enterprise development in macro- and micro-level development policy.

The purpose of this chapter is to raise questions about the implications of recent development experience on the place of small and microenterprises in Africa. In order to capture the possible place of SSE in a dynamic context (in a changing world economy and technological environment) questions will be raised about the implications of new and emerging technologies on policies for SSE development. In this context, the paper examines some policy issues for sustaining direct assistance programmes to these enterprises and raises some issues for further research in technology policy.

Small- and microenterprise sectors: a typology

The place of small enterprises is likely to vary according to the type of sector and the way the sector is influenced by technological developments, economies of scale, linkages and other relationships with other sectors. The following categories of SSE could have different policy implications:

(1) sectors where SSEs predominate (e.g. furniture, garments, footwear) are usually characterized by demand for individualized products, are manufactured in short runs, their processes are not intensively technological and investments are modest. Innovations to improve productivity originate outside the sector but they may spread fast through the sector (e.g. the use of modern adhesives, more efficient dyeing and painting techniques);

(2) sectors where there is a division of labour between small and large firms, mainly in the form of sub-contracting, face downstream influences whereby it is mainly the large firms that control innovation, expecting their sub-contractors to adapt their products to trends in the larger unit. In such cases, policies on SSE would need to be formulated in consideration of the development of large-scale industries (and policies which influence their development) with which they have sub-contracting relationships.

(3) sectors in which SSEs stand side by side in competition with large enterprises. These face various lateral influences whereby they are forced by the presence of large enterprises to seek out particular markets, usually small specialist ones where they make maximum use of their flexibility and scope for adaptation. The position of such enterprises is likely to be changing with changes in demand structures and technological possibilities.

In general, but to varying degrees, the three categories of SSE seem to be firmly integrated into a technological and economic system in two directions: vertically and horizontally. Vertically, SSEs may face upstream and/or downstream influences on their production decisions and on prospects of technological development. For instance, in footwear and furniture the introduction of new forms of varnish and glue has induced some SSEs to change their production decisions on products and processes. Downstream influences are more common where SSEs function as sub-contractors to large firms. Horizontally, SSEs face lateral influence through competition, large companies, research and technological institutions, training institutions and more generally, government macro- and sectoral policies and other regulations. Policymaking for SSE development will need to take into account the fact that different types of SSE are influenced differently by various policy instruments.

Position of small enterprise development in new and emerging technologies

In the era of new and emerging technologies (e.g. micro-electronics, new materials, energy and biotechnology) the position of small enterprises is likely to be influenced by these developments by way of introducing new constraints and/or new opportunities. It would be useful to anticipate the implications of some of these developments.

Influences of new technologies on scale and organization

The implications of new technologies on the scale of production is a debatable issue. The evidence on this matter is mixed. However, there is evidence that setting up times and costs of changing over from one product in the production line to another are being reduced with implications of descaling at the product level (Alcorta, 1992). At plant and firm level, there are indications that increasing requirements of capital, R. & D. and marketing and management are contributing to increasing optimal scale in some industries (Alcorta, 1992).

The meshing of new technology with organization design, process strategy and external relationships appears to be one of the most important issues for the future. Integration of technological innovation across various functional areas is a major strategic issue. Some have argued that the new technologies integrating microelectronic processing with electronic communication (collectively known as information technology) tend to increase the degree of freedom available for organizational design (Child *et al.*, 1987), facilitating networking and communications and better production scheduling and inter-firm co-ordination. Organizationally, these new technologies seem to facilitate the gradual removal of the zero-sum nature of the balance between centralization and decentralization, permitting much more flexibility in design in this aspect and in respect to the role individuals can play.

New technologies could have implications on product quality improvements and on efficiency of small-scale processes. For instance, the use of integrated circuits in the production process has reduced differences in manufacturing capability and quality of products between firms of different sizes (Hayashi, 1990). In some industries there is evidence that there is no one-to-one relationship between the type of product manufactured and the efficient organization of production. For instance, Levy (1990b) found that jogging shoes of similar quality and design were produced in both large and small firms in Korea and Taiwan. In some cases, the balance of relative competitiveness between SSEs and large firms may be shifted in favour of small enterprises. A substantial part of the management literature seems to predict that the winners in the 1990s will be smaller, more specialized factories competing on the basis of quality and responsiveness to niche markets (Tidd, 1991).

In some of the less technologically advanced industries, and especially those in which the importance of economies of scale is on the decline, the recent trend has favoured small enterprises. Taiwanese footwear is organized via a subdivision among independent firms of the various processes of production. It has been suggested that the role of government policy in facilitating workable sub-contracting arrangements and reducing transaction costs between them has been significant

(Levy, 1990b). In the case of the newly-industrialized economies of South-east Asia, the rise in the role of small enterprises in this context has been explained in terms of government support for these enterprises combined with increasing promotion provided by business associations, co-operatives, banks and private firms, especially in the fields of training, technology, development finance and venture capital (Regnier, 1990). A relevant policy implication which emerges from the South-east Asian experiences is that through government support, there could be consideration of policies and programmes which would reduce the costs of market transactions. Such government interventions could contribute to reducing the obstacles to industrialization and technology development via the proliferation of small enterprises.

The evidence available so far does not render concrete support to generalization one way or the other. The outcome here may be influenced by results of a sector-by-sector analysis, age of the industry, type of innovation and possibilities of new venture approaches (e.g. spin-off technique). The relevant policy implication here is that new and emerging technologies are bound to influence the position, the prospects and constraints of SSEs. Policy making for SSE should be made with ample consideration of the implications of these technologies.

New industries and opportunities for SSE

Most new technologies, however, are knowledge-intensive and/or skill-intensive. The rise of some new industries could represent windows of opportunities for science- and skill-based small enterprises. These could represent potential grounds for the establishment of new ventures led by skilled managers and technical personnel (e.g. engineers, computer programmers) spinning-off from the civil service, public enterprises or multinational corporations. Such enterprises are capable of being quite technologically dynamic. For instance, in the case of semi-conductors, much of the dynamic growth and market diffusion in the advanced economies is reported to have resulted from the formation and rapid expansion of new (and usually small) technology-based firms (NTBFs) (e.g. as noted by Rothwell and Zegveld, 1985). In these cases, the technological entrepreneurs often came from established corporations bringing much of the relevant know-how with them. In both cases, the interaction between small and large firms was instrumental to the evolutionary dynamic. A system of dynamic complementarity is apparent.

In some of the more advanced developing countries, small enterprises are occupying a strategic position in some of the frontier industries. For instance, Levy and Kuo (1991) have pointed out that Taiwanese firms in keyboard and personal computer assembly were started small by young engineers recently graduated from university with a few years' experience in other companies. These firms not only procured all components from independent vendors but also sub-contracted the mounting of electronic components on printed circuit boards and a significant fraction of the keyboard assembly operation itself. The relative ease with which Taiwanese firms could enter into sub-contracting arrangements with one another and the presence of Taiwanese traders willing and able to explore the international market prospects for SSEs imply the Taiwanese entrepreneurs could initiate production at a relatively small scale with little up-front investment for production facilities or marketing information.

The likelihood that such complementary interactions between large and small enterprises could be promoted in the African situation seems to be favoured by recent developments where skilled entrepreneurs are already emerging as spinoffs, at varying degrees, from the civil service, public enterprises and foreign-owned enterprises (located locally or abroad). These entrepreneurs could form the core of a new generation of technological entrepreneur bringing much of the know-how from their previous employers. Findings from surveys of metalworking SSEs in Rwanda and Mali render support for the observation that greater capacity to innovate is associated with linkages to the large-scale sector and with previous experience in large-scale, modern enterprises (Bhalla, 1991). It would be useful to explore the macro- and sectoral policy implications and/or prerequisites of promoting such complementary interactions between enterprises of different sizes in the levels of technologies that are feasible in the African context.

Prospects and possibilities of blending new and traditional technologies

Prospects and possibilities of integrating new technologies with traditional economic sectors could be explored. The process of blending new technologies and traditional technologies in a complementary fashion can lead to outcomes ranging from marginal effects of infusion of new technologies to radical restructuring of traditional production. Some studies have found that the proportion of successful cases of upgrading technologies in traditional activities through blending with new technologies while preserving much of their core characteristics (institutions, skills, know-how and supporting infrastructure) is encouraging (Bhalla *et al.*, 1984; Bhalla and James, 1988). However, it has also been found that there is an absence of specific policies to encourage or promote such blending.

There is some evidence to suggest that there are opportunities for blending new and traditional technologies such as biotechnology, photovoltaic technology and information technology. Biotechnology applications to some African fermented foods like kaffir beer, Nigerian *ogi* and *gari*, and cloning of tea in Malawi have been reported as promising cases (Bhalla *et al.*, 1984 citing Steinkreus, 1982). The literature available on this aspect suggests that photovoltaic technology is a viable option for providing electricity in the rural areas of developing countries in activities like waterpumping, refrigeration, telecommunications, lighting and multipurpose systems (Stevens, 1988). The scope for using information technology in SSEs is also promising. Selective use of new information technologies can facilitate quicker response of SSEs to changes in demand, quicker adaptation of production equipment and processes to new uses, faster dissemination of technological and market information to enterprises and facilitate information flow about whatever supportive programmes may be available.

In the context of Africa, there is an absence of specific policies to encourage the application of new technologies in traditional activities. Considering the policy implications of blending new and traditional technologies, two broad policy areas deserve further research: policies towards encouraging the adaptation of the organization of traditional production to facilitate the application and absorption of new technologies; and policies for adapting the various new technologies to suit the needs of SSE operations.

Technology policy for small and microenterprise development

It is now widely recognized that direct technical assistance to small and microenterprises is not likely to achieve sustainable levels of technological development without also putting in place a supportive policy environment and technology policy (e.g. Heklund, 1991). While larger enterprises can afford to incorporate an explicit technology function (e.g. in the form of R. & D. departments) it is difficult for SSEs to incorporate such functions as selecting and sourcing, adaptation and absorption or undertaking local innovations. It is in this context that government policy could facilitate meeting the technological requirements of SSEs, provision of technical services and creating a supportive environment for SSEs.

Potential for innovations

There is evidence that small and microenterprises in Africa have the potential and willingness to undertake and to benefit from technological innovations. For instance, in Sierra Leone, a survey of entrepreneurs of SSEs (USAID/MSU/ILO) found that 48 per cent of them had introduced some kind of technical change in their products or production processes between 1975 and 1980 (Bhalla, 1991). Other studies of SSEs manufacturing metal windows and doors in Mali and Rwanda found that considerable effort had been put in making some tools and equipment on their own. In Rwanda about half of SSEs had made some of their tools or equipment for themselves. In the case of Mali the proportion of such SSEs was 67 per cent (Bhalla, 1991).

An important policy issue arises from the fact that although SSEs have been found to have considerable potential and willingness to undertake technological innovations, fuller utilization of that potential has been limited by problems of access to technology and related resources, incentives, and various contextual factors.

Access to technology

Technology and technological change can be accessed through various methods through acquiring, developing or modifying technology in the form of the make-or-buy decision (in terms of a dichotomy between R. & D. strategy versus purchase strategy). There are various alternative sources from which firms may acquire new technologies. Some of these are indigenous R. & D. activity, purchasing new capital equipment, acquisition of firms through mergers, licensing from domestic firms, licensing from international firms and R. & D. conducted under government contract (Bozeman and Link, 1983). All these sources are candidates for consideration in respective circumstances.

Available evidence on sourcing technology by SSEs indicates that most equipment is imported. For instance, results from ILO-WEP surveys in Mali and Rwanda and several technical assistance projects in activities related to SSEs in Tanzania have given indications that technology was largely imported and that straight technology imports seem to discourage local technological innovations and adaptations (Bhalla, 1991 and Wangwe, 1991).

Technology imports can be complementary to local technologies if they are utilized to augment and upgrade existing technologies in SSEs. However, in many cases such technology imports have been introduced to replace rather than to build on local technologies. Sourcing of technology in many countries in Africa has been overdependent on foreign sources even when domestic alternatives could have been sought. The resulting relationship between imported technology and local technology has been that of replacement or pre-empting the latter by the former. Such relationships have been demonstrated for instance by Coughlin (1988) in the case of Kenya, Mytelka (1992) in the case of Cote d'Ivoire, by Adubifa (1990) in the case of Nigeria, Bhalla (1991) in the case of Mali and Rwanda, and in the case of Tanzania by Wangwe (1992), UNDP (1991). Bagachwa (1991), and Wangwe, (1991).

This raises the policy question of how SSE can be assisted to access technology that is generated locally and sourced from imports in a manner which enhances complementarity between them and in the process of which local technology is upgraded and developed further. The role and relationship between local and imported technologies needs to be revised as an important policy matter, especially with a view to attaining fuller utilization and development of domestic technological capabilities. In this context, a relevant policy implication can be drawn from a study of ten multilateral and bilateral aid projects in Tanzania which have corroborated this weakness (Wangwe, 1991). In that study the experience of several projects has shown that the approaches which recognized the existence of local technology and capabilities, and started by addressing the issue of upgrading that technology, stood a better chance of increasing endogenous capacity building (ECB). Although it should not be assumed that all external technical assistance activities must necessarily involve upgrading traditional technology, it is important to recognize systematically and make a detailed study of existing local capabilities so as to define the place and role of external technical assistance and the gaps it is envisaged filling.

Encouraging and promoting technological change: towards generation of local technologies

As has been indicated in the foregoing sections, SSEs have the potential and desire to undertake technological innovations. The problem is that this potential is often not utilized for lack of relevant resources and supportive technical services, infrastructure and policies. For instance, in the case of SSEs producing metal windows and doors in Mali and Rwanda it was found that many attempts to make tools and equipment for themselves had been abandoned for lack of finance, raw materials or equipment, skills and experience, and limited access to markets (Bhalla, 1991).

The small size of SSEs makes it difficult to carry out the technological development and innovation involved in upgrading local technologies or designing and manufacturing various equipment and other production facilities. Hence, much of the technological research and innovation effort and development of local technologies should be expected to take place in separate R. & D. institutions which could develop prototype equipment. The role of SSEs would be to take up these prototypes for commercial production for sale to various users including SSEs.

The effectiveness of R. & D. institutions in carrying out this function has been limited by the failure to enable these institutions to do technological research and development and the failure to commercialize the technologies which are developed in these institutions.

One aspect in which R. & D. institutions have not been enabled to carry out technological development and innovation functions is financing. Inadequate financing not only limits the activities that R. & D. institutions can perform but it often diverts the attention of these institutions from research and development into various income-generating activities in order to 'survive'. In the case of Tanzania, for instance, it has been shown that the financing policy of R. & D. institutions has diverted the attention of these institutions to income-generating activities (Wangwe, 1991). Since technological innovation activities are often not good candidates for commercial profitability the pursuit of income generation encourages R. & D. institutions to divert their meagre resources to activities which are not central to technological innovation. This kind of competition has not been particularly desirable partly because many R. & D. institutions are subsized, partly because R. & D. institutions are supposed to develop innovative rather than production capabilities. For manufacturing enterprises, venturing into unproven technologies is quite risky. It is reasonable to suppose that competition with the innovator makes the venture into such technologies even more risky.

The resulting tendency to strive for 'survival' has a further adverse effect on the relationship between the R. & D. institutions and the production units which are supposed to use the prototypes for commercial production. The relationship between them tends to be competitive rather than complementary. For instance, in the case of R. & D. institutions in Tanzania, the response to the financial squeeze has been to try to produce commercially their own prototypes (Wangwe, 1991).

Sustaining direct assistance programmes for SSEs requires that the form and level of such assistance be consistent with the capacity of the SSEs to absorb the assistance and augment the technological capabilities in the SSEs or in the institutions which are providing technical services and other forms of support to the SSEs. There are many cases where technical assistance projects failed to improve the technological capability in SSEs because such projects required a higher level of technological capability than that which was available locally in the enterprises and in the technological institutions (Wangwe, 1991).

In some cases, technical assistance programmes have not taken adequate stock of existing capabilities in SSEs and in institutions providing supportive technical service. Such omissions have resulted in the provision of external technical assistance elements which could have been provided by local institutions. For instance, a study of technical assistance projects in Tanzania indicated that although some local enterprises had the capability to manufacture waterpumps, technical assistance programmes tended to include their own waterpump-producing units without first addressing the question of what capabilities existed in the local enterprises and whether such capabilities could be upgraded and developed (Wangwe, 1991).

One factor which has been found to inhibit the realization of the potential for technological innovations among SSEs is the lack of appropriate financing. Enterprises avoid the risk of making investments in unproven technologies. Technological innovations are usually unproven and risky. Part of the risk involved could be reduced by paying greater attention to a more thorough evaluation of these technological innovations for commercial profitability. More importantly, however, it will be necessary to make the necessary arrangements to provide for risk capital within the development finance institutions.

Some issues for further research

By way of conclusion four main issues may be singled out from the above analysis which require further investigation.

First, the place of small enterprises is likely to vary according to the type of sector and the way the sector is influenced by technological developments, economies of scale, linkages and other relationships with other sectors. Policymaking for SSE development will need to take into account the existence of typologies of SSEs to the extent different types of SSE are influenced differently by various policy instruments. Research into the technological development implications of various typologies of SSEs would be useful in guiding policy on this matter.

Second, new and emerging technologies are bound to influence the position, the prospects and constraints of SSEs. Policymaking for SSE should be made with ample consideration of the implications of these technologies. The rise of some new industries could represent windows of opportunities for science- and skill-based small enterprises. The process of blending new technologies and traditional technologies in a complementary fashion can lead to outcomes ranging from marginal effects of infusion of new technologies to radical restructuring of traditional production. Prospects and possibilities of integrating new technologies with traditional technologies need to be explored further.

In the context of Africa, there is an absence of specific policies to encourage the applications of new technologies in traditional activities. Considering the policy implications of blending new and traditional technologies, two broad policy areas deserve further research: policies towards encouraging the adaptation of the organization of traditional production to facilitate the application and absorption of new technologies; and policies for adapting the various new technologies to suit the needs of SSE operations.

Third, although SSEs have been found to have considerable potential and desire to undertake technological innovations, a fuller utilization of that potential has been limited by problems of access to technology and related resources, incentives, and various contextual factors. More systematic research into the factors inhibiting or discouraging local technological innovations could yield useful results for policymaking in this area. More specifically, the fact that in many cases technology imports have been introduced to replace rather than to build on local technologies calls for further research into the kinds of macro- and sectoral policies and incentive structures which favour such competitive rather than complementary relationships between imported and local technologies.

Finally, financing technology is one important factor which has been found to inhibit the realization of the potential for technological innovations among SSEs and R.& D. institutions which could be supportive of the innovative efforts made by SSEs. Enterprises avoid the risk of making investments in unproven technologies. Technological innovations are usually unproven and risky. Financing of R.& D. activities are so dependent on the government budget that they have been victims of budget cuts. This has forced them to undertake income-generating activities, most of which do not form the core of innovative activities. There is a need to undertake further research of the appropriate alternative financing arrangements for funding technological innovations and for providing risk capital for investments in unproven but promising local technologies.

Private-sector organizations and support for small and microenterprises

JAKE LEVITSKY

Background

Until now, most major efforts of governments assisted by donor agencies to support the promotion and development of SSE have concentrated on building up centralized institutions which were supposed to offer an array of forms of help involving advice and training, among others. The detailed organizational structure has varied at times from country to country depending to some extent upon its degree of development, geographical character and the particular advice received from experts sent by donor agencies to help design a support system. The institutions set up were always publicly financed as well as staffed and managed by government appointees. It did not seem to matter whether the pervading ideology of the government favoured private sector development as in the Philippines or Kenya, or whether the policies supported aimed at a socialist organization as in Tanzania and Zambia, for the approach remained the same, namely the creation of a government-sponsored institution to support small enterprise development (Levitsky, 1989).

In general, these publicly-supported institutions adopted a supply-side approach by offering programmes and services which they believed, or were led to believe, small-scale enterprises wanted and then waited for clients to come forward and avail themselves of the support activities offered. Only later was some effort made by these institutions to respond to the demand of the small business community for particular types of help.

The institutions suffered, as most government bodies do in developing countries, from incompetent and inexperienced management (usually political appointees with little or no qualifications for the post), weak staffing as well as irregular and inadequate budgets. Such assistance as was given reached only a few of the entrepreneurs who needed help. Their facilities tended to be utilized mostly by those with good political connections and who were thus well-placed to take advantage of any assistance offered. Viewed as appendages of government, they failed to win the confidence of the small business community and of the financial institutions whose co-operation was badly needed to provide parallel finance for the development of the SSE.

Such evaluation studies as were made (relatively few in number) assessed the impact of the institution on small enterprise development as poor in relation to the costs involved. This was the conclusion of a major study undertaken by UNDP and the specialized agencies UNIDO and ILO which commissioned a team of experts to review the effectiveness of multilateral and bilateral donor support for rural small-scale enterprises in developing countries (UNDP *et al.*, 1988). This study found the general purpose small- and medium-size industrial development agencies (SMIDA) to be suffering from 'over-centralization, rigidity and over emphasis on hardware with a largely urban focus'. This report subsequently pointed out that these agencies tended to place unwarranted emphasis on large, costly, impressive buildings and offices, technical centres, demonstration workshops and laboratories, industrial estates, and fleets of vehicles rather than on the intrinsic quality, competence, dedication and motivation of the staff that were to deliver the services offered.

A major reason for low effectiveness of these national agencies was in fact their over-centralized organizational structure which could have been replaced by smaller more dynamic local branches and regional agencies much closer to the enterprises they were trying to help (UNDP, *et al.*, 1988). While the comprehensive national government-supported institutions have failed to provide cost-effective programmes in support of SME, there have been some examples of smaller local agencies which – even when publicly supported – have achieved more positive results. It is becoming clear that training, advice and assistance in such fields as subcontracting, export and new technologies introduction can be better delivered on a local or regional basis, except possibly in very small countries where a centralized organization might be justified. An optimum cost-effective framework can best be achieved through systems of referral via smaller agencies or centres staffed with experienced, less specialized staff – where appropriate operating on a sectoral basis – who are able to diagnose the problems and overall situation of an enterprise and then refer the case to other more specialized sources of assistance, be it a public-supported research centre or institute, a university, a large enterprise, a local private consultant or an NGO.

In the light of the difficulties encountered in public agency support of SME, it is clearly time to explore ways of involving private sector institutions in delivering assistance to SME in developing countries a priori in the long run[1]. Such organizations are more likely to be accepted by the small-scale entrepreneurs they are trying to help, as well as have a better understanding of the real problems of the small enterprise they are trying to promote. They also do not suffer from the suspicion and, in some cases, contempt with which the small business community views government.

Support for SME by private-sector organizations

In searching for a private sector model of a support system for SME it is worthwhile looking at the situation in developed countries. The approach in these countries is that a large variety of support services can be offered by non-governmental organizations (NGOs) – an umbrella term that usually means non-profit private sector organizations. (In theory, the term NGO could apply also to commercial for-profit organizations.)

Among not-for-profit NGOs that become actively engaged in providing support services for SME are:

1. Foundations: usually NGOs set up by larger business organizations, by the business community, by wealthy individuals or by social organizations whose aim is to assist smaller or weaker business units.
2. Membership Organizations: associations, federations, enterprises, trade or business organizations, Chambers of Commerce. Sometimes this group of organizations is referred to as 'self-help' or representative bodies.

In addition to the above, in developed countries a number of private consulting organizations, private commercial research and development institutions and training firms offer services at a fee which renders a profit to the providers.

In some developed countries large enterprises play a direct role in setting up local development agencies to provide support for entrepreneurs and in particular for new small businesses. An example of this are the Enterprise Agencies in the UK and similar local initiatives in France and the Netherlands as well as in other European countries. Assistance is given by these agencies with management and business training, technical and market information, help in obtaining access to finance (usually special schemes or credit lines with banks) and to new technologies. Sometimes help is provided in obtaining suitable premises or office services (EEC, 1988).

The foundations referred to are often set up by large businesses to improve relations with local regional or central governments and to improve their general image in the community. In some cases they offer assistance in the creation of small businesses as a direct compensation for employment losses and the adverse impact on local communities of restructuring activities undertaken by the corporation.

Membership organizations

Most support provided for SMEs by private sector NGOs in developed countries in Europe comes from associations, federations and Chambers of Commerce – in other words from representative private sector organizations.

Small companies have different interest profiles than large businesses. In all European countries, as well as in North America, Japan and elsewhere, there is a strong movement to create small firm representative bodies which are distinct from larger business associations. Clearly the main purpose of these bodies is 'advocacy', namely to lobby governments and to take account of the interests of small-scale businesses in the formation of national policies (Levitsky, 1989).

Even in industrialized countries, the proportion of small firms which take an active part in promoting their interests through representative bodies is very small. Most studies show that only about 10 per cent or less of small businesses are active members of such representative bodies compared to with perhaps over 50 per cent or higher which are members of trade associations — bodies which have a direct relationship to the commercial activities of the enterprise.

The low level of membership is partially explained by the independent character of small business proprietors and the limited time that they perceive to have available for participation in group activities. The independent, individualistic character of small-scale entrepreneurs tends to make them believe that they have little to gain from seeking the protection of a group. This proves to be a short-sighted view when the benefits that can accrue from membership in such representative bodies are compared to the payment of a modest membership fee.

By far the most active representative bodies for small firms are the local Chambers of Commerce. Since the vast majority of the members of such chambers are small firms, one would expect that these bodies should devote a considerable amount of their activity to looking after the interests of SMEs. Usually such chambers are local bodies affiliated with a central Federation of Chambers headquartered in the main city.

Chambers of Commerce are set up with the aim of promoting and protecting the interests of commerce and industry. They consider their main function to be represention of the interests of the business community to the governing authority at the local, regional and national level.

However, Chambers of Commerce operate differently in different countries (Forster, 1983). The major difference seems to lie in the fact that in European countries, specifically in France, Germany, the Netherlands and Italy, membership in the Chamber of Commerce is obligatory. These bodies have 'public law status' and are financed by an obligatory tax on all businesses. In these countries all new businesses are obliged to register with their local chamber and thus coverage of the business sector is complete.

In Japan, chambers are half-way between the voluntary character of the Anglo-Saxon countries and the public law status of mainland Europe. Membership is not obligatory but because of strong social pressures from the Societies of Commerce, as they are called, about 95 per cent of small firms are members. High levels of membership are largely due to the fact that a great deal of assistance is given by the government to SMEs through these bodies, such as loan guarantees, various forms of special financing, preferences in government procurement, sub-contracting arrangements and industrial estates. Projects are implemented through the chambers making it highly advantageous for SMEs to be members. This may indicate the way in which chambers in developing countries can increase their memberships.

Voluntary and obligatory membership

This discussion is also important to developing countries. There are arguments on both sides. Obligatory membership would increase the power and revenues of the chambers. Chambers could operate more in the general interest since they would not have to fear withdrawal of membership when members oppose particular decisions or actions. Obligatory membership also eliminates resentment of members when membership is voluntary and non-members benefit from the chambers' efforts or programmes.

Those in favour of voluntary membership argue that such chambers have a greater degree of independence from the government and that the leadership is more responsive to members since they have to work to retain membership.

In most developing countries it is probably too early to speak of obligatory membership. Paying taxes in general is less accepted and the collection of dues by a public chamber with obligatory membership would pose problems. However, if the chambers are to be given an enhanced role, they must increase their resources. Therefore, a way has to be found for them to enhance their revenues so that they can operate effectively.

Craft Chambers – *Handwerkskammer* in Germany

Unique among developed countries, Germany has a special Chamber of Commerce for smaller or craft-sector enterprises referred to in German as the *Handwerkskammer*. All such craft-sector enterprises must register locally with the *Handwerkskammer* (Chamber of Crafts). The legal basis for the *Handwerkskammer* organization is a code developed in 1953. The structure of the *Handwerkskammer* organization is set out in Figure 19.1 (see also Doran, 1984).

The *Handwerkskammer* grew out of the guild system in Germany -whereby self-employed craftsmen from the same trade formed a '*Handwerkskammer*' or Craft Guild, which aimed to look after the interests of members. At the national or federal level the associations for each state (Land) form an occupational affiliate or national guild association. There were 65 such associations in 1980. All self-employed craftsmen and owners of '*handwerk*'-related firms must be members of these chambers. The main task of these chambers as defined by public legal status is to represent the interests of the *handwerk* sector, to supervise training and to issue and control the regulations for the examination and certification of all craftsmen.

The Central Association of German Handwerk (ZDH) is the headquarters organization of the *handwerk* sector. It fulfills the role of presenting uniform policy recommendations and of representing interests of *handwerkskammer* to the federal government of Germany. The ZDH is powerful and one of the largest central organizations in the domestic economy. It is organized in departments to cover such areas as economic policy, business promotion, finance, social policies, labour laws, training, information and public relations. The *handwerk* support network for the sector covers:

(1) Technical education and training
(2) Insurance
(3) Information, advice, consultancy and management education
(4) Business promotion
(5) Research, development and innovation
(6) Finance and savings.

The education and training activities are among the most important of the *hand-*

Figure 1 GERMAN HANDWERK ORGANIZATIONAL STRUCTURE

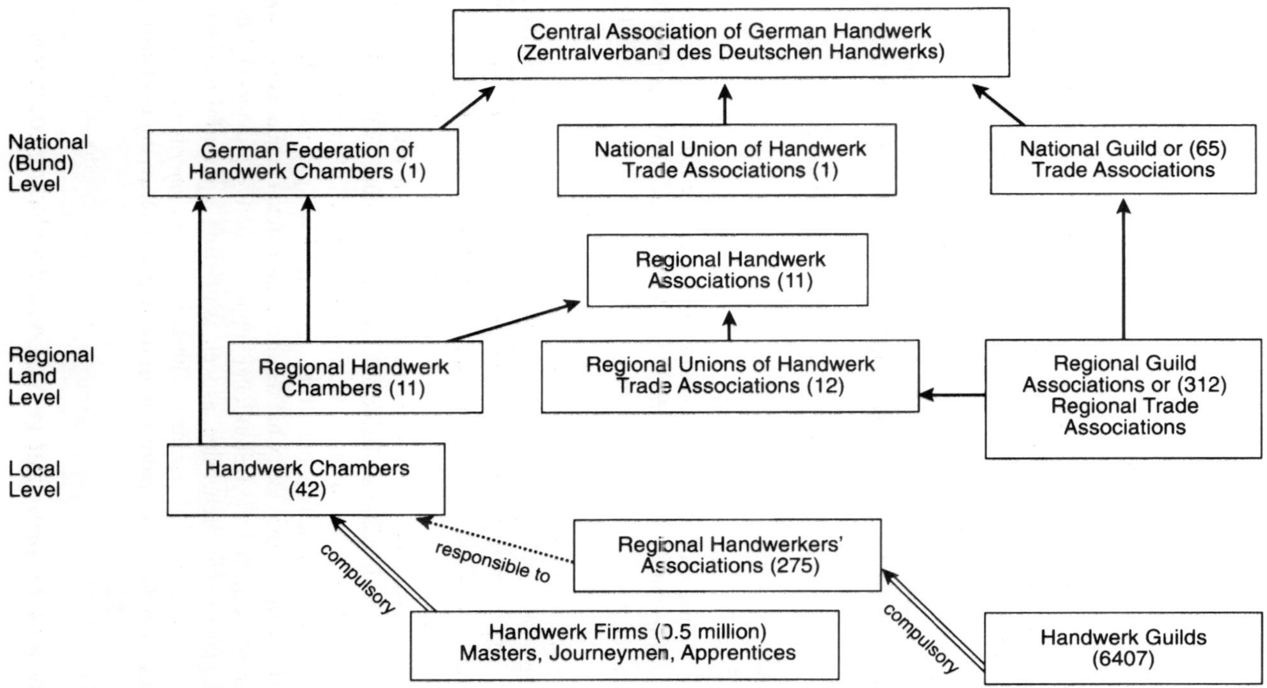

Note: Figures given are for 1979
Source: Doran, A (1984). *Craft Enterprises in Britain and Germany – a sectoral study.*

werkskammer since they form the basis for the education, examination and certification of craftsmen.

In the information, advice and consultancy field the *handwerk* chambers operate free consultancy services and employ several hundred consultants who carry out tens of thousands of individual consultancy assignments annually. In this activity, more than 80 per cent of the costs of these *handwerk* consultants are covered by federal or state budgets, the larger part coming from the state government. The free consultancy service is limited to two days per year, but new firms have three lots of two days per year over the course of five years. There is also a programme of subsidized consultancy beyond these two days which may be extended for up to 50 days for new firms. The rate of subsidy is on a sliding scale depending on turnover, ranging from 25 to 75 per cent.

The *Handswerkskammer* also operates a comprehensive programme of management education for entrepreneurs offering hundreds of hours of training courses mostly carried out through the ITB – The Institute for Management Techniques in *Handwerk* – based in Karlsruhe.

Apart from the above, the *handwerkskammer* also operates programmes in business promotion, research and development and in the provision of finance for its member firms.

In the field of business promotion, the *handwerkskammer* publicizes and supports the inclusion of *handwerk* products at various international exhibitions and also assists in the sale of output from *handwerk* firms through purchasing programmes of the Federal and Land governments. Furthermore, the *handwerkskammer* also helps firms by operating computer centres for the use of members at various convenient locations.

Perhaps the most important support of the *handwerkskammer* is in the field of finance and particularly through the operation of credit guarantee schemes through the formation of Craft Credit Guarantee Associations (*Kredit Garantie Gemeinschaften*). These are formed from trade associations and *handwerk* chambers although the institutional arrangements may vary from region to region. The guarantee funds are made available by contributing banks, by the federal government and by the Länder (states). Guarantee associations offer guarantees to lending banks to cover usually about 80 per cent of the loans provided to the *handwerk* firms. The borrower provides what security (s)he can to the guarantee association.

It can be seen that the institutional support structure provided by the *handwerkskammer* is comprehensive, as well as offering a powerful representational function at all levels of government. The *handwerkskammer* has an enhanced public status, also due to its major role in training and certifying craftsmen (Doran, 1984).

Private sector representative NGOs in developing countries

Private sector representative organizations do exist in developing countries. In practically every developing country, Chambers of Commerce and Industry and associations of small enterprises are active in promoting the interests of the business sector in general, and of small enterprises in particular. In most cases, they regard advocacy for the SSE section and trying to influence government policies as their principal roles.

In all developing countries membership representative organizations, whether the Chamber of Commerce and Industry or the Association of Enterprises is entirely voluntary. Not surprisingly, most of them are only able to recruit a small percentage of the actual number of businesses that are eligible. The low level of membership means in turn that the revenue from membership fees is low and the organizations are therefore unable to offer services or assistance programmes. This in turn means that many enterprises are reluctant to join since they see little advantage in becoming members.

Table 19.1 gives some figures on representative bodies for SME in selected developing countries. It can be observed that full-time staff available for carrying out programmes and implementing services is very limited. Budgets are also minimal. The annual 1989 budget for the association in Malaysia was the equivalent of US$6000 and US$11,500 in Thailand. As can be seen from the figures most of these organizations cover only 5 to 25 per cent of expenditure via membership fees. Two of the more active institutions, the Chamber in Cebu, the Philippines and ASSI in Ghana have 30 and 40 per cent of their budgets provided by German donors.

Finance was named by nearly all of these bodies as the most important constraint that prevented them from expanding services for which they see considerable potential demand. Low membership seems to be a general feature of these representative organizations.

As can be seen from Table 19.1, most of the associations are too weak and inadequately staffed to offer services of value to their members. Donor efforts to work with and through private sector representative organizations have invariably come up against the reality that these organizations only manage to recruit less than 5 per cent of the potentially eligible membership. In some Asian countries they are fragmented into several separate small-enterprise organizations, for example six in Indonesia and a number of different sectorial organizations in the Philippines. In Latin America, associations of small industries such as those in Peru, Colombia, Brazil, Argentina and Mexico are relatively stronger. ACOPI in Colombia and FENAPI in Peru operate effective information services and bulk purchasing schemes for their members and participate in credit guarantee schemes for small scale borrowers.

Organizations of this type in Latin America tend to enjoy greater recognition vis-à-vis the governments which consult with them on policy matters.

In Africa, most countries now have active Chambers of Commerce and associations of small enterprises. However, they generally have very low membership and are strongly politically-oriented and are able to function properly only with outside donor help.

Still, in the last five years there has been a significant increase in the activities

Table 19.1 SME Associations in Selected Developing Countries

Country	*Association*	*Year of Establishment*	*No. of Full-time Staff*	*Source of Financing* A B C D*	*Constraint for Expanding Services*
ASIA					
Bangladesh	National Association of Small & Cottage Industries (NASIB)	1985	10 (256 in branches)	70 branches	Finance
Indonesia	Association of SME Enterprises	1979	10	1 15 60 20	Finance
Malaysia	SME Enterprises Association of Malaysia	1981	2	n/a	Low membership
Philippines	Chamber of Commerce and Industry (Cebu)	1981	24	26–30–	Finance Low membership
Thailand	Small Industries Association	1976	19	n/a	Finance
AFRICA					
Ghana	Association of SSE (ASSI)	1986	5	10–50 40	Finance
Kenya	Association of Kenya Small Enterprises and Traders	1988	7–8	20 20–50	Finance Professional staff
Nigeria	Nigerian Association of SSI (NASSI)	n/a	646 (in 23 branches)	20 15 40 20	
Uganda	Uganda Small-Scale Industries Association	1979	6	5 n/a n/a n/a	Finance
Zambia	Association of Zambian Small-Scale Enterprises	1983	2	90 10 – –	Low Membership Finance

*Code: A — Membership fees
B — User fees and commissions for services
C — Government direct — indirect import
D — Donor support

Note: Drawn from paper present by Chee Peng Lim to International Conference on Small Business Development, Singapore, October 1989 (based on replies to questionnaires), Technonet Asia, 1990.

and interest in associations of small business in Africa. Although weak in resources and capacity relative to the tasks, active organizations of small enterprises are operating in Nigeria, Ghana, Kenya, Uganda, Lesotho, Zimbabwe[2], Zaire, Senegal and Togo.

Overcoming weakness of representative organizations in developing countries

The main weaknesses of representative organizations in developing countries are:

1. Low membership which makes them unrepresentative, resulting in little influence and weak contacts with the sector and with policymaking circles. The low levels of membership fee income mean few and poor services which in turn fail to attract more members.
2. Poor leadership. The private sector agencies are often run by small cliques with political ambitions who can manipulate the organization for their own purposes. Seldom are they persons with the vision to build up strong organizations to serve the sector.
3. Inefficient management and administration. Either due to incapacity or lack of time of those in leading positions as well as limited staff resouces, the agencies are usually ineffectively managed. Most agencies are run by part-time managers who have their own businesses to manage and can only devote inadequate time to administrative matters. Even when there are full-time paid managers they are seldom of high calibre but rather are often political appointees.
4. Non-acceptance as full partners by government. Sometimes for political reasons, sometimes for reasons mentioned in 1–3 above, governments have shown reluctance or even outright opposition to supporting these agencies or fully accepting a role for them in determining policies. This in turn lowers the enthusiasm of enterprises in participating actively in the organizations.
5. Inadequate finance. For all the reasons given above (low membership fees, poor leadership, inadequate government support, etc.), these agencies end up without any real financial resources, thus making it impossible for them to offer effective services.

This is the general picture in most African and Asian countries where government agencies still dominate SME support programmes.

Given the present weakness of most private sector organizations, efforts have to be made to enhance their role in supporting the SME sector by taking steps to solve the problems causing this weakness.

The low membership of these private sector agencies, particularly in Chambers of Commerce raises the question of whether it might not be appropriate to make membership or chambers obligatory in developing countries as in most European countries.

As already stated, those who support voluntary membership (particularly in the US and UK) argue that obligatory membership would tend to bring these chambers more under government control. In fact, the problem in some developing countries may be that these agencies are too often in conflict with government and a closer relationship might be of advantage to both sides.

In considering the low level of membership of representative bodies, it should be recognized that there is a need to educate the small entrepreneurs to appreciate the benefits that can accrue from membership in, and support of, representative bodies and that the reluctance to participate because of a desire to avoid payment of a relatively modest membership fee is short-sighted.

Is the introduction of compulsory membership in Chambers of Commerce or other representative bodies a feasible option for developing countries? There are some considerations here that are different from those that apply in developed countries. In developing countries there is a tendency for representative bodies to become politicized, so there might be a serious danger that compulsory membership could serve to cement an even closer political relationship with government. In the end, these organizations might not really represent the sector but rather serve the interests of a particular government. Also, even if membership is obligatory by law, it is by no means certain whether within the prevailing conditions of developing countries this obligation would be enforceable.

It is important to explore the possibilities of obligatory membership and how this proposal would be accepted by government and by the business community. The other option would be to attempt something closer to the Japanese approach, namely not to impose a statutory obligation, but rather to transfer to Chambers of Commerce and representative bodies a number of functions which enable them to provide distinct commercial advantages to their members, such as involvement in government purchasing schemes, credit guarantee schemes, sub-contracting arrangements, and so on.

In the short term, efforts should be made to have these bodies first become more involved in commercial activities such as those mentioned above as well as encourage them to develop mutual aid funds, to engage in certification of origin and provide simple office facilities (faxes, photocopying and computer services) which would make members feel that they are getting some value for their membership fees. This would, in the course of time, raise active membership levels probably more effectively than the introduction of a law making it obligatory for all SME to be members.

Poor leadership

It is either expected that the leaders of these representative private-sector agencies are of the same political persuasion as the government of the day or that they are totally repudiated by the government and are regarded as opposition or dissidents. In both cases the tendency is for the individuals concerned to provide poor leadership since their aims in operating the agencies are not really to serve the members' interests. Small-scale enterprises have to be educated to demand that their leadership deal with the real problems of the sector, that they exert an influence on the government to follow policies that would provide incentives for SME growth, and that they offer services to small enterprises that respond to their real needs.

Upgrading the level of management in private sector organizations is difficult. In private sector membership organizations, the members generally determine who will be in charge and full-time effective management has to give way in most circumstances to the special interests of part-time member representatives. Assistance given by foundations and external donors to these private sector organizations can help to implement training programmes. Raising the level of management of the institutions is an appropriate target for donor aid to these bodies.

Non-acceptance as full partners by government

Where governments regard the private sector with suspicion they will inevitably reject the idea that private-sector institutions can act as full partners with government in determining and implementing policies. Even in situations where the prevailing ideology of the government is in support of the private sector, there is also a vested interest of government in not giving over too many of its functions to the private sector. In other cases the rejection by the government of a partnership with these organizations may be legitimately based on the poor quality of the organizations or even more likely, on its low membership and unrepresentative character.

It is vital to create a collaborative relationship between government and these institutions. All efforts must be made to attain mutual recognition and respect. This requires also from the private-sector organizations and the small-business community an acceptance of the role of the government and an eschewing of the tendency to attack the government constantly as wasteful and bureaucratic. As efforts are made to raise the level of these private sector organizations one may expect that more can be achieved in attaining partnership with government.

Inadequate finance

Most view this as a key issue but in reality it is a reflection to a great extent of the problems already referred to. Low membership produces low revenue from fees, poor leadership undermines the possibility of obtaining greater help from large businesses and from the government, and inadequate government support also reflects a reluctance to provide finance for such private sector organizations. Without adequate finance these institutions are unable to obtain the staff they need and so cannot offer services or employ the qualified professionals they need.

The following are possible sources of finance for organizations such as Chambers of Commerce or associations of businesses or small enterprises:

(1) Membership fees
(2) Fees from activities undertaken by the organization
(3) Government subsidies
(4) Support from large businesses or foundations
(5) Special projects
(6) Help from external donors

Most Chambers of Commerce and associations in developing countries have only a very small income from activities fees. This fee income can come from payments by participants who take part in training or from payments for advisory services or for information or sale of publications. It may also arise from activities of the chamber or association in arranging missions abroad, participation in exhibitions, certification of origin of products or commissions from loan request preparation activities. In the course of time, income from user fees such as for fax, telex, auditing, secretarial, legal and computer services could be substantial depending upon the capacity of the organization to offer reliable services. This would depend on a higher level of competence in the administration and management of the organizations concerned.

Initially, income from user fees would probably not reach more than 10 or maximum 15 per cent of the overall budget of the organization but, if activities were expanded, could in the course of time reach 25 to 30 per cent or even higher.

Finally, in addition to the income from membership fees or user fees, private sector organizations may require additional sources of funds such as a direct or indirect public subsidy or grant. Such a grant should for a variety of reasons not exceed 50 per cent of the budget of the organization. Above this level there would be a danger of the organization becoming overly-controlled by the government. Furthermore, public grants should not come exclusively from the national government but also from the regional and local authorities concerned. Subsidies and grants can be directly linked to training (for example funding to cover a proportion of training costs depending on numbers trained) to export promotion activities or to the carrying out of specific programmes or projects.

Grants to these bodies could also include support from foreign donors. Such finance from external donors will be needed in the earlier phases of the development of a private sector organization, but here too care should be taken not to swamp these organizations with grants above the level which they could reasonably absorb into productive activities. Excessive donor support could lead to an element of corruption within the organization's management. It therefore should be limited exclusively to the provision over a period of some advisory or staff support or equipment, presumably of the type which could help in the dissemination of information and in the improvement of office operations. There may also be some direct subsidies relating to specific training programmes. Global grants of the sort that would result in the rapid increase of the sums to be handled and disbursed by the management without prior conditions and controls are to be discouraged.

One should not ignore the possibility of some funding for chambers being directly given by larger enterprises or multinational corporations specifically for support activities for small enterprises. Clearly this is more likely to occur in a larger representative organization in which both large and small enterprises participate but it should not be ignored as a possible source of revenue in all SME representative bodies.

Government support for private-sector bodies assisting SMEs

It is clear that the representative bodies and 'self-help' organizations of the small business community, whether associations or Chambers of Commerce or federations comprising also large enterprises, are not of themselves able to mobilize the financial resources necessary to carry out a major programme of support for small enterprises. Advisory services, training, promotion and information usage all require professional staff and there is little likelihood in the short term of being able to pay for this staff from membership fees, even if supplemented by fees and commissions for services rendered.

The government may channel some of the funds that it makes available for small enterprise support through these private-sector organizations. This may be a political problem. There are bureaucratic vested interests in most countries that are reluctant to make large portions of the public treasury available to NGOs and particularly to representative bodies of the private sector.

Training and counselling for small business is an expensive matter, and the participants and beneficiaries cannot be expected to cover all, or even most, of the costs. The government must help in one way or another, either by some general form of assistance to approved organizations, either private-sector bodies or academic institutions, or by a provision for special programmes. A regular budget avoids prolonged annual negotiations over the size of the subsidy but on the other hand, where subsidies are related to particular activities, there is a greater incentive for the institutions to produce results in relation to the support that they are receiving.

Thus in European countries and Japan, the implementation of programmes for training and counselling are primarily given over to Chambers of Commerce and associations, and the government therefore directs its grants and subsidies to these agencies, while in the English-speaking countries the government provides funding more to academic institutions such as universities and business schools and to a lesser extent to consulting and representative organizations.

Neither of the above approaches by government needs to be exclusive. In practice, it is a question of emphasis, and the programmes in developing countries may combine both approaches.

Prevailing opinion tends to see merit in a situation in which both the private sector through the business community as a whole and the direct participants in training or counselling programmes each make some contribution to cover the costs of the support programme as well as relying on government subsidies. There are also those who believe that there are benefits in linking government financial support to the outputs of specific programmes, such as the number of persons trained, or the number of consultancy assignments undertaken. There are of course dangers in this approach too, since where an overall grant might weaken control and encourage lax management, the linking to specific activities could encourage quantity rather than quality.

In the end, if a private-sector organization or representative body, whether it be an association or a Chamber of Commerce, is to carry out an effective programme, it must be guaranteed adequate financing, and the ideal situation would be for this financing to be drawn from a variety of different sources which would include membership fees, government grants, fees for users and beneficiaries, special projects and support from the business community and possibly some forms of external donor assistance whether direct or through government channels.

If an NGO wishes to maintain a degree of independence from government, then it should not become overly dependent on financial support from governmental sources.

There is some merit in the view that at least partial payment, possibly more than a 'token' contribution, should be made by those who take part in a training course or workshop or receive consultation from an advisory service. Beneficiaries take assistance for which they have paid something more seriously. Free advice is rarely valued. Furthermore, those who provide counselling or training will have a more disciplined approach when they are aware that their efforts are being paid for directly by the recipient.

There should be a cost-effective approach to all support services. There can be no question of creating a large, unwieldy service attempting to do everything and thus replicating the worst inefficiencies of the public sector agencies. Private-sector support agencies must be kept small by behaving more as referral agencies than as actual implementors of programmes themselves. A certain amount of short-term training in the form of workshops and seminars could be carried out directly by any private-sector agency or a representative self-help organization that wants to offer services to SME. The same would apply to some relatively short diagnostic or problem-solving consultancies but the main aim should be to help SME overcome difficulties whether technical, managerial or marketing through directing them to where they can obtain the most effective help. This may mean referral to another institution – possibly a specialist sectoral research and development centre, either public or private – an academic institution, private or non-profit consultancy organizations or even individuals in larger enterprises. In such referrals the private-sector organization could monitor developments to ensure that the SME obtain the required services and might help finance the assistance where necessary through funding received from public sources for that purpose. To ensure that costs are kept at a reasonable level an efficient referral system is essential. Attempts to create institutions or agencies whether in the public or private sector that try to do everything with their own staff are bound to be bureaucratic, expensive and less effective. This can only result in a smaller number of enterprises actively being helped.

Decentralization

SME programmes are more effective when implementation is carried out by small organizations locally, either decentralized geographically or operating along sectoral lines. The exact structure must conform to the degree of development of the country and its economy, the size and nature of the territory involved and the maturity and capacity of the national and local governments, the business community and the entrepreneurs. Decentralization of private institutions is desirable, and more effective, but must take account of the feasibility of the number of small businesses in a particular locality, region or sectoral group to justify independent programmes. Decentralization of support services should be the objective to the maximum degree feasible.

Although geographical decentralization is most important and can help make support services more acceptable to SME and more cost effective, wherever possible sectoral groups should also be considered. Of course this will depend on whether there are enough enterprises in a region within a particular sector to make it feasible to operate separate sectoral representative self-help agencies, for example an Association of Leather and Footwear Enterprises. In some cases larger sectoral groups where there are similar backgrounds (e.g. woodworking and metalworking) may be a pragmatic solution. Sectoral groups, along with local and regional decentralizations, will certainly make communication easier with the potential beneficiaries and can make services more cost-effective through use of collective approaches.

Central national body for SME development

In most developing countries, until now, direction of development policies and programmes for the SME sector has been allocated to the Ministry of Industry, or the Department of Industry within the Ministry of Commerce and Industry. In several developing countries, there is a Small Industry Division within this ministry that is charged with formulating policies for the sector. In fact, where donor agencies have established projects to assist this sector with the help of the World Bank, UNIDO, or some bilateral agencies, there usually has been a recommendation either to set up such a division or to strengthen it if it exists.

Unfortunately, several years of attempting to establish or strengthen such divisions in the Ministry of Industry have been relatively ineffective. In virtually all cases, this division has been small, weak, inadequately staffed, and managed usually by inexperienced people who have little relationship with the sector. In many of the cases, the policymaking function has been merged with the regulatory function.

Thus these divisions have become involved in the regulations governing the registration of enterprises, foreign currency procurement, import licence issuance, approval of capital development plans and so on. In only a very few cases have they exerted any serious influence on the formulation of policies in relation to the sector.

An alternative would be for a central national body to be set up, composed of representatives of the government and the public and private sectors involving participants from financial, training, technical and scientific institutions who are engaged in one form or another in programmes or activities in support of the SME sector. Such a National Council would act as a central supervisory body for the SME sector and would have responsibility through a smaller executive committee and a small full-time secretariat for co-ordination and monitoring of the various public and private NGOs engaged in programmes in support of the SME sector. It would act as a conduit for government financial support for this purpose. The National Council and its executive committee should have at least 50 per cent representation of the private sector.

Political problems of private-sector organizations

There are those who argue that more comprehensive organizations comprised of both large and small enterprises have greater prospects of developing responsible leadership answerable to the membership. There are, however, others who hold the opposite view and argue against an organization which is dominated by a small number of representatives from large firms.

This body is replete with examples of splits in representative organizations, of conflicts between provincial chambers and associations and the headquarters, of the development of different private-sector organizations, each linked to their own specific political grouping. Such has, over the years, been the experience in various countries of the developing world.

Similarly, it is known, particularly in many Latin American countries, that the representatives' organizations of employers and industrialists have been the stepping stones to important political office, both on the regional and the national level, and that these organizations have often been callously manipulated to these ends.

It would be extreme to conclude that, because of these unfortunate experiences, there was no possibility of building up strong, independent and democratic organizations in developing countries, but it is as well to recognize the difficulties which will need to be surmounted before strong organizations of these types can be developed. It must be continuously brought home to the SME, and to the entrepreneurs who are members of the organizations, that the behaviour of the leadership of the organization and their response to their needs will depend in great measure on the readiness of members to be active and vigilant and to press for the organization's leadership to act at all times on their behalf. In this respect the National Council will have an important role to play by constantly reviewing the behaviour of the management of the private organizations that have been entrusted with implementation of programmes with public funds and intervening where necessary.

Transition phase to support services delivery by private-sector organizations

One may conclude that all organizations and agencies, both public and private, that seek to provide support and services to small enterprises should be encouraged to keep the headquarter organizations as small as possible. These agencies, whether implementing programmes in training, consultancy, information or in special projects in the fields of sub-contracting, industrial estates, or exporting, should rely to a great extent on other groups to carry out the activities rather than on their own staff. Thus, training activities could be carried out by instructors drawn from the business community, academic institutions and consultancy organizations. Arrangements can be made for consultancy and advisory services to be offered through referral to consultants or research or technical institutions.

In keeping with this concept of the SME support organizations as primarily a small group involved in referrals rather than in actual implementation, some activities can be transferred early on to the private-sector organizations who can make use of the same outside resources as any private-sector agency. In seeking a transition from public agencies to private-sector bodies, training activities could be among the first to be increasingly devolved. Similarly an information service might be offered by private-sector agencies including both technical information and economic information.

There could be a phase in which some public, national or local agencies or academic institutions might continue to offer advisory services while the private-sector representative organization tries to further develop its activities in the same field. During the transition, despite the appearance of overlap, it might make sense to have services offered by different organizations, both private and public. As the capacity and competence of the private-sector organization improves and a proven record of performance is achieved in the field, more and more government funding for this purpose can be transferred to the private-sector organization concerned. The private-sector organization, whether Chamber of Commerce or association or confederation would need to set up a suitable organizational structure to handle this situation. A special division or department would *need to* be set up to deal with training or to handle an information service for clients.

In this transition stage the large public SMI development agencies, where they exist, would need to be slimmed down and up into more efficient decentralized local organizations or smaller institutions focused sectorally or specialized in the context of services offered, such as management, training, technology, marketing or some suitable combination. Close working arrangements between public specialized agencies and the developing private-sector bodies should help strengthen the latter in order to the enable them to overcome their administrative weakness.

One could envisage a fairly long, drawn-out period of collaboration between the private and public sector agencies on a local basis with some degree of overlap in fields such as training. Since both would probably use the same outside resource persons, to which there would be limited availability locally, one could reasonably expect that a co-operative relationship would of necessity develop. The public SMI development agencies should gradually be integrated with the local and regional government and would assume a more promotional role in providing information on facilities, incentives and special assistance in such matters as provision of factory accommodation, special credits, export promotion assistance and training grants where available. Gradually, the private-sector organization would become the major local provider of direct support services for SMI, as least in the field of training and extension services. Table 19.2 gives one possible model of how the breakdown could take place in the provision of services to SMEs between government and the private sector in the transitional phase.

In addition to the development of training programmes the private-sector organizations can slowly develop financial services for SME. A financial service unit could try to link members with commercial banks who are prepared to lend to small enterprises or who may be in a position to put credit lines at the disposal of the sector. The unit would in the course of time establish links with venture capital organizations and possibly develop a credit guarantee scheme although many believe – as indicated in the table – that the source of the guarantee fund would have to be mainly the government.

A consultancy unit would need to be developed slowly. Probably the best approach would be for the government, through the National Council, to make available small amounts of funding to private-sector organizations to start advisory and consultancy services using, wherever possible, outside resources rather than the in-house staff. In the course of time, after reviewing the ability of the organizations to respond to the needs of its SME members in their field, further development of these services could be considered to the point at which a large scale comprehensive type of advisory and consultancy service – based on referrals – could be offered in management, technology, marketing, export as well as in legal and tax matters.

As a final stage the organizations could start special projects in support of SME such as bulk purchasing, government procurement and export promotion, industrial estates or special development and research programmes. Each of these steps should be subject to careful study and implemented only after it is clear that they can be justified economically and that there is demand for the assistance offered.

A major question to be faced in the course of time would be whether services are to be made available only to members or to all SMEs in the district, sector or group covered. A possible way out might be to provide services to all clients, but giving members priority by providing them services at a discounted rate. If the services gradually are valued by the clientele, this can of course become a major attraction for new members.

Thus, during the transitional phase, support services will be offered to SME both by public agencies and private sector organizations. One could envisage a country-wide network of organizations on a local or sectoral basis which would all offer services. Each would offer different types of services. Some would be more involved in technology, others might more specifically be working on resolving marketing problems and yet others involved in providing management training. One would assume that during this phase government support would be available – through the National Council – to all organizations (both public and private sector) who request support and can show they are able to provide the services. Gradually the volume of support provided by the private-sector organizations would increase to a point – within five years or so – when the overwhelming majority of

Table 19.2 Roles of Service Providers to SMEs

	GOVERNMENT	*PRIVATE SECTOR*	*TAs, CHAMBER etc.*
FINANCE	Grants, soft loans Subsidies, tax relief Export insurance Credit guarantees Savings facilities	Export & other insurance Banking Hire purchase/leasing Factoring Credit rating Securities markets	Tailored insurance policies Credit unions Credit assessment Joint purchasing
ADVICE AND INFORMATION	Information on regulation Economics & statistics Management advice (basic) Referrals to appropriate body Contact services (specialized, e.g. export)	Legal & accounting Specific market data Consultancy (tailored) Personnel recruitment	Information on regulation, especially export documentation Market & export information Referrals to appropriate body Contact services in broadest service
TECHNOLOGY	Basic technology transfer Signposting (Referrals)	Licensing Contract R.&D.	Signposting (Referrals)
TRAINING	Basic commercial & management skills Owner training Basic technical skills, e.g. machine shop	Basic education Specific commercial & management skills, e.g. languages, secretarial, export management	All, including setting of qualifications and standards. Emphasis on trades
CHARACTERISTICS: Driven by:	Social needs	Market needs	Membership needs
Firm size:	Micro-small	Small-medium	All

Acknowledgement: Prepared in collaboration with Graham Bannock, Graham Bannock and Partners, London.

Note: The above is a proposal for breakdown of roles in provision of services to SME suitable for a middle-income developing country in a transitional phase of transferring more responsibilities of services to the private sector. It is based mainly on experiences in the UK and other European countries. Some of the roles assigned to the 'private sector' may suit the situation in more advanced developing countries. The 'Private Sector' in African countries would certainly be too weak to undertake most if not all these roles. However, it should be regarded as the desirable breakdown of roles (with minor variations) for which to aim.

services are offered by the non-governmental organization, such as Chambers of Commerce, associations or consulting organizations.

Policy framework and donor support

It is vital for governments to fully recognize the important role to be played in economic development by the private Small and medium-sized industrial SMI sector. This recognition must be manifested in a readiness to accept the representative bodies of the private and SMI as partners who have to be consulted in deciding on policies, measures and regulations which will directly affect the operations of these enterprises. One could summarize the preconditions on the part of a government that need to be satisfied before one could expect a private-sector representative organization to fulfil a major role in supplying support services for the SMI sector. They are:

(1) Not pursuing policies and enacting regulations that would create disincentives to SME growth and development.
(2) Recognition of the important role of the SMI private sector and a readiness to accept a partnership with the sector in formulating policies that affect the welfare of the SMI sector.
(3) Preparedness to consult with the sector through its representative bodies and the acceptance of the importance of fostering strong independent organizations to represent SMI.
(4) Recognition that public agencies are not always the most effective in delivering services and assistance to the private SMI sector and a readiness to help the private-sector organization to play a major role in implementing assistance programmes even when financed in whole or part by government.
(5) Making available within the resources at the disposal of the government, bearing in mind the many demands on it, finance to enable the private-sector organizations to implement effective programmes in support of the SMI sector, always accepting that the organizations must show evidence of being willing and able to match government funding with an equal amount of resources mobilized from other non-governmental sources through their own efforts.
(6) Co-operation in instituting a decentralized system for delivering support services to the SME sector, accepting an important role in this respect of local and regional authorities.
(7) Co-operating in allowing private-sector organizations to have access to a reasonable share of external donor funds for the implementation of support programmes for SME.

Only if all these preconditions are satisfied can one expect that private-sector representative 'self-help' organizations would have the resources and capacity to fulfil the role outlined for them in this paper. Needless to say the pre-conditions apply equally to the attitudes, behaviour and policies of state, provincial, regional and local government.

Donor support for private-sector organizations

In the past few years as part of the general move towards a greater recognition by all donor agencies of the role of the private sector in economic development, more aid has been directed by external donors in setting up and strengthening the representative bodies and 'self-help' organizations of the private sector. This is in keeping with a parallel trend of donors to channel more of its assistance through NGOs.

Most prominent in these efforts have been the German aid organizations. In 1985 the GTZ (German Technical Coporation) launched its partnership or 'twinning programmes' between the *Handwerkskammer* (Craft Chambers) of Germany and selected representative organizations in certain developing countries. One of the earlier examples of the 'twinning' was the project to strengthen the Chambers of Commerce and Industry in Cebu and Cagayan de Oro in the Philippines to enable them to deliver improved services to member firms. This project, which started in 1986, is scheduled to continue through 1992. At the start the GTZ grant covered more than 50 per cent of the operating budget but by 1990 it had fallen to 30 per cent. It is anticipated that after 1992 the Chamber will finance itself without donor assistance (GTZ, 1989)

The German foundations have been most active in supporting SME associations in Africa. The Konrad Adenauer Foundation has assisted the ASSI (Association of Small Scale Industries of Ghana). Another German aid foundation has provided an adviser and equipment for the Ugandan Small Scale Industries Association (USSIA) while the Friedrich Naumann Foundation has for the past four years been engaged in helping private-sector organizations in Kenya and Nigeria. In Kenya the Friedrich Naumann Foundation has financed five local Kenyan professional workers for the Small Scale Traders and Entrepreneurs Society which claims it has over 5000 members. This society has, with this German help, developed a training programme for its members. The Friedrich Naumann Foundation enters into long-term agreements with the private-sector organization it assists, offering to cover a considerable part of the operating budget for a period if the recipient organization works towards building up its income from other sources over a number of years.

The case of the Nigerian Association of Small Scale Industrialists is indicative of the type of aid that can be given to these African self-help associations. This Association now has a staff of six persons, including three professionals, in its head office in Lagos and 40 persons throughout its branches in 21 states and in the federal capital Abuja. It claims that 40 per cent of its budget is covered by government support via indirect funds from external donors, mainly the German Friedrich Naumann Foundation. The Nigerian Association, while still restricted in its activities because of limited resources, runs an active programme of short courses and claims to offer an advisory service on financial management, legal matters and exporting. Membership fees cover only 25 per cent of its budget.

A different picture is given by the Zambian Association of Small Scale Enterprises. Although officially established in 1982, it has failed to obtain any support from either the government or external donors. Its membership has dropped from

300 to around 100 in 1991. Only recently has it managed to open a small part-time office.

The Ghanian ASSI, assisted by the Konrad Adenauer Foundation, received 40 per cent of its budget in 1990 from the Foundation. It has a staff of five professionals and claims 2100 members.

Donor aid should be tailored to the needs and capacity of the recipient institutions. Some equipment can be useful and help raise efficiency but excessive help in such items as vehicles, computers or costly office furnishings could be counterproductive as could an overall grant to cover operating expenses. Subsidies may be appropriate as long as matched by the organization's own efforts to raise revenue and based on a programme to eliminate the subsidies over a number of years and to make the organization self-financing from domestic sources, mainly from income earned directly by the organization.

In some cases, such as in the Philippines and some other South-East Asian countries, donors (in this case mainly the GTZ) have contributed funding as well as specialized consultants to help local sectoral associations develop special common service facilities for members, e.g. an improved kiln for potters, a timber-seasoning plant for woodworking and a modern toolmaking facility for engineering workshops. Donors could also help set up an export-marketing service to provide up-to-date information on overseas marketing outlets and opportunities. Due to severe shortages of operating funds, donors will have to be prepared to supplement local operating budgets. However, this should always be given in a transparent fashion, clearly identifying the purpose of the funding given and insisting continuously on matching funds, however modest, from local sources.

The most important help that donors can give is to improve administration and management and help in initiating, if even on a limited scale, the delivery of high-quality services to members. During the transition phase of transferring the provision of support services for SMI to private-sector organisations, help from donor agencies could play an important role. The assistance could best be given by NGOs, particularly by persons with experience in chambers and associations and in operating support programmes for SMI. In most cases, building up local 'self-help' organizations will be a slow process and projects may have to go on for five to ten years but it would be better to maintain foreign inputs at minimal levels and to build up local competence gradually.

Notes on Contributors

Aredo, Dejene, Lecturer, Department of Economics, Addis Ababa University, Ethiopia

Aryeetey, Ernest, Researcher, Institute of Social Statistics & Economic Research, University of Ghana, Ghana

Baah-Nuakoh, Amoah, Researcher, Department of Economics, University of Ghana, Ghana

Bagachwa, Mboya S.D., Senior Research Fellow, Economic Research Bureau, University of Dar es Salaam, Tanzania

Buvinic, Mayra, Deputy Director of the International Center for Research on Woman, Washington, USA

Dawson, Jonathan, Consultant, Development Initiatives, Planning and Management (DPIM), Ardington, UK

Gaidzanwa, Rudo Barbra, Senior Lecturer, Department of Sociology, University of Zimbabwe, Zimbabwe

Helmsing, A.H.J. (Bert), Senior Lecturer, Institute of Social Studies, The Netherlands

Kessous, Jean-Claude, Consultant, Etude Economique Conseil Canada Inc., Canada

Kolstee, Theo, Head of the Special Programme on Urban Poverty, Directorate General of International Cooperation, Ministry of Foreign Affairs, The Netherlands

Lessard, Giles, Head Enterprise Sector, Canadian International Development Agency, Canada

Levitsky, Jake, Consultant, formerly at the World Bank, London, UK

Liedholm, Carl, Professor, Department of Economics, Michigan State University, USA

Mumbengegwi, Clever, Senior Lecturer and Chairman, Department of Economics, University of Zimbabwe, Zimbabwe

Mwarania, Kirimi, Lecturer, Department of Accounting, University of Nairobi, Kenya

Oyejide, Ademola, Professor, Department of Economics, University of Ibadan, Nigeria

Osei, Barfour, Researcher, Department of Economics, University of Ghana, Ghana

Sowa, Nii Kwaku, Head, Department of Economics, University of Ghana, Ghana

Steel, William, Senior Economist, the World Bank, Washington, USA

Teszler, Roger, Lecturer, Department of Agricultural and Development Economics, University of Amsterdam, The Netherlands

Tutu, Kwadwo, Researcher, Department of Economics, University of Ghana, Ghana

Uribe-Echevarría, Francisco, Senior Lecturer, Institute of Social Studies, The Netherlands

Wangwe, Samuel, Researcher Fellow, United Nations University, Institute of New Technologies (INTECH), The Netherlands

Endnotes

Steel

1. The views expressed in this article are those of the author and should not be attributed to the World Bank. The author has benefited greatly from discussions with and papers by Paul Ballard, Jake Levitsky, Carl Liedholm, Don Mead and Leila Webster, among others, and from comments by Lynn Bennet, Hans-Peter Brunner, Malcolm Harper and Carl Jayarajah.
2. This chapter deals only with those facilitating institutions that channel resources and that are directly affected by government policies. Complete analysis of the context for small enterprise development would include an appraisal of institutions that provide direct support, which include information systems, technology institutions, marketing agencies, chambers of commerce and industry, business associations, training programmes, community development and welfare agencies, and non-governmental organizations (NGOs). Such institutions can fill gaps, help firms cope with policy changes in transitional periods, provide services that are costly for individual firms, and build capabilities for sustained development. But they can also waste resources, especially if they are driven by outsiders' perceptions of what is needed rather than by effective demand from the entrepreneurs themselves. An appropriate additional analytical question to ask is: how effectively do supporting institutions meet the needs of small enterprises?

Osei, Baah-Nuakoh, Tutu and Sowa

1. This paper has been written out of a project financed by the British Overseas Development Administration (ODA).
2. The only difference between our definition and that of Steel and Webster is the exclusion of 'micro' enterprises in their definiton of SSEs.
3. *Kenkey* is a popular local staple food made from maize.
4. In 1988 the average compensation received by a redeployed person was about ¢178,000, which included severance pay and end-of-service award. See ILO/JASPA (1989, pp.36).
5. On 1 January 1991, the GEDC was absorbed by the NBSSI.
6. It is possible that some enterprises established in periods earlier than the ERP might have collapsed during the ERP era. Thus, a more comprehensive assess-

ment would require looking also at mortality rates of enterprises. However, such an assessment is not possible due to lack of available data on mortality rates.

7. *Oburoni Wawu* is a local expression for imported second-hand clothing.
8. The survey was conducted before the two agencies were merged on January 1991.
9. Recent pronouncements of the National Investment Centre suggest that this idea is being planned for large-scale industries. It is hoped it will be implemented also for SSEs.

Bagachwa

1. The World Bank (1987b) estimates that average levels of effective protection for Tanzanian industry declined from about 500 per cent in early 1984 to about 50 per cent in 1985 and that some firms became effectively disprotected.
2. Maliyamkono and Bagachwa (1990) estimated that parallel market (second economy) sales for maize and paddy accounted for an average of 67 per cent and 78 per cent of total marketed surplus respectively in 1986.
3. With the exception of six traditional export crops (i.e. coffee, cotton, cashew nuts, tea, tobacco and pyrethrum).
4. There is no common definition of a small-scale enterprise in Tanzania. In this chapter, the term is used to cover all establishments employing up to 50 persons. The terms microenterprise and informal-sector enterprises are used interchangeably to refer to the Small Industries Development Organization (SIDO) non-factory units employing up to 10 persons.

Kessous and Lessard

1. The authors thank Diane Marleau and Caroline Cambourieu from the Etude Economique Conseil Canada Inc. for the computer and statistical processing of the survey data. The ideas given in this article are those of the authors and cannot be attributed to the Canadian International Development Agency (CIDA) which financed this study.
2. Certain measures were taken before that year. In particular, this is the case with respect to the abolishment of export monopolies.
3. Project for the support of the creation of companies and the insertion of young graduates.
4. The financial needs of the nuclear and extended family make it difficult for many enterprises to adequately manage their working capital. In general, except for rare exceptions, no distinction is made between family needs and business funds, which leads to a chronic shortage of working capital and an incapacity to procure raw materials or other consumables on a regular basis.

Mumbengegwi

1. Peter Kunjeku, Executive Officer (Projects) CZI, personal communication.
2. See Dr Kombo Moyana, Governor of the Reserve Bank's statement whose full text is published in the *Financial Gazette*, 12 September 1991.

3. See the proceedings of the Workshop on Small Scale Enterprises held at Brondesbury Park Motel, Nyanga. July 10-12 1991.

Uribe-Echevarría

1. 'Easy import substitution' industries received protection since the 1897 tariff law and most of the substitution was already completed before the Second World War, (Behrman 1976).
2. For example, CORFO performs a number of important functions for both LSI and SSMIs: (i) research and development through the Fondo de Desarrollo Productivo, Comisión de Bienes de Capital and INTEC (Instituto de Investigación Tecnológica); (ii) training through INACAP (Instituto Nacional de Capacitación; and (iii) control through INN (Instituto Nacional de Normas), (Cárcamo 1989).
3. This law, approved in December 1989, is particularly resented by small entrepreneurs because it cancelled the significant tax benefits they had obtained for specific industries in each region in May 1989.
4. The effect of comparative advantage, internal effective protection and effective subsidy to export was estimated in a regression equation of the form IA(i) =f(IVC)(i), SEFEX(i), PIN(i) where: IA(i)= Index of external openness; IVC(i) Index of comparative advantage: SEFEX(i)= Effective subsidies to exports; PIN(i)= Effective protection to internal sales.
5. In Chile, the 10–49 worker stratum occupied 29.2 per cent of the industrial workers in 1979 and 29.7 per cent in 1984. This compares with about 20 per cent in Colombia and Ecuador. However, it appears that the overall protectionist environment may have been the driving force since the industrial sector in general was favoured over other sectors. In fact, the large-scale sector was initially the hardest hit and recuperated only after restructuring was well advanced.
6. The enhanced capacity, due to new information technology, to manage effectively and co-ordinate large groups of specialized small producers is one important element. Others are the new 'time saving' production philosophy, the re-evaluation of flexibility etc.
7. The OTIR are formed through the association of enterprises to administer their common training needs.

Oyejide

1. Revised version of paper prepared for conference on 'Small and Micro Enterprise Promotion in a Changing Policy Environment: A Focus on Africa' held at the Institute of Social Studies, The Hague, 30 Sept.-2 Oct. 1991. The revision has benefited from helpful comments of participants in general and those of Bert Helmsing in particular.

Teszler

1. Major efforts in this field as far as sub-Saharan Africa is concerned include

SIDO in Tanzania, which received more than US$10 million between 1974 and 1989 from a variety of official Dutch programmes and a large number of individual small amounts of direct assistance via Small Project Funds of the local Netherlands Embassy.

2. FMO Annual Report, 1990, p.22. In 1991 further agreements were signed with the Banco del Desarrollo in Chile and with the Caisse Commune d'Epargne et d'Investissement in Cameroon. The two discontinued agreements referred to in the text allude to SSE financing in Liberia and Peru.
3. Jacob Levitsky (1988) mentions a number of cases in The Netherlands, Colombia, Korea, Turkey and Pakistan (but not one in Africa). These banks have, however, either been the victim of strict government regulations such as artificially low interest rates, or have prospered by taking on other activities. Thus, the NMB (Nederlandse Middenstands Bank) in The Netherlands developed into a general bank, and CFP (Corporación Financiera Popular) in Colombia became involved in the provision of export credit, for which it receives a fixed management fee from the government.
4. Hernando de Soto overemphasizes the inefficiencies of the formal system and neglects other more profound gaps in (Peruvian) economy and society. For a more balanced view see Germidis *et al.*, 1991. This latter study proposes to tackle financial dualism by transforming the formal sector and substituting it for the informal sector *(integration)* and at the same time by organizing closer links between a more systemized informal sector and the renewed formal sector *(interlinkage)*.
5. J. Keddie, S. Nanjundan and R. Teszler (1988) p.52. Although it would appear that microenterprise is best served by demand-side policies, if only because institutional outreach in this case is both costly and time-consuming, this is not an argument for concentrating on supply-side activities for the larger and more modern small businesses.
6. World Bank (1991) World Development Report, makes a case for government and market working in harmony rather than as alternatives; in other words, government should only step in when the market fails to address important issues, such as basic education, extreme poverty and the environment. The World Bank maintains the view (pp.70–87) that private enterprise develops best under competitive conditions. All SSEs are private-sector operations.
7. When the Netherlands discontinued its funding of SIDO Tanzania (December 1989), this was taken over by the other major donor, Sweden, without any apparent policy change to make SIDO economically viable.
8. Groups of microentrepreneurs working together in ROSCAs-type associations can also be considered in a similar approach.

Aredo

1. The reduction of the waiting time is significant. If the amount of the kitty is equal to the sum needed for the planned expenditure, the average waiting time

'W' can be expressed as a fraction of the duration of the entire cycle of the *tontine* required from each of the 'n' members of the *tontine*:

$$W = \frac{n + 1}{2n}$$

According to this formula it is possible to reduce the average waiting time by close to 50 per cent of the time which would be needed if all savers had to save in isolation.

2. Some scholars argue that the *iqqub* was first practised by the Gurage people of Ethiopia (Levine, 1972; Pankhurst and Eshete 1958, Mamo 1983).
3. The Bank of Abyssinia issued the first bank notes in 1914 (Belay 1987).

Liedholm

1. This chapter reports on work supported by the GEMINI project of the US Agency for International Development, Office of Small, Micro, and Informal Enterprise Development. An earlier version of this chapter will appear in *Informal Finance in Low Income Countries*, Dale Adams and Del Fitchett (eds), 1992.
2. Small scale is defined in this paper in terms of employment and generally refers to those firms with up to 50 workers. The term 'microenterprise', which is defined in this paper as a firm with 10 or fewer workers, is used to depict the lower end of the spectrum. 'Modern' small firms are defined as having more than 10 employees. The establishments examined in this study include those specifically engaged in the production and repair of manufactured goods (ISIC codes 31–39 and 95). Excluded are establishments engaged in mining, construction, trading, transport, financial, social and personal services.
3. See, for example, Chuta (1989) for Nigeria; Steel and Webster (1990) for Ghana; Parker and Aleke Dondo (1991) for Kenya; Liedholm and McPherson (1991) for South Africa; Fisseha and McPherson (1991) for Swaziland. A general overview of the empirical evidence on enterprise dynamics is found in Liedholm and Mead (1991).
4. See Pan-Thuy *et al.* (1981) for a discussion of the various studies as well as a treatment of the distinction between excess capacity (i.e. how close to its desired, efficient level of output a firm is operating) and 'capital utilization' (i.e. the proportion of the total time a productive capital stock is operated).
5. The true need for finance, particularly working capital, however, is lower than the proprietor's perceived demand for it. This is because working capital shortages are often the symptom of some other problem. For instance, a raw-material delivery bottleneck may force proprietors to keep their raw material inventories at unduly high levels. Similarly, managerial inefficiencies, such as those that slow throughput, waste material, or siphon off funds to non-business activities, can appear as a working capital shortage. Consequently, one must distinguish valid needs for working capital from the specious demands that only serve to

sustain temporarily a fatally-ill enterprise or reflect some other underlying problem (Kilby *et al.*, 1984).

6. In answering this question, the enterprises were asked to describe the three most serious obstacles they would face when expanding, *under the assumption that they could sell all they produce*; thus demand constraints were not examined in this question. It should also be noted that for the firms with up to three workers, lack of credit for raw materials was also the most frequently cited constraint to expansion, but the percentage listing it was only 52 per cent.
7. The constancy of the inventory-sales ratio for bread is, no doubt, strongly related to the perishability of the commodity.
8. Indirect evidence from lenders on the relative importance of fixed capital at this stage can be derived from the recent review of microenterprise support programmes by USAID. In this review of 32 AID projects, the fixed capital component of loans comprised only 20 per cent in microenterprise expansion schemes, but 45 per cent in enterprise 'transformation' schemes. (Boomgard, 1989). Yet, small firms often attempt to minimize their demand for fixed capital by renting (leasing) or by buying used equipment. (Chuta and Liedholm, 1985; and Cortes *et al.*, 1987).
9. The credit extended to other customers on delivery must be subtracted from this figure to arrive at the net supply of working capital by customers. In Jamaica 34 per cent of the sample entrepreneurs reported granting loans on sales, while in Haiti, the comparable figure was 71 per cent. In Egypt less than 10 per cent of the sales were on credit.

Levitsky

1. This presentation is based on a more comprehensive paper prepared on the subject for the BMZ (Ministry of Economic Cooperation) and GTZ (German Technical Cooperation) of Germany. The author gratefully acknowledges the assistance of these organizations.
2. In Zimbabwe recently (1991) the Indigenous Business Development Centre was formed as a voluntary membership organization to represent several Zimbabwe businesses. It claims a membership of 4000 mainly small trading services and manufacturing businesses. The new Centre works alongside the Confederation of Zimbabwe Industries (CZI) and the Zimbabwe National Chamber of Commerce (ZNCC).

Bibliography

Acevedo, A., Quirós, G. and Restrepo, R., (1985) 'Una aproximación sobre el desarrollo industrial colombiano. 1958–1980' in J.A. Bejarano (ed.), *Lecturas sobre Economía Colombiana'*, Procultura, Bogotá, D.E.

Adams, D. and Fitchett, D. (1991) *Informal Finance in Low Income Countries*, Westview Press, Boulder, Colorado.

Adubifa, A. (1990) *Technology Policy in Nigeria*. NISER, Ibadan.

Alcorta, L. (1992) 'The Impact of New Technologies on Scale in Manufacturing Industry: Issues and Evidence', INTECH Paper, Maastricht, May 1992.

Alemayehu, S. (1969) 'Eder in Addis Ababa: A Sociological Study' *Ethiopian Observer*, Vol.12, No.1.

Altaye A. (1991) 'Mutual Assistance Network: The Case of Wolaita'. Paper prepared for the XIth International Confernce of Ethiopian Studies, Addis Ababa, April 1-6.

Aluko, S.A., Oguntoye, O.A. and Afonja, Y.A.O. (1972) 'Small Scale Industries: Western State of Nigeria', Industrial Research Unit, University of Ife.

Anderson, D. (1982a), 'Small Industry in Developing Countries: A Discussion of the Issues,' *World Development*, Vol.10, No.11, pp.913–48.

Anderson, D. and Khambata, F. (1981) 'Small Enterprises and Development Policy in the Philippines: A Case Study'. World Bank Working Paper No.468, July, Washington.

Anderson, D. and Leiserson, M.W. (1980) 'Rural non-farm employment in developing countries', *Economic Development and Cultural Change*, No.28, p.2.

Anderson, D. and Khambata, F. (1985) 'Financing Small-Scale Industry and Agriculture in Developed Countries: The Merits and Limitations of Commercial Policies', *Economic Development and Cultural Change*, Vol.32.

Anheier, H. K. and Seibel, H.D. (1987) *Small-Scale Industries and Economic Development in Ghana: Business Behaviour and Strategies in Informal Sector Economics*. Cologne Development Studies No.3. Breitenbach Publishers, Saarbrucken, Germany.

Arrighy, G. (1970) 'Labour supplies in historical perspective: a study of the proletarianization of the African peasantry in Rhodesia', *Journal of Development Studies*, No.6 and 3, pp.197–234.

Aryee, G. (1976) 'Effects of Formal Education and Training on the Intensity of Employment in the Informal Sector: A Case Study of Kumasi, Ghana'. ILO, WEP 2-18/WP 14, Geneva.

Aryee, G. (1977) 'Small-Scale Manufacturing Activities: A Study of the Interrelationships between the Formal and Informal Sectors in Kumasi, Ghana'. ILO, WEP 2–19/WEP 23, Geneva.

Aryee, G. (1981) 'The Informal Manufacturing Sector in Kumasi' in S.V. Sethuraman, (ed.) *The Urban Informal Sector in Developing Countries: Employment, Poverty and Environment*, ILO, WEP Study, Geneva.

Aryeetey, E. (1991) 'The Relationship Between Formal and Informal Segments of the Financial Sector in Ghana'. Paper presented at the AERC Research Workshop, Nairobi, May.

Aryeetey, E., Asante, Y., Gockel, F. and Kyei, A.Y. (1990) 'Mobilizing Domestic Savings for African Development and Diversification: A Ghanaian Case Study'. Research report presented at a workshop of the International Development Centre, Queen Elizabeth House, Oxford University, July.

Asfaw D. (1958) 'Ekub', Ethnological society, University College of Addis Ababa, Quarterly Bulletin No.8, July, pp.63-76.

Aspen, H. (1989) 'Present Forms of Traditional Associations and Institutions in Mafud', Northern Shoa. (mimeo)

Assefa A. (1987) 'Some Factors Influencing Agricultural Credit Use Among Peasant Farmers in Ethiopia', M.Sc. Thesis, Addis Ababa University.

Bagachwa M.S.D. and Stewart, F. (1990) 'Rural Industries and Rural Linkages in Sub-Saharan Africa: A Survey', International Development Centre, Oxford University.

Bagachwa, M.S.D. (1981) 'The urban informal enterprise sector in Tanzania — a case study of Arusha region', ERB paper No. 81, Dar es Salaam.

Bagachwa, M.S.D. (1990a) 'Small Enterprise Development in Tanzania'. Report to ILO/JASPA, Dar-es-Salaam.

Bagachwa, M.S.D. (1990b) 'The Nature and Magnitude of the Informal Sector in Tanzania', University of Dar es Salaam.

Bagachwa, M.S.D. (1991a) *Choice of Technology in Industry: The Economics of Grain-milling in Tanzania*, International Development Research Center, Ottawa.

Bagachwa, M.S.D. (1991b) 'Zanzibar: the Informal Sector Survey'. A report to UNDP/ILO/Zanzibar Government.

Bagachwa, M.S.D. and Ndanshau, M.O. (1988) 'Rural Informal Mutual Credit in Tanzania', University of Dar es Salaam.

Bagachwa, M.S.D. and Ndulu, B.J. (1988) 'The Urban Informal Sector in Tanzania', Dar es Salaam (mimeo).

Baker, (1986) *The Rural-Urban Dichotomy in the Developing World: A case study from Northern Ethiopia*, Norwegian University Press.

Bakarra, B. *et al.* (1982) *Development Strategies in Semi-industrialized Economies*, Baltimore MD, Johns Hopkins University Press.

Bank of Ghana (1980) *Annual Report*, Accra.

Bank of Ghana (1982) *Annual Report*, Accra.

Behrman, J.R. (1976) '*Foreign Trade Regimes and Economic Development: Chile*', National Bureau of Economic Research, New York.

Belay G. (1987) *Currency and Banking in Ethiopia*, A.A. Commercial Press, Addis Ababa.

Berry, A. and Pinell-Siles, A. (1979) 'Small-Scale Enterprises in Colombia: A Case Study'. World Bank Studies on Employment and Rural Development No.56, Washington DC.

Berry, S. (1977) 'Custom, class and the informal sector; or why marginality is not likely to pay', Working Paper No.1, African Studies Center, Boston University.

Berry, S. (1984) 'From peasant to artisan: motor mechanics in a Nigerian town'. Working Paper No.76, African Studies Center, Boston University.

Bevan D., Collier, P., Gunning, J. and Karlstrom, B. (1988) 'Kenya Macroeconomic Events', April.

Bhalla, A.S. (ed.) (1991) *Small and Medium Size Enterprises: Technology Policies and Options*, Greenwood Press, Westport.

Bhalla, A.S. *et al.* (eds) (1984) *Blending of New and Traditional Technologies*. Tycooly International Publishing Ltd., ILO, Dublin.

Bhalla, A.S. and James, D. (eds) (1988) *New Technologies and Development: Experiences in Technology Blending*, Lynne Rienner Publishers, Boulder/London.

Biggs, T., Snodgrass D., and Srivastava, P., (1990) 'On Minimalist Credit Programs', Harvard Institute for International Development Discussion Paper No.331. Cambridge, Massachusetts.

Boomgard, J. (1989) 'A.I.D. Microenterprise Stock-taking: Synthesis Report', USAID, Washington.

Boomgard, J.J. (1989) 'AID Microenterprise Stock-taking: Synthesis Report', AID Evaluation Special Study No.65, USAID, Washington DC.

Boon, E.K. (1989) 'Women in SMEs: An African Example', *The Courier*, 155 (May-June) pp.74–6.

Bozeman, T. and Link, A.N. (1983) *Investments in Technology: Corporate Strategies and Public Policy Alternatives*, Praeger, New York.

Bruce, J. and Dwyer, D. (eds) (1988) *A Home Divided: Women and Income in the Third World*, Stanford University Press, California.

Brusco, S. (1989) 'A policy for industrial districts', in Goodman & Banford (eds) *Small Farms and Industrial Districts in Italy*, Routledge, London, pp.259-69.

Buvinic, M. (1986) 'Projects for women in the Third World: Explaining their misbehavior', *World Development*, Vol.24, No.5.

Buvinic, M. (1990) *Women and Poverty in Latin America and the Caribbean: A Primer for Policy Makers*, International Center for Research on Women, Washington DC.

Buvinic, M. and Berger, M. (1990) 'Sex Differences in Access to a Small Enterprise Development Fund in Peru', *World Development*, Vol.18, No.5.

Buvinic, M., Berger, M. and Jaramillo, C. (1989) 'Impact of a Credit Project for

Women and Men Microentrepreneurs in Quito, Ecuador', in M. Berger and M. Buvinic (eds) *Women's Ventures: Assistance to the Informal Sector in Latin America*, Kumarian Press, West Hartford, Connecticut.

Callier, P. (1990) 'Informal Finance: The Rotating Saving and Credit Association: An Interpretation'. KYKLOS, Vol.43, Fasc.2, 273-76.

Callier, P. (ed.) (1991) 'Financial Systems and Development in Africa', EDI Seminar Series, World Bank.

Cárcamo, R. (1989) '*Las principales instituciones y programas de fomento productivo nacional*, Documento de Trabajo No. 15, SERCAL, Santiago.

Carr, M. (1989) 'Creative Donor Interventions', in A. Gosses, K. Molenaar and R. Teszler (eds) *Small scale enterprise development. In search of new Dutch approaches*. Proceedings of a workshop, 6–7 March, 1989. DGIS, Ministry of Foreign Affairs, The Hague.

Castillo, M., and Cortellese, C. (1989) 'La pequeña y mediana industria en el desarrollo de América Latina' in *Revista de la CEPAL*, No. 34, Santiago.

Cazar, S. (1989) 'Políticas para el fomento de pequeña y mediana industria en el Ecuador' in Fopial (ed.) *Industrialización en América Latina y el rol de la PYMI*, Instituto de Investigaciones Socio-económicas y Tecnológicas (INSOTEC).

Central Bank of Nigeria, *Annual Report, 1980-90*, Lagos.

Centre d'Etude et de Promotion Industrielle (1991) 'La situation de l'artisanat et de la petite industrie au Mali: Problèmes et Perspectives', Février.

Checchi, *et al.* (1976) 'Small-Scale Industry Development in Ghana'. Report prepared for the Government of Ghana, Checchi and Company, Washington DC.

Chica, R. (1990) 'El estancamiento de la industria colombiana' in *Coyuntura Económica*, Vol. XX, No. 2, Fedesarrollo y FES, Bogotá, June.

Child, F.C. (1977) 'Small-scale rural industry in Kenya', Occasional Paper, No.17, African Studies Center, UCLA, Los Angeles.

Child, J., Ganter, H.D. and Kieser, A. (1987) 'Technological innovation and organizational conservatism' in J.M Pennings and A. Buitendam (eds) (1987) *New Technology as Organizational Innovation*, Ballinger, Cambridge, Mass.

Chuta, E. (1989) 'A Nigerian Study of Firm Dynamics,' Draft Paper, Michigan State University, East Lansing.

Chuta, E. and Liedholm, C., (1979) *Rural non-farm employment. A review of the state of the art*, Michigan State University, East Lansing.

Chuta, E. and Liedholm, C. (1982) 'Employment Growth and Change in Sierra Leone Small Scale Industry: 1974–1980', *International Labour Review*, Vol.121, No.1, Jan.-Feb., pp.101–12.

Chuta, E. and Liedholm, C. (1985) *Employment and Growth in Small-Scale Industry: Empirical Evidence and Policy Assessment from Sierra Leone*, St. Martin's Press, New York.

CINSET (1990) 'Condiciones de Entorno al Desarrollo de la Pequena Empresa en Colombia', mimeo, Bogotá.

Clark, D.G. (1980) *Foreign companies and international investment in Zimbabwe*. CIIR/Mambo press, London/Gwelo.

Collier P., Radwan, S. and Wangwe, S. (1986) *Labour and poverty in rural Tanzania. Ujamaa and rural developemnt in the United Republic of Tanzania*. Clarendon Press, Oxford.

Comité Interministerial de Desarrollo Productivo (1991) '*Pequeña y mediana empresa: Políticas de fomento y modernización productiva*'. Documento para discusión, mimeo, unpublished, Santiago, May.

Comhaire, (1966) 'Wage pool as a form of Voluntary Association in Ethiopia and other African Towns' in Proceedings of the Third International Conference of Ethiopian Studies, Institute of Ethiopian Studies, Haile Selassie I University, pp.44–8.

Commission of European Communities (1988) 'Partnership Between Small and Large Firms'. Proceedings of a Conference in Brussels, Brussels.

Cornea, G.A. (1991) 'Is adjustment conducive to long term development? The case of Africa in the 1980s', Centre Studi d'Agliano, Queen Elizabeth House Development Studies working papers, No.42, November.

Cortes, M., Berry, A. and Ishaq, A. (1987) *Success in Small and Medium-Scale Enterprises: The Evidence from Colombia*, Oxford University Press, New York.

Coughlin, P. (1988) 'Development policy and inappropriate product technology: the case of Kenya' in P. Coughlin and G. Ikiara (eds) *Industrialization in Kenya. In search of a strategy*, Heinemann, Nairobi.

Coulson, A. (1974) 'The Automated Bread Factory' in A.Coulson (ed.) *African Socialism in Practice: The Case of Tanzanian Experience*, Spokesman Books, Nottingham.

Courcelles, M. and Lattre, A. de (1989) 'Le secteur privé au Mali', OCDE[5C]Club du Sahel, Sahel D(89) 334, Septembre.

CSO (1982) Statistical Abstract, Addis Ababa.

CSO (1985) *Results of the Survey of Manufacturing Industries 1974 E.C.*, CSO, Statistical Bulletin No.48.

CSO (1988) National Rural Household Survey, Addis Ababa.

DANE, (1985) '*Plan Nacional de La Micro-empresa*', Bogotá.

Davies, R. 'Trade, Trade Management and Development in Zimbabwe', University of Zimbabwe, Department of Economics, Working Paper No.3 1988.

Davies, S. *et.al.* (1984) 'Small Enterprises in Egypt: A Study of Two Governorates', MSU International Development Working Paper No.16, Michigan State University, East Lansing.

Dawson, J. (1965) 'Area Sample Survey of Small Manufacturing Establishments — 1963', Central Bureau of Statistics, Accra.

Dawson, J. (1988) 'Small-Scale Industry Development in Ghana: A Case Study of Kumasi', Overseas Development Administration, ESCOR, Processed, London.

Dawson, J. (1990) 'The Wider Context: The Importance of the Macroenvironment for Small Enterprise Development,' *Small Enterprise Development*, Vol.1, No.3.

Dawson, J. (1991a) 'The Development of Small-Scale Industry in Ghana: A Case Study of Kumasi', in *Small-Scale Strategies For Industrial Restructuring*, H. Thomas *et al.* (eds), IT Publications, London.

Dawson, J. *et al.* (1991b) 'Small Enterprise Development in Tanzania', Consultancy Report to the Overseas Development Administration, London.

Dawson, J. (1991c) 'Rural Travel and Transport in Morogoro Region, Tanzania', I.T. Transport, Oxford.

de Groot, H., van Kooten, C., Wills, F. and Chávez, E. (1989) '*Las ONG y el sector productivo en el Perú y Chile. El rol de la generación de ingreso y empleo en las estrategias de las ONG*', Gobierno de Holanda y NOVIB, La Haya.

Dessalegn, R. (1989) 'Rural Women in Ethiopia: Problems and Prospects' (mimeo) Directorate General for International Cooperation (1992) Nota Kleinbedrijf. DGIS, The Hague.

Doran, A. (1984) 'Craft Enterprises in Britain and Germany – a Sectoral Study', Economics Advisory Group, Anglo-German Foundation, London.

Downing, J. (1990) 'Gender and the growth and dynamics of microenterprise', GEMINI Project, MSU, East Lansing.

Duggleby, T. (1991) 'Recommendations for Improving Performance of Lenders and Borrowers Under SME Credit for Ghana', Consultancy Report submitted to the World Bank.

Echavarría, J.J. (1990) 'Cambio técnico, inversión y reestructuración industrial en Colombia' in *Coyuntura Ecónomica*, Vol.XX, No.2, Fedesarrollo y FES, Bogotá, June.

Echavarría, J.L. and Perry, G. (1990) 'Aranceles y subsidios a las exportaciones. Análisis de su estructura sectorial y de su efecto en la apertura de la industria colombiana' in *El Trimestre Económico*, Vol.1, No.197, Jan.-Mar.

ECLAC (Economic Commission for Latin America and the Caribbean) División de Desarrollo Social (1989) *Proyectos Productivos de Mujeres en América Latina:Una Compilación*, ECLAC, Santiago.

ECLAC (1990a) *La Transformación Productiva con Equidad*, ECLAC, Santiago.

ECLAC (1990b) *Transformación Productiva con Equidad: La tarea prioritaria del desarrollo de América Latina y el Caribe en los años noventa*, ECLAC, Santiago.

ECLAC (1991a) 'Balance Preliminar de la Economía de América Latina y el Caribe', *Notas sobre la Economía y el Desarrollo* No.519/520, ECLAC, Santiago, Diciembre.

ECLAC (1991b) 'Panorama Social de America Latina, Edicion 1991' en *Notas sobre la Economia y el Desarrollo*, No.517/518, ECLAC, Santiago.

Economist Intelligence Unit (1987) *Country Profile: Ghana*, London.

Elkan, W. (1988) 'Entrepreneurs and Entrepreneurship in Africa', *World Bank Research Observer*, Vol.3, No.2.

ENDA (1990) *The informal sector in Zimbabwe: The role of women,* Harare.

Ettema, W. (1984) 'Small scale industry in Malawi', *JMAS*, Nos 22 and 23, pp.487-510.

Ettema, W. (1987) 'De informele sector in Malawi: dynamische ondernemers of scharrelaars', *Internationale Spectator*, Nos 51 and 3, pp. 125–31.

Farbman, M. and Lessik, A. (1989) 'The Impact of Classification on Policy', in A.H. Gosses *et al.* (eds) *Small Enterprises New Approaches*, DGIS, The Hague.

Fernández, F. (1990) '*Condiciones de entorno de las pequeñas empresas en el Ecuado*r', INSOTEC, Quito.

Fisseha, Y. (1991) 'Small Scale Enterprises in Lesotho: Summary of a Country-Wide Survey'. GEMINI Technical Report No.14. DAI, Washington DC.

Fisseha, Y. and Davies, O. (1981) 'The Small-Scale Manufacturing

Enterprises in Jamaica: Socioeconomic Characteristics and Constraints', MSU Rural Development Series Working paper No.16, Michigan State University, East Lansing.

Fisseha, Y. and McPherson, M. (1991) 'A Country-Wide Study of Small Scale Enterprises in Swaziland', Gemini Working Paper (forthcoming), DAI, Washington DC.

Forster, N. (1983) 'Chamber of Commerce — A Comparative Study of their Role in the UK and in other EEC Countries', Industrial Aids Ltd., London.

Fransman, M. (ed) (1982) *Industry and Accumulation in Africa*, Heinemann, London

Freeman, D.B. and Norcliffe, G.B. (1985) 'Rural enterprise in Kenya', Research Paper No.214, University of Chicago.

Freeman D.B. and Norcliffe G.B. (1985b) 'Relations between the rural non-farm and small farm sector in Central Povince, Kenya', TESG, Nos 75 and 1, pp.61–75.

Frischman, A. (1988) 'The Survival and Disappearance of Small Scale Enterprises in Urban Kano, 1973–1980'. Draft paper.

Frischtak, C. (1990) 'Adjustment and constrained response: Malawi at the threshold of sustained growth', World Bank, Industry and Energy Department Working Paper, Industries Series Paper No.41, October.

Fyle, Magbaile, C. (1987) 'Culture, technology and policy in the informal sector', *Africa*, Nos 57 and 4, pp.498-509.

Gaidzanwa, R.B. (1984) 'The policy implications of women's involvement in the informal sector' in *MISS. Journal of the Ministry of Manpower Planning and Development.* Vol.1, No.1.

Gaidzanwa, R.B. (1985) *An evaluation of Oxfam-America projects in Zimbabwe*, Oxfam-America, Harare.

Gaidzanwa, R.B. (1991) 'Ideologies of domesticity'. Paper presented at the workshop on Women Organizing in the Process of Industrialization at the Institute of Social Studies, The Hague, April.

Garzón López, F., (1979) 'Evaluación del Efecto Económico Regional de las Tasas Diferenciales de Interes de los Fondos Financiero Industrial y de Inversiones Privadas', Departamento Nacional de Planeacion, Unidad de Desarollo Regional Urbano, Bogotá.

Germidis, D., Kessler, D. and Meghir, R. (1991) 'Financial Systems and Develop-

ment: What Role for the Formal and Informal Financial Sector', OECD Development Centre, Paris.
Ghana Enterprises Development Commission (1976) 'The Policy and Guidelines of the GEDC for the Administration of the Small Business Loan Scheme', GEDC, Accra.
Goodman, E.A.J. and Bamford, J. (eds) (1989) *Small firms and industrial districts in Italy*, Routledge, London.
Gordon, H. (1989) 'An Overview of Grain Marketing in Tanzania 1974/75 to the Present', unpublished paper of the World Bank, Washington.
Gould, D. (1980) *Bureaucratic Corruption and Underdevelopment in the Third World: The case of Zaire*. Pergamon Press, New York.
Government of Botswana (1984) Report on Evaluation of FAP. Ministry of Finance and Development Planning, Gabarone.
Government of Kenya (1986) 'Economic Management for Renowned Growth'.
Government of Kenya Sessional Paper No.1, various years. Economic Survey of Kenya.
Government of Kenya (1989a) *A Strategy for Small Enterprise Development in Kenya: Towards the Year 2000*, Government Printers, Nairobi, May.
Government of Kenya (1989b) *1989–1993 Development Plan*, Government Printers, Nairobi.
Government of Kenya (1992) 'Small Scale and Jua Kali Business Development in Kenya', Sessional Paper No.2.
Government of Kenya, *Central Bank Reports*, various years.
Government of Kenya, Central Bureau of Statistics, various reports.
Government of Tanzania (1987) *National Accounts of Tanzania, 1976–1986*, Dar es Salaam Bureau of Statistics, Ministry of Finance, Economic Affairs and Planning.
Government of Tanzania (1991) *Economic policy framework for 1991/92 — 1993/94*.
Government of The Netherlands (1990) 'A World of Difference'. Policy document on small enterprise development, forthcoming, The Hague.
Government of Zimbabwe (1991) *IMBABWE: A Framework for Economic Reform (1991-95)*, Government Printers, Harare, January.
Government of Zimbabwe (1992) *Second National Five Year Development Plan 1991–95*, Government Printers, Harare, January.
Green, R.H. and Iladhani, X.M. (1986) 'Zimbabwe: Transitions to Economic Crisis, 1981–1985; Retrospect and Prospect', *World Development*, Vol. 14, No. 8, pp. 1059–83
GTZ Gmbh. (1989) 'Philippines — German Chamber Co-operation Programme', Terminal Report Phase 1, Germany.
Haggblade, S., Defay, J. and Pitman, R. (1979) 'Small Manufacturing and Repair Activities in Haiti: Survey Results', MSU Rural Development Working Paper No.4, Michigan State University, East Lansing.
Haggblade, S., Liedholm, C. and Mead D. (1990) 'The Effect of Policy Reforms on

Non-agricultural Enterprises and Employment in Developing Countries: A Review of Past Experience' in *The Other Policy,* F. Stewart, H. Thomas and T. de Wilde (eds.) IT Publications, London.
Haimanot, A. 1990, Agricultural Credit in Ethiopia (Senior paper), Department of Economics, Addis Ababa University.
Hakam, A.N. (1978) 'Technology Diffusion from the Formal to the Informal Sector: The Case of the Auto-Repair Industry in Ghana', ILO, processed, Geneva.
Hardy, C. '(1987) *Organizarse para vivir, pobreza urbana y organización popular*', Programa de economía del trabajo (PET), Santiago.
Harper M. and Jong, M.F. de (eds) (1986) *Financing Small Enterprise*, IT Publications, London.
Harris, J.R. (1967) 'Industrial entrepreneurship in Nigeria'. PhD Thesis Northwestern University.
Hart, J.K. (1973a) 'Informal Income Opportunities and the Structure of Urban Employment in Ghana', *Journal of Modern African Studies*, Vol.11, No.1, March, pp.61–89.
Hart, K. (1973b) 'Informal Income Opportunities and Urban Employment in Ghana' in *Journal of Modern African Studies*, Vol.13.
Hayashi, T. (1990) *The Japanese Experience in Technology: from transfer to self-reliance*, UNU Press, Tokyo.
Heklund, J.M. (1991) 'Building Indigenous Technological Capacity Through Foreign Assistance to Small/Medium Enterprises' in A.S. Bhalla (ed.) *Small and Medium Size Enterprises: Technology Policies and Options*, Greenwood Press, Westport.
Helmsing, A.H.J. (1986a) 'Rural Industries and Growth Points: issues in an ongoing debate', University of Zimbabwe, Department of Rural and Urban Planning, Occasional Paper No.2, May.
Helmsing, A.H.J. (1986b) 'Rural industries in the Communal Lands of Zimbabwe', TESG, Nos 78 and 2, pp.139–50, reprinted in N.M. Mutizwa-Mangiza and A.H.J. Helmsing (eds) (1991) *Rural Development and Planning in Zimbabwe*, Avebury, Aldershot.
Helmsing, A.H.J. (1991a) 'Non-agricultural enterprises in the communal lands of Zimbabwe' in N.D. Mutizwa-Mangiza and A.H.J. Helmsing (eds) (1991) *Rural Development and Planning in Zimbabwe*, Avebury, Aldershot.
Helmsing, A.H.J. (1991b) 'Small scale rural industries in Zimbabwe: an overview', Zimbabwe Energy Research Organization (ZERO) Publications Working Paper No.17, Harare.
Holtermann, S. (1979) *Intermediate Technology in Ghana: The Experience of Kumasi University's Technology Consulting Centre*, IT Publications, London.
ILO, (1972) *A Strategy For Increasing Productive Employment in Kenya*, ILO, Geneva.
ILO (1972) *Employment, incomes and equality: a strategy for increasing productive employment in Kenya*, ILO, Geneva.

ILO (1986) *Women's employment patterns' discrimination and promotion of equality in Africa: The case of Zimbabwe*. ILO-SATE, Lusaka.

ILO (1987) 'Report of International Labour Conference 72nd. Series', The Promotion of Small and Medium Enterprises Report VI, Geneva.

ILO/JASPA (1989) 'From Redeployment to Sustained Employment Generation: Challenges for Ghana's Programme of Economic Recovery and Development', Addis Ababa.

Indigenous Business Development Centre (1991) 'The Indigenous Business Development Programme: A Framework for Implementation', Harare.

Ingram, W.D. and Pearson, S.R. (1981) 'The Impact of Investment Concessions on the Profitability of Selected Firms in Ghana', *Economic Development and Cultural Change*, Vol.29, No.4, July, pp.831–39.

Interamerican Development Bank (1987) '*Colombia: Informe Socio-económico*', Departamento de Desarrollo Económico y Social, División de Estudios de Países, Washington.

ISSAS (1989) '*Basis Document Andean Region*', ISS, The Hague.

Itao, A. 1980. 'A Study on Mortality Rates and Causes of Failure of Small-Scale Industries in the Philippines', Research Department, Institute for Small-Scale Industries, University of the Philippines, Quezon City, Manila.

Jackelen, H.R. (1989) 'Banking on the Informal Sector' in J. Levitsky (ed.), 'Financing of Small and Medium-Scale Enterprises', UNIDO mimeo, Vienna, pp.131-43.

Joekes, S. and Roxana, M. (1987) 'Women and Export Manufacturing: A Review of the Issues and AID Policy', International Center for Research on Women, Washington DC.

Kaplinsky, R. (1982) 'Capitalist accumulation in the periphery: Kenya' in M. Fransman (ed.) *Industry and accumulation in Africa*, Heinemann, London.

Keddie, J., Nanjundan, S. and Teszler, R. (1988) 'Development of Rural Small Industrial Enterprise (RSIE), Lessons from Experience', UNIDO for UNDP/ Neth./ILO/UNIDO, Vienna, pp.116–17.

Kennedy, P.T. (1977) 'Indigenous capitalism in Ghana', *Review of African Political Economy*, January.

Kennedy, P.T. (1980) 'Ghanaian Businessmen: From Artisan to Capitalist Entrepreneur in a Dependent Economy,' *Weltforum Verlag*, 4 IFO-Institute for Economic Research, Africa-Studien No.106, Munich.

Kennedy, P.T. (1981) 'Role and Position of Petty Producers in a West African City', *Journal of Modern African Studies*, Vol.19, No.40, December, pp.565-94.

Kilby, P. (1965) *African enterprise: the Nigerian bread industry*, Stanford University Press, The Hoover Institution.

Kilby, P. (1988) 'Breaking the Entrepreneurial Bottleneck in Late-Developing Countries: Is there a Useful Role for Government?', *Journal of Development Planning*, Vol.18, pp.221-49.

Kilby, P., Liedholm, C. and Meyer, R. (1984) 'Working Capital and Nonfarm

Rural Enterprises' in Adams, D.W., Graham, D.H., and Von Pischke J.D. (eds) *Undermining Rural Development With Cheap Credit*, Westview Press, Boulder.
King, K. (1974) 'Kenya's machine makers: a study of small scale industries in Kenya's emergant artisan society', *World development*, Vol.2, No.4, pp.9-28.
King, K. (1977) *The African artisan: education and the informal sector in Kenya*, Heinemann, London.
King, K. (1977) *The African artisan: education and the informal sector in Kenya*, Heinemann, London.
Kleiterp, N. (1991) 'SSE DFIs, Long-term Strategies and Sustainability', FMO: The Hague, mimeo.
Krueger, A.O. (1978) *Liberalization Attempts and Consequences*, National Bureau of Economic Research, New York.
Kulessa, M. (ed.) (1990) *The Newly Industrializing Economies of Asia: prospects of cooperation,* Springer-Verlag, Berlin, Heidelberg, New York, Tokyo.
Kunjeku, P. (1991) 'What can big business do to help small business?', Confederation of Zimbabwe Industries, mimeo, March.
Landuber, A. (1983) 'The Development of Savings and Credit Co-operatives in Ethiopia', (Senior Paper) Department of Economics, Addis Ababa University.
Levine, D. N. (1972) *Wax and Gold; Tradition and Innovation in Ethiopian Culture*, University of Chicago Press, Chicago.
Levitsky, J. (1988) 'Financing of Small and Medium-Scale Enterprises', UNIDO mimeo, Vienna.
Levitsky, J. (1989a) 'Training for SSE Managers and Enterprises: A Review of International Experience' in P. Ickis and J. Levitsky, *Educating Managers for Business and Government*, World Bank Discussion Paper No.54, Washington DC.
Levitsky, J. (1989b) 'Review of Effectiveness of Donor Agency Support for Small Enterprise Development'. Paper presented at Conference on Policies for Small Enterprise Development, NORAD, Oslo, Norway.
Levitsky, J. and Prasad, R. (1987) 'Credit Guarantee Schemes for Small and Medium Enterprises', World Bank Technical Paper No.58., World Bank, Washington DC.
Levy, B. (1990a) 'The Role of Government in the Development of Support Systems for Small and Medium Enterprises: A Research Proposal', World Bank, Washington DC.
Levy, B. (1990b) 'Transactions Costs, the Size of Firms and Industrial Policy: lessons from a comparative case study of the footwear industry in Korea and Taiwan', *Journal of Development Economics*, Vol.32 Nos 1 and 2, pp.151–78 November.
Levy, B. and Kuo, W.J. (1991) 'The Strategic Orientations of Firms and the Performance of Korea and Taiwan in Frontier Industries: lessons from comparative case studies of keyboard and personal computer assembly', *World Development*, Vol.19, No.4, April.
Leys, C. (1982) 'Accumulation, class formation and dependency: Kenya', in M.

Fransman (ed.) *Industry and accumulation in Africa*, Heinemann, London, pp. 170-92.

Liedholm, C. (1990) 'The Dynamics of Small Scale Industry in Africa and the Role of Policy', Gemini Working Paper No.2., DAI, Washington DC.

Liedholm, C. (1991) 'Small Scale Industry in Africa: Dynamic Issues and the Role of Policy' in F. Stewart, S. Lall and S. Wangwe (eds) *Alternative Development Strategies in Africa*, Macmillan, London.

Liedholm, C. and Kilby, K. (1989) 'Nonfarm Activities in the Rural Economy' in J. Williamson and V. Panchamukhi, (eds) *The Balance Between Industry and Agriculture in Economic development, Volume II*, St. Martin Press, New York.

Liedholm, C. and McPherson, M. (1991) 'Small-Scale Enterprises in Mamelodi and Kwazakhele Townships, South Africa', GEMINI Technical Report No.16. DAI, Washington DC.

Liedholm, C. and Mead, D.C. (1985) 'Small scale industry in Africa: an overview', 28th annual meeting African Studies Association, New Orleans, 23-26 November.

Liedholm, C. and Mead, D.C. (1986) 'Small-Scale Industry in Sub-Saharan Africa: Empirical Evidence and Strategic Implications' in R.J. Berg and J.S. Whitaker (eds) *Strategies for African Development*, Berkeley, University of California Press.

Liedholm, C. and Mead, D.C. (1987) 'Small Scale Industries in Developing Countries: Empirical Evidence and Policy Implications', MSU International Development Paper No.9, Michigan State University, East Lansing.

Liedholm, C. and Mead, D.C. (1991) 'Dynamics of Microenterprises: Research Issues and Approaches', GEMINI Working Paper No.12., DAI, Washington DC.

Liedholm, C. and Parker, J. (1989) 'Small Scale Manufacturing Growth in Africa: Initial Evidence', MSU International Development Working Paper No.33, Michigan State University, East Lansing.

Link, A.N. (1987) *Technology Change and Productivity Growth*, Harwood Academic Publishers, London/New York.

Little, I.M.D. (1987) 'Small Manufacturing Enterprises in Developing Countries', *World Bank Economic Review*, Vol.1, No.2, pp.203–35.

Little, I.M.D., Mazumdar, D. and Page, J.M.Jr. (1987) *Small Manufacturing Enterprises: A Comparative Analysis of India and Other Economies*, Oxford University Press, New York.

López, H. (1986) 'El Sector Informal Urbano: Estructura, Dinámica y Políticas', Misión de Empleo, DNP, Bogotá.

López, H., Corchuelo, A. and Zorro, C. (1991) 'El Impacto del crédito sobre el empleo y los ingresos de las microempresas en Colombia' in '*Lecciones sobre el crédito al sector informal*', Bogotá.

López H., Henao M.L. and Sierra O. (1982) 'El Empleo en el Sector Informal: El

Caso de Colombia' in *La Problemática del Empleo en América Latina y en Colombia*, CIE, Medellín.

Lora, E. (1990) 'Las 'encuestas arancelarias' y la apertura económica' in *Coyuntura Económica*, Vol.XX, No.2, Fedesarrollo y FES, Bogotá, June.

Luna Osorio, L. (1991) '*Ecuador: Hacia la definición de una política de industrialización*'. Paper read at the Seminar on Policies for Small-Scale Industries, Quito, May.

Lyberaki, A. and Smyth, I. (1990) 'Small is Small: The Role and Functions of Small-Scale Industries' in M.P. van Dijk and H.S. Marcussen (eds), *Industrialization in the Third World: The Need for Alternative Strategies*, Frank Cass, London.

MacGaffey, J. (1983) 'How to survive and become rich amidst devastation: The second economy in Zaire' in *African Affairs*, Vol.82, No.328, July.

Mahtsentu, F. (1989) 'An Assessment of the Role of The Commercial Bank in Savings Mobilization and Utilization in Post Revolutionary Ethiopia', M.A. Thesis, Addis Ababa University.

Maliyamkono, T.L. and Bagachwa, M.S.D. (1990) *The second economy in Tanzania*, James Curry, London; Ohio University Press, Athens; Heinemann Kenya, Nairobi; and ESAURP, Dar es Salaam.

Mamo, W. (1983) *Iqqubtegnoch*, Addis Ababa, in Amharic.

Mauri, (1987) 'The Role of Financial Intermediation in the Mobilization and Allocation of Household Saving' in *Developing Countries: Interlinks between Organized and Informal Circuits: The Case of Ethiopia*, International Experts Meeting on Domestic Savings Mobilization, East-West Center, Honolulu, 2–4 June 1987.

Maybaile F. (1987) 'Culture, technology and policy in the informal sector: attention to endogenous development', *Africa*, Nos 57 and 4, pp.498-509.

McCleod, R. (1986) 'Financing Small Business in Indonesia'. Paper Presented at the Conference on Financial Research in Indonesia, Indonesia, August 1986.

McNamara, R.S. (1990) 'Africa's Development Crisis: Agricultural Stagnation, Population Explosion and Environmental Degradation'. Address to the African Leadership Forum, Ota, Nigeria.

McPherson, M. A. (1991) 'Micro and Small Scale Enterprises in Zimbabwe: Results of a Country-Wide Survey', GEMINI Technical Report 25.

Mead, D. (1985) 'Sub-Contracting Systems and Assistance Programs: Opportunities for Intervention', MSU International Working Paper No.24, Michigan State University, East Lansing.

Mead, D. (1989) 'Policy Reform and the Informal Sector in Africa'. Paper prepared for Conferences on The Informal Sector: Issues in Policy Reform and Programs, Abidjan and Nairobi.

Meerendonk, H.vd and Picavet, R. (1990) 'Export oriented rural small scale industrialization in Pakistan', ISS Industrialization Seminar, No.90/6, ISS, The Hague.

Meghir, R. (1991) 'Formal and Informal Financial Support for Small and Micro Enterprises', *Development*, Vol.1, 102-108.

Meier, G.M. and Steel W.F. (eds) (1989) *Industrial Adjustment in Sub-Saharan Africa*, OUP, London.

Meyer, R. (1988) 'Financial Services for Microenterprises: Programs or Markets?'. Paper prepared for the World Conference on Support of Microenterprises, Washington DC, June, 1988.

Meyer, R. and Cuevas, C. (1990) 'Reducing the Transactions Costs of Financial Intermediation: Theory and Innovations'. Paper from the International Conference on Savings and Credit for Development, Copenhagen.

Mihyo, P. and Kurian, R. (1991) 'Work organization, motivation, time management and the economic recovery in Eastern Africa', I.S.S. (project proposal), The Hague.

Milimo, J.T. and Fisseka, Y. (1986) 'Rural small scale enterprise in Zambia: results of a 1985 country wide survey', MSU Nor International Development Papers, Working Paper No.28., MSU.

Ministry of Agriculture (1984), 'General Agricultural Survey'. Preliminary Report 1983/84, Vol.1, Ethiopia.

Ministry of Planning and International Co-operation, National Department of Statistics and Information Processes (1989) 'Informal Sector Enquiry'.

Miracle, M.P., Miracle, D. and Cohen, (1980) 'Informal Savings Mobilization in Africa', *Economic Development and Cultural Change*, Vol.28, No.4, July, pp.701-24.

Monette, M. (1990a) 'Ajustement structurel et secteur privé au Mali', Bamako, Juin.

Monette, M. (1990b) 'Un aperçu de la situation macroéconomique au Mali en 1990 et perspectives pour 1991', Bamako, Décembre.

Moyo, N. *et al.* (1984) 'The informal sector in Zimbabwe: Its potential for employment creation', mimeo, Dept. of Economics, University of Zimbabwe.

Muñoz Goma, O. (1989) 'El estado y la pequeña y mediana empresa: Hacia un nuevo enfoque de política industrial' in *Serie de estudios sobre la pequeña y la mediana empresa*, No.3, Corporación para el fomento de la pequeña y mediana empresa, CEFOPE, Santiago.

Mutambirwa, S. (1989) 'Entrepreneurship and small scale enterprise development for women in Zimbabwe', ILO, Lusaka.

Mwarania, K.M., (1988) 'Why the banks collapsed', *Journal of Accounting*, Jan.-Mar. 1988.

Mytelka, L.K. (1992) 'Ivorian industry at the crossroads' in F. Stewart, S. Lall, and S. Wangwe (eds) *Alternative development strategies in African development*, Macmillan, London.

Nanjundan, S. (1987) 'Small and Medium Enterprises: Some Basic Development Issues', *Industry and Development*, Vol.20.

National Bank of Ethiopia (1975) *Quarterly Bulletin, New Series*, Vol.1, No.2.

National Bank of Ethiopia (1986/87) *Annual Report 1986/87*, Addis Ababa.

Netherlands Development Cooperation (1989) 'Small Enterprises, New Approaches' Proceedings of the Workshop on Small Scale Enterprise Development in Search of New Dutch Approaches, The Hague.

Ngirabatware, A., Murembya,L. and Mead, D. (1988) 'Large Private Manufacturing Firms in Rwanda: Current Situation and Policy Impact'. Draft paper, July.

Niccolini, F. (1989) 'Fomento de la Pequena y Mediana Empresa. Analisis de la ley No.17.386' en *Serie de Estudios sobre la Pequena y Meadiana Empresa* No.1, Centro de Fomento de la Pequena y Mediana Empresa (CEFOPE), Santiago.

Nigerian Bank for Commerce and Industry (1985) *Annual Report*, Lagos.

Nigerian Institute of Social and Economic Research (1987) *Towards the Development of Small Scale Industries in Nigeria*, Rosprint Press, Ibadan.

Norcliffe, G. (1983) 'Operating characteristics of rural non-farm enterprises in Central Province, Kenya', *World Development*, No.11, pp.981-94.

NOVIB (1989) Evaluation of the Manicaland Development Association project (internal document) NOVIB, The Hague.

Ocampo, J.A. and Lora, E. (1987),'Stabilization and Adjustment Policies and Programmes: Case Study of Colombia', WIDER, Helsinski.

OECD (1982) *Innovation in Small and Medium Firms: background reports,* OECD, Paris.

Olashore, O. (1985) 'Role of Commercial Banks in Financing Small and Medium Enterprises in Nigeria', *The Nigerian Accountant*, July/September.

Ominami, C. (1991) 'Programa de apoyo a la pequeña y mediana empresa'. Speech given by the minister at the launch of the programme, mimeo, unpublished, Santiago, July.

ONCCP, (1984) *Ten Years Perspective Plan 1984/85–1983/94*, Addis Ababa.

Pack, H. and Westphal, L. (1986) 'Industrial Strategy and Technological Change: Theory versus Reality' in *Journal of Development Economics*, Vol.22, pp.87–128.

Page, J.R.Jr. (1978) 'Economies of Scale, Income Distribution, and Small-Enterprise Promotion in Ghana's Timber Industry', *Food Research Institute Studies*, Vol.16, No.3, pp.159-82.

Page, J.M.Jr. and Steel, W.F. (1984) 'Small Enterprise Development: Economic Issues from African Experience', Technical Paper No.26, World Bank, Washington, DC.

Pan-Thuy, N., Betancourt, R., Winston, G. and Kabaj, M. (1981) *Industrial Capacity and Employment Promotion*, Gower Publishing, Hampshire.

Pankhurst, R. and Eshete, A. (1958) 'Self-help in Ethiopia', *Ethiopian Observer* Vol.II, No.XI, pp.354–64.

Parker, J. and Aleke Dondo, C. (1991) 'Kenya: Kibera's Small Enterprise Sector — Baseline Survey Report', GEMINI Working Paper No.17. DAI, Washington DC.

Patrick, H.T. (1966) 'Financial Development and Economic Growth in Developing Countries', *Economic Development and Cultural Change*, Vol.14, No.2.

Pennings, J.M. (1987) 'Technology innovations in manufacturing' in J.M. Pennings and A. Buitendam (eds) *New Technology as Organizational Innovation*, Ballinger, Cambridge, Massachusetts.

Pennings, J.M. and Buitendam, A. (eds) *New Technology as Organizational Innovation*, Ballinger, Cambridge,Massachusetts.

Phillips, B.D. and Kirchhoff, B.A. (1988) 'Analysis of New Firm Survival and Growth'. Paper presented at the Babson Entrepreneurship Research Conference, Calgary, Canada, May.

Phillips, B.D. and Bruce, – (1986) *The State of Small Business – 1986*. Washington DC, US Government Printing Office.

Piore, M. and Sabel, C. (1984) *The second industrial divide: possibilities for prosperity*, Basic Books, New York.

PRAL/SERCAL/SUR (1990) *La capacidad de emprender puesta a prueba*, Germinal Ltda., Santiago.

Raczynski, D. (1989) 'Apoyo a Pequeñas Unidades Productivas en Sectores Pobres: Lecciones de Políticas'. Notas Técnicas No.133, CIEPLAN, Santiago.

Regnier, P. (1990) 'Development of Small and Medium-sized Enterprises in the Asian NIEs: business opportunities for western Europe?' in M. Kulesa (ed.) *The Newly Industrializing Economies of Asia*, Springer-Verlag, Berlin/Heidelberg, New York, Tokyo.

Republic of Ghana (1974) 'Report on the Role and Activities of the Office of Business Promotion' Ghana Publishing Corporation, Accra.

République du Mali, Ministère de l'Industrie, de l'Hydraulique et de l'Energie, Direction Nationale des industries (1990) 'Recensement industriel 1988', Juillet.

République du Mali, Ministère des Finances et du Commerce et Ministère du Plan (1990) 'Actes du séminaire sur la promotion du secteur privé', Bamako 10-24 Décembre.

République du Mali, Ministère du Plan, Direction Nationale de la Statistique et de l'Informatique (1989) 'Enquête secteur informel (1989): analyse préliminaire et résultats'.

République du Mali, Ministère du Plan, Direction Nationale de la Statistique et de l'Informatique (1990) 'Comptes économiques du Mali 1989, Résultats préliminaires', Décembre.

Rhyne, E. and Otero. M. (1991) 'A Financial Systems Approach to Microenterprises'. GEMINI Working Paper No.18, DAI, Washington DC.

Riddell, R. (1988) 'Industrialisation in Sub-Saharan Africa: Country Case Study — Zimbabwe', ODI Working Paper.

Riddell, R.C. (ed.) (1990) *Manufacturing Africa: Performance and Prospects in Seven Countries in SSA*, James Currey, London and Heinemann, Portsmouth.

Román, E. (1990) 'Regional Industrial Performance in an Opening Economy: Small-Scale Industry in Chile 1975–1986' M.Phil. Thesis ISS, The Hague.

Romijn, H. and de Wilde, T. (1991) 'Appropriate technology for small industry. A review of issues' in H. Thomas, F. Uribe-Echevarría and H. Romijn (eds) *Small*

scale production: Strategies for industrial restructuring, IT Publications, London, pp.86–113.
Rothwell, R. and Zegveld, W. (1985) *Re-industrialization and technology*, Longman, London.
Sabel, C. (1986) 'Changing Role of Economic Efficiency and their Implications for Industrialization in the Third World' in A. Foxley, M. McPherson and G. O'Donell (eds) *Development, Democracy, and the Art of Trespassing*, University of Notre Dame Press, Paris.
Samper, E. (1991) Speech delivered at the 'Seminar for Industrial Restructuring in the Andean Region', organized by the Industrialists National Association (ANDI), Bogotá, May.
Schadler, K. (1968) *Crafts, Small-Scale Industries and Industrial Education in Tanzania*, Weltform Verlag, Munich.
Schmitz, H. (1982) 'Growth Constraints on Small-scale Manufacturing in Developing Countries: A Critical Review', *World Development*, Vol.10, No.6, pp.429-50.
Schmitz, H. (1989) 'Flexible specialization — a new paradigm of small scale industrialization?' Discussion paper 261, IDS, Sussex.
Schmitz, H. (1990) 'Small Firms and Flexible Specialization in Developing Countries' in *Labour and Society*, Vol.15, No. 3.
Scott, A.J. (1988) 'Flexible Production Systems and Regional Development: the rise of new industrial spaces in North America and western Europe' in *Journal of Urban and Regional Research*, Vol.12, No.2.
Seibel, H.D. (1989) Linking Informal and Formal Financial Institutions in Africa, in J. Levitsky (ed.) *Microenterprises in Developing Countries*, IT Publications, London, pp.97-118.
Seibel, H.D. and Parkusip, U. (1990) 'Financial innovations for micro enterprise — linking formal and informal financial institutions', *Small Enterprise Development*, No.1 and 2, pp.14–26.
Selowsky, M. (1970) 'Politica Cambiaria y Asignacion de Recursos'Santiago, Centro de Investigaciones Economicas, Universidad Catolica de Chile.
Sengenberger, W. (1988) 'Economic and social purspectives of small enterprises' in *Labour and Society*, Vol.13, No.3, pp.249–59.
Sengenberger, W. and Pyke, F. (1991) 'Small firm industrial districts and local economic regeneration: research and policy issues' in *Labour and Society*, Vol.16, No.1, pp.1-24.
Sibanda, B. (1986) 'Evaluation of the Mzarabani goat project' Oxfam-America/ World Bank.
Soto H. de. (1986) *El Otro Sendero*, ILD (Instituto de Libertad y Democracia), Líma. English translation: *The Other Path*, New York, 1989.
Stallmann, J. (1984) 'Rural manufacturing in three regions of Honduras', unpublished, Michigan State University, East Lansing.
Steel, W.F. (1977) *Small-Scale Employment and Production in Developing Countries: Evidence from Ghana*, Praeger, New York.

Steel, W.F. (1979) 'Development of the Urban Artisanal Sector in Ghana and Cameroon', *Journal of Modern African Studies*, Vol.17, No.2, June, pp.271–84.

Steel, W.F. (1981) 'Female and Small-Scale Employment under Modernization in Ghana', *Economic Development and Cultural Change*, Vol.30, No.1, October, pp.153-67.

Steel, W.F. and Takagi, Y. (1983) 'Small Enterprise Development and the Employment-Output Trade-Off', *Oxford Economic Papers*, Vol.35, No.3.

Steel, W.F. and Webster, L. (1990) 'Small Enterprises in Ghana: Responses to Adjustment', Industry and Energy Department Working Paper No.33, World Bank, Washington DC.

Stein H. and Nafziger, E.W. (1991) 'Structural adjustment, human needs and the World Bank agenda', *Journal of Modern African Studies*, Vol.19, No.1, pp.173–89.

Steinkreus, K.A. (1982) 'Applications of bio technology and genetic engineering to African fermented food processes', UNIDO/IF-336, Vienna.

Stevens, Y. (1988) 'Photovoltaic Applications in Rural Areas in Developing Countries: a survey of the evidence' in A.S. Bhalla and D. James (eds) *New Technologies and Development: Experiences in Technology Blending*, Lynne Rienner Publishers, Boulder/London.

Stewart, F. (1987) *Macro-policies for Appropriate Technology in Developing Countries*, Frances Pinter, London.

Stewart, F. (1990) 'Macro-policies for Small-scale Industry and Appropriate Technology', *Small Enterprise Development*, Vol.1, No.3.

Stewart, F., Thomas, H. and de Wilde, T. (1990) *The Other Policy*, IT Publications, London.

Storper, M. (1990) 'Industrialization and the regional question in the Third World: lessons of post-imperialism; prospects of post-fordism', IJURR, Nos 14 and 3, pp.423–45.

Storper, M. and Scott, A. (1990) 'Work organization and local labour markets in an era of flexible production', *International Labour Review*, Nos 129 and 5, pp.573-91.

Summary of Meeting of Researchers (1991) Donors and Government representatives on Small Scale Enterprises in Zimbabwe held at Brondesbury Park Motel, Nyanga 10–12 July Zimbabwe

SUR, (1988) '*Cuatro años de talleres de experiencia con talleres populares*', SUR, Santiago.

Sverrisson, A. (1990) 'Entrepreneurship and industrialization: a case study of carpenters in Mutare, Zimbabwe'. Research policy studies discussion paper No.186, University of Lund.

Swedish Development Consulting Partners AB (1991) 'Evaluation of SIDA Supported Small Industry Programmes in Tanzania', report to SIDA, Stockholm.

Taylor, L. (1991) 'Economic Openness: Problems to the Century's End' in E. Amadeo and T. Banuri (eds) *Economic Liberalization: No Panacea. The Expereinces of Latin America and Asia*, Clarendon Press, Oxford.

Technonet Asia – Central Association of German Handwork (1990) 'Small Scale Business Development Conference October 1989 Report', Singapore.
Tejeiro, J.D. and Elson, A. (1973) 'The Export Promotion System and the growth of Minor Exports in Colombia', IMF Staff Papers, No.20, Washington DC, July.
Tendler, J. (1982) 'Turning private voluntary organizations into development agencies: Questions for evaluation', AID Program Evaluation Paper No.12, USAID, Washington.
Teszler, R. (1989) 'Small Scale Industry's Contribution to Economic Development', mimeo.
Teszler, R. (1991) 'SSE and Development Finance in Four African Countries; the Point of View of the Small Entrepreneur', mimeo. p.40ff. (a summary of the work of four African consultants during the autumn of 1990).
The Financial Gazette (1991) 'Reserve Bank increases interest rates to curb inflation', 12 September.
Tidd, J. (1991) *Flexible Manufacturing Technologies and International Competitiveness,* Pinter Publishers, London.
Tokeshi, S.A. (1989) 'Programas de fomento a la microempresa: la experiencia peruana', *Finanzas Públicas* 5, No.7, April.
Trigilia, C. (1989) 'Small firm development and political subcultures in Italy' in E.A.G. Goodman and A. Banford (eds) *Small Firms and Industrial District in Italy*, Routledge, London, pp. 174–97.
Tripp, A.M. (1988) 'Defending the right to subsist: the state vs the urban informal economy in Tanzania'. Paper presented at the African Studies Association Annual Meeting, Chicago, Illinois.
Tripp, A.M. (1989) 'Defending the right to subsist: the state versus the urban informal economy in Tanzania', Working Paper No.59, WIDER, Helsinki.
UNDP (1989) Development cooperation report on Tanzania for 1989, UNDP, Dar es Salaam, May.
UNDP (1990) *Human Development Report*, OUP, New York
UNDP/Government of the Netherlands/ILO/UNIDO (1988) *Development of Rural Small Industrial Enterprise: Lessons from Experience*, UNIDO, Vienna.
UNDP/UNIDO/ILO/The Netherlands (1988) 'The Thematic Evaluation of Technical Co-operation in Support of Rural Small Enterprises in Tanzania', Vienna.
UNIDO (1986) 'Zimbabwe industrial sector study', UNDP, Harare
UNIDO (1989), 'Environment Conducive to Sustained Growth of Small- and Medium-Scale Enterprises'. Discussion Paper ID/WG.492/4 for the First Consultation on Small- and Medium-Scale Enterprises including Co-operatives, UNIDO, Bari, Italy.
UNIDO (1969) *Small-Scale Industry in Latin America,* Vienna.
Uribe-Echevarría, J.F. (1983) 'Evaluation of the Performance of Deconcentration Policies in Colombia: Towards an Alternative Explanation', paper presented at the International Conference on *Small and Intermediate Cities and National Development*, UNCRD/NIUA, New Delhi.

Uribe-Echevarría, J.F. (1985) 'Algunas Notas sobre las Políticas de Promoción de las Actividades Urbanas Informales', ISS, The Hague.

Uribe-Echevarría, J.F. (1989) 'The Role of the Informal Sector in Labour Absorption: A Case Study of the Period Between 1976 and 1985 in Colombia', paper presented at the International Conference on Informal Sector and Employment, Erasmus University/ILO, Rotterdam.

Uribe-Echevarría, J.F. (1991) 'Small-Scale Industrial Development' in H. Thomas, F. Uribe-Echevarría and H. Romijn, *Small-Scale Production: Strategies for Industrial Restructuring*, IT Publications, London.

Valarezzo, H.M. (1991) 'Propuesta del Ministerio de Industria, Comercio, Integración y Pesca a través de la subsecretaría de Pequeña Industria y Artesanía, sobre Políticas para Desarrollo de la Pequeña Industria Ecuatoriana'. Paper presented to the Primer Encuentro Nacional de la Pequeña y Mediana Industria y el Ministerio de Industria, Comercio, Integración y Pesca, Puembo, July.

Villarreal, M. (1991) 'Gender Dimension in Social Development Projects', unpublished manuscript, PREALC, Santiago.

von Braun, J. (1989) 'Effects of New Export Crops in Smallholder Agriculture on Division of Labour and Child Nutritional Status in Guatemala' in J. Leslie and M. Paolisso (eds) *Women's Work and Child Welfare in the Third World*, AAAS Selected Symposium 10, Westview Press, Boulder, Colorado.

von Pischke, J.D. (1991) *Finance at the Frontier: Debt Capacity and the Role of Credit in the Private Economy*, EDI Development Studies, World Bank, Washington DC.

Wangwe, S.M. (1991) The Impact of External Assistance on Endogenous Capacity Building in Science and Technology, UNCSTD, New York.

Wangwe, S.M. (1992) 'Building indigenous technological capacity – A study of selected industries in Tanzania' in F. Stewart, S. Lall and S. Wangwe (eds) *Alternative development strategies in African development*, Macmillan, London.

Wangwe, S.M. and Bagachwa, M.S.D. (1988) 'Impact of economic policies on technological choice and development in Tanzania'. Paper prepared for Conference on the Implications of Technology Choice on Economic Development. Nairobi, 29–31 August.

Webster, L. (1991) 'World Bank Lending for Small and Medium Enterprises', World Bank Discussion Papers, No.113, Washington DC.

Weiss, J. (1988) *Industry in Developing Countries:Theory, Policy and Evidence*. Routledge, London and New York.

Wibaux, H. (1986) Agriculture in the Highlands of Hararghe, Kombolcha Area: A Study of Six Farms, unpublished material, Alemaya Agricultural University.

Wogart, J.P. (1978) '*Industrialization in Colombia: Policies, Patterns, Perspectives*, J.C.B. Mohr (Paul Siebeck), Tubingen.

Wolgin, J.M. (1990) 'Fresh Start in Africa: AID and Structural Adjustment in Africa', mimeo, August.

World Bank (1987a) 'Parastatals in Tanzania: Towards a Reform Program'. Report No.7100-TA, World Bank, Washington DC.

World Bank (1987b) 'Project Performance and Audit Report Tanzania: Second National Sites and Services Project', World Bank, Washington DC.

World Bank (1987c) 'Tanzania: An Agenda for Industrial Recovery'. Report No.6357-TA., World Bank, Washington DC.

World Bank (1987d) *World Development Report*, World Bank, Washington.

World Bank (1987e) *Zimbabwe. A strategy for sustained growth,* Nov.

World Bank (1978) *Rural enterprise and non-farm employment*, World Bank, Washington.

World Bank (1989a) *Sub-Saharan Africa: From Crisis to Sustainable Growth*, World Bank, Washington DC.

World Bank (1989b) *World Development Report 1989*, Oxford University Press, New York.

World Bank (1990a) *Ethiopia's Economy in the 1980s and Framework for Accelerated Growth*, Report No.8062-ET, Washington DC.

World Bank (1990b) 'Republic of Mali, Structural Adjustment Credit (SAL1)', Report No.P-5318-MLI, September 27.

World Bank (1990c) *World Development Report 1990,* Oxford University Press, New York.

World Bank (1991a) *Tanzania Economic Report Towards Sustainable Development in the 1990s*, World Bank, Washington DC.

World Bank (1991b) *World Development Report 1991*, Oxford University Press, New York.

Yankson, P.W.K. (1983) 'Employment and Income Generation in the Petty Commodity Sector of the Urban Economy: The Case of the Central Region of Ghana', *Africa Development* Vol.8, No.3, pp.75–97.

Yankson, P.W.K. (1986) 'Small-Scale Industries in the Implementation of a Growth Centre Strategy of Regional Development: A Case Study in Ghana'. Industry and Development 17 (UNIDO/E.86II.B.1).

Yeshitla Y. (1989) 'Agricultural Credit and Rural Financial Markets' in *Towards a Food and Nutrition Strategy for Ethiopia*, ONCCP, Addis Ababa.

Yoshikuni, I. (1984) 'The origins and development of the Salisbury Municipal location: a study of municipal control of African workers in colonial Harare, 1892–1923', Henderson Seminar Paper, Dept. of History, mimeo, University of Zimbabwe, Harare.

Yung W. R. and Soulier, Ch. (1989) 'Small trading companies and a succesful export response: lessons from Hong Kong', Industry Series Paper No.16, Industry & Energy Department, World Bank, Washington.

Zewdie S. (1986), Forderung von Klein-und Mittelbetrieben im Produktionsbereich als Instrument der regionalen Entwicklung Äthiopiens, Institut für Raumordnung und Entwicklungsplanung der Universität Stuttgart, Stuttgart.